Photoshop 6 / ImageReady 3 | H·O·T
Hands-On Training

lynda.com/books

By Lynda Weinman and Jan Kabili

Design: Ali Karp

Photoshop 6 / ImageReady 3 | H·O·T
Hands-On Training

By Lynda Weinman and Jan Kabili

lynda.com/books | Peachpit Press
1249 Eighth Street • Berkeley, CA • 94710
800.283.9444 • 510.524.2178 •
510.524.2221 (fax)
http://www.lynda.com/books
http://www.peachpit.com

lynda.com/books is published in
association with Peachpit Press,
a division of Pearson Education
Copyright ©2002 by lynda.com

ISBN: 0-201-72796-X

0 9 8 7 6 5 4 3 2 1

Printed and bound in the
United States of America

H•O•T | Credits

Original Design: Ali Karp, Alink Newmedia

Peachpit Editor: Cary Norsworthy

Peachpit Project Coordinator: Suzie Lowey

Copyeditors: Dave Awl, Rebecca Pepper

Peachpit Production: Lisa Brazieal, Myrna Vladic

Peachpit Compositors: Rick Gordon, Deborah Roberti

Beta Testers: Michelle Bauer Carpenter, Rosanna Yeung, Ellen Norgard

Cover Illustration: Bruce Heavin (`bruce@stink.com`)

Indexer: Steve Rath

H•O•T | Colophon

The preliminary design for the H•O•T series was sketched on paper by Ali Karp | Alink Newmedia. The layout was heavily influenced by online communication–merging a traditional book format with a modern Web aesthetic.

The text in Photoshop 6 / ImageReady 3 H•O•T was set in Akzidenz Grotesk from Adobe, and Triplex from Emigre. The cover illustration was painted in Adobe Photoshop and Adobe Illustrator.

This book was created using QuarkXPress 4.1, Adobe Photoshop 6, Microsoft Office 2001, and ImageReady 3 on a Macintosh G3, running Mac OS 9.1.

Photoshop 6 / ImageReady 3 | H•O•T _____ Table of Contents

Introduction

Photoshop 6 / ImageReady 3

For the Web

A Note from Lynda and Jan

We were motivated to continue this Hands-On Training book series because it's our experience that people buy computer books to educate themselves. Most books and manuals are reference based, and while there is nothing wrong with reference books in general, it seemed that a book with hands-on tutorials would be of great value. We are the type of learners who learn by doing. We enjoy a reference manual or book after we know our way around a program, but those types of materials don't help us get up to speed as quickly as we like. We at lynda.com wrote this series of books with our own learning styles in mind. We know we're not alone in our impatience to get productive in a tool as soon as humanly possible.

In this book, you will find carefully developed lessons and exercises that have been tested in lynda.com's digital arts training center to help you learn Photoshop 6 and ImageReady 3. If you are new to Photoshop or even if you've owned Photoshop for years, this book will teach you many new things that you didn't know. That's mostly because there are so many new features in Photoshop and ImageReady that even experienced Photoshop users will be on new ground.

This book is targeted toward beginning–to intermediate–level Web developers who are looking for a great tool to create graphics and Web content. The premise of the hands-on exercise approach is to get you up to speed quickly in these programs, while actively working through the book's lessons. It's one thing to read about a product, and an entirely different one to try the product and get measurable results.

Many exercise-based books take a paint-by-numbers approach to teaching by offering instructions that tell you what to do, but not why or when the instruction will apply to your work later. While this approach sometimes works, it's often difficult to figure out how to apply those lessons to a real-world situation, or understand why or when you would use the technique again. What sets this book apart is that the lessons contain lots of background information for each given subject, which is designed to help you understand the process as well as the particular exercise.

At times, pictures are worth a lot more than words. When necessary, we have also included short QuickTime movies to show any process that's difficult to explain in writing. These files are located on the **H•O•T CD-ROM** inside a folder called **movies**. We approach teaching from many different angles because we know that some people are visual learners, while others like to read, and still others like to get out there and try things. This book combines a lot of teaching approaches so you can learn Photoshop and ImageReady as thoroughly as you want to.

We didn't set out to cover every single aspect of these programs. The manual and many other reference books are great for that! What we saw missing from the bookshelves was a process-oriented book that taught readers core principles, techniques, and tips in a hands-on training format. We've been making graphics for the Web since 1995, and it used to be a lot tougher than it is today. These versions of Photoshop and ImageReady in particular are oriented toward making Web graphics faster to download and easier to make. Additionally, ImageReady even writes JavaScript code and HTML, something which traditional imaging programs have seldom broached.

It's our hope that this book will raise your skills in Web design and digital imaging. If it does, then we have accomplished the job we set out to do!

• We welcome your comments at
commentspsirhot@lynda.com

• Please visit our Web site as well at
http://www.lynda.com

• The URL for support for this book is
http://www.lynda.com/books/psirhot

> Lynda Weinman
> Jan Kabili

How This Book Works

This book has several components, including step-by-step exercises, commentary, notes, tips, warnings, and movies. Step-by-step exercises are numbered, and file names and command keys are bolded so they pop out more easily. When you see italicized text, it signifies commentary.

- At the beginning of each exercise you'll see the notation **[IR]** if the exercise takes place in ImageReady, or **[PS]** if the exercise takes place in Photoshop.

- Whenever you're being instructed to go to a menu or multiple menu items, it's stated like this: **File > Open...**

- Code is in a monospace font: **<HTML></HTML>**

- URLs are in a bold font: **http://www.lynda.com**

- Macintosh and Windows interface screen captures: Most of the screen captures in the book were taken on a Macintosh. Windows shots were taken only when the interface differed from the Macintosh. We made this decision because we do most of our design work and writing on Macs. We also own and use Windows systems, so we noted important differences when they occurred.

Exercise Files and the H•O•T CD-ROM

All of your course files are located inside a folder called **exercise_files** on the **H•O•T CD-ROM**. These files are divided into chapter folders. Please copy the chapter folders to your hard drive because you will be required to alter them, which is not possible if they stay on the CD.

WARNING | Platform Concerns

Windows: Locked Files

Unfortunately, when files originate from a CD-ROM, the Windows operating system defaults to making them write-protected (read-only). This means that by default you will not be able to alter and resave any exercise files you copy from the H•O•T CD-ROM to a Windows hard drive. If you are working on Windows, you must remove the read-only setting from each copied exercise file as follows:

1. Open the **exercises** folder on the **H•O•T CD-ROM**, and copy one of the subfolders (for example, the **chap_05** folder (to your desktop.

2. Open the **chap_05** folder you copied to your desktop, and choose **Edit > Select All**.

3. Right-click on one of the selected files, and choose **Properties** from the pop-up menu.

4. In the **General** tab of the **Properties** dialog box, uncheck **Read-only**. This will unlock all of the files in the **chap_05** folder on your desktop.

Windows: Missing File Extensions

By default, **Windows 98/ME/2000** users will not be able to see file extension names, such as .gif, .jpg, or .html. Don't worry, you can change this setting.

Windows 98/ME Users:

1. Double-click on the **My Computer** icon on your desktop. (**Note:** If you or someone else has changed the name, it will not say **My Computer**.)

2. Select **View > Folder Options** to open the **Folder Options** dialog box.

3. Click on the **View** tab at the top. This will allow you to access the different view settings for your computer.

4. Uncheck the checkbox inside the **Hide file extensions for known file types** option. This will make all of the file extensions visible.

Windows 2000 Users:

1. Double-click on the **My Computer** icon on your desktop. **Note:** (If you or someone else have changed the name, it will not say **My Computer**.)

2. Select **Tools > Folder Options**. This opens the **Folder Options** dialog box.

3. Click on the **View** tab at the top. This opens the **View** options screen so you can change the view settings for Windows 2000.

4. Make sure there is no checkmark next to the **Hide file extensions for known file types** option. This makes all of the file extensions visible.

Software Files on the CD-ROM

The **H•O•T CD-ROM** includes a Mac and Windows version of Netscape 6, as well as QuickTime 5.0. All software is located inside the CD's software folder (imagine that!).

Troubleshooting FAQ

If you find yourself getting stuck in an exercise, be sure to read the Troubleshooting FAQ in the back of the book. If you don't find your answer there, send an email to **psirfaq@lynda.com** and we'll post an update on the companion Web site for the book, **http://www.lynda.com/books/psirhot/** as quickly as we can. Obviously, we can't offer personal technical support for everyone who reads the book, so be sure to refer to this FAQ before you request extra help.

Note: This FAQ is intended to support the exercises in this book. If you have other questions about Photoshop or ImageReady, as a registered owner of the program you can call Adobe's technical support line at 206-675-6203 (Mac) or 206-675-6303 (Windows), or visit their excellent Web site at **http://www.adobe.com**.

Skill Level

This book assumes that you possess a basic knowledge of Photoshop. If you have never used Photoshop before, you should go through the tutorial in the manual before you begin this book. Web design and digital imaging are challenging, somewhat technical, creative mediums. You must have good general computer skills to work with Web applications, as they require that you save and open numerous files and often work in multiple programs at the same time.

RAM, RAM, and More RAM

It's ideal to keep Photoshop, ImageReady, and a Web browser open at the same time. To do this, we recommend that you have at least 128 MB of RAM. This book assumes that you can open all these programs simultaneously. If you cannot, you will need to quit whichever program you're in whenever you are requested to enter another. This is possible to do but will grow tiring, we assure you. Photoshop and ImageReady are professional tools and require professional-level systems to run optimally.

System Requirements

This book requires that you use either the Mac OS operating system (on a Macintosh running System 8.5 or later) or Windows 98, 2000, ME, or NT. That's another reason we suggest that you have at least 128 MB of RAM. More RAM is better, especially on Macintosh computers, which do not offer dynamic RAM allocation like Windows.

About lynda.com

lynda.com is dedicated to helping Web designers and developers understand tools and design principles. lynda.com offers training books, CDs, videos, hands-on workshops, training seminars, and on-site training. The Web site contains online tips, discussion boards, training products, and a design job board. Be sure to visit our site at **http://www.lynda.com** to learn more!

Check out Lynda's other books at: **http://www.lynda.com/books**

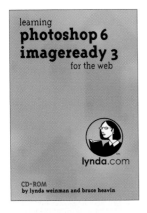

Check out Lynda's training DVDs and CDs at: ***http://www.lynda.com/videos***

About Lynda

I've been practicing computer design and animation since 1984, when I bought one of the first Macintosh computers. I worked as an animator and motion graphics director in the special-effects industry for seven years before having a daughter in 1989. At that time, I was asked to teach my first workshop in multimedia animation, and eventually became a full-time faculty member at Art Center College of Design in Pasadena, California. I've worked as a beta tester for imaging and animation software packages since 1984, and have worked as a consultant for Adobe, Macromedia, and Microsoft. I've conducted workshops at Disney, Microsoft, Adobe, and Macromedia, and have been a keynote speaker and/or moderator at numerous design, broadcast-design, animation, Web-design, and computer-graphics conferences. With my husband Bruce Heavin (who is responsible for the beautiful covers of all my books!), I cofounded lynda.com, Inc., which specializes in Web-design training via hands-on classes, seminars, training videos, books, Web tips, and CD-ROMs. The list could go on and on, but I basically love teaching and sharing knowledge, and that's what I spend most of my waking hours doing. I hope you'll visit **http://www.lynda.com** to learn more.

About Jan

I've had the amazing opportunity to teach, write, and speak for lynda.com ever since I had the good fortune to meet Lynda a couple of years ago at a digital arts program in Aspen, Colorado. I'm now head of the Adobe training program at lynda.com and a lead instructor at the Ojai Digital Arts Center. I've spoken at national Web design conferences, authored Web design articles and training manuals, and taught Web design at the University of Colorado. I'm an Adobe Certified Expert in Photoshop 6 and ImageReady 3, and hold way too many advanced degrees, including a Master of Fine Arts degree in Electronic Media, and a J.D. from Stanford Law School (yes, I'm a recovering lawyer ☺). I live in beautiful Boulder, Colorado with my three cool kids, and commute to work in Ojai, California. The bottom line is that learning the Web has changed my life, and I love teaching others about it!

lynda.com offers hands-on training in Ojai, California. The classrooms have the latest Web-design software, plus state-of-the-art networked Mac and Windows computers utilizing a T1 Internet connection. **Lynda** *is shown above, teaching color theory to a group of Web-design professionals.*

Lynda *and her husband/partner* **Bruce Heavin**.

Lynda *and her beautiful 12 year old daughter,* **Jamie**.

Jan and her great kids, Ben (17), Coby (12), and Katie (11).

Acknowledgments

We could not have written this book without the help of many key people.

Lynda sends special thanks to...

Jan Kabili for her dedication to this project, and everything that she touches! Jan, you are da bomb! Your attention to detail and commitment to excellence is inspiring, and it is an honor to work with you.

Garo Green, our Director of Publications, who knows how to wear a lot of hats and still have cute hair! It is a gift to have the opportunity to work with you and to count you as a friend.

Tony Winecoff, our COO/Business Developer, who holds our ship together and also wears so many hats so well. You don't have much hair to worry about, but you have a cute head too. In all seriousness, it is a joy to work with you and I am filled with gratitude as I think of how important you are to our company, and how much value you have brought to this book series and everything else at lynda.com.

To the **staff** at lynda.com for helping with everything.

To **David Rogelberg**, my book agent (http://www.studiob.com), for helping make the Hands-On Training book series dream a reality.

To my daughter **Jamie** for her support, humor, and beautiful spirit.

To my husband **Bruce** for his support, humor, art, and patience. I know I am not an easy person to live with, and I'm grateful for your understanding.

To **Cary Norsworthy**, **Nancy Ruenzel**, and **Victor Gavenda** at Peachpit for their hard work and commitment to this series.

To **Adobe**, for making software that is just so damn good. To all the engineers and support team who keep making a great tool greater.

To you, the reader, for supporting this series. I hope this book is helpful to you, and that you enjoy creating Web graphics in this most amazing tool!

Jan sends special thanks to:

Her fellow Adobe course instructors at lynda.com and good friends, **Grace Hodgson** and **Ellen Norgard**.

The beta-testing team, **Michelle Bauer Carpenter**, **Rosanna Yeung**, and **Ellen Norgard**.

Her colleague, **Garo Green**, whose production assistance helped get this book to press.

Her son **Ben**, who is proof that living with a teenager can be a wonderful thing.

Her son **Coby**, who no doubt will support the whole family in our old age.

Her daughter **Katie**, the coolest and most gorgeous hip-hop dancer on the planet.

Her awesome partner **David Van de Water**, who has made life grrrreat again.

Her friend and mentor **Alex Sweetman**, who got her started down this road.

Her parents **Sy** and **Barb Feldman**, who always trusted and helped her.

Her brother, **Peter Feldman**, who let her sleep on his couch many times as she flew back and forth to Ojai over the last two years.

The **staff** at lynda.com, who work hard and are good folks.

Cary Norsworthy and staff at Peachpit Press.

And, of course, **Lynda** and **Bruce**.

I.

Interface

Disabling Color Profiles	Adobe Gamma
Preference Settings for the Web	Interface Overview
Photoshop / ImageReady Toolbars	Jump To
Moving Palettes and Tabs	Options Bar and Palettes	Shortcuts

Photoshop 6 / ImageReady 3
————————————————
For the Web

Adobe has always been known for is its consistency in interfaces. An Adobe application feels like just that—once you learn one product, it's a lot easier to learn another. Still, this version of Photoshop has many new features and workflow changes, so even seasoned Photoshop users will have some new things to learn.

This chapter includes information and advice on color settings, gives an overview of the interfaces of Photoshop and ImageReady, and shows how to set up Photoshop preferences for Web graphics. We chose not to go in depth into each palette and tool, because that's best left to each chapter so you can try features in context with what you're learning. Instead, this chapter focuses on the overarching principles of the interface and shows how to optimize your settings for Web graphics workflow.

Color Profiling in Photoshop 6

Color profiling was introduced into Photoshop with version 5.0 to help Web and print developers manage color consistency between printers, scanners and computer monitors. Adobe shipped Photoshop 5.0 and 5.5 with color profiles turned on, which was greeted by end users with some controversy and confusion. In Photoshop 6 color profiles are *not* on by default, which is a good thing, in our humble opinion.

What are color profiles, anyway? Computer color reliability has always been an inexact science. Digital artwork looks different on the computer monitor than it does once it's printed. A number of computer software and hardware vendors, such as Adobe, Apple, Hewlett Packard, and Microsoft, got together to form some standards around computer color, and came up with the concept of color profiles. The premise was that computer files could carry information about where they were created and how they were supposed to look, and that printing devices could read the information and duplicate the intended settings. Sounds good so far, right?

The trouble is, unless there's a receiving device that understands color profiles, they are of little use to anyone. Sadly, that is the case on today's Web, though at some point it will potentially change for the better. Today, if you use color profiles in your Web graphics, not only will no other software or hardware recognize them, but the result is that your images will look different in Photoshop than they do anywhere else – even in other Adobe Web products such as ImageReady, GoLive or LiveMotion!

While we think color profiles could ultimately be a great thing, we don't advocate using them just yet. We believe it will be more damaging to turn them on because you won't have an accurate idea of how your artwork looks in other applications, such as Explorer, Fireworks, FreeHand, GoLive, Illustrator, ImageReady, Netscape, etc. Photoshop's display will be adjusted, actually changing the appearance of otherwise absolute RGB pixel colors into something completely different. Your document will look the same in every other program except Photoshop, effectively ruining Photoshop's ability to integrate with other applications.

sRGB in Photoshop 6

We're grateful that Adobe chose to leave color profiles turned off in Photoshop 6, allowing advanced users to turn them on, and leaving those who don't know how to use them less bewildered and frustrated. However, there's still one gotcha for Macintosh users only that we recommend you change from the way the program ships, and that has to do with sRGB. If you are not on a Macintosh, you can skip this sRGB section, as it will not affect you.

sRGB is the default color setting of Photoshop 6 when you first launch the program. The sRGB color setting emulates the appearance of the average PC monitor, which is generally darker than the average Macintosh monitor. Adobe claims that sRGB is endorsed by many hardware and software manufacturers, although we haven't run across this in our own experience. Adobe, however, claims in its documentation that sRGB is becoming the default color space for many scanners, low-end printers, and software applications. Adobe recommends this color space for Web work, but we do not.

While choosing this color setting will make your screen emulate a PC while you're in Photoshop, it will not change the way your screen looks in other Web applications, such as browsers, ImageReady, GoLive, LiveMotion, Dreamweaver, etc. It's rather disconcerting to choose colors in Photoshop, and then have those colors look different in other applications on the same computer.

It should be noted that Photoshop is not actually changing the colors of the real pixels in sRGB mode. Instead, it is changing the way the colors are previewed in Photoshop. We personally don't see the advantage of having our artwork preview differently in Photoshop than in our Web browser or in ImageReady. Adobe's thought was that this preview is more accurate to how your Web graphics will be viewed from PCs, which have a higher market share than Macintoshes. In our opinion, there are other, better ways to preview your artwork, which we will recommend instead in this chapter, such as changing your gamma.

For this reason, the next section will cover how to change the Color Settings in Photoshop 6 from sRGB to Monitor RGB.

[PS]

I. —————————— Setting Photoshop Color Settings (MAC)

This exercise is for Macintosh users only. If you are using a Windows machine, skip ahead! The purpose of this exercise is to disable the sRGB settings, so that the colors you choose in Photoshop will look the same as they do in ImageReady, other Web applications, and your browser.

1. Launch Photoshop, and choose **Edit > Color Settings.**

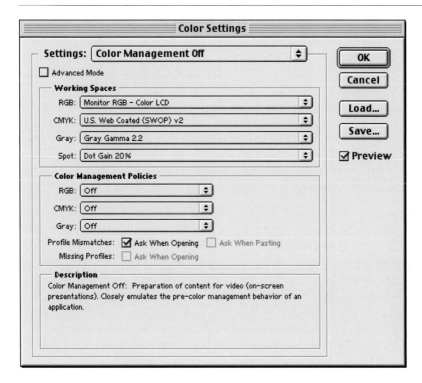

2. In the **Color Settings** dialog box, choose **Settings: Color Management Off**. Click **OK**.

Note that this change sets the RGB field to Monitor RGB, which effectively leaves the appearance of your monitor set to its defaults (just like in browsers, graphics applications other than Photoshop, and HTML editors.) The artwork on your screen will appear without any alteration, like it did in the days of Photoshop 4.0 and earlier, before color profiles were introduced. By the way, your Monitor RGB setting may read a little differently than the one in this example - Monitor RGB - Color LCD - depending on what kind of monitor you're using.

Now that you've finished these steps, all the color profile and preview options will be turned off, and your images will look exactly like they did in Photoshop 4.0 and in every other graphics and browser application you use.

TIP | Additional Color Help

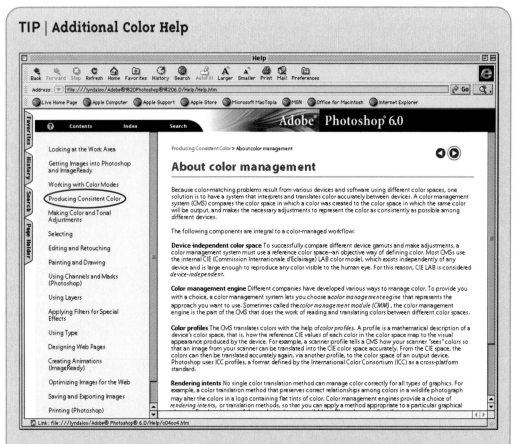

Photoshop 6 ships with additional documentation about color management, which you can access by choosing **Help > Help Contents** and clicking **Producing Consistent Color**. We're intentionally not bogging you down with all the technical details of this highly complex subject, so that the book stays focused on the Web instead of print. However, if this subject piques your curiosity, be sure to give this **Help** file a read. Additional Color Management information is also available in the **Adobe Photoshop 6.0 User Guide Supplement**.

NOTE | Adobe Gamma on Macintoshes

The "gamma" of your monitor sets a midpoint for gray, meaning that it affects not the white point or black point display, but the grays or values in between white and black. Windows has a setting of 2.2 gamma, while Macintosh uses a setting of 1.8. This is why Web graphics look darker on Windows than they do on Macintoshes. Many Web developers who work on Macs like to change their gamma settings to match that of Windows. If you make this change, it will affect all applications, not just Photoshop. We leave our gamma settings alone, because we primarily design Web graphics for the **lynda.com** site, which has a large Mac audience. If you think that your site might have a larger Windows audience, this change might save you from potential unanticipated revisions to lighten your graphics so they read better on Windows machines.

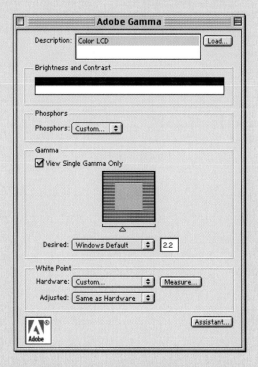

You can access **Adobe Gamma** by going to the **Apple** menu and choosing **Control Panels > Adobe Gamma**. Select the **Control Panel** button, since this can be accessed at any time from within any application, not just Photoshop or ImageReady. This opens the **Adobe Gamma** control panel, where you can choose **Desired: Windows Default 2.2**, which is the setting you want if you do a lot of Web authoring for a Windows audience. The beauty of changing your system to match a Windows system this way instead of through Color Settings is that it will affect all applications, including Photoshop, ImageReady, GoLive, etc.

[PS]

2. ————————Setting Photoshop Color Settings (WIN)

This exercise is for Windows users only. If you are using a Macintosh machine, skip ahead! The purpose of this exercise is to make sure that color profiles for print graphics are not invoked when you are working on Web graphics.

1. Launch Photoshop 6, and choose **Edit > Color Settings.**

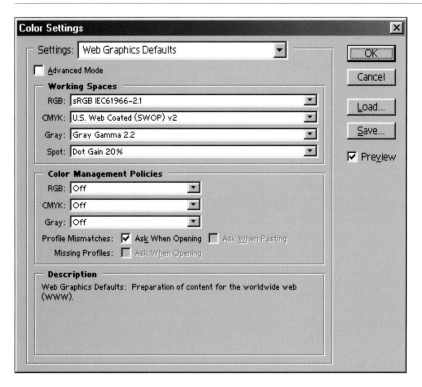

2. In the **Color Settings** dialog box, choose **Settings: Web Graphics Defaults**. Click **OK.**

Even though this setting leaves sRGB active, that's immaterial on Windows machine. Your colors will still match between Photoshop, ImageReady and other Web applications, since sRGB is the native color space on Windows machines.

3. ————————— Changing Your Photoshop Preferences for the Web

There are numerous **Preference** settings in Photoshop, and many of them are related to workflow, while others will directly impact whether you are set up properly for the Web or print. The following setup emulates how we prefer to change our Photoshop preferences for the Web. For a complete list of preferences and their settings, refer to the Adobe Photoshop manual.

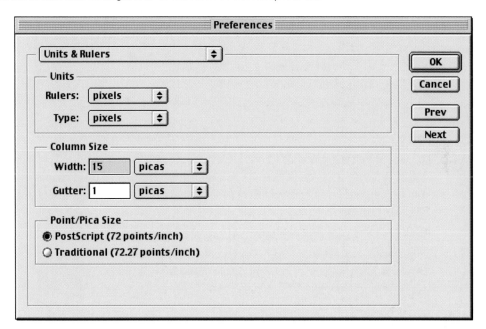

1. In Photoshop, choose **Edit** > **Preferences** > **Units & Rulers....** In the **Preferences** dialog box, change the Rulers units to **pixels**, and click **OK**.

When you work on the Web you measure everything by pixels and points, not picas, as you would in print.

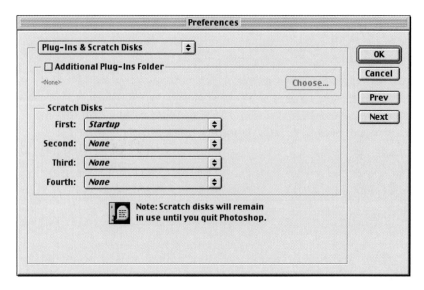

2. Choose **Edit > Preferences > Plug-Ins & Scratch Disks….** This illustration shows the default settings for this preference. If you have more than one hard drive, choose the drive with the most space on it for your **First** setting, and click **OK. Note:** This change will not take effect until you quit and reopen Photoshop.

Scratch disk space helps Photoshop manage memory, so you want as much free space on your primary disk as you can get. There's only one hard drive on the laptop on which this chapter is being written, so our First Scratch Disk is set to Startup.

Interface Overview

Photoshop and ImageReady began their lives as separate applications. Although they are still separate, now they ship together and are designed to work together. The good news is that, from an interface standpoint, you're in for an easy learning curve. That's because Photoshop and ImageReady's toolbars, palettes, and menu items are organized in a very logical way, and support your workflow to a higher degree than just about any other software tool we can think of.

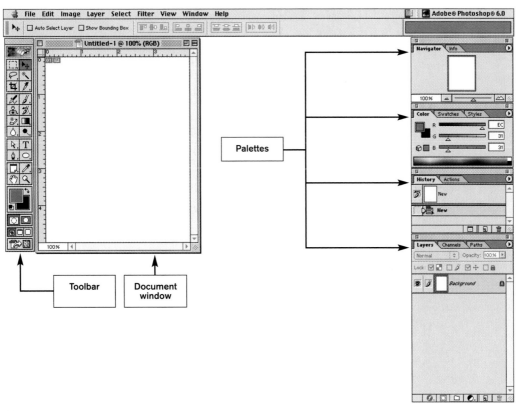

Photoshop 6

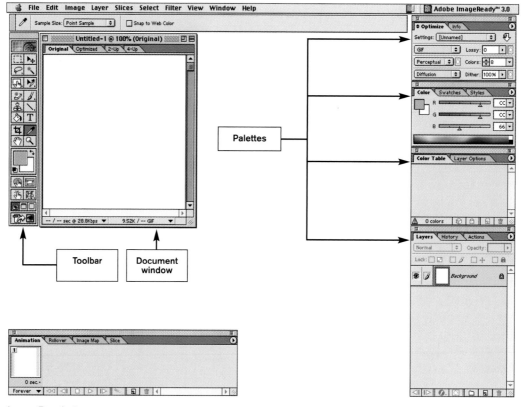

ImageReady 3

When you first open Photoshop or ImageReady, they default to showing the Toolbox and a few key palettes. The figures above also show an open, untitled document, which you can create by choosing File > New. Pressing the Tab key toggles all the palettes on and off in either application. Even though you'll see a few different palettes, it's obvious from first glance that these two programs have a very similar interface. If you know Photoshop already, you'll have a huge advantage when learning ImageReady.

The Photoshop 6 and ImageReady 3 Toolboxes

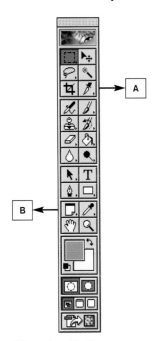

Photoshop Toolbox

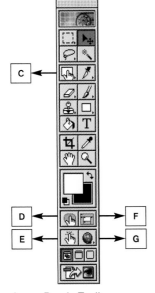

ImageReady Toolbox

The toolbar is almost identical in Photoshop 6 and ImageReady 3. There are a few key differences, as well as a few new tools, which are outlined in the following chart:

Photoshop 6	
A	*Slice and Slice Select Tools:* Slicing tools are new to Photoshop 6. You'll get to try them out in Chapter 10, "*Slicing.*"
B	*Annotation Tools*: It's possible to leave notes or audio voice messages to yourself or other team members now in Photoshop 6 using the annotation tools.

ImageReady 3	
C	*Image Map Tools*: ImageReady 3 has a few new image map tools, which you can try in Chapter 9, "*Image Maps.*"
D	*Toggles Image Map Visibility*: Image Maps can be previewed, or the preview can be turned off, using this tool.
E	*Rollover Preview:* You can preview rollovers without going to the browser by using this tool. You'll get to try this tool in Chapter 11, "*Rollovers.*"
F	*Toggles Slice Visibility:* Slice previews can be turned on or off using this tool. You'll get to try this tool in Chapter 10, "*Slicing.*"
G	*Preview in Default Browser*: You can preview an ImageReady document with a click of this button. You'll get to try this tool in many chapters.

Fly Out Menus

Whenever you see a little right-pointing arrow on a tool in Photoshop or ImageReady (or any Adobe application for that matter), it means there are other tool choices. Simply hold your mouse down on the tool, and other choices will fly out. Sometimes it's hard to find that one tool you're looking for because it's hidden under a fly-out menu icon. These handy illustrations should help you in both Photoshop and ImageReady.

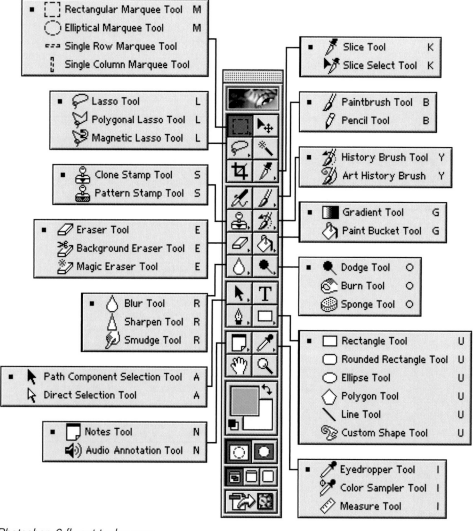

Photoshop 6 fly-out tool menus

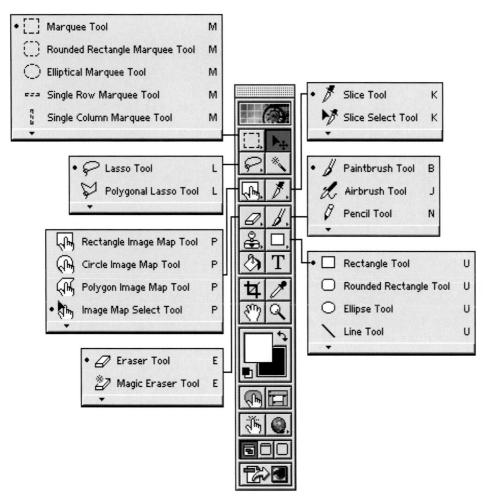

• ⬚ Marquee Tool		M
◌ Rounded Rectangle Marquee Tool		M
◯ Elliptical Marquee Tool		M
⚏ Single Row Marquee Tool		M
⦀ Single Column Marquee Tool		M

• 🔪 Slice Tool		K
🔪 Slice Select Tool		K

• ⌇ Lasso Tool		L
⌇ Polygonal Lasso Tool		L

• 🖌 Paintbrush Tool		B
🖌 Airbrush Tool		J
✎ Pencil Tool		N

🖑 Rectangle Image Map Tool		P
🖑 Circle Image Map Tool		P
🖑 Polygon Image Map Tool		P
• 🖑 Image Map Select Tool		P

• ⬜ Rectangle Tool		U
◻ Rounded Rectangle Tool		U
◯ Ellipse Tool		U
╲ Line Tool		U

• ⌫ Eraser Tool		E
⌫ Magic Eraser Tool		E

ImageReady 3 fly-out tool menus

Jump To Buttons

The **Jump To** button is located at the bottom of both toolboxes. It lets you switch between Photoshop and ImageReady with a convenient click of a button.

Jump To ImageReady button in Photoshop

Jump To Photoshop button in ImageReady

You'll have plenty of opportunities to use the Jump To button throughout this book. When you have an open document and click this button, the same document reopens in the other application. If you don't have a document open, the Jump To button will not work.

[PS/IR]

_____**Using Flexible Palettes and Tabs**

What's distinctive about Photoshop and ImageReady is that you can reorganize items by docking or undocking a tab to form a new palette. This is a very convenient thing to do if you find that you are only working with a few palettes that are not grouped together, or if you don't want to crowd your work-space with palettes you don't use.

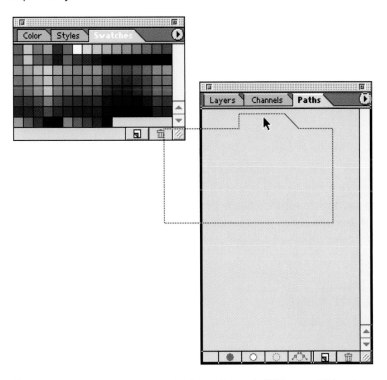

1. In either application, click on the **Swatches** tab (if it's not visible, choose **Window > Show Swatches**), and drag the **Swatches** palette by its tab into the group of palettes that includes the **Layers** palette (if not visible, choose Window > Show Layers).

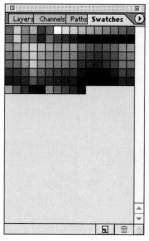

By dragging the Swatches palette by the tab area, you can drag it into another palette group. We do this often when we're working in Photoshop or ImageReady because we find ourselves using just a few features, and we don't want to clutter up the screen with all the default palettes.

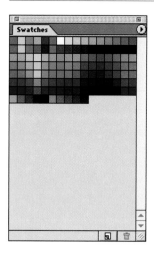

2. You can also create a palette with just one item if you want to, rather than nesting several items into a palette group. Drag the **Swatches** palette out of the **Layers** palette group and it will form its own palette all by itself.

[PS]

5. _____Docking Palettes to Each Other in Photoshop

There's a new way you can dock palettes in Photoshop, creating a vertical grouped palette. Here's how.

1. The **Swatches** palette should be on its own right now, if you followed the last exercise. If not, drag the **Swatches** palette by its tab away from any palette group in which it might be nested, so that it forms its own single palette.

2. Drag the **Color** palette by its tab away from its palette group so that it also forms a single palette.

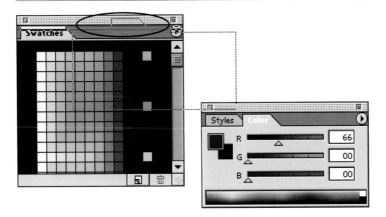

3. Drag the **Color** palette by its tab, and position it so it is in the top-most title bar of the **Swatches** palette.

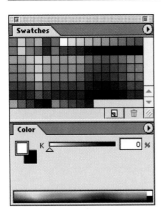

This should result in the palettes being docked to each other in a vertical fashion. We like to do this with certain palettes that relate to one another.

[IR]

6. —————————— Docking Palettes to Each Other in ImageReady

It's possible to dock palettes to each other in ImageReady as well, but it's done a little differently.

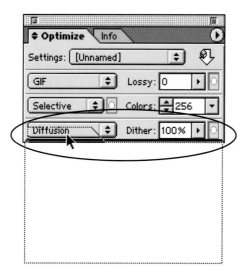

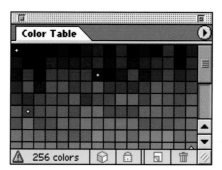

1. Drag the **Color Table** palette by its tab onto the bottom of the **Optimize** palette so only the bottom line of the Optimize palette becomes highlighted, as shown above.

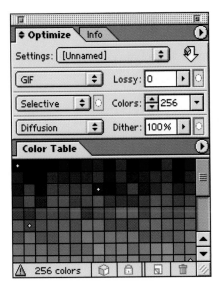

The result is that these two palettes form a vertical docked configuration. We like to compare these two palettes often when we're optimizing images, and find this docking technique very helpful.

[PS/IR]

 7. ———————**Returning the Palettes to Default Settings**

The fact that you can rearrange palettes and tabs is wonderful until you wish you could set them back to the way Photoshop or ImageReady had them in the first place. We often create our own custom groupings of tabs and palettes to support a single project, and then return to the defaults when we're finished. The procedure for both applications is similar, as you'll see in this short exercise.

1. In Photoshop, choose **Window > Reset Palette Locations**. In ImageReady, choose **Window > Arrange > Reset Palettes**.

This restores the default positions of all your palettes. Easy!

[PS/IR]

8. Using the Options Bar

New to Photoshop 6 and ImageReady 3 is the Options bar, which contains setting options for each tool in the Toolbox. This feature is an improvement over the Options palette, which was present in older versions of these two applications. Often the same information that is on the Options bar used to be found in the Options palette. The advantage of the Options bar over the palette is that it is always in the upper part of the screen, and you don't have to hunt for it, as was the case with the older Options palette. The palette is not completely gone, however. This next exercise will show you how to access the Options bar, and when necessary, the palettes that resemble the Options palette. This exercise is shown in Photoshop, but it works the same in ImageReady.

1. Choose **File > New**. Enter any size value, and click **OK**.

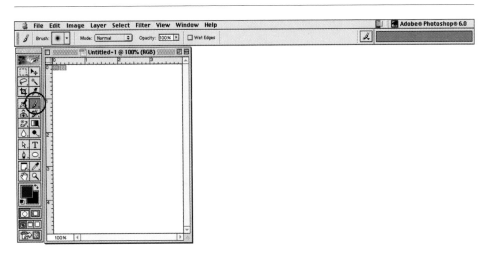

2. Click the **Paintbrush** tool in the Toolbox.

Notice that the settings for the Paintbrush tool (Brush type and size, Mode, Opacity and Wet Edges) are visible in the Options bar, which is located at the top of the Photoshop 6 screen.

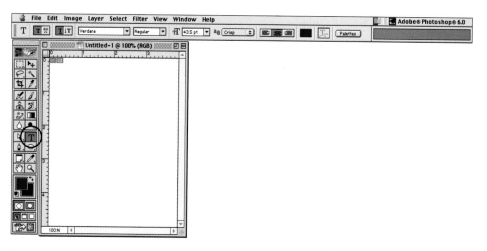

3. Click the **Type** tool in the Toolbox.

Notice that the settings have changed to show the options for the Type tool.

---

4. Click the **Palettes** button in the Options bar.

This brings the older style of Options palette forward, which has additional Type settings (Character and Paragraph settings) some of which are not found on the Options bar. Though this new way of accessing settings through the Options bar and Options palettes might seem minor, it's one of our favorite improvements to Photoshop 6. We used to spend extra time searching for the right palette for a tool, and now these settings are always close at hand and easy to locate.

---

5. Close the file. You don't need to save it.

[PS]

9. ———————Docking Palettes to the Photoshop Options Bar

There's a spot to the far right of the Photoshop Options bar called the **Palette Well,** where you can dock one or more palettes that you use often. This is another small, yet significant, improvement in keeping often-used palettes within easy arms reach. For example, we use the Swatches and the Layers palettes all the time. Because of this, they are great candidates to dock on our Options bar. Here's a short exercise to show you how.

Note: You won't be able to see or use the Palette Well unless your screen resolution is set to 800x600 resolution or greater and you have a big enough screen (set your working area to Maximize on Windows). It's important that your screen resolution matches the resolution for which you're designing, so that your images are the correct size in the end. So don't change your resolution just to be able to use the palette well.

1. Make sure the **Swatches** and the **Layers** palettes are both open. If they are not on your screen already, choose **Window > Show Swatches,** and **Window > Show Layers.**

2. Drag the tab of the **Swatches** palette to the **Palette Well** in the upper right corner of the **Options** bar.

3. Drag the tab of the **Layers** palette to the **Palette Well** too.

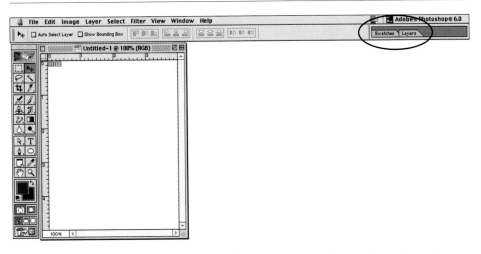

Now, both these palettes are docked inside the Options bar and are easier to locate than by going to the Window menu to find them. You can click either tab in the docked Options bar location, and those palettes will pop up and become active.

Shortcuts

Next are some of the most useful shortcuts when doing Web work in Photoshop 6 and ImageReady 3. Here are two big ones.

• The Tab key shows/hides all palettes and the toolbox. To show or hide only the palettes, leaving the toolbar as is, press **Shift+Tab**.

• To select a tool quickly, press its shortcut key on your keyboard. To see a tool's shortcut key, point your mouse over the tool in the Toolbox.

The two charts below give the keyboard letter shortcuts to the most commonly used tools when doing Web design.

Photoshop	
Tool	Shortcut Key
Eraser	E
Eyedropper	I
Hand	H
Move	V
Switch Colors	X
Type	T
Zoom	Z

ImageReady	
Tool	Shortcut Key
Slice	K
Slice Selection	K
Hide/Show Slices	Q

How to Set a Tool's Default Settings in Photoshop

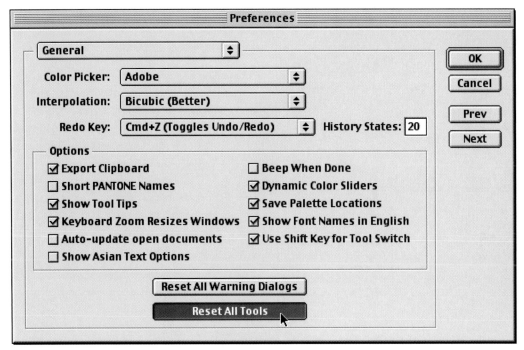

Photoshop's Option bar and palettes are "sticky," meaning they remember the settings that were last used. If you want to reset the values of the settings back to defaults, choose Edit > Preferences > General, and click Reset All Tools.

2.

Web Color

Web-Safe Color	Hexadecimal Color
Information Palette	Copying Color	Dithering
Lock Transparent Pixels	Ditherbox	Gamma

chap_o2

Photoshop 6 / ImageReady 3
H•O•T CD-ROM

Photoshop and ImageReady offer great tools for working with Web-safe color, from palettes to swatches to hexadecimal readouts in the Info palette. If you don't know what those terms mean, then this chapter will help a lot. You'll get the lowdown on Web color—what Web-safe color is, why you need to care about it, when to use it, and how to use it in Photoshop and ImageReady.

Aside from Web-safe color, there are numerous techniques for manipulating color in these two applications. In this chapter we share our favorite tips for picking, editing, and changing colors. You will learn how to load swatch palettes, convert RGB to hexadecimal, limit the Photoshop Color Picker to Web-safe colors, change the Color palette to Web-safe colors only, copy HTML color, shift non-safe colors to Web-safe ones, work with hybrid colors, and use Lock Transparent Pixels to color artwork. Color has probably never sounded so scary and technical before, but Photoshop and ImageReady make this process as fun and creative as possible by offering the best Web-color picking tools around.

What Is Web-Safe Color Anyway?

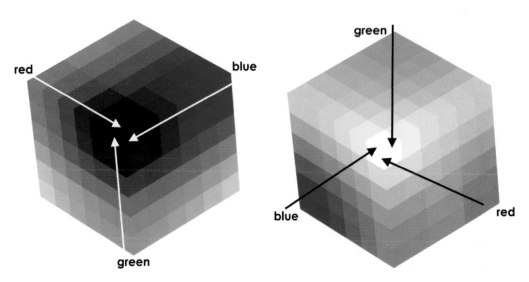

If you've been around the Web for a while, you might have heard the term Web-safe color. Perhaps you've heard other terms, too, such as browser safe, Web palette, 216 palette, the 6 x 6 x 6 cube, Netscape cube, Explorer colors, Web colors, etc. These all refer to the same 216 colors whose numerical definition forms a mathematical cube. We don't know about you, but our minds don't think in mathematical cubes, so when we first learned of this concept we were confused.

You probably have never thought that color was mathematical before now, and if you are not fond of math we're certain that you will not welcome this news. We'll do our best to explain it, but before we do, let us assure you that you don't have to understand the math to use and benefit from Web-safe color picking. Photoshop and ImageReady take the pain out of understanding this math and make it easy to choose Web-safe colors visually and intuitively. This section of this chapter is really here to give you an understanding of the whats, whys, and wherefores of Web-safe color. If you prefer to skip over this background information you won't offend us in the least.

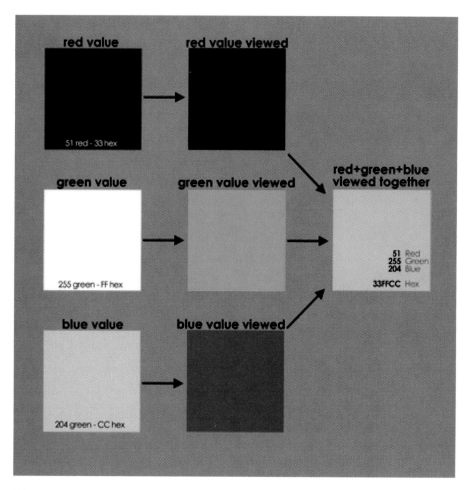

Printed colors are formed from pigments that combine cyan, magenta, yellow, and black (CMYK). For those of you who are curious, the K in CMYK stands for black. Strange, huh? Screen colors are formed from three colors of light: red, green, and blue (RGB). Because the focus of this chapter is Web color, understanding how pixels create color is the first step toward comprehending this stuff.

A computer forms a pixel by projecting three lights to a single location on your screen. The lights vary in intensity, measured in 256 steps from 0 to 255. This color process is also sometimes called additive light, because it involves adding these three colored lights together. When the lights of all three colors (red, green, and blue) are fully on, white is created. When all lights are off, black is created. Colored pixels are created with various combinations of these three lights.

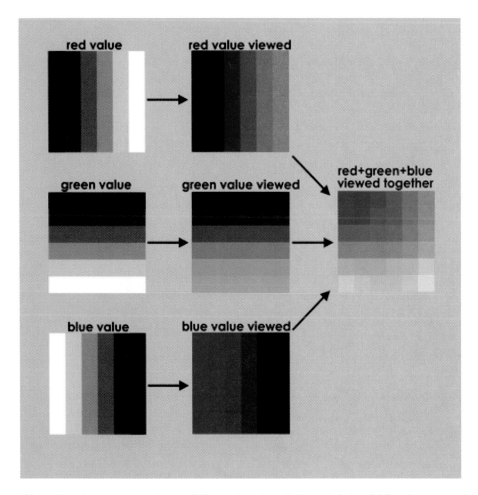

Web-safe colors are derived from distinct values from light to dark, by dividing the potential values of these lights into six equal parts for each of the red, green, and blue elements. If you divide the scale for a given color into six equal parts, the resulting values are 0, 51, 102, 153, 204, and 255. If you then translate this mathematical formula into percentages, the results are 0%, 20%, 40%, 60%, 80%, and 100%. Web-safe colors are created by mixing six values of red, six values of green, and six values of blue. So there are 216 Web-safe colors because that is the total number of combinations of 6 x 6 x 6; or six reds, times six greens, times six blues.

Is Web-Safe Color So Important?

When you publish your images to the Web, people's computer screens, in effect, are your printing press. Your images are subjected to whatever type of monitor and color card your audience is using. If one part of your audience can see your Web site in millions of colors, another audience sector can see your site in thousands of colors, and another part in hundreds, your site is going to look different to different audiences. Welcome to the frustrating world of Web color.

Web-safe color specifically deals with color limitations on 8-bit systems. This term, 8-bit, refers to the number 256, and in the past many computer systems shipped with the limitation of only being able to display 256 colors.

Today, you would be hard pressed to buy a computer that was limited to 8-bit color. When the Web became popular about five to six years ago, this was a much bigger issue. At that time, you couldn't buy a laptop that had thousands or millions of colors (it's still not uncommon to see 8-bit laptops), and you had to buy special video cards and monitors that would support more colors. Many desktop systems didn't have 16-bit (thousands of colors) or 24-bit color cards (millions of colors) like they do today.

Even though most laptop and desktop systems today include color cards that can show more than 256 colors, many of them are set to 256 colors when you buy them at the store. This is not true of Macintosh computers, but it is true for Wintel computers. Most consumers buy computers for word processing, spreadsheets, database work, and games. It is not necessary that these systems view more than 256 colors, so many people never even know to check their settings to change from 256 colors to thousands or millions.

Regardless of all the warnings we're raising here, the truth is that the number of people with 8-bit systems decreases every year. There will come a day when Web-safe color will be a thing of the past. In fact, many people believe that day is already here. We are not among them. Even as computer displays become more powerful, other devices with limited color displays, like PDAs, cell phones, and Internet appliances, are becoming popular.

Although the 8-bit audience is much smaller than it used to be, it's not that difficult to make pages that look just as good to those viewers as to the more fortunate audiences with newer machines and more colors. If you know that your audience is composed mostly of people with newer computers, or you are designing an Intranet for systems that you know can see millions or thousands of colors, then you can ignore all the problems with 8-bit color and not be concerned about Web-safe palettes. If you want to have maximum control over how your pages are seen, even on less powerful systems than your own, then you will benefit by using these colors.

What happens when you don't use Web-safe colors and your pages are viewed on a system with an 8-bit color limitation? Some colors will shift to ones that you didn't choose, and some may have unwanted dots all over them. If that doesn't concern you, then you can skip to the next chapter.

We are not here to judge whether you should or should not use Web-safe color. If you make the informed decision not to use these colors in your work, you will not be alone. We know many Web designers who choose to do this. Our job is simply to inform you of the issues. Your job is to know

whether the issues are pertinent to your publishing needs or not. We believe that creative professionals are judged by how good their images look. If your images shift to a color that you didn't choose or
appear with unwanted dots all over them, and we could have taught you something that you could
have done to avoid those problems, then we did not do our job.

What Is Hexadecimal Color?

When you specify color in HTML, you cannot use decimal values or the base 10 math that we all grew
up learning. The decimal system that you are already familiar with uses 10 digits (0, 1, 2, 3, 4, 5, 6, 7,
8, and 9). HTML requires that you convert the decimal values to hexadecimal values, or base 16, which
uses 16 digits (0, 1, 2, 3, 4, 5, 6, 7, 8, 9, A, B, C, D, E, and F). Letters are used for the digits greater
than 9. Base 10 is natural for humans, who have a total of 10 fingers with which to count, and hexadecimal is natural for computers, which readily work with multiples of two.

Therefore, the Web-safe RGB decimal values of 0, 51, 102, 153, 204, or 255 need to be converted
for use on the Web. This handy chart shows how this conversion works.

RGB Color Translation Values		
Decimal	**Percentage**	**Hexadecimal**
0	0%	00
51	20%	33
102	40%	66
153	60%	99
204	80%	CC
255	100%	FF

Fortunately, Photoshop and ImageReady don't require that you use math to create Web-safe color. This
chart is here merely to explain the concept.

RGB Color Translations															
Decimal Digits															
0	1	2	3	4	5	6	7	8	9	10	11	12	13	14	15
Hexadecimal Digits															
0	1	2	3	4	5	6	7	8	9	A	B	C	D	E	F

What Happens If You Don't Use Web-Safe Color?

Two big problems occur to your images if you don't use Web-safe colors. The first has to do with the hexadecimal values that are used in the **BODY** tag of HTML pages. The **BODY** tag specifies which colors are used for the background color, text color, link color, active link color, and visited link color of Web pages.

If you don't use Web-safe colors, then the colors you choose for the **BODY** of your Web pages will shift on systems that are limited to 256 colors. We've had people write to us who published their pages and then didn't understand why they couldn't see the colored links or text that they specified. Their link or text color had shifted to the same color as their background color, rendering their text unreadable! This is a potential penalty of using any color in the spectrum on a Web page. If you stick to Web-safe colors, your colors will not be unexpectedly shifted on 8-bit systems. If you don't use Web-safe colors, you run the risk of not knowing what color the browser will use for those colors you specified in the **BODY** element of your HTML.

You won't need to program the **BODY** tag in HTML in this book because Photoshop 6 and ImageReady 3 will write all the code for you. You'll learn more about this in Chapter 7, *"Background Images."* The thing is, within Photoshop and ImageReady you'll have the choice of whether or not to choose Web-safe colors for these aspects of HTML. Our suggestion is to always use Web-safe colors for background colors in HTML, to avoid unexpected color shifting on 8-bit systems.

Graphic viewed in 24-bit.

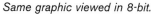
Same graphic viewed in 8-bit.

Close-up 24-bit.

Close-up 8-bit.

The second problem has to do with color in images. If you don't use Web-safe colors on certain types of images, you might get unwanted dithering in them. Here are some examples of what that looks like.

Notice the unwanted dots in the image viewed in 8-bit? They're the result of dithering, and they only happen because the colors of the hat and skin tone were not chosen from Web-safe colors. If the colors chosen for this illustration were Web safe to begin with, they would not dither at all, regardless of whether they were viewed in 24-bit or 8-bit.

The only time not to use Web-safe colors in Web graphics is with photographs or continuous-tone content. When the browser views these types of images, it converts them to 8-bit on the fly and does a better job than if you'd converted them yourself. The following images demonstrate what we're talking about.

JPEG image viewed on 24-bit or 16-bit system.

JPEG image viewed on 8-bit system.

GIF image saved with a Perceptual palette in Photoshop or ImageReady viewed on 24-bit or 16-bit system.

GIF image saved with a Selective palette in Photoshop or ImageReady viewed on an 8-bit system.

GIF image saved with Adaptive palette in Photoshop or ImageReady viewed on 8-bit system.

GIF image saved with Web palette in Photoshop or ImageReady viewed on 24-bit or 16-bit system.

This demonstrates that the browser does just as good a job of converting the photograph on an 8-bit system as you could if you forced the image to a Web palette. We never use Web palettes on photographs for this reason. The browser does just as good a job as we could, and if we leave the image in a 24-bit or adaptive format, it will look better on systems that can view it in 24-bit or 16-bit. **Perceptual**, **Selective**, and **Adaptive** are "adaptive" style palettes that will be described in detail in Chapter 3, *"Optimization."*

To summarize:

• Web-safe color is something you use to make your images look best on 8-bit systems.

• 16-bit and 24-bit systems can see any color you publish without dithering or shifting color.

• Use Web-safe colors for your hexadecimal **BODY** elements in HTML.

• Use Web-safe colors for areas of solid colors in your graphics.

• Never use Web-safe color palettes for photographic or continuous-tone artwork.

[PS]

 I. ——————————**Changing the Info Palette**

The Info palette in Photoshop offers a lot of valuable feedback about your image's colors. You can change the setting to offer RGB and hexadecimal readouts so that you can read the values of your color images in the context of the Web.

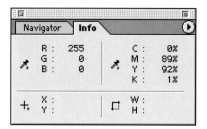

1. Launch Photoshop and click on the **Info** tab on your screen, or choose **Window > Show Info** if it isn't visible. Click on the **Info** palette's upper-right arrow and choose **Palette Options...** from the pop-up menu. The **Info Options** dialog box will appear.

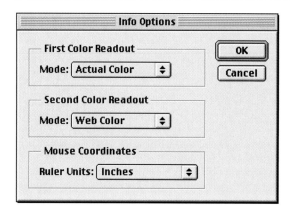

2. Make sure that your **Info Options** match the settings shown here, and click **OK**.

3. Open **color.gif** from the **chap_02** folder you transferred to your hard drive from the **H•O•T CD-ROM**.

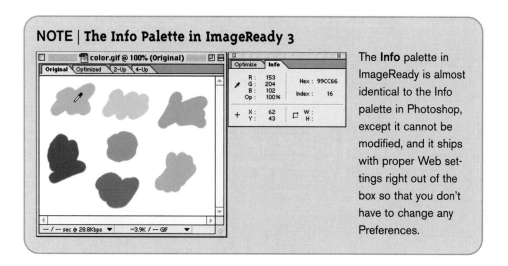

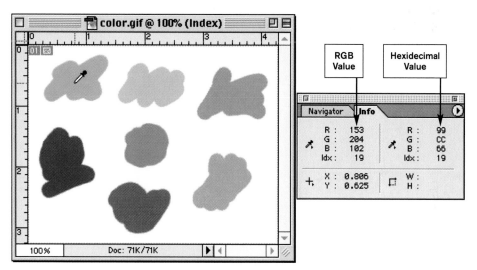

4. With any tool selected, move your cursor over the colors in this image. Look at the **Info** palette and notice that the readout on the right is giving you the hexadecimal value of each RGB color.

In the example on the preceding page, the RGB value is R:153, G:204, B:102, *and the hexadecimal value is* 99CC66. *The readout for* Idx *(under the RGB column in the hexadecimal readout) stands for* Index. *An indexed graphic is one that contains a maximum of 256 colors, and the* Idx *number is the mathematical position of each color in the* Color Table. *We know of no use for the* Idx *values readout, except that it alerts you to the fact that you are working with an index-mode graphic. In fact, whenever you are editing a 256-color document in Photoshop, it is referred to as "Indexed" color mode.*

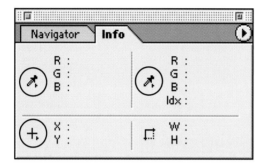

Tip: The circled items above contain pop-up menus that offer alternative access to the Info Options settings in Photoshop. This is not available in ImageReady.

5. Close this file. You won't need it again.

[PS/IR]

2. ―――――――――**Copy Color as HTML**

If you want to get the hexadecimal value of a color from Photoshop or ImageReady into an HTML or text editor, you might find the **Copy Color as HTML** feature useful. This feature converts an RGB color value to a hexadecimal color value in text (for example, **#663300**), and puts that color value into your computer's clipboard so you can paste it as text into other applications. This is a handy feature if you are writing HTML from scratch and want to quickly and easily get a color value from Photoshop into your code.

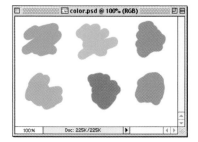

1. Open **color.psd** from the **chap_02** folder that you transferred to your hard drive from the **H•O•T CD-ROM**.

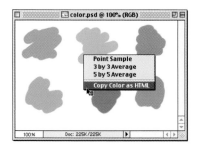

2. To copy the hexadecimal color of an image so you can paste it into an HTML editor, select the **Eyedropper** tool from the Toolbox (the shortcut is the letter **I** on your keyboard). In Photoshop, **Control+click** (Mac) or **right-click** (Windows) on a color in a document, and choose **Copy Color as HTML** from the contextual menu. If you're working in ImageReady, first click on a color in the document; then **Control+click** (Mac) or **right-click** (Windows) anywhere in the document and choose **Copy Foreground Color as HTML**. **Note:** The Eyedropper tool must be selected for this to work in either program.

3. When you go to paste this color into a text editor or HTML program, it will look like this:
`COLOR="#336633"`

4. Close the file. You won't need it again.

3. ——————Only Web Colors

In past versions of Photoshop, it was difficult to choose a Web-safe color from the **Color Picker** without manually typing in Web-safe RGB values. This hassle has been removed since Photoshop 5.5, because the native **Color Picker** can now be set to display **Only Web Colors**. Here's how.

Note: The same **Color Picker** you'll learn about in this exercise also exists in ImageReady. The only exception in ImageReady is that there are no L.a.b. and CMYK color values, and no shifting to the nearest print color. However, everything related to Web color is the same.

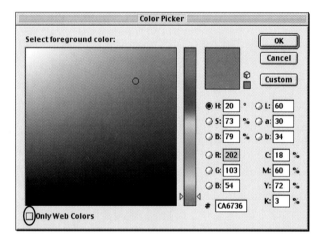

1. Click on the **foreground** color swatch in the Photoshop Toolbox. This will open the **Color Picker**.

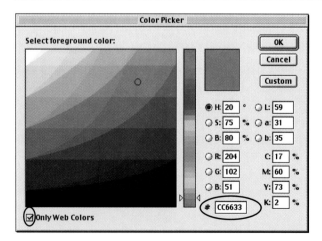

2. Make sure that you check **Only Web Colors** in the lower left corner of this dialog box.

Notice the hexadecimal readout at the bottom of the Color Picker? If you move the arrows up the vertical hue slider you'll see these readout numbers and the colors on the screen change.

*H, S, and B stand for **H**ue, **S**aturation, and **B**rightness. The above Color Picker is set to view by hue. All the different radio buttons offer different ways of seeing and picking colors. You may find that these different choices help you find colors that go together more quickly. It's very interesting to see how Web colors spread across the spectrum if you actively move the slider when exploring these different settings of **H, S, B, R, G, B,** or **L, a, b.***

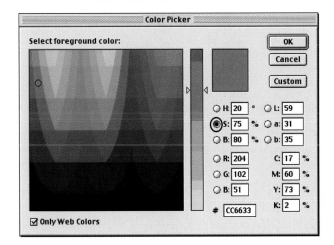

3. Click **S** to view the **Color Picker** by saturation. Saturation is the measure of color intensity. Try moving the vertical slider or clicking on a different color in the rainbow area to view Web-safe colors by this criterion. Move the slider arrows up to view more highly saturated Web colors, and down to view the desaturated ones.

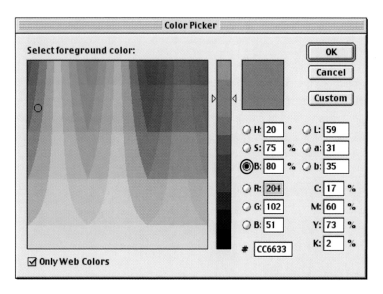

4. Click **B** to view the **Color Picker** by brightness. Brightness is the measure of light to dark values. Try moving the brightness slider or clicking on a different color in the rainbow area to view Web-safe colors by this criterion. Move the slider arrows up to view brighter Web color values, and down to view darker ones.

Try clicking on the R, G, and B buttons as well. These stand for Red, Green, and Blue. Click on the L, a, and b buttons next. These stand for Lightness, a Axis (green to magenta), and b Axis (blue to yellow). Aside from the psychedelic color experience, these methods offer some other interesting color formations from which to view or pick Web colors.

5. Click **Cancel** to get out of the color-picking mode, and move on to the next exercise to learn more about Web-color-picking options.

NOTE | Only Web Colors in ImageReady 3

The **Color Picker** in ImageReady 3 is almost identical to that of Photoshop 6, except that it lacks feedback about L.a.b. or CMYK color. This is because Photoshop has a dual purpose—it can be used for print or Web. ImageReady was developed for screen graphics only.

[PS]

4. _____Snapping to Web Colors

The thing about Photoshop is that there are often numerous ways to achieve the same goal. Instead of viewing Only Web Colors, you can use the standard **Color Picker** and then snap a non-Web-safe color to a safe one. This feature is also available in ImageReady.

1. This exercise takes place in Photoshop. Click on the foreground color swatch in the toolbox again to access the Photoshop **Color Picker**.

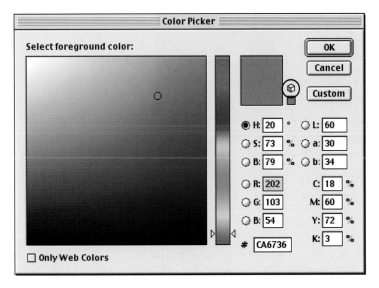

2. Uncheck the **Only Web Colors** box and move and click your cursor around inside the red area. Notice the cube icon that appears to the right of the color preview. The cube alerts you when you've selected a color that's not safe for the Web. If you click on the cube, the color selection will jump to the closest Web-safe color and then the cube will disappear.

3. Click **OK**, and the Web-safe color will appear in the foreground color area of your toolbox.

Note: This feature works identically in ImageReady. If you decide to try it out in ImageReady now, be sure to return to Photoshop for the next exercise.

[PS]

5. ———————————Setting the Color Palette to Web Colors

There are yet more ways to access and view Web-safe colors from Photoshop. How do you know which way to use? It's often a matter of convenience and/or habit. Sometimes, you'll find yourself intuitively wanting to click on the foreground color swatch to access the Photoshop Color Picker, as you just did in Exercises 3 and 4. Other times, it's more convenient to pick a color more quickly. The Color palette is a great alternative to using the Color Picker because it can stay open on the screen all the time and is faster to access. Here's how to set it to Web-safe colors.

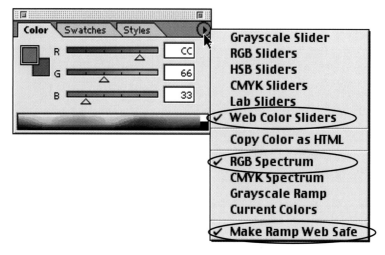

1. Locate the **Color** palette on your screen. If it is not visible, choose **Window > Show Color**. Click on the upper-right arrow and choose **Web Color** sliders from the pop-up menu. Make sure that **RGB Spectrum** is also selected. If it isn't, click on the upper-right arrow again to select it.

2. Click on the upper-right arrow again and choose **Make Ramp Web Safe**.

3. Try moving the sliders and you'll see them snap to the Web color markers. If you move your mouse over the color ramp and click around, you'll see the sliders move to different Web-safe colors.

That's the end of this exercise. You can leave the Color palette set this way until you choose to change it. **Note:** *ImageReady's Color palette looks and functions identically.*

[PS]

6. _____ Setting the Swatches Palette to Web Colors

The last way to set Web colors is by using Photoshop's **Swatches** palette. This palette defaults to displaying the system palette: If you are on a Mac, it will show the Mac system palette; if you are on Windows, it will show the Windows system palette. However, it's possible and preferable to load in Web-safe palettes, and that's just what you'll learn to do next. This exercise takes place in Photoshop, but would work in ImageReady almost the same way.

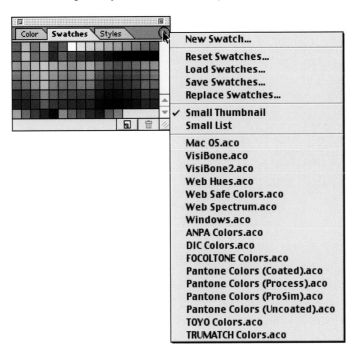

1. Click on the **Swatches** tab, and then press on the upper-right arrow to display a pop-up menu.

Notice the list of swatches at the bottom of the menu. All you have to do is select a swatch you want to load from the list, and it will replace the default swatches.

2. Choose **Web Hues.aco** from the list of swatches that appear. At the prompt, click **OK** (or **Replace** in ImageReady).

The Web Hues palette will replace the Photoshop default system palette.

3. You can leave the **Swatches** palette set up this way. Next time you open Photoshop, it will still be set.

[PS/IR]

7. ———————————Loading the lynda.com Swatch

Lynda and Bruce Heavin wrote a book together in 1997 called *Coloring Web Graphics*, which is now in its second edition. Bruce developed a series of Web-color swatches for that book which he organized aesthetically for picking Web colors. We've included one of these palettes inside the **chap_02** folder of the **H•O•T CD-ROM** for you to try. **Note:** Future exercises require that you have loaded this swatch into both Photoshop and ImageReady, so be sure to load it in both applications as instructed below.

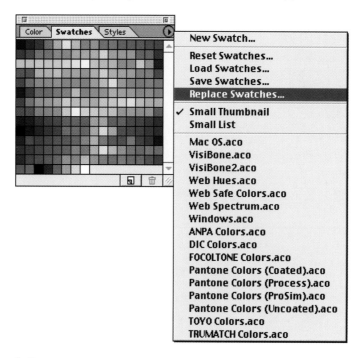

1. Press the upper-right arrow of the **Swatches** palette and choose **Replace Swatches…**. Navigate to the **chap_02** folder that you transferred to your hard drive from the **H•O•T CD-ROM** and choose **color.aco**. Click **Load** (or **Open** in ImageReady).

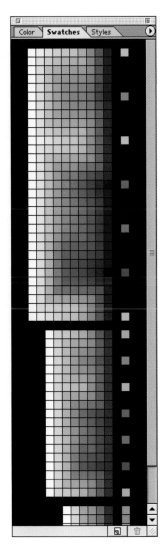

2. Drag the **Swatches** palette window as long as it will go, and then use the scroll bar to view the entire swatch document. This swatch is organized by hue (up and down), by value (right to left), and saturation (up and down).

---

3. Follow the same procedure in ImageReady.

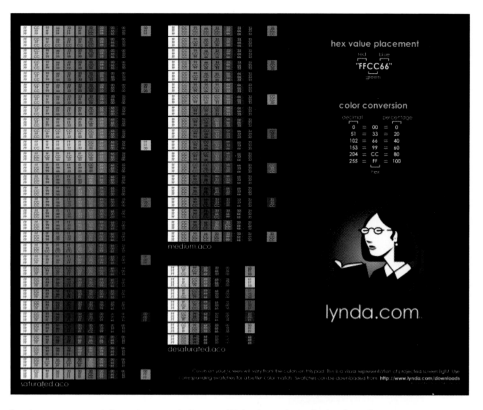

lynda.com created the mouse pad above, which shows hexadecimal readouts for each color within the color.aco swatch set, as well as a conversion chart from RGB to hexadecimal values. You can purchase the pad from our site, or just refer to the values printed here when you need to.

Note: Many of the colors are repeated for the sole reason of presenting an array that is organized efficiently for color picking. It's nice to see all the hues together. If you want to pick a red, for example, you can view the choices easily. It's also helpful to easily see all the dark colors and/or colors of equal saturation together. Once you use this palette, you will likely never remove it from the Swatches palette because it is so useful. Exercise 9 will show you how to use this Swatches palette in the context of editing browser dither from a color document.

[PS]

8. ———————Previewing Browser Dither

Unwanted dithering can look bad, but if you don't have an 8-bit system how can you preview whether your images will have it or not? Both Photoshop and ImageReady can preview how an 8-bit browser will dither. This exercise shows you how to preview dithering in Photoshop.

1. Make sure you are in Photoshop. Open **notsafe.psd** from the **chap_02** folder on your hard drive. This image contains non-Web-safe colors. On your system, it probably doesn't show any dithering.

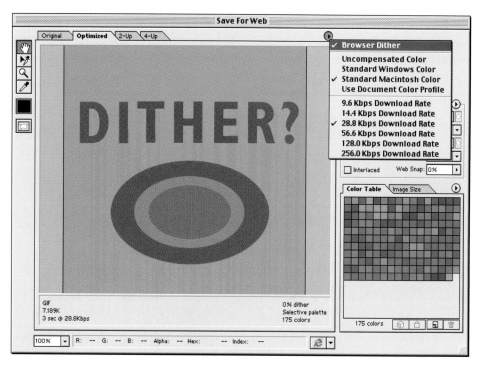

2. To preview how this file will appear on an 8-bit system, choose **File > Save for Web....**
Click on the arrow at the upper-right of the preview image to access the menu and choose
Browser Dither. Zoom into the image so you can see the dithering more clearly by selecting
the **Zoom** tool in the **Save for Web** Toolbox and clicking on the image. (It's not necessary to
use the Zoom tool, but we're suggesting it so you can see the problem more clearly.) This
book will cover the Save For Web feature in great detail in Chapter 3, "*Optimization*," so don't
worry if you are curious about any of the other features found in this new area of the program.

*Yuck! Look at all those unwanted dots in the image. Even though you don't see the image
this way on your system, this is the way some people will view it. The next exercise will
show you how to fix the image so the colors will look good on anyone's system, regardless
of color bit depth.*

3. Leave this image and the **Save For Web** dialog box open for the next exercise.

NOTE | Previewing Browser Dither in ImageReady 3

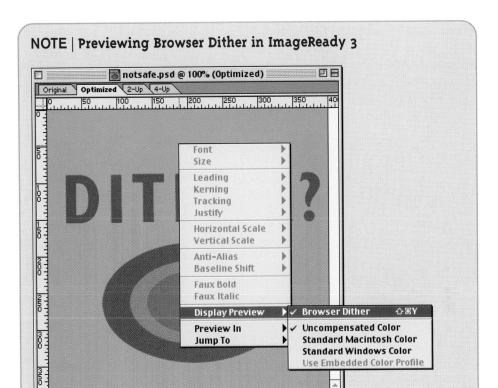

There are two ways to preview dither in ImageReady. If you are on the **Optimized** tab in the document window and you've selected the **Eyedropper** tool, choose **View > Preview > Browser Dither**. You can also **Control+click** (Mac) or **right-click** (Windows) on the document to access a contextual menu, and choose **Display Preview > Browser Dither**.

[PS]

9. ————————Fixing a Non-Safe Image

Not everyone knows to create graphics with the 216 colors in the first place, so it's likely that a day will come when you'll have to fix a graphic that was made with colors that appear dithered when displayed on an 8-bit system. Both Photoshop and ImageReady allow you to shift the colors to Web safe easily. Here's how to do this in Photoshop's **Save For Web** dialog box.

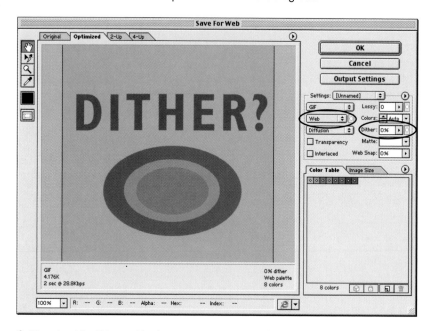

1. You should still have this document open in the **Save For Web** dialog box from the last exercise in Photoshop. If not, return to Photoshop, open **notsafe.psd** from the **chap_02** folder, and choose **File > Save for Web**. Change the **palette** setting (located on the right side of the dialog box below the GIF format setting) to **Web**, and make sure that **Dither** is set to **0%**. Notice that all the unwanted dots from the dithering went away! Also, notice that each swatch in the **Color Table** has a diamond? The diamond indicates that the color is web safe.

Don't worry about understanding the various palettes for now. You'll learn lots about them in Chapter 3, "Optimization."

2. Click **OK**. Photoshop will prompt you to save this document as **notsafe.gif**. Click **OK** again. Now you can close the document in Photoshop to go on to the next lesson. If you are prompted to save changes to **notsafe.psd**, click **No**.

The beauty of Photoshop's Save For Web feature is that you can adjust the image you plan to optimize and never alter the original .psd file.

NOTE | Fixing a Non-Safe Color in ImageReady 3

The process of fixing color in ImageReady is almost identical to that of Photoshop, with the following differences.

1. Open **notsafe.psd**. Be sure that you are on the **Optimized** tab and that the fields in the **Optimize** palette are set to **GIF**, **Selective**, **Dither 0%**.

Tip: If you're having trouble seeing your image with the **Optimize** settings, go to the top-right corner of the **Optimize** palette and make sure that **Auto Regenerate** is checked off in the pull-down menu.

2. Choose **View > Preview > Browser Dither**.

3. Make sure the **Color Table** palette is visible. If you can't see it, choose **Window > Show Color Table**. (We like to dock the **Color Table** to the **Optimize** palette, as you learned to do in Chapter 1, *"Interface."*)

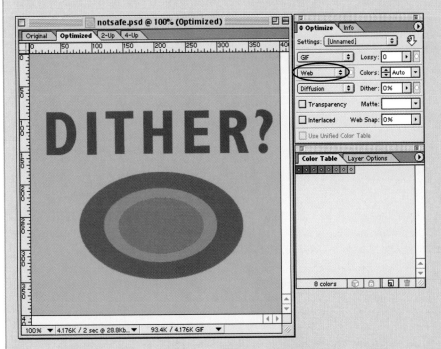

4. In the **Optimize** palette, change the setting from **Selective** to **Web**.

5. When you're ready to save the image, choose **File > Save Optimized As…**. This will save a GIF, but will leave the .psd untouched, just like the **Save For Web** feature in Photoshop.

[PS]

IO. _____Recoloring Layered Documents

Now that you've learned how to view Web color in a variety of different ways within Photoshop, how do you make images that use these colors? You could use a brush and paint with any of these colors at any time. You could also use fill tools to color artwork. This next exercise focuses on how to recolor an existing Photoshop document, and introduces you to some of the new types of layers, including gradient and object layers. The exercise gives you a chance to work with the **Lock Transparent Pixels** feature, which is the new term for Preserve Transparency (used in Photoshop 3 through 5.5). Lock Transparent Pixels allows you to easily recolor layered documents with any color you want.

1. This exercise takes place in Photoshop but will work in a similar fashion in ImageReady, except where noted. Open **recolor.psd** from the **chap_02** folder on your hard drive.

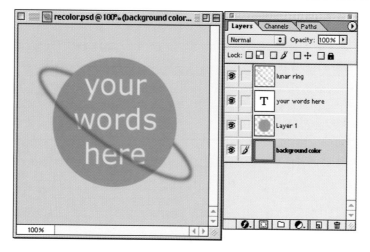

2. Look at the **Layers** palette (Window > Show Layers), and you'll notice that this document is composed of multiple layers. It's helpful to set your files up with separate layers like this and give them names, so you can color each layer separately and keep track of it.

3. Right now, this document is colored using greens and blues. To change this color scheme to reds and yellows (or any other color choice you'd prefer), you'll be working on a layer at a time. To begin, select the layer at the bottom of the **Layers** palette called **background color**.

4. Make sure the **Swatches** palette is visible (Window > Show Swatches). The **color.aco** swatch is still loaded from Exercise 7 in this chapter. Use the **Eyedropper** to pick a **red**.

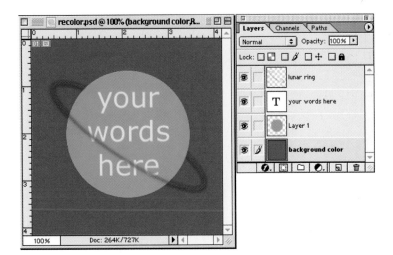

5. To fill the **background color** layer with this red, press **Option+Delete** (Mac), or **Alt+Backspace** or **Alt+Delete** (Win).

This is one of our favorite shortcuts for filling a layer with a color, because it is faster than using the menu command Edit > Fill or the paint bucket. Using a color from the color.aco swatch, ensures that the color fill is Web safe.

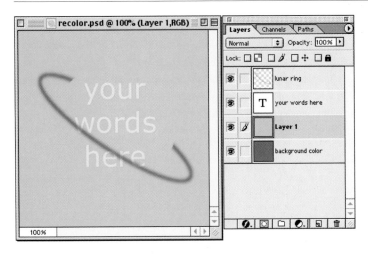

6. Next, select the layer called **Layer 1** that contains the circle. Pick an **orange** color from the **Swatches** palette, and use the fill shortcut again by pressing **Option+Delete** (Mac), or **Alt+Backspace** or **Alt+Delete** (Win). Notice that the entire layer filled with this color. In order to recolor the circle, and not the entire contents of the layer, there's a new and valuable trick you'll learn in the following step.

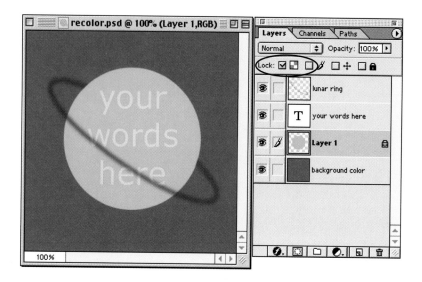

7. Undo the fill you just created by using the shortcut key **Command+Z** (Mac) or **Control+Z** (Win). Click the **Lock Transparent Pixels** checkbox on the **Layers** palette, and press **Option+Delete** (Mac), or **Alt+Backspace** or **Alt+Delete** (Win). This time, only the contents of the layer changed color. **Tip:** The shortcut key to toggle Lock Transparent Pixels on or off is the **/** (forward slash) key.

Lock Transparent Pixels means that Photoshop will protect the transparent areas of this layer. When you fill the layer with a new color, Photoshop only fills the area of the layer that contains an image, and preserves the transparent areas. We can't tell you how many students we watch try to use the magic wand or other selection tools to select shapes on layers in order to fill them. This technique works much better because it's easier, it only fills areas of the layer that contain information, and it doesn't leave rough edges on color fills.

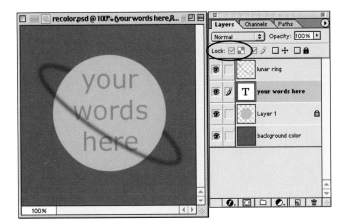

8. Next, select the editable type layer (signified by the letter **T** on the layer). Choose a red color from the **Swatches** palette, and press **Option+Delete** (Mac) or **Alt+Backspace** or or **Alt+Delete** (Win).

Note that the Lock Transparent Pixels *checkbox is active, even though it's dimmed out. This is a default behavior for an editable type layer.*

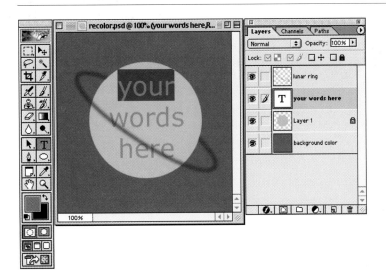

9. There's something else you can do on editable type layers now, that's new to Photoshop 6. You can color individual letters or words. Click the **Type** tool from the Toolbox. Select the word **your** in the type layer by clicking and dragging on it. Select a different color from the **Swatches** palette. Once you deselect the type choosing a different tool on the toolbox, you'll see that the word **your** changed color.

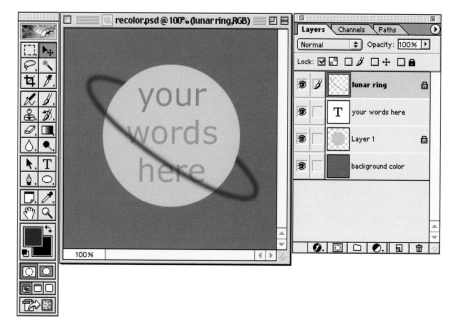

10. Select the layer called **lunar ring**. Choose a new color from the **Swatches** palette. Click the **Lock Transparent Pixels** checkbox and use the shortcut keys **Option+Delete** (Mac) or **Alt+Backspace** or **Alt+Delete** (Win) to fill with the new color. Leave the file open for the next exercise.

What's really cool about this last step, is that the artwork in this layer is slightly blurry. There's no other way to make a clean selection of blurry artwork than activating Lock Transparent Pixels.

The skills covered in this exercise will help you recolor artwork that is on layers at any point in your Web design or Photoshop design life. You'll probably use this technique more than most others in the book. When we've shown this technique at conferences, many people have told us it was worth the price of admission for the time it saved. For those of you who read the last edition of this book, or have seen us show this technique before, it replaces Preserve Transparency.

NOTE | Lock Checkboxes in Photoshop 6

You might have noticed a few other checkboxes in the Layers palette. There are four: **Lock Transparent Pixels**, **Lock Image Pixels**, **Lock Position**, and **Lock All**. Here's a handy chart to explain what these terms mean, and when to use locking features.

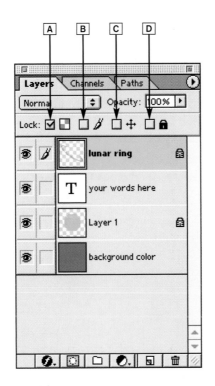

Lock Checkboxes in Photoshop 6 and ImageReady 3

A. Lock Transparent Pixels	Protects the transparent pixels on a layer. Use this feature on layers that have transparency when you want to edit only the colored pixels and mask the transparent ones.
B. Lock Image Pixels	Prevents you from editing any pixels in a given layer. This is good to check when you don't want anyone changing the content of a layer.
C. Lock Position	Prevents you from moving a layer.
D. Lock All	Does all of the above, preventing you from moving or editing a layer. It's good to use when you want to lock the content and position of a layer.

[PS]

II. _____Filling with DitherBox™

There are going to be times when you want a color that isn't Web safe, but you still want it to look good on systems that are limited to 8-bit colors. Photoshop and ImageReady include a great filter called **DitherBox**™ that fills by creating a checkerboard pattern of two or more Web colors. By putting two or more colors so closely together, this filter achieves the effect of a secondary color that isn't present in the Web-color palette.

1. This exercise in Photoshop will work identically in ImageReady. With **recolor.psd** still open from the last exercise, select the **background color** layer.

You don't have to check Lock Transparent Pixels on this layer to change its color because the content fills the entire screen and doesn't have any transparent areas that need preservation.

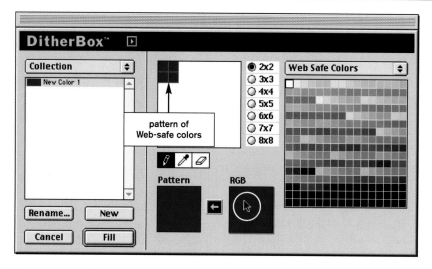

2. Choose **Filter > Other > DitherBox**™.... When the **DitherBox**™ dialog box appears, click inside the **RGB** square shown above.

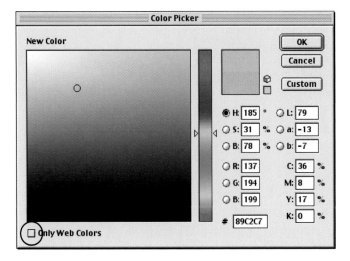

3. This takes you to the **Color Picker**. Make sure that **Only Web Colors** is **unchecked**, and select a light blue color.

You can tell that the color is not Web safe because it has a cube symbol next to it. That's good. You want to pick a non-safe color on purpose. The idea of the DitherBox™ filter, which you are about to use, is to take non-safe colors and mix a combination of two safe colors to simulate non-safe color.

4. Click **OK**.

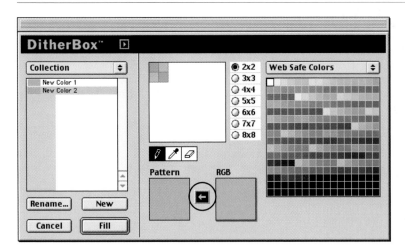

5. Click on the **arrow** that is circled above to create a pattern of Web-safe colors. The pattern is composed of two different Web-safe colors. Click the **Fill** button.

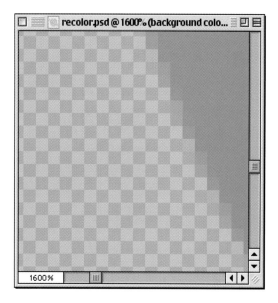

6. The image's background will fill with a light blue. If you click the **Zoom** tool and zoom into the image as tightly as possible, you will see that it is filled with a checkerboard pattern. This pattern is not visible when shown at 100%, yet it produces the illusion of a secondary color that is not within the Web-safe spectrum. **Tip:** To zoom back out to 100%, hold the Option key (Mac) or Alt key (Win) down as you click the Zoom tool on this image.

7. Save and close this file.

Note: This exercise will work identically in ImageReady.

[PS]

12. _____Previewing Gamma

As if dithering problems and color-picking techniques weren't enough to think about in Web publishing, there's another cross-platform issue to consider—gamma. Gamma refers to the midpoint values on a computer system. Pure black and pure white are identical on all the systems, but the intermediary grays appear lighter on Macs and darker on Windows. In general, Mac and Unix systems tend to have lighter displays than Windows. There's nothing that you can do about this sad fact, but at least Photoshop and ImageReady allow you to preview how your work will appear differently on the opposite platforms. This exercise will show you how.

1. This exercise takes place in Photoshop and works a little differently in ImageReady (as the next exercise will demonstrate). Open **cactus.psd** from the **chap_02** folder on your hard drive.

2. Choose **File > Save for Web...**. Make sure you select the **JPEG** setting so the color stays true to the original.

3. Click on the arrow at the upper right of the preview image to access the menu. You can preview the image with four kinds of color: **Uncompensated Color**, **Standard Windows Color**, **Standard Macintosh Color**, and **Use Document Color Profile**. Try each setting and notice the differences.

You can also preview gamma without being in the Photoshop Save For Web dialog box. Choose View > Proof Setup > Macintosh RGB, Windows RGB, or Monitor RGB.

4. Click **Cancel** to exit the **Save For Web** dialog box.

There's not a lot that you can do about the gamma shifts, but the ability to preview these changes is helpful in showing you whether you need to adjust your image so it is lighter or darker. If you did want to permanently make your image lighter or darker, you would choose Image > Adjust > Levels... and move the slider to lighten or darken your image accordingly.

6. Close this file.

NOTE | What Do the Four Color Settings Mean?

You may be wondering what these settings mean. First of all, these are previews only. If you leave one of these previews checked, it will not affect how the image is stored once it is saved, only how it is previewed. Here's what each means.

Color Settings	
Uncompensated Color	Color without any alteration
Macintosh Color	How the image will appear on a Macintosh
Windows Color	How the image will appear on Windows
Use Document Color Profile	If you had any color profiles set (and we hope you don't!), the settings would affect this preview

[IR]

13. —————————Previewing Gamma in ImageReady

You learned how to preview gamma in Photoshop's **Save For Web** dialog box earlier. It's possible to do this in ImageReady as well, only it differs just enough to warrant its own exercise. Here's how it's done.

1. Launch ImageReady, and open **cactus.psd** from your **chap_02** folder. Click on the **Optimized** tab and make sure that the format is set to **JPEG** in the **Optimize** palette.

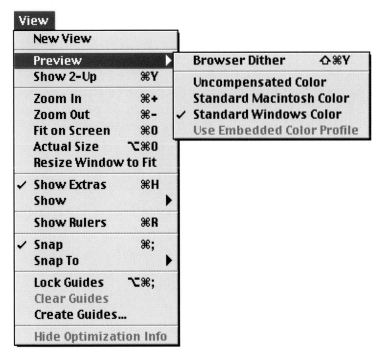

2. Choose **View > Preview > Standard Windows Color**. Try all the preview settings to see how this same image will display on different platforms.

3. Save and close this file. You're finished with this chapter.

Bet you never knew there was this much to Web color before now! The good news is that Photoshop and ImageReady make working with Web color easier than ever before. Had you worked with these concepts in earlier versions of this product, you would have had to do a lot more work to get the same results.

3.
Optimization

GIF, JPEG, and PNG	Bit Depth	Optimizing in Photoshop
Optimizing in ImageReady	Palette Descriptions
Matte Color on JPEG	Previewing and Writing HTML

chap_03

Photoshop 6 / ImageReady 3
H•O•T CD-ROM

Anyone who has ever used the Web has surely been frustrated by slow-loading Web pages. There's never been a design medium before where the file size of your artwork translates into the speed at which someone can view it. Making small Web graphics is both an art and a science. Fortunately, Photoshop and ImageReady are the ideal tools with which to master this craft.

Prepare for a long chapter, because optimization is a fairly complex subject that both Photoshop and ImageReady handle with great detail. If terms like dither, adaptive palettes, bit depth, JPEG, and GIF are unfamiliar to you, they won't be for long. Even if you're a pro at optimizing Web graphics, you will be impressed by Photoshop's and ImageReady's superb optimization capabilities.

Every image you work with is different and each has its own challenges. We've intentionally selected images that expose you to different optimization principles, so that you'll be able to apply a wide variety of tips and techniques that you learn here once you start optimizing images of your own.

What Affects Speed on the Web?

We wish that we could tell you that making your file sizes small in Photoshop or ImageReady guarantees fast Web site performance, because that would be so easy. Sadly, there are more factors involved than just your images' file size. Here are some of the other factors that slow down Web sites:

• Slow Web-server connection speed.

• Clogged arteries in the Information Highway (otherwise known as router problems "somewhere" in the system).

• Large service providers, such as AOL, Earthlink, or GeoCities, sometimes have so much traffic that your site's performance might slow down during heavy usage hours

• Sometimes small local providers can't offer fast connections either, because they don't have the resources to handle their heaviest traffic periods.

Solutions? Make sure that you run your Web site off of a fast connection or that you hire a hosting company that guarantees a fast connection. If you have a serious business site, get a dedicated hosting service instead of a large consumer-based Web service. If the Web is slow because of router problems, it affects everyone. Such is life. The best thing you can do is to control the things that you can (like file size) and accept that you can't control everything. The only predictable thing about the Web is that it won't always perform in a predictable manner. You can make your mark on speed by making images that are small in file size, which is what this chapter is going to get to as soon as some of this background information stuff is out of the way.

GIF or JPEG?

GIF stands for **Graphic I**nterchange Format and **JPEG** stands for Joint **Photographic E**xperts **G**roup. We've intentionally bolded the words "graphic" and "photographic" to point out what each file format handles best. It isn't that GIF is better than JPEG or JPEG better than GIF, but that each of these compression schemes is best suited for certain types of images.

• GIFs are best for flat or simple graphic images that contain a lot of solid areas of color, including but not limited to logos, illustrations, cartoons, line art, etc.

• JPEGs are best for continuous-tone images, including but not limited to photographs, landscapes, glows, gradients, drop shadows, etc.

Of course, some images don't fall into either category because they are hybrids of line art and continuous-tone artwork. In those cases, experiment with GIF and JPEG to see which works better.

GIF Transparency and Animation

Whether a graphic contains line art or continuous tone is not the sole deciding factor for whether to choose GIF or JPEG. The GIF format can do a couple of things that the JPEG format cannot—transparency and animation. This book has a chapter devoted to each, but we thought we'd provide a brief explanation of these terms in this chapter, too, because it may factor into your optimization strategy.

GIF Definitions	
GIF Transparency	What if you have a button design that's circular instead of square or rectangular? You would need to use transparency to mask the shape so it would appear in a circle inside the Web browser. The GIF file format supports 1-bit masking, meaning that the image can be turned off in specified areas, making it possible to create irregularly-shaped images. Because the file format only supports 1-bit transparency, there are no degrees of opacity except on or off (visibility or no visibility). For more information, check out Chapter 8, "*Transparent GIFs.*"
GIF Animation	A single GIF document can contain multiple images and display them in a slide-show fashion. GIF files that contain multiple images are called animated GIFs. For more information on how the GIF file format supports animation, check out Chapter 13, "*Animated GIFs.*"

Lossy or Lossless?

In past books we've reported that the JPEG file format is **lossy** and the GIF file format is **lossless**. That's what everyone thought until the release of Photoshop 5.5, and now 6. Those crafty Adobe engineers figured out a way to apply lossy compression to the GIF file format. Although this may mean nothing to you, it was quite exciting to us, because no one had figured out a new way to make GIF files smaller until this breakthrough. So what do lossy and lossless mean? Lossy means that the compression scheme reduces file size by discarding information, while lossless means that it reduces file size without throwing away information. Traditionally JPEG was a lossy compression method, and GIF was a lossless method. Now GIF can contain both methods.

WARNING | Don't Recompress a Compressed Image

Because JPEG compression is lossy, this format will cause your image to lose quality each time it is compressed. This is perfectly controllable as long as you start with a clean original. Unwanted compression artifacts that cause the image to look distressed can appear if you apply JPEG to an image that has already had JPEG compression applied to it. Always start with an uncompressed file, and your JPEGs will look as good as it gets.

This same warning applies to the GIF format when lossy compression is added. If you recompress an image that already contains lossy compression, it will look much worse than if you began with an uncompressed original image.

How Can You Make Small JPEGS?

The JPEG file format best compresses images that are continuous tone. Here is a handy chart that shows what can be done to compress an image most effectively in this format.

JPEG Compression	
Start with an image that has tonal qualities, such as a photograph, blurry graphic, or image that incorporates effects such as glows, drop shadows, etc.	The JPEG file format looks for the type of data it's best at compressing: areas of low contrast, subtle variation, and slight tonal shifts. It can't compress areas of solid color well at all, and it doesn't work well for graphic-style artwork.
Add blur	Unlike GIF, the JPEG format compresses blurry images well.
Add more JPEG compression	The more JPEG compression you add, the smaller the file size becomes. Too much JPEG compression can cause unwanted compression artifacts to appear when you are using the optimization features of Photoshop or ImageReady. It's your job to find the balance between making the file small and making it look good.
Decrease the saturation	If you decrease the color saturation of a JPEG, it will most often result in greater file savings.
Decrease the contrast	Decreasing a JPEG's contrast usually reduces file size.
Use an Alpha Channel	New to Photoshop 6 is the ability to compress a single image with two different levels of JPEG compression. The two areas are delineated by a mask called an alpha channel. You'll learn to do this later in the chapter.

How Can You Make Small GIFs?

The principles of making a small GIF are almost opposite from those of making a small JPEG. The GIF file format works best on areas of solid color—and that's why it's best for line art, logos, illustrations, and cartoons.

GIF Compression	
Start with an image that has large areas of solid color	The GIF file format looks for patterns in artwork, such as large runs of a single color that span in a horizontal, vertical, or diagonal direction. Note: The moment a color changes, the file size increases.
Reduce the number of colors	Reducing the number of colors in a GIF image also reduces the file size. At some point during the color reduction process the image won't look right, and that's when you'll have to back up and add some colors. The objective is to find that exact threshold where the image looks good but contains the fewest number of colors.
Reduce the amount of dithering	Dithering is a process in which the computer adds different colored pixels in close proximity to each other to simulate secondary colors or smooth gradations of color. A dithered image often looks noisy or has scattered pixels. Some images have to contain dithering to look good, but it's best to use the least amount of dithering necessary in order to see better file-size savings.
Add lossy compression	Lossy compression was new to Photoshop 5.5 and ImageReady 2.0. Adding a little to your GIF file will likely reduce your file size.

NOTE | Recompressing GIF Images

Compression artifacts are not an issue with GIF as they are with the JPEG format. You can recompress a GIF with no ill compression effects, though it's sometimes preferable to begin with a clean original .psd, .pict, or .bmp rather than to recompress an already compressed GIF. If, for example, you recompressed a GIF that had been set to six colors, you wouldn't be able to introduce any more colors even if you wanted to. You would have more latitude with your choices if instead you compressed a GIF from an original image source.

What About PNG?

Both Photoshop and ImageReady write the **PNG** file format, which stands for **P**ortable **N**etwork **G**raphics. Many people, ourselves included, believe that PNG is a superior file format to GIF and JPEG, but sadly it still isn't supported fully by the two major browsers, Explorer and Netscape. PNG is superior because it supports better transparency than GIF, plus it can achieve smaller file sizes than JPEG for photographic and graphic-based images.

Another reason why PNG is attractive is that the GIF file format is patented by the company that developed it, Unisys. For this reason, technically you are supposed to pay a royalty to use the GIF compression scheme. The good news is that Adobe has a license for GIF that covers anyone using Photoshop or ImageReady, so this patent shouldn't concern you. Still, many people are looking to PNG as an alternative to GIF, so the patent issue can go away completely.

Until PNG is supported by the main Web browsers, however, the penalty of using it could result in broken images on your Web pages. That's just not acceptable, so we would say the risks of PNG outweigh the benefits right now. We hope this changes soon, and frankly we thought it would have already. The good news is that once PNG is supported by Web browsers, both Photoshop and ImageReady will be able to write the format perfectly.

What is Bit Depth?

Bit depth has to do with the number of colors in a graphic file. For your information, GIF is an 8-bit file format and JPEG is a 24-bit file format. We're not suggesting that you memorize these numbers, but if you ever need to refer to a chart that lists bit depth, here you go.

Bit-Depth Chart	
32-bit	16.7 million colors plus an 8-bit masking channel
24-bit	16.7 million colors
16-bit	65.6 thousand colors
8-bit	256 colors
7-bit	128 colors
6-bit	64 colors
5-bit	32 colors
4-bit	16 colors
3-bit	8 colors
2-bit	4 colors
1-bit	2 colors

JPEG and GIF Photoshop Options

You are probably wondering what all the options mean inside the GIF and JPEG settings area of the **Save For Web** dialog box. The following descriptions might be helpful for quick reference until you try out the majority of these features in later chapters.

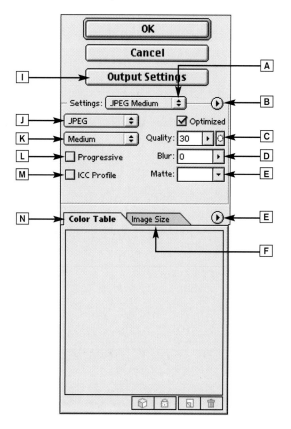

	JPEG Context-Sensitive Properties	
A	**Settings menu**	Settings contain preset compression values. You can choose from the ones that ship with Photoshop, or you can make your own by choosing *Save Settings…* in the *Optimize* menu (B).
B	**Optimize menu**	To see it, hold your mouse down on the arrow. This is where you are able to save and load settings for the *Settings menu* (A).
C	**Optimized**	Highly recommended for making the smallest possible JPEG files.

continues on next page

	JPEG Context-Sensitive Properties *continued*	
D	**Quality**	Enter the quality value in this field. You can type it in manually—or, if you hold your mouse down on the arrow, a slider will appear, which you can then drag to the desired value. Click the small circle to access a window in which you can use channels to modify quality in different parts of the image.
E	**Blur**	Blurry images compress better as JPEGs than sharp images. This value field allows you to blur the image by typing a value or by holding your mouse down on the arrow to access a slider. We prefer using the slider because it's easier to make small incremental changes to the blur, which is usually what you'll want to prevent the image from appearing too blurry.
F	**Matte**	If you begin with an image that is against a transparent background, you can change its matte color. Exercise 14 in this chapter shows you how to set the matte color for a JPEG.
G	**Color Palette menu**	This has no effect on JPEG settings.
H	**Image Size**	You can change the pixel dimensions of your image if you click on this tab and enter changes to the values.
I	**Output Settings**	This opens the Output Settings dialog box, where you can choose options for how your file will be saved, such as how HTML files will be written, how files made from slices will be named, and whether the image will be a background or a foreground image. You can also access Output Settings from the *Save Optimized As* window in Photoshop.
J	**File Format**	This controls whether you're going to apply JPEG, GIF, or PNG compression to an image.
K	**Quality**	Preset quality values for the JPEG format. Alternatively, you can enter values into the *Quality* setting (D).
L	**Progressive**	Progressive JPEGs are like Interlaced GIFs, in that they appear chunky and come into focus as they download. We don't recommend this format because it won't work on browsers below Netscape 3.0 or Explorer 3.0.
M	**ICC Profiles**	ICC (**I**nternational **C**olor **C**onsortium) Profiles work with some printing devices, but not with Web browsers (unless you use proprietary plug-ins). They add a lot of file size to a compressed image. We don't recommend them at present. However, there might come a day when browsers recognize this setting.
N	**Color Table**	When you select this tab, the *Color Table* displays GIF and PNG-8 colors. There is no Color Table for JPEGs.

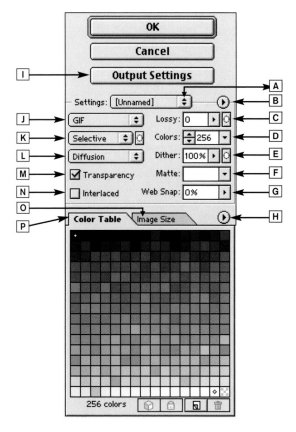

GIF Context-Sensitive Properties		
A	**Settings menu**	Settings contain preset compression values. You can use the ones that ship with Photoshop, or you can make your own by choosing *Save Settings...* in the *Optimize* menu (B).
B	**Optimize menu**	To see it, hold your mouse down on the arrow. This is where you can save and load settings for the *Settings* menu (A).
C	**Lossy**	Changing the value in this field will add *lossy* compression to your GIF images. We almost always find that small values of lossy decrease the file size of any GIF. It works much better on continuous-tone GIF files (such as photographs that you want to make transparent or animate). The channel symbol to the right of this field allows you to use alpha channels to vary lossiness in different parts of the image.

continues on next page

GIF Context-Sensitive Properties *continued*

D	**Colors**	Reducing the number of colors in a GIF image always results in file-size savings. The trick is to find the threshold where it has the fewest colors but still looks good.
E	**Dither**	Controls the amount of dither. Adding dither to a GIF always increases file size but is sometimes necessary for the image to look its best. The channel symbol to the right of this field allows you to use alpha channels to vary dither in different parts of the image.
F	**Matte**	If you begin with an image that is set against a transparent background, you can change its matte color. You'll get a chance to do this in Chapter 8, *"Transparent GIFs."*
G	**Web Snap**	If an image contains non-Web-safe colors, you can set a threshold so that any colors which are close will "snap" to become Web safe. We prefer to change colors to Web safe one at a time, as discussed in Chapter 2, *"Web Color."*
H	**Color Palette Menu**	This menu allows you to sort the colors in your palette, to load and save color palettes, and to create new colors in your palette.
I	**Output Settings**	This opens the Output Settings dialog box, where you can choose options for how your file will be saved, such as how HTML files will be written, how files made from slices will be named, and whether the image will be a background or a foreground image.
J	**File Format**	This menu controls whether you're going to apply JPEG, GIF, or PNG compression to an image.
K	**Color Reduction Algorithm**	The Adobe engineers give you a lot of options as to which type of algorithm (palette) to use for best compressing your GIF images. You'll try them out in several upcoming exercises. The channel symbol to the right of this field allows you to use alpha channels to influence the palette applied to different parts of the image.
L	**Dithering Algorithms**	Bet you didn't know that your dithering could have algorithms! This is just a fancy way of saying that there are a few types of dithering options. You'll get to try these out in this chapter, too.

continues on next page

		GIF Context-Sensitive Properties *continued*
M	**Transparency**	Check this box when you want to make transparent GIF images. You might find that it won't work, and that is most likely because your image doesn't contain any transparent areas. You'll learn all about how to make perfect transparent GIFs in Chapter 8, *"Transparent GIFs."*
N	**Interlaced**	Check this box if you want your GIFs to be interlaced, which means they will look chunky until they finish downloading. Interlaced GIFs work on all browsers, so you don't have to worry about backwards compatibility. We don't like to use interlacing on text because we think it is frustrating to wait for an image to appear in focus when you have to read it. If we were ever going to use interlacing, it would be on graphics that contain no text; but the truth is we don't ever use interlacing because we don't like the way it looks. To each his or her own preference.
O	**Image Size**	You can change the pixel dimensions of your image if you click on this tab and enter changes to the values.
P	**Color Table**	This area displays the colors that are being assigned to the GIF image. You explored this setting in great depth in Chapter 2, *"Web Color."*

[PS]

I. ————————————Saving For Web Using JPEG

This first exercise will walk you through saving a JPEG. It will introduce you to a feature in Photoshop called **Save For Web**. You used this feature briefly in the last chapter, but this chapter will demonstrate the numerous nuances of this function. The Save For Web feature gives you control over so many options that you will be able to make the smallest possible Web graphics once you master its nuances.

1. Open Photoshop and choose **File > Open** to select **cactus.psd** from the **chap_03** folder you transferred to your hard drive from the **H•O•T CD-ROM**.

2. Choose **File > Save for Web….**

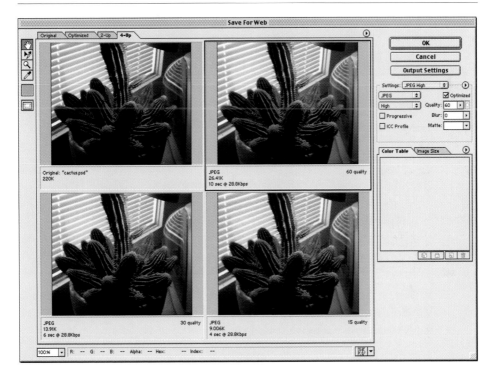

3. Click on the **4-Up** tab in the **Save For Web** dialog box, as this will let you compare different compression settings.

Notice that the upper-left preview has the term "Original" in it? This allows you to compare compression choices to how the image looked in its original, uncompressed state. If you have already used the Save For Web feature before reading this book, your version of Photoshop might default to a different setting. That's because this feature memorizes whichever compression settings were last set.

4. Click on the upper-right preview (it is probably selected already), and change the pop-up menu that reads **GIF** to **JPEG** (if it needs to be changed).

Notice that the JPEG is better looking than any of the other previews that are GIFs? This is what we were talking about earlier when we wrote that continuous-tone images always compress better as JPEGs than as GIFs.

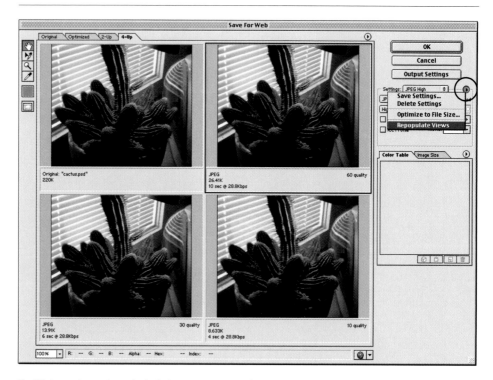

5. Click on the **arrow** circled above to access the pop-up menu, and choose **Repopulate Views**. This will change the other previews in the two frames at the bottom of the dialog box to the same file format as the selected preview JPEG in this case.

Notice the readout below each preview? It tells you the quality (compression levels) and file size of each preview. Photoshop also estimates how long this graphic will take to download over a slow connection. Note that this is a theoretical estimate of speed, and it might not be accurate due to other factors such as server speed and bottlenecks in the Internet. Your read-outs may have different numbers than those in the example above, because Photoshop remembers the compression levels from the last time you saved for Web with JPEG settings.

*Judging the quality and file-size savings of all the choices in the example above, it looks like the best quality would lie between a JPEG setting of **30** and **10**. Every image that you optimize will have a different threshold of quality versus size, but isn't this readout handy for making your final decision?*

6. Use the **slider** by clicking on the arrow next to the **Quality** field and try some settings between **30** and **10**. **Note:** You must release the slider for the results of the new setting to take effect.

The slider is useful because it lets you easily experiment with different settings instead of requiring you to use the keyboard to type in different values.

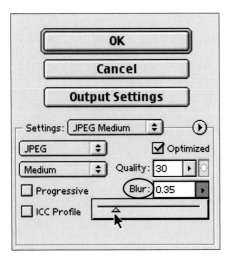

7. Try adding a tiny amount of **blur** to the image. It will result in a slight file savings, but you should avoid adding too much or you will adversely affect the quality. When you're happy with the result, click **OK**.

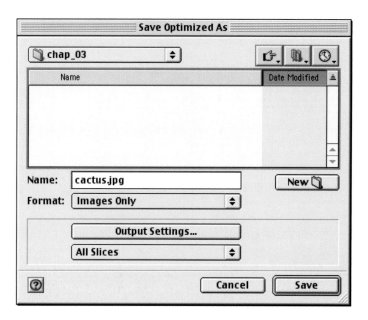

The Save Optimized As dialog box will open. Notice that it puts a .jpg suffix on the file name for you? It also automatically generates a file name, which you can change.

Notice the setting "Format: Images Only" (Mac) or "Save as type: Images Only" (Windows)? It is possible to access this setting as a pop-up menu and choose HTML and Images instead, in which case Photoshop would generate an HTML file that places this image at the upper-left corner of a Web page. You could upload this HTML file to the Web or open it in any HTML editor to further modify it.

8. Navigate to the **chap_03** folder on your hard drive, and click **Save**.

Notice that when you click Save, the original, uncompressed cactus.psd file remains open in your program? That's because you haven't altered the original a bit. When you choose Save for Web..., it saves a copy on your hard drive and does not harm the original file.

9. Close the original **cactus.psd** image without saving.

[PS]

2. ———————Selective JPEG Optimization with Alpha

A new addition to Photoshop 6 and ImageReady 3 is the ability to isolate a part of the image using an alpha channel to allow for selective compression. If that mouthful of words caused your eyes to glaze over, here's a brief explanation. An alpha channel is a mechanism that Photoshop uses to produce a mask. If you use a mask (alpha) on an image, Photoshop allows you to selectively optimize parts of an image with different compression settings. This next exercise will show when this technique will come in handy, and will walk you through how to do it in Photoshop.

1. Open **dotcom1.psd** from the **chap_03** folder you copied to your hard drive. This is an image that contains blurry areas that might best be optimized as a JPEG, and crisp areas that might not look so great as a JPEG.

If you get a warning that fonts are missing, you can ignore it for now.

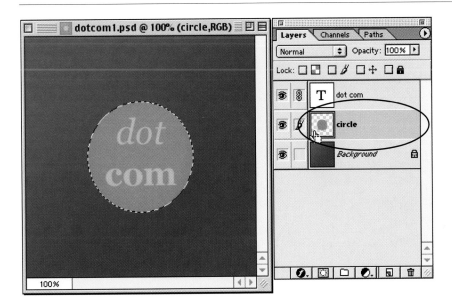

2. Hold down the **Command** key (Mac) or **Control** key (Win) and click on the **circle** layer in the **Layer** palette. This should result in the cursor changing to a hand (as seen above), and cause the selection marquee to appear around the content of this layer only.

This is one of our favorite shortcuts for creating a perfect selection around artwork on a layer. It's much better than using the magic wand or any of the other selection tools in Photoshop, because it will always give you a perfect selection. Any time you have a layer with content and transparency, this is the best method with which to get a selection.

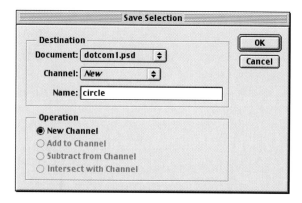

3. Once you have the selection, you can save it as an alpha channel. Choose **Select > Save Selection...**, and the **Save Selection** dialog box will appear. This is all there is to saving the circle shape as an alpha channel. Give it a name (circle makes the most sense, but any name will do) and click **OK**. You can deselect the circle now, by pressing **Command+D** (Mac) or **Control+D** (Win).

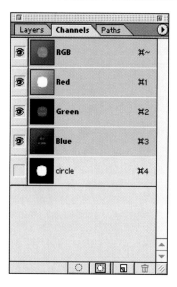

4. If you want to check to see if the alpha channel was made correctly, click on the **Channels** tab in the **Layers** palette group, and you'll see the new channel at the bottom. Click on the **circle** channel to see the alpha mask in the document. Be sure to select the **RGB** channel, and to return to the **Layers** tab once you've finished checking this. You do not need to check to see if the alpha channel exists for it to work, this was simply a suggestion if you've never seen one before.

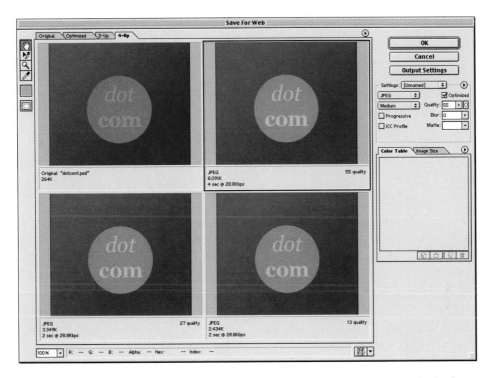

5. Choose **File > Save For Web...**. Notice that as the JPEG quality goes down, the background looks fine, but the content in the circle contains unwanted JPEG artifacts. By having an alpha channel, which is a stored mask, you can add different amounts of compression to the different parts of the image. Select the preview on the upper right.

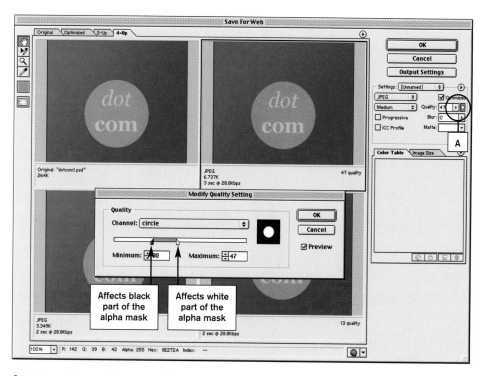

6. Click on the small button to the right of the **Quality** field (A, above). This will open the **Modify Quality Setting** dialog box. It will open to a default setting of Channel: None. Select **Channel: Circle**. When you move the white slider bar (on the right) it affects the quality setting for the content that is inside the white alpha mask (in this case, the circle shape). The black slider bar affects the quality of what is outside of the white mask. By moving these two sliders you can see a live preview of setting two different optimization settings for this one image. Click **OK** when you're happy with the way the image looks.

---

7. Click **OK** in the **Save For Web** dialog box, and you will be prompted in the **Save Optimized As...** window to save this image as **dotcom1.jpg**. Click **Save**.

---

8. Close the **dotcom1.psd** file, and do not save changes.

Saving Options in Photoshop

In the last exercises, you learned how to use Photoshop's **Save For Web** feature. You might be familiar with a feature called **Save As....** In addition to plain old **Save**, there is a fourth way to save from Photoshop, **Save a Copy....** Here's a useful chart to show you when you would use each of the four Photoshop save options.

Which Type of Save Is Best?	
Save	To write over an existing file. If, for example, you have a .psd file open and you make a change that you want to keep, all you need to do is choose *File > Save* and the file will be overwritten. It's important to note that the .psd format will save layers, filter effects, adjustment layers, etc. The GIF and JPEG formats will not save these things.
Save As a Copy...	When you want to choose a file format other than the type of file you've opened. For example, if you have a .psd open but you want to save a version of it as a TIFF, EPS, PICT, BMP, or something else. This is also useful for when you want to keep an alternate version with a different name while not overwriting the original. It's a good way of keeping snapshots of different versions of a project. It leaves the original open and saves a copy to the hard drive. For example, if you were working on *orangeflower.psd* and saved a copy as *orangeflower.tif*, *orangeflower.psd* would remain open and unsaved. To access this setting, choose *File > Save As...*, and put a checkmark next to *As a Copy*.
Save As...	To save the same type of file you already have open as another name. In effect, this creates a copy of the file but it will only create a copy in the identical format that you have open. For example, if you have a file called *orangeflower.psd* and want to save a purple version of it as *purpleflower.psd*, you would choose *Save As...* In this example, *purpleflower.psd* would remain open, and *orangeflower.psd* would close.
Save for Web...	To optimize graphics and create a copy of your file in a Web format, such as GIF, JPEG, or PNG, and leave your original open and unchanged.

NOTE | Issues with Save

If you are using the **Save** function to overwrite an image, Photoshop will honor whichever file format you are starting with, such as a GIF, JPEG, TIFF, EPS, etc. The only time it will not let you write over an existing format is when you add attributes that aren't supported by that format, such as layers, masks, adjustments, etc. It will then force you to write a .psd unless you choose **Save a Copy...**, and then you can change the file format.

[PS]

3. ————————————Saving For Web Using GIF

The GIF file format is far more complex than the JPEG file format in terms of optimizing because there are so many more settings that affect file size. This exercise will expose you to some of the key settings to optimize a GIF, such as lowering the number of colors, adjusting the dither options, and choosing a palette.

1. Open **monkey.psd** from the **chap_03** folder you copied to your hard drive, and choose **File > Save for Web....**

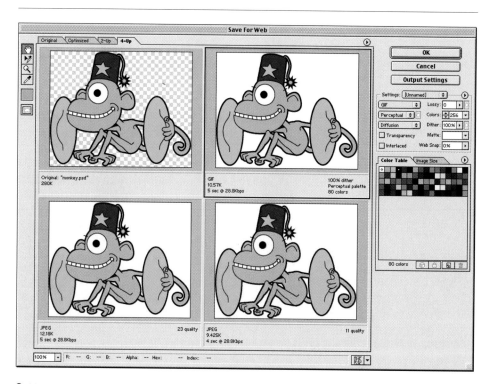

2. You still should be seeing the 4-Up view—if not, click on the **4-Up** tab. Notice that all the views are in JPEG? The upper-right preview might still be set to JPEG. Click on the **JPEG** pop-up menu and choose **GIF**. Change the **Colors** to **256** and make sure that all the other settings match those above.

Although the preview on the bottom-right (set to JPEG) is smaller in file size than the upper-right preview (now set to GIF), notice that the bottom-right preview doesn't look very good.

3. Click on the **Zoom** tool inside the toolbox in the **Save For Web** dialog box. Click once on the bottom-right image to select it and two more times to change the magnification to **300%**.

Notice how the two bottom JPEG images look distressed upon closer examination, and the top-right image set to GIF looks much more like the original on the upper left? As we mentioned before, flat-style graphics such as this image are better suited for the GIF format.

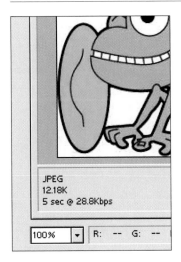

4. Click on the **arrow** next to the size readout on the bottom left of the **Save For Web** dialog box, and choose **100%** from the pop-up menu to return the view to normal size. (As an alternative, you could also type 100% into this field.) No one will ever see your Web images at anything other than 100%, so don't fuss too much with an image at a high magnification. Next, select the **hand** icon from the Toolbox in the **Save For Web** dialog box.

5. Click on the **upper-right GIF** preview. Notice that lots of settings change on the far right of the Save For Web dialog box? Click on the **bottom-left** preview and again keep your eye on the settings at the far right of the window. As you switch from a JPEG to a GIF, notice the additional options available for GIF.

When the image is set to a GIF, the feedback of this window changes drastically. This is called a context-sensitive interface. When a preview is set to GIF, the Save For Web dialog box shows you all the compression options for GIF; when a preview is set to JPEG, it displays all the options for JPEG. Notice that when a preview is set to GIF there is a color palette, but when it's set to JPEG there is not? That's because the GIF file format supports a maximum of only 256 colors, which are mapped to whichever palette appears in this window. A JPEG file supports up to millions of colors and doesn't need to map to a palette.

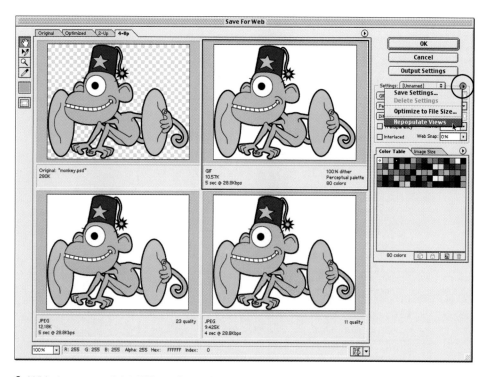

6. With the **upper-right** GIF preview selected again, hold your mouse down on the arrow circled above and choose **Repopulate Views** from the pop-up **Optimize** menu. This changes all the views to the same format as the selected preview(GIF.

You can always choose to use Repopulate Views when you want to see variations on one compression setting, as you just did with the GIF format, to which it should now be set.

---

7. Leave this file open in the **Save For Web** dialog box for the next exercise.

Note: If you press Cancel, the Save For Web dialog box will not remember all of these settings. For the purposes of this exercise, it is best if you leave the Save For Web dialog box open. If you cannot do so, expect to re-enter the settings.

[PS]

4. ——————Choosing the Right Palette

In the classes that we teach, we find that palette settings are among the most confusing things to our students. We thought it best to start with these mysterious settings, so you can cut to the chase and get through the confusing parts of optimizing GIFs.

1. Make sure that the **upper-right** preview is selected in the **Save For Web** dialog box containing **monkey.psd** from the previous exercise.

2. Change the palette setting from **Selective** to **Perceptual**, then **Adaptive**, and then **Web**, just to see the effect that these settings have on the file size and the image.

Adaptive

Selective

Perceptual

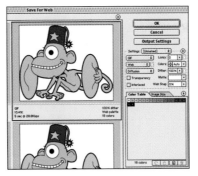

Web

Notice how most of the Color Table feedback looks almost identical? Although the Web palette setting resulted in a smaller file size, it also had fewer colors and didn't look very good. We almost always use Adaptive, Perceptual, or Selective instead of Web.

3. Once you've looked at all of them, change the setting back to **Selective**. Make sure that the **Dither** method is set to **Diffusion**.

4. Leave the **Save For Web** dialog box as it is and move to the next exercise. If you have to quit Photoshop right now to start the next exercise later, be sure to save the .psd file. The next time you enter the **Save For Web** dialog box, the last settings will still be remembered.

The Meaning of Perceptual, Selective, Adaptive, and Web

If you are wondering what these four terms mean, here's a chart that shows how the Photoshop manual differentiates them.

Definitions	
Perceptual	Gives priority to colors for which the human eye has the greatest sensitivity.
Selective	Similar to perceptual, but favors broad areas of color and the preservation of Web colors.
Adaptive	Samples colors from hues that appear most commonly in the image.
Web	Limits the *Color Table* to the 216 Web-safe colors that make the most sense in relation to the image.

We always think of the **Perceptual, Selective,** and **Adaptive** palettes as variations of the same thing—algorithms that look to the colors in the image and build a different palette for each image to which they're applied. In contrast, the Web palette is made up of fixed colors that sometimes don't relate to the image being compressed.

[PS]

5. ——————Reducing the Colors

In order to make a GIF image small in file size, it's necessary to reduce the number of colors until you arrive at the fewest that are necessary to ensure that the image looks good. The battle between looking good and having a small file is always present when you're optimizing Web graphics.

1. While still in the **Web** setting from the previous exercise, change the number of colors to **64** by accessing the pop-up menu next to the **Colors** setting. You'll see the file size get smaller right away. Compare this image to the original, and it still looks great. Try smaller values until the image stops looking good.

We're satisfied with this image at 8 colors, which results in a file size of about 6.12K. Notice when you take this image down to 4 that some of the colors start looking dotted with other colors? Those dots are called dithering, and in this example they don't look good. We still think this image can be coaxed to go smaller, though.

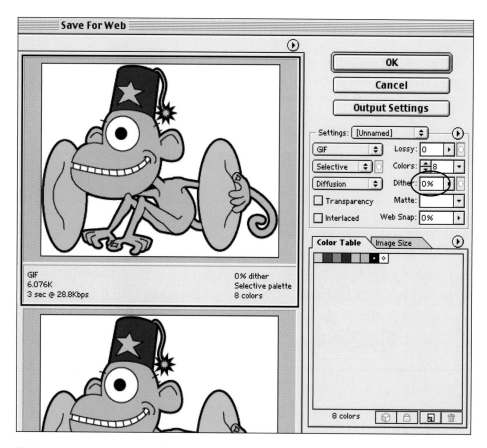

2. Move the **Dither** slider to **0%**.

Notice that the file size is now slightly smaller. Different types of images realize different amounts of file savings with dithering set to zero.

3. Click **OK** to save the GIF, and close the original .psd file without saving.

[PS]

6. _____When Dithering is Good

So far, dithering has gotten a bum rap in this book. You might think that it should always be avoided, but that's really not true. Sometimes a dithered image looks better than a non-dithered one. The rule of thumb is that dithering looks bad in solid colors (like what you witnessed in the last exercise) but it is required on areas of an image that contain glows, drop shadows, blurs, or anything that produces a gradient. This next exercise will demonstrate when to use dithering.

1. Open **glow.psd** from the **chap_03** folder you copied to your hard drive, choose **File > Save for Web...**, and click on the **2-up** tab.

If you get an alert that fonts are missing, just ignore it for now.

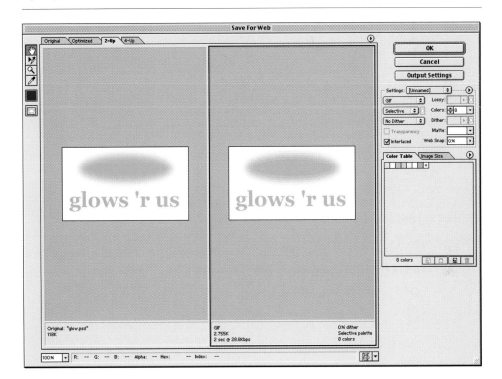

2. Change your settings to reflect what is shown here: **GIF, Selective, No Dither, Lossy: 0, Colors: 8**.

This particular image would look better and be smaller as a JPEG, but if you have to save an image like this as a GIF (for reasons of animation or transparency) you should understand how dithering can help things out. Notice the banding in the image? Even though the file is small (approximately 3K), it doesn't look good.

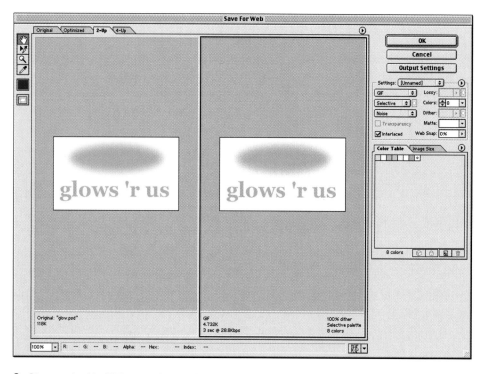

3. Change the **No Dither** setting to **Noise** and watch the image improve.

The file size also increased, but the image looks so much better now that the increase was worthwhile.

4. We have a trick to share, though! Change the settings to **No Dither**, **Lossy: 27**, and **Colors: 16**. The image is now around **2.5K** and the dithering looks good.

Lossy compression reduces the file size of some images saved in the GIF format, especially images like this one that contain a glow or gradient.

5. Click **OK**. You'll be prompted to save the optimized file as **glow.gif**. Click **Save** to do so.

6. Close **glow.psd**, and do not save it.

[PS]

7.————————Locking Colors

One of the great features of Photoshop and ImageReady is the fact that you can influence which colors are stored with an image, even when you greatly reduce the number of colors in the Color Table.

1. Open **dotcom2.psd** from the **chap_03** folder you copied to your hard drive. Choose **File > Save For Web**.

If you get a warning that fonts are missing, you can ignore it for now.

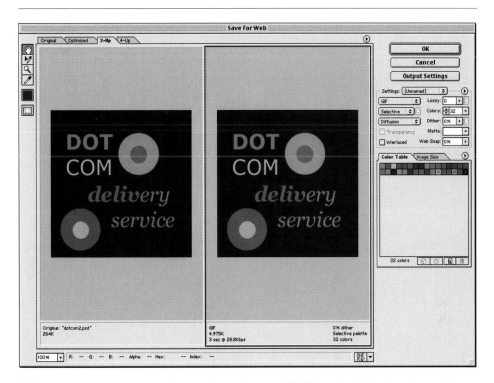

2. Click on the **2-up** tab, and change the settings to **GIF, Selective, Diffusion, Lossy: 0, Colors: 32, Dither: 0%**.

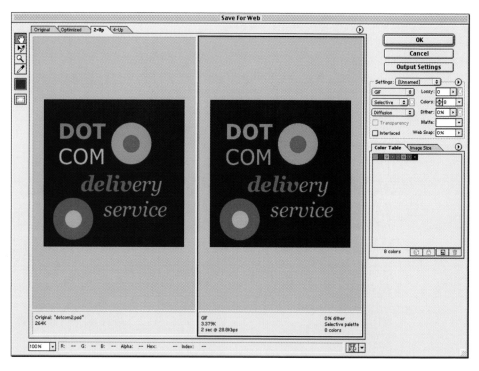

3. Reduce the number of colors to **8**. Even though this image may not look like it has more than eight colors in it, when you make this change some of the colors change in the preview. That's because Photoshop is making a decision about which colors to throw away, and the program didn't throw away the colors you would expect.

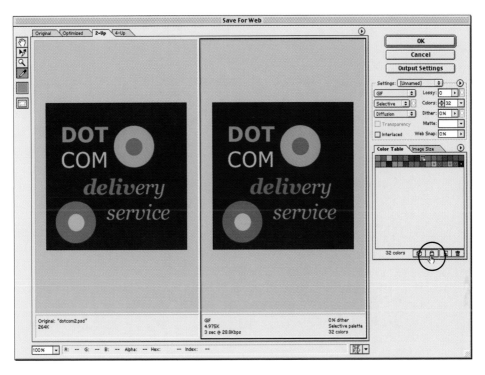

4. Return the **Colors** setting to **32** colors. Using the **Eyedropper**, click on the **brown** color in the word **DOT**. Its corresponding color chip in the **Color Table** should be highlighted. Click on the **Lock** symbol to lock it. Once the color has been locked, a small white square will appear in the lower right corner of the color chip.

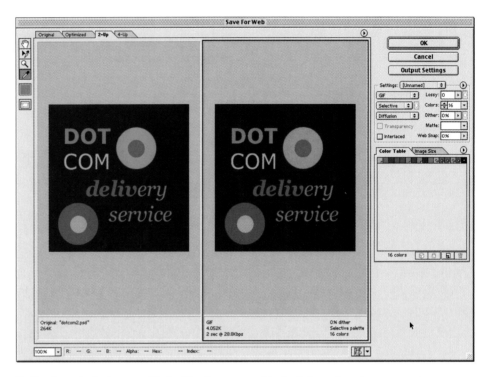

5. Go through the image with the **Eyedropper** and lock all the colors that you want to pre-serve. Once you have all the colors locked, change the setting back to **16** colors.

This time all the important colors in the image were preserved. Being able to lock colors is a great feature in the Save For Web dialog box.

6. Leave the file open in the **Save For Web** dialog box for the next exercise.

[PS]

Changing the Dimensions of a Graphic

There is only one more thing that can make this image smaller—changing its dimensions. This isn't always an option, because you might have sized it to the perfect dimensions before you started optimizing. The cool thing is that you can change the dimensions and you don't even have to leave the **Save For Web** dialog box. Another advantage is that doing so leaves the original untouched and only resizes the Web version of the graphic.

> **1.** With **dotcom2.psd** still open in the **Save For Web** dialog box from the previous exercise, click on the **Image Size** tab to the right of the **Color Table** tab.

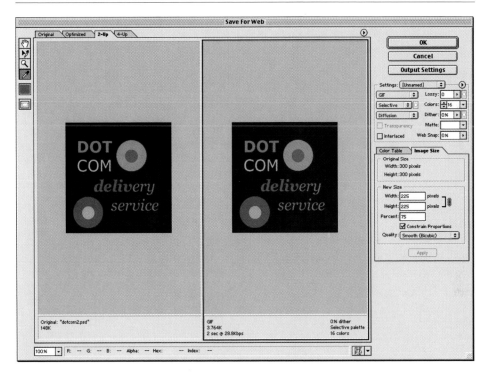

> **2.** Enter **Percent: 75%**, click the **Apply** button, and watch the image get smaller.

> **3.** Click **OK** to save this image as a **GIF**, and close the original **.psd** file without saving.

[PS]

9. ——————Selective GIF Optimization with Alpha

Earlier, you learned how to create selective optimization using alpha channels in the JPEG file format. You can also apply selective optimization to GIF files. In this context however, you can control the color reduction, dither, and lossy compression via your alpha channel mask. This exercise will review how to create an alpha channel, and how to use it for selectively optimizing the color reduction, dither, and amount of lossy compression.

1. Open **queen.psd** from the **chap_03** folder that you transferred to your hard drive. Make sure that you select the layer **jamie_face**, as shown above.

2. Command+click (Mac) or **Control+click** (Win) on the layer **jamie_face** in the Layers palette. A perfect selection should appear around the periphery of Jamie's outline

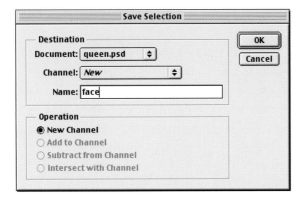

3. With the selection still active, choose **Select > Save Selection**. The Save Selection dialog box will appear. Name the selection **face**, as shown above. Click **OK**.

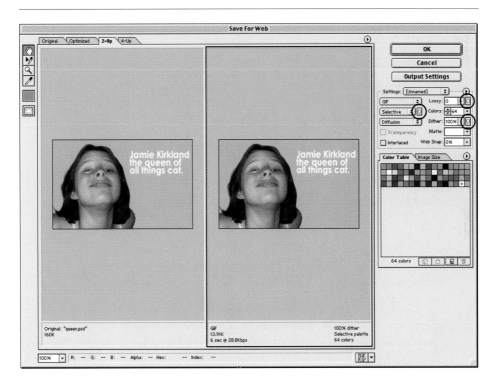

4. Choose **File > Save For Web**. Click the **2-up** tab, and set the **File Format** to **GIF**, as shown above. Choose a **Selective** palette, **Diffusion**, Dither **100%**, and **64** colors. Notice the buttons to the right of the Palette, Lossy, and Dither settings that are circled above. They indicate that an alpha channel can be used to independently control these settings.

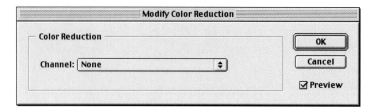

5. Click the **channel symbol** icon to the right of Selective. This will open the **Modify Color Reduction** dialog box.

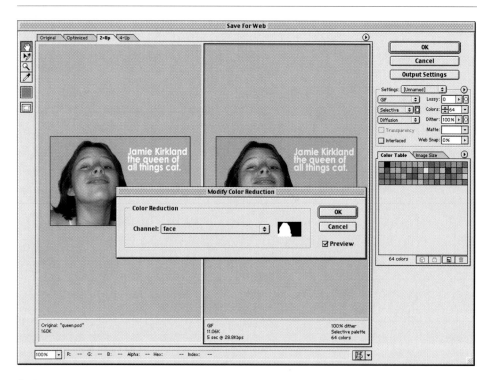

6. Choose **Channel: face**. Notice that the colors in the color table change when you do this? The Color Table is now weighting this palette towards the colors found inside the mask (the skin tones) instead of uniformly across the entire image. If you toggle the Channel menu from **face** to **None**, you'll see the colors weighting more towards the blues in the **None** setting and more towards skin tones in the **face** setting. Click **OK.**

Use this setting whenever you want to influence the Color Table by the content inside an alpha channel. In this case, that meant weighting it in favor of the skin tones instead of the solid blue background.

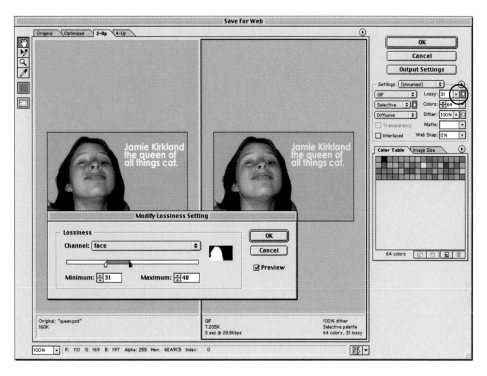

7. Click the **channel symbol** icon to the right of Lossy. This will open the **Modify Lossiness Setting** dialog box. Choose **Channel: face**, and adjust the white and black sliders to where you think they look best. This allows you to change the amount of lossy compression, with the black slider indicating the compression for outside the mask, and the white slider for inside the mask. Click **OK**.

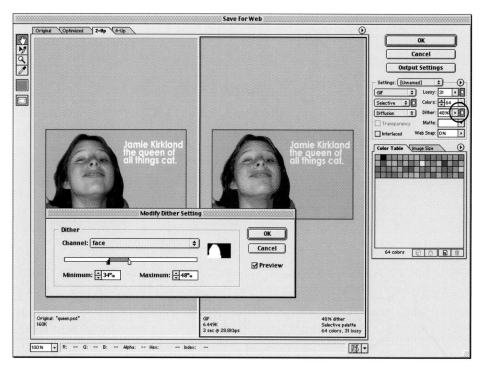

8. Click the **channel button** icon to the right of Dither. This will open the **Modify Dither Setting** dialog box. Choose **Channel: face** and adjust the white and black sliders to where you think they look best. This allows you to change the amount of dither, with the black slider indicating the compression for outside the mask, and the white slider for inside the mask.

After making these modifications based on the alpha channel, the GIF file was reduced from 13k to 7k. You won't always use these selective optimization masking features, but on certain images where parts might compress differently than others (such as this example that mixes continuous tone and flat color), this feature is great!

9. Leave this file open in the **Save For Web** dialog box for the next exercise.

[PS]

10.—————————Previewing in a Browser

Photoshop is capable of previewing in a browser, right from the **Save For Web** dialog box.

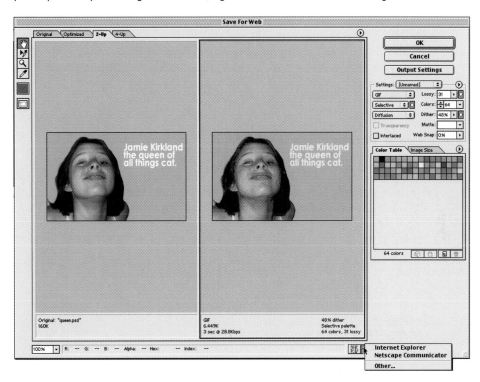

1. With the **queen.psd** file open in the **Save For Web** dialog box, choose a browser by clicking on either the symbol for **Internet Explorer** at the bottom of the **Save For Web** dialog box or the **arrow** to its right to access a pop-up menu for other browser choices. We chose **Netscape Communicator** instead of the default Internet Explorer by using this technique.

The square that is highlighted in the Save For Web dialog box will be the image that is previewed inside the browser. Notice the table that contains information and HTML code? This contains references to a temporary image and HTML file. If you want to use the HTML that Photoshop generates in final form with path names that work, it's best to save the HTML when you save the file. You will learn to do this in future exercises.

2. Return to Photoshop to click the **OK** button at last. You'll be prompted to save this image as **queen.gif**. Save it into your **chap_03** folder and close the **queen.psd** image, too. When asked if you want to save **queen.psd**, click **Don't Save**.

You just optimized a Photoshop graphic without altering or saving the original. This can be useful because you can save a master document that remains untouched and save copies as Web graphics. This is ideal because, as you've learned, documents in the Photoshop .psd format store information about layers, layer effects and adjustment layers, but the Web formats GIF and JPEG do not.

ImageReady versus Photoshop Workflow

We want to show you how to do the same processes in ImageReady that you just learned in Photoshop so you know how to optimize in either application.

You might wonder *why* you would optimize a graphic in ImageReady when you can do it in Photoshop. The only reason we can think of is because you might be in one program or the other. Let's say you're in ImageReady creating animations or rollovers. Those are things that you can't do in Photoshop because they're unsupported there. While you're in ImageReady doing those tasks, it would be awfully convenient to complete the task by optimizing and saving a GIF or JPEG. We find that we spend more time optimizing Web graphics in ImageReady than in Photoshop, because we're often using a feature that's only found in ImageReady. Regardless, it's essential to know how to do the optimization in either application, so this book shows you how.

The bigger question is, which program should you use for which tasks? Here's a chart based on our experiences with these applications and personal preferences.

When to Use Which Program?		
Task	Photoshop 6	ImageReady 3
Adjustment Layers	•	
Animation		•
Background Images		•
Batch-Processing	•	•
Color Profiles	•	
Color Swatches	•	•
Custom Brushes	•	
Editable Type	•	•
Filters	•	•
Image Maps		•
Importing Vectors	•	•
Layer Effects	•	•
Layers	•	•
Masking	•	
Optimizing Graphics	•	•
Rollovers		•
Slices	•	•
Styles		•
Transparency	•	•
Web Photo Gallery	•	

[PS/IR]

II. —————————Jump to ImageReady

You could quit Photoshop and open ImageReady, but if you have enough RAM to support it there's a much better way with Photoshop and ImageReady's **Jump To** feature. Go ahead and try this next exercise, and if you run low on memory your computer will complain. If you don't have enough memory, simply quit Photoshop, open ImageReady, and open the requested files manually. Otherwise, the Jump To feature is a very good way to manage workflow between the two applications.

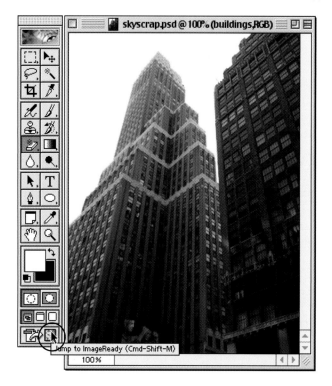

1. In Photoshop, open the file **skyscrap.psd** from the **chap_03** folder that you transferred to your hard drive. Click the **Jump To** button.

This will launch ImageReady, and leave the file skyscrap.psd open in both programs.

You can jump back to Photoshop using the same button in ImageReady if you want to. This is a great way to go between the two applications. If you make changes in one program, the change will appear when the image is viewed in the other program when you use the Jump To button feature.

2. Make sure you're in ImageReady with the **skyscrap.psd** file open and go to the next exercise.

[IR]

I2. _____ImageReady Palettes and Preference Settings

ImageReady matches Photoshop for optimization capabilities feature for feature. Don't worry about the results being different in these two programs; the underlying code is identical. The only true difference is in the two interfaces. In Photoshop, when you choose **Save for Web...**, a single dialog box appears. In ImageReady, the settings are spread across several palettes.

We prefer to arrange our palettes in a specific way that groups them together. Here's how we do it in ImageReady.

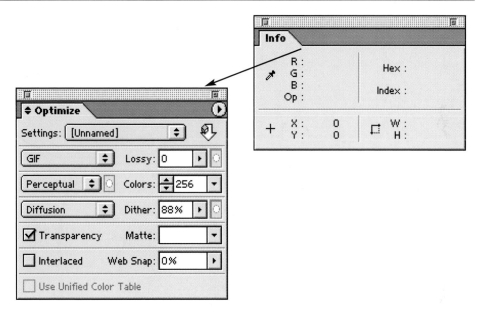

1. Make sure you're in ImageReady. If your **Optimize** palette is not already visible, choose **Window > Show Optimize**. Click and drag the **Optimize** tab off its palette so it separates as a stand-alone palette. **Hint:** If your palette doesn't offer all the choices shown below, click on the arrow on the top-right corner and choose Show Options.

2. Do the same with the **Color Table** palette.

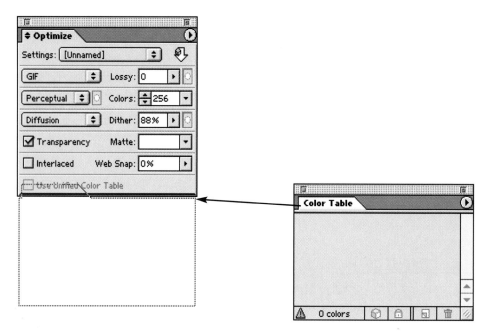

3. Drag the **Color Table** palette by its tab so that it touches the bottom of the **Optimize** palette and turns the bottom dark, as shown above. The two palettes should now be joined when you move them around by the top bar of the **Optimize** palette.

If you ever want to separate them, you can drag either one by its name tab. We really like this kind of docking, and we'll recommend you do it with other palettes later in the book whenever it makes sense.

Why did it make sense to do it just now? Because the only reason you'd ever want to look at the Color Table is in the context of saving GIFs.

We also like to change the ImageReady Optimization Preferences before we start with optimization.

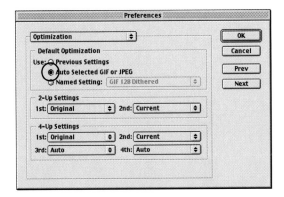

4. Choose **Edit > Preferences > Optimization…**. In the **Preferences** dialog box, change the **Default Optimization** setting to **Auto Selected GIF or JPEG**.

This instructs ImageReady to make a best guess as to which type of compression format (GIF or JPEG) to select. You can override its guess, but why not have ImageReady make it for you as a good starting point?

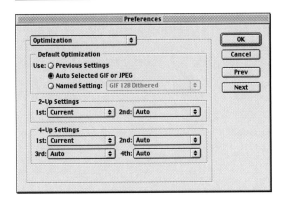

5. In the **2-Up Settings**, enter **1st : Current** and **2nd: Auto**. For the **4-Up Settings**, enter **1st: Current, 2nd: Auto, 3rd: Auto**, and **4th: Auto**. Click **OK**.

Notice that we suggested you change all of your 1st settings from Original to Current and everything else to Auto? Original means that the Photoshop file format would be used, and Current means that whatever format you open would be used. Therefore, if you open a GIF or JPEG, it will display as such instead of in the Photoshop file format. Auto, as explained before, allows ImageReady to make a best guess as to which type of compression to use.

[PS]

13. ————————————————Optimizing a JPEG

Everything in this exercise ought to be pretty familiar to you. ImageReady and Photoshop are almost identical for optimization purposes. We'll show you a few new tricks along the way and you can do them in either application if you want to.

1. The file **skyscrap.psd** should still be open from the preceding exercises. Notice that it appears in a window that already has tabs that read **Original**, **Optimized**, **2-Up**, and **4-Up**.

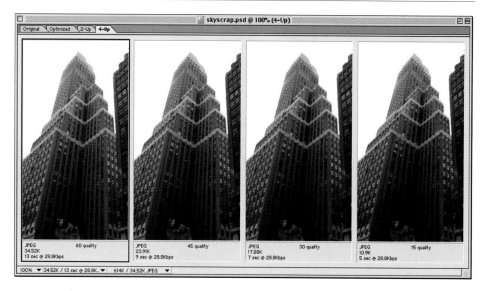

2. Click on the **4-Up** tab and the image should appear in four small preview windows.

Notice that they all defaulted to JPEG? That's the result of the Preference setting you made in the last exercise. ImageReady made a best guess that this photo would best be optimized as a JPEG.

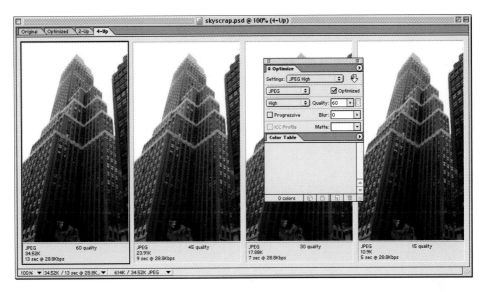

3. Move the **Optimize** palette to position it where you want on the screen. (It should bring the Color Table along with it if you completed the last exercise properly.)

4. Try all the things we covered in the Photoshop section of this chapter. Change the **Quality** setting, add **Blur**, and see what makes the smallest file size.

You already know how to use this program, because most of it is identical to Photoshop.

5. When you're ready to save this JPEG, choose **File > Save Optimized**. The **Save Optimized** window will appear with the name **skyscrap.jpg** already filled out. Save the file and leave it open for the next exercise.

This saved an optimized version of this file. Whenever you want to save a file in a Web format, choose Save Optimized or Save Optimized As…. Whenever you want to save the original Photoshop file, choose Save or Save As….

You might wonder what all the other settings are for in the Save Optimized window. Using the Format setting, you can save HTML just as you can from Photoshop. You'll learn how to do this in future chapters.

[IR]

14. —————————Using a Matte Color on a JPEG

One major difference between Photoshop and ImageReady is that you can edit this image easily in ImageReady, which was not true of the Save For Web feature in Photoshop. You would have had to click Cancel in the Save For Web dialog box to return to Photoshop's image-editing environment. Here in ImageReady, you can edit whenever you want. It's best to click on the Original tab, or else ImageReady will try to optimize the graphic while you're working, which can take a long time. In this exercise you will edit the image by erasing the background and inserting a new color by using the **Matte** feature.

1. With **skyscrap.psd** still open from the previous exercise, click back on the **Original** tab. This will cause the 4-up view to collapse into a single view of just the original.

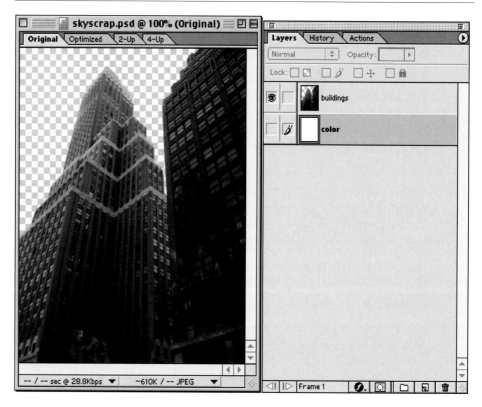

2. Choose **Window > Show Layers** if you cannot locate the Layers palette. Turn off the **Eye** icon for the layer named **color**. This should cause the checkerboard pattern to appear behind the skyscrapers, indicating transparency.

3. Click on the **Optimized** tab.

Notice that the checkerboard background disappeared and turned white? That's because you didn't specify a matte color, and ImageReady defaults to using white. You'll learn how to assign a different matte color in the next few steps.

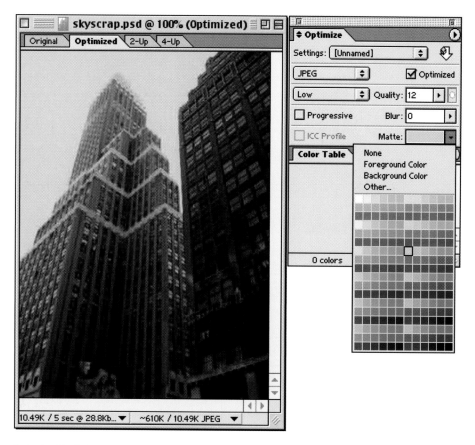

4. In the **Optimize** palette, click on the arrow next to the **Matte** field, and select a color off the pop-up color palette. **Note:** if you don't see the Matte field, either click the double-arrow symbol on the left of the Optimize tab or click the upper-right arrow of this palette to choose Show Options.

5. The image will now have behind it whichever color you chose. Click **OK**. Keep the file open for the next exercise.

If you click back on the Original tab, you'll see the matte color disappear. It is only a function of the JPEG that the matte color exists. You have not permanently altered the file except to turn off visibility on the color layer.

[IR]

I5. _____Previewing and Writing HTML

If you're an experienced Photoshop user, you might be wondering why you would choose to use the Matte color to insert a background color into a JPEG. You could have easily made a new layer in ImageReady, filled it with this color, and achieved the same effect. The only advantage is that because you used the Matte feature, ImageReady now knows to write this same color into the background color element of an HTML page, as well as the image. This exercise will show you how to set Matte color for the background color of your Web page.

However, you should note that there are times when the JPEG color will not perfectly match your HTML background color. If this happens to you, it would be better to create a transparent GIF, which you will learn about in Chapter 8, "*Transparent GIFs.*"

1. Choose **File > Preview In** and select the browser of your choice.

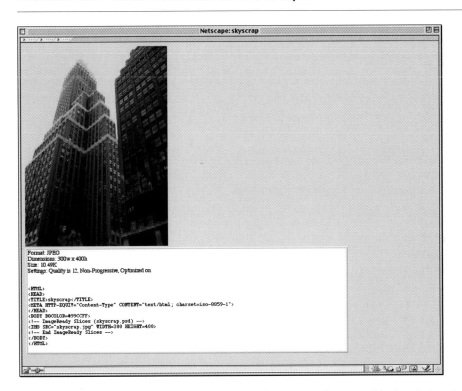

Notice that ImageReady creates a preview in the browser and puts a white box below the image that displays the HTML code that has been automatically written. You can actually copy and paste this code into an HTML editor, if you want. Better yet, you can have ImageReady write the HTML for you. You'll learn to do that next.

2. Return to ImageReady and choose **File > Save Optimized As....**

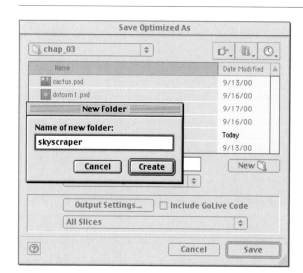

3. In the **Save Optimized As** window that appears, create a folder for this artwork named **skyscraper** by clicking **New** (Mac) or the yellow **Create New Folder** button (Windows). **Note:** Windows users should open the new folder *skyscraper* after you create it.

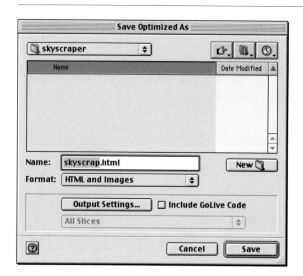

4. In the **Save Optimized As** window, change the **Format** field (Mac)or **Save as type** field (Windows) to **HTML and Images**, and click **Save**. A separate folder is not required, but it helps to keep your files organized.

5. Look on your hard drive for the folder **skyscraper** or for the directory where you chose to save the **skyscrap.jpg**. Notice that there are two files, an HTML file and the JPEG file?

6. Double-click on the **HTML** file, and you'll see the page open in the browser without the white information box that the preview generated before. It also contains references to the real file names instead of the temporary names that were assigned in the white information box.

This page can be opened in any HTML editor or uploaded directly to the Web. If you wanted to format it differently, such as to center the picture or put a headline at the top, you could easily add to the HTML in an editor or, if you know how, code HTML by hand.

7. Return to **ImageReady**. Leave the image open for the next exercise, which is the last one in this long chapter!

[IR]

16. _____Using Lossy Compression

You already learned the nuances of saving a GIF in Photoshop. All the same techniques you used before will work identically in ImageReady. In earlier exercises, when you saved a graphic image as a GIF, we purposely didn't show you how to apply lossy compression. You can apply lossy compression to graphics in small amounts, but you'll only see a minimal file savings, if any. Where lossy compression really shines is when you add it to a GIF that is photographic in nature, such as the skyscraper image that should still be open from the previous exercise. Here's how.

1. Revert the image so it's not transparent anymore. You can do this by choosing **File > Revert**.

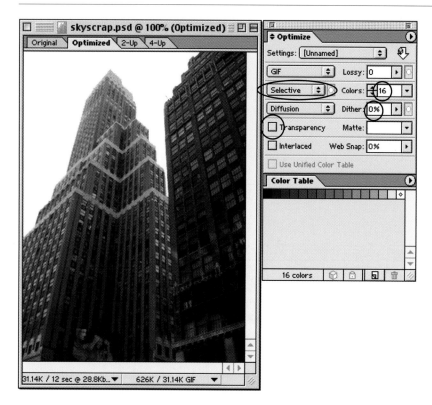

2. Click on the **Optimized** tab and choose **GIF** as the file format in the **Optimize** palette. Set the palette to **Selective** and **Colors: 16, Dither: 0%. Uncheck** the **Transparency** checkbox (you'll learn all about transparency in Chapter 8, *"Transparent GIFs"*).

The image is about 31K at this point. In the past this was the best you could have done. That was before Adobe introduced lossy compression!

3. Click on the **arrow** next to the **Lossy** field and start moving the slider up until you don't like the effect it's having on the image. ImageReady won't calculate the new image size or preview the results until you release the slider.

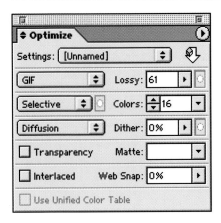

We settled at a lossy value of 61. The GIF is almost half the file size now at 14K! As we mentioned early on in this chapter, there are a few instances when you would want to save a photographic style image as a GIF, such as when you make animated or transparent GIFs. Most of the time, you'd save an image like this as a JPEG, and it would be just fine. For those few instances when you do have to save this type of image as a GIF, lossy compression simply rocks.

4. Close the file, congratulate yourself for doing so much in this chapter, and take a break.

NOTE | A GIF with Lossy Compression Is Still a GIF

Even though lossy compression in GIF files represents a relatively new capability, once you write the GIF it is a normal, healthy GIF–just like any other GIF you've ever met. The lossy compression was part of the processing you used to make the file small, but the GIF format is just the same as any other GIF format on the Web. There is absolutely no penalty to using lossy compression–in fact, the only penalty is a smaller file size and faster download.

4

Layers on Steroids

Layer Basics	Solid, Gradient, and Pattern Layers
Linking and Aligning Layers	Layer Sets	Layer Masks
Adjustment Layers	Clipping Groups

chap_04

Photoshop 6 / ImageReady 3
H·O·T CD-ROM

Understanding layers is one of the most important cornerstones of mastering Photoshop, because when you use layers, you can separate elements of your artwork so they can be independently edited. With this version of Photoshop, both layer novices and veterans will be on new ground, because of the introduction of many new types of layers.

By using layers, you can isolate image areas and apply special effects, or change the image's location, color, or opacity without affecting the rest of your art on the other layers. Now, in Photoshop 6, you can create even more specialized types of layers, such as solid, pattern, and gradient layers. These new types of layers help you in your workflow to create artwork more efficiently. Layers are powerful and sometimes even mysterious, but by the time you work through these exercises, you should be comfortable with most layering tasks.

What are Layers?

When the **Layers** palette was introduced in Photoshop a few years ago, it revolutionized the way that digital artists created, edited, and saved their work. Photoshop is a raster application. So every image was created in pixels, or bitmaps, which would be canceled out if another pixel was placed on top of them. This changed when layers came along. Suddenly, by separating areas of your work into layers, you could have stacks and stacks of bitmap images on separate layers that you could change or move without altering the pixels in the image areas below them. As long as you didn't "flatten" your layers, each one of them would remain independent of the others to allow you to make your changes. Although layers were introduced originally to help artists edit specific areas of artwork, they have grown to be more powerful with each new version. Now, layers not only isolate artwork, but they can contain special types of artwork, such as masks, patterns, solid fills and vectors. It all might seem a bit abstract. We suggest you follow the exercises, and that should make these concepts come to life for you.

[PS]

I. —————————————Layer Basics

We joke in class that if something doesn't work as expected in Photoshop, check to see if you're on the correct layer. Even seasoned Photoshop users get mixed up with layers sometimes, we assure you. This first exercise teaches the stacking order of layers, how to alter that order, how to rename a layer, and how to change the Background layer from being fixed to being flexible. **Note**: Everything you learn in this chapter is applicable in ImageReady 3 as well.

1. In Photoshop, open **layers.psd** from the **chap_04** folder that you transferred to your hard drive from the **H•O•T CD-ROM**.

2. In the **Layers** palette, click and drag the **cactus** layer below the **house** layer. You should see your cursor change to a **hand** icon and the lines between the layers change as this movement is accepted.

This is the way to change the stacking order of a layered Photoshop document. You don't touch the image at all; you just move the layers around via the Layers palette. At this point, you should see the cactus leaves poking out behind the house. Notice the stacking order goes from background to foreground as you move from the bottom of the palette to the top.

3. In the **Layers** palette, click the **Eye** icon on the **cactus** layer to turn it off. Notice that you don't see images on the **cactus** layer in your document window any longer. The process of clicking the Eye icon toggles on and off the visibility of that layer.

Try moving the Background layer above the clouds layer. You will discover that this layer cannot be moved. That's because by default, when a layer is called Background it's immovable unless you rename it.

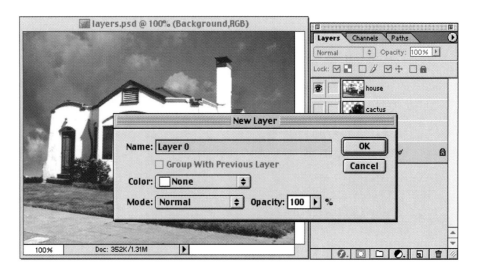

4. Double-click the **Background** layer to open the **New Layer** dialog box. You can leave the default name **Layer 0** in the **Name** field and click **OK**. Now move **Layer 0** above the **clouds** layer and it will move just like the cactus layer did in Step 2.

5. With **Layer 0** selected, move the **Opacity** slider to **44%**.

Because Layer 0 *is solid white, before you reduced its opacity from 100% to 44%, it completely covered the* cloud *layer, and the* house *layer looked washed-out. Sometimes this kind of washed-out effect is desirable, as it creates a nice screened-back look. Now you know how this sort of effect is achieved!*

6. Layer 0 isn't a terribly descriptive name for the white layer. To rename it, select **Layer 0**, and press **Option+double-click** (Mac) or **Alt+double-click** (Win). The **Layers Properties** dialog box will appear. Enter **white** in the **Name** field, and click **OK**.

This technique of renaming a layer is new to Photoshop 6. In the past, you could simply double-click on any layer to rename it. Now, you must hold down the Option (Mac) or Alt (Win) key to invoke the Layers Properties dialog box, unless you are renaming the Background layer, as you did in Step 4. Go figure!

Note: *In ImageReady there is only one way to change the name of a layer—just double-click on it.*

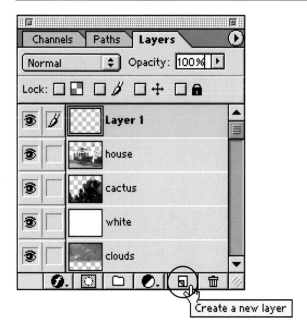

7. Click on the top layer in the stacking order, the **house** layer, to select it. Click the **New Layer** icon at the bottom of the **Layers** palette. Notice that a new empty layer appears in the Layers palette, but nothing has changed on your screen inside the document window.

When you add a new layer, by default the layer is empty and transparent. Next, you'll draw on the empty layer. The benefit to drawing on this layer, as opposed to drawing on any of the other layers, is that it can be isolated on its own—turned on or off, opacity lowered or raised, reordered, etc.

8. Make sure that the new empty layer is selected. Using the **Paintbrush** tool from the Toolbox, select a color, and start drawing lines around the house. Rename the layer **drawing** (you learned this in Step 6).

The benefit to drawing on this new empty layer is that it can be turned off if you don't like what you draw. Whew!

---

9. Experiment more with the techniques you just learned. Turn the **Visibility** (Eye) icons on and off, move layers around, reduce opacity, and change layer names. The more you play with this document, the more you'll build your layer skills.

---

10. Close and save the file.

Note that this exercise would function identically in ImageReady, with the exception of Step 6, where differences are noted.

NOTE | Flattening Photoshop Files

You are learning to work with layers in this chapter, and you will likely appreciate the flexibility they offer, as type and art elements can be separated and edited independently. In Photoshop, the term "flattened" means that the document's layers have been compressed into a single layer. There are times when you might want to flatten a Photoshop document—to send it to a client, or to make the file size smaller. If you plan to do this, it's always best to save a non-flattened version as well as a flattened one. You never know when having access to the layers will be important. It's possible to flatten all the layers, or just flatten certain layers to simplify a layered document that has grown to be very complex.

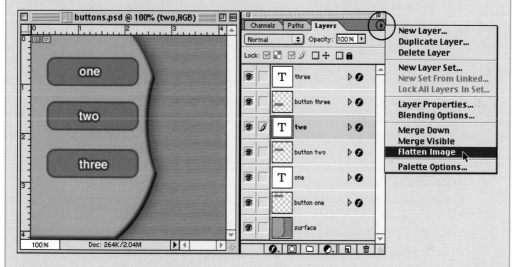

To flatten an image or layer, hold down the arrow button on the upper right corner of the Layers palette and select one of the following items:

Merge Down: Combines (or flattens, to use Photoshop's terminology) the selected layer and the layer directly below it.

Merge Visible: Combines (or flattens) any layers that have the Eye icons turned on. This is a great method to selectively flatten layers that aren't next to each other in the Layers palette.

Flatten Image: Combines all layers in the document.

2. ———————————**Moving and Linking Layers**

In the last exercise, you learned to move the stacking order of layers from front to back, but what if you want to move a layer's position on the screen? This next exercise will teach you how to link layers together so they can be moved and aligned.

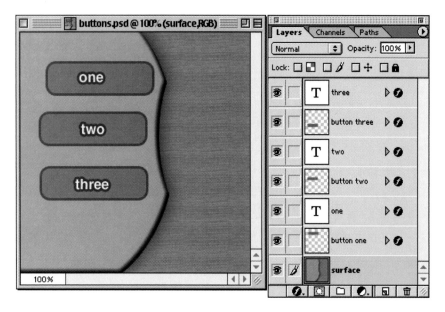

1. In Photoshop, open **buttons.psd** from the **chap_04** folder on your hard drive. Notice that there are three buttons on the screen, which are represented by seven layers in the Layers palette.

If you are wondering what the ƒ symbol means to the right of most of the layers, it denotes that a layer style is in use. You'll learn more about the new layer styles feature in Chapter 6, "Layer Styles."

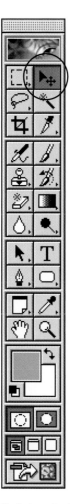

2. Select the **Move** tool from the Toolbox. This is a tool that is used so often with Photoshop work that you'll save a lot of time by using the shortcut key for it. Just press the letter **V** on your keyboard and this tool will become selected. Try clicking on a different tool, then press the letter **V** to try it out. This is one of our favorite and most frequently used tools and short-cut keys in Photoshop.

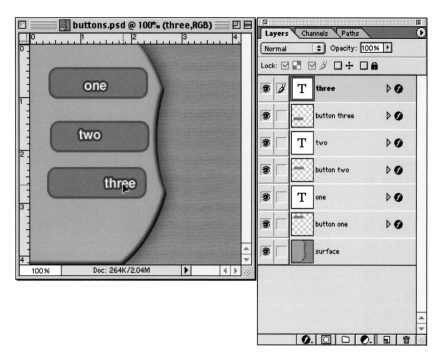

3. Click on the **three** layer in the **Layers** palette to select it. Move your mouse to the document window and click and drag. The word **three** should move with your movements.

You've just hit one of the biggest hurdles of being adept in Photoshop. A layer must be selected first before it can be moved on the screen. This is a difficult concept for most new Photoshop users because there's a disconnect between wanting to move something on the screen, and having to first consciously think about which layer contains that artwork. Next, you'll learn a shortcut to selecting layers that doesn't involve the Layers palette.

4. Click to put a checkmark in the **Auto Select Layer** checkbox, which is on the left of the **Options** bar at the top of your screen. Using the **Move** tool, click on different areas of your screen and watch the **Layers** palette selections change. This is much easier than going to the **Layers** palette to select a specific layer that you want to move. Sweet!

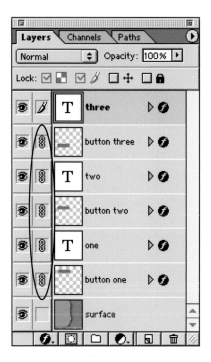

5. To move more than one layer at a time, you'll need to link your layers using the **Link** icon. In the **Layers** palette, click inside the **Link** region, directly to the left of the layer thumbnail, on all the layers except the surface layer. Notice that your active layer (the one that is currently selected in the Layers palette) has a **Paintbrush** icon instead of a link icon in the link region. This means that all the other layers in which you've put a link icon are linking to it.

6. With the **Move** tool selected, click and drag on your screen. You'll see all the layers move together. The next exercise will show you how the Link icon is helpful when aligning layers.

7. Leave this file open for the next exercise.

This exercise works identically in ImageReady.

[PS]

3. ——————————Aligning Layers with the Link Icon

The link function in Photoshop is useful for more than just moving your layers as a group. You can also use it to align linked layers by specific measurements, such as left, center, right, and distribution distances.

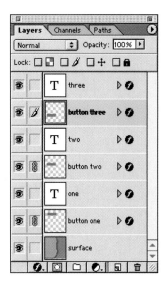

1. First, you might want to get the buttons to align left. Select the layer **button three**. You'll see a **Paintbrush** icon in the **Links** region that confirms this is your selected layer. Because this file has all the buttons and text linked from the previous exercise, you'll have to unlink the text layers. All you have to do is click again inside the **Link** region on layers **one**, **two**, and **three** and the **Link** icons on those layers will toggle off. Make sure your **Layers** palette looks like the one we show in this step.

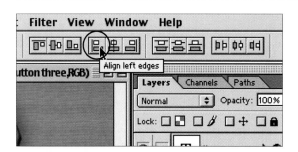

2. Click the **Align left edges** button in the **Options** bar to align the buttons vertically. You'll see all the button shapes line up to the left.

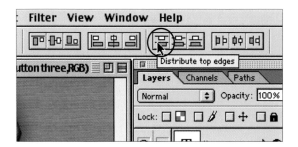

3. Click the **Distribute top edges** button in the **Options** bar to distribute the buttons vertically. All the button shapes will be evenly spaced.

With the Move tool selected, you can move these three perfectly aligned and spaced buttons around and they'll stay grouped this way.

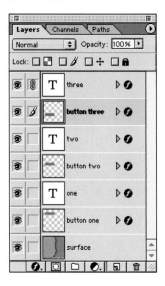

4. Now you'll want to align the text to the buttons. Select **button three** in the **Layers** palette and link the **three** layer to it. Unlink all the other links.

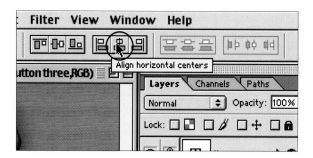

5. Click the **Align horizontal centers** button. The lettering will be centered on the button. See if you can get the other labels to align center to their buttons.

Hint: Select the button artwork first, then link the lettering to it before you align. Alignment is always based on the selected layer as the starting point, as indicated by the Paintbrush icon. If you select the text first and then the button layer, your button will move instead.

6. Save and close the file.

This exercise works exactly the same way in ImageReady.

What are Layer Sets?

Layer sets are new to Photoshop 6 and ImageReady 3, and one of our favorite new features because they offer new freedom and flexibility in documents that contain multiple layers. A layer set is a folder that you can add to the Layers palette in which other layers can be stored. This makes it easy to organize your Layers palette when you are using a lot of layers. It means that you could turn multiple layers on and off at once, because the Visibility(eye) icon can control everything that's inside the layer set folder. You can also lower and raise the opacity of multiple layers this way, because the opacity will affect the entire contents of the layer set folder.

What are Layer Sets Good For?

Old Way	Layer Set Way
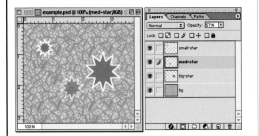	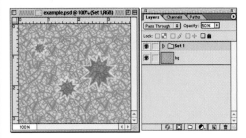
In previous versions of Photoshop, you had to lower the opacity of each layer, one by one.	If, instead, you put all the layers into a layer set, you could adjust the opacity of the layer set and all the nested layers within it would be affected at once.
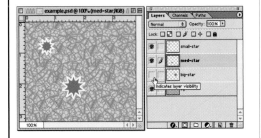	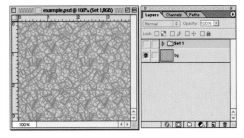
In previous versions of Photoshop, you had to turn the visibility of layers off, one by one.	Using a layer set, you could turn its visibility off and affect multiple layers' visibility at once. This is great for organizing documents that have dozens of layers.

continues on next page

What are Layer Sets Good For? *continued*

Old Way

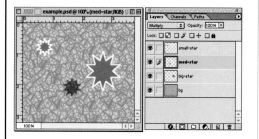

Layer Set Way

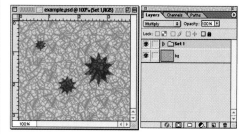

In previous versions of Photoshop, you had to change the layer blending mode (Multiply is shown here) one layer at a time.

By putting all the layers into a layer set, you could set the layer blending mode one time and it would affect all the nested layers.

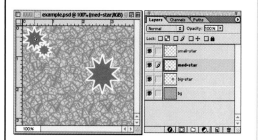

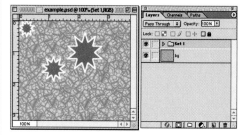

Without linking (which you learned about in Exercise 2), you can only move a layer at a time.

Using a layer set, you could move all the layers within a set at once by first selecting the layer set and then using the Move tool inside the document window. Note: This technique only works if Auto Select Layer is turned off on the Options bar.

[PS]

4. ————————Layer Sets

Layer sets offer a great way of grouping multiple layers into a single folder. In this exercise you'll learn to create layer sets and how to change their opacity, their visibility, and their position. In the end, you might wonder why and when to use layer sets. They are useful for everything shown here, with the exception of aligning artwork. You'll get to link layers within a layer set to see how to get around that limitation. This exercise also works in ImageReady.

1. Open **circle_layers.psd** from the **chap_04** folder you copied to your hard drive.

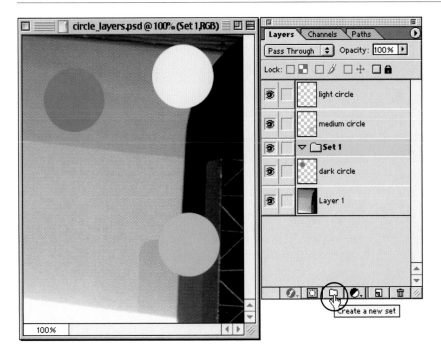

2. Click the **New Set** icon at the bottom of the **Layers** palette. A folder called **Set 1** will appear above whatever layer was active when you clicked the icon.

A layer set can be moved in the stacking order just like any other layer.

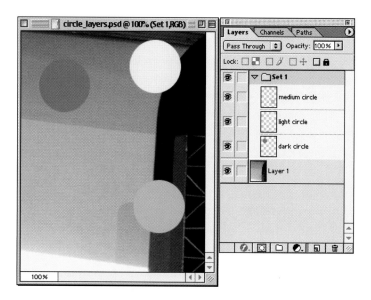

3. Move the layers **light circle**, **medium circle** and **dark circle** into the folder called **Set 1** by clicking and dragging the layers from the **Layers** palette onto its folder icon. **Note:** Once the layers are inside the folder, the folder arrow can be twirled up or down to show its contents.

4. Uncheck the **Auto Select Layer** checkbox in the **Options** bar at the top of your screen, which was left on from the previous exercise, or this step will not work properly. Select **Set 1** in the **Layers** palette. Using the **Move** tool (**V**), move the three circles around on the screen together.

Layer sets can be used to group objects, and can provide an alternative to using the Link icon for moving multiple layers.

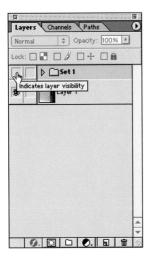

5. Turn off the **Visibility** icon for **Set 1**, and you'll see all three circles disappear. In this example, the **Set 1** arrow is turned up so its contents are not visible. If you click to twirl the arrow down you'll see all three of the layers with their **Visibility** icons dimmed out.

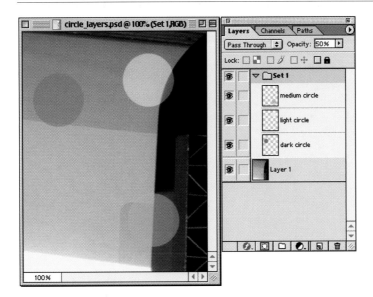

6. Turn the **Visibility** of **Set 1** back on, and click the arrow so the set is revealed again. It really doesn't matter if the set reveals its contents in the **Layers** palette for most operations. With **Set 1** selected, change the **Opacity** slider to **50%**. Layer sets are useful for changing the opacity of multiple layers at one time.

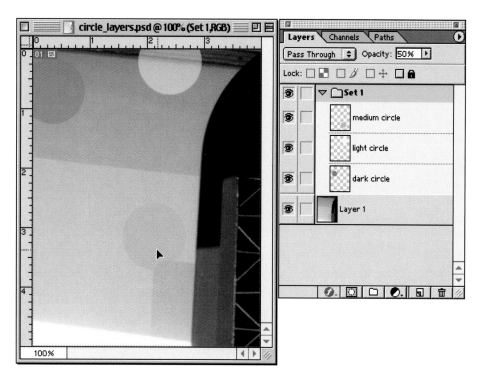

7. Make sure the **Move** tool is selected in the Toolbox, and that **Set 1** is selected. Click on any of the circles inside the document window, and move it to a new location. All the other circles should follow, as they are grouped together via this layer set. **Note:** this will not work if **Auto Select Layers** is checked in the **Options** bar!

Notice that all of the alignment options on the Options bar are dimmed out. That's because you have to use the Link icon to align artwork, even when it's inside a layer set. The next step will show you how.

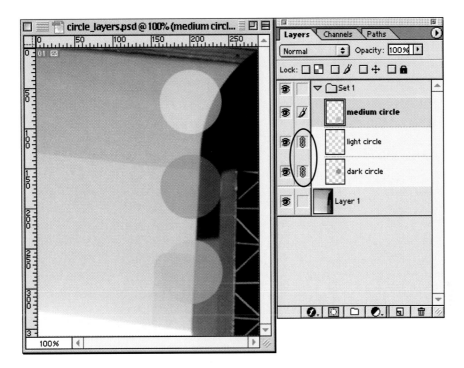

8. Select any one of the layers in the set, and activate the **Link** icons for the other layers in the set. Use the **align** buttons on the **Options** bar to set the alignment of the layers to the left and distribute from top. The circles should align as shown in this illustration, with the layers containing a Link icon aligning to the selected layer.

Layer sets are useful for organizing layers so they can be easily turned on and off. They are also useful for moving layers around in a group or changing the opacity of a group. Layer sets do not help with alignment, however, like the Link icons. We like to use them for organizing large layered documents, for moving multiple layers at once, and for adjusting the opacity of multiple layers. We still use those Link icons, however, as layer sets don't offer alignment options without them.

9. Save and close this file.

5. ————————————Solid Color Layer

This exercise will show you how to quickly generate a **solid color layer**, which is useful for backgrounds to images. It's new to Photoshop 6 and is also supported in ImageReady 3.

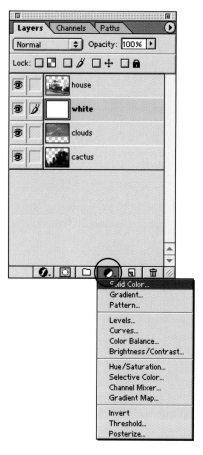

1. Open **layers2.psd** from the **chap_04** folder, and select the layer **white**. Press the black and white circle icon for the **New Fill** or **Adjustment Layer** menu at the bottom of the **Layers** palette, and select **Solid Color...**. This will open the **Color Picker**.

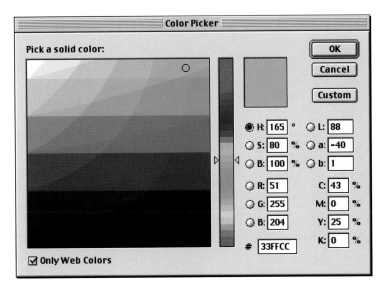

2. Click **Only Web Colors** (this ensures that the color you pick will be Web-safe), select a color, and click **OK**.

Notice that a new layer, Color Fill 1, that has two thumbnails and a link symbol associated with it, has been added to the Layers palette. The thumbnail on the left is a solid color fill. The white thumbnail on the right is a layer mask, which you'll learn about later in this chapter. The reason for using a solid color layer is that it gives you the flexibility to easily change a solid fill. The next step will show you how easy it is to change your mind about a color when using a solid color layer.

3. In the **Layers** palette, double-click on the thumbnail on the left side of the **solid color** layer. This will open the **Color Picker**. Choose a new color and notice the live preview of the color changes to the layer. Click **OK**.

4. Leave the document open for the next exercise.

Note that the solid color layer will appear and behave identically in ImageReady. It cannot be created from within ImageReady, however. Of the two tools, only Photoshop allows you to create a solid color layer.

6. ——————Gradient Layer

Next, you'll get to create a **gradient layer**. Gradient layers are great for quickly creating backgrounds that contain a gradient, and for their flexibility if you ever want to change the colors or blend of the gradient. Like solid color layers, gradient layers cannot be created in ImageReady, but ImageReady will support gradient layers made in Photoshop.

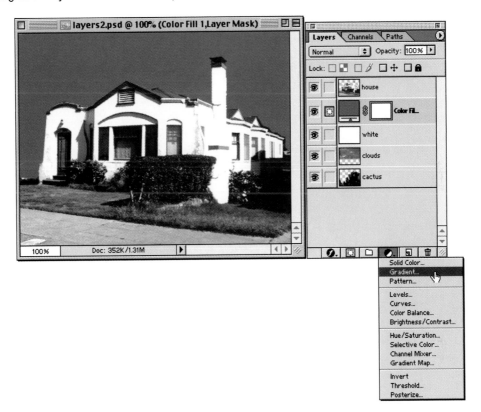

1. In the **Layers** palette, select the **Color Fill 1** layer that you created in the last exercise. This ensures that the next layer you create will appear above this layer in the stacking order. Press the black and white circle icon at the bottom of the **Layers** palette to create a new layer, and from the pull-down menu, select **Gradient...**. This will open the **Gradient Fill** dialog box.

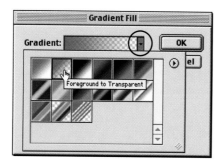

2. Click the **arrow** to the right of the **Gradient** field to open the default **Gradient** library. Click around on different choices and you'll see them update automatically in your document. Once you've chosen a gradient from this library, click back inside the **Gradient Fill** dialog box and your choice will be accepted.

3. Change the **Style**, **Angle**, and **Scale** options in the **Gradient Fill** dialog box to see different effects. Click **OK** once you've explored this dialog box.

If you've ever worked with gradient backgrounds before using the Gradient tool from the Toolbox, we think you'll agree that this gradient layer is very valuable. What if you want to make your own custom gradient, however? That's possible too, as you'll learn from the following steps.

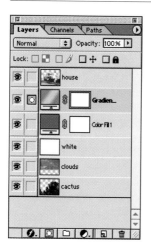

If you look at the Layers palette, you'll see that like the solid color layer, the gradient layer also has two thumbnails: the gradient and the layer mask thumbnail. The layer mask is another type of layer that can change the shape of the layer it's associated with. You'll learn to work with a layer mask, which will help you to understand it better, later in this chapter.

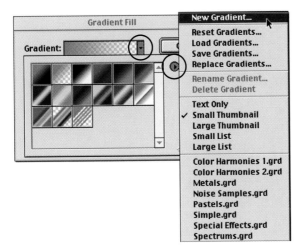

4. Double-click on the left thumbnail to re-access the **Gradient Fill** dialog box. Click on the **arrow** to the right of the **Gradient** field, and then click on the **arrow** to the right of the **Gradient** library to access the pop-up menu. Choose **New Gradient…**. The **Gradient Name** dialog box will appear.

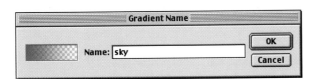

5. Enter **sky** into the **Name** field of the **Gradient Name** dialog box. Click **OK**.

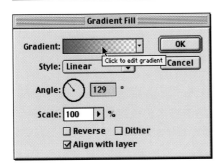

6. Click inside the gradient area, as shown here. This will open the **Gradient Editor**.

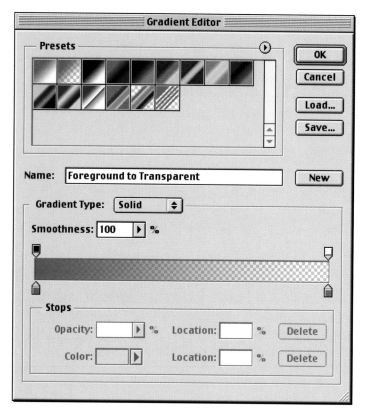

7. Experiment with changing the colors or moving the start and end points of the gradient. When you're finished, click **OK**.

---

8. Leave the file open for the next exercise.

 MOVIE

To see a movie that shows how to edit the gradient, open **gradient.mov** from the **movies** folder that you transferred to your hard drive from the **H•O•T CD-ROM**.

[PS]

7. ———————Pattern Layer

A **pattern layer** allows you to fill a layer with . . . you guessed correctly, a pattern! Later in Chapter 7, "*Background Images*," you'll learn how to make your own pattern to simulate a background image on a Web page. For now, this exercise will simply introduce you to the feature. A pattern layer is another kind of layer that is supported by, but cannot be created in ImageReady.

1. In the **Layers** palette, select the **Gradient Fill 1** layer that you created in the last exercise. This ensures that the next layer you create will appear above this layer in the stacking order. Press the **New Fill** or **Adjustment Layer** icon at the bottom of the **Layers** palette, and from the pop-up menu, choose **Pattern….** This will open the **Pattern Fill** dialog box.

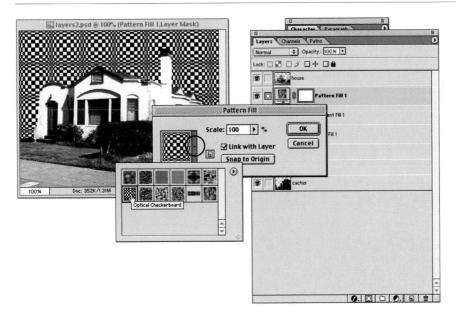

2. Click the **arrow** to the right of the **Pattern** thumbnail, which will access the **Pattern** library. Click around and try different patterns until you're ready to accept one by clicking **OK**.

Chances are, you'll be wondering right about now if you can create and add your own patterns. The answer is yes, but you'll learn how later, in Chapter 7, "Background Images."

3. Most patterns will look pretty silly when layered behind the house, but you get the idea. Any of these **solid**, **gradient**, or **pattern layers** in the document can be re-accessed by double-clicking on their thumbnails in the **Layers** palette.

4. You're finished learning about these new types of layers. Save and close the file.

8. _____Layer Masks

The term **mask** is common in most digital imaging programs. A mask will determine whether an image is visible, invisible, or partially visible. Masks are common because, by default, all computer images are in square or rectangular shapes. Without a mask, you would never be able to make artwork in irregular shapes! Making masks is something that Photoshop excels at, and there are lots of ways to make them, so it's one of the more advanced aspects of the program. Our favorite way to make a mask involves using a **layer mask**. This next exercise will show you how to make and edit these great masking devices. It works the same way in ImageReady.

1. Open **mtn_clds.psd** from the **chap_04** folder that you transferred to your hard drive. Turn on and off the **Visibility** icons in the **Layers** palette so you can familiarize yourself with the two layers in this document. The goal of this exercise will be to mask out the real clouds in the **mountain** layer to reveal the **other_clouds** layer.

2. In the **Layers** palette, select the **mountain** layer and click the **New Layer Mask** icon (shown circled above). This will make an empty white **layer mask** thumbnail appear to the right of the picture thumbnail. Notice that the layer mask thumbnail is highlighted? When it is highlighted, it means you can paint inside of it to create a mask that will affect the image. You'll learn how to do this next.

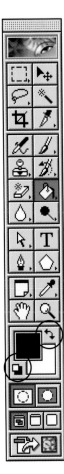

3. Make sure you have the color **black** as your foreground color. **Hint:** You can click on the small squares icon circled above to force your palette to white and black. Then click on the double-pointed arrow circled above to switch the foreground color to black.

It's imperative that you draw with black in the masking layer. Black allows you to paint out content, and white allows you to paint content back in. For now, just trust us on this! You'll see how it works shortly.

4. Select the **Paintbrush** tool from the Toolbox. Select a large hard-edged **Brush** from the **Brush** pop-up palette, which you access by clicking the arrow next to the **Brush** sample on the **Options** bar at the top of your screen. Start to paint on the image along the outline where the sky meets the mountain. As you paint, you will see the layer below show through your paint stroke.

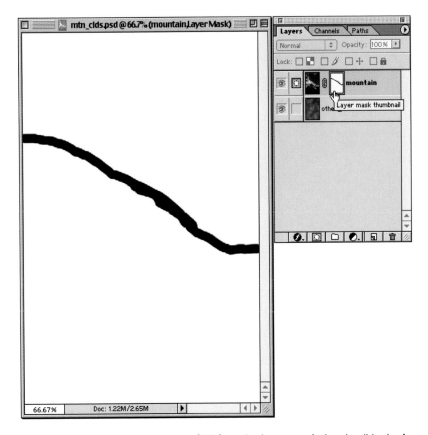

5. Option+click (Mac) or **Alt+click** (Win) on the **layer mask** thumbnail in the **Layers** palette. This will cause the mask to appear inside the document window, and will turn off the image layer. Be sure to click on the *layer mask thumbnail* when you use this keyboard shortcut, and not the document window, or else you will get the Eyedropper tool.

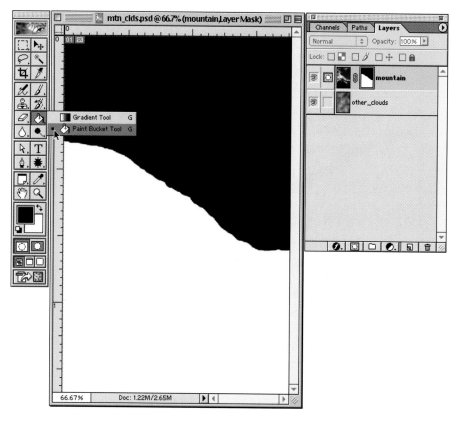

6. Select the **Paint Bucket** tool from the Toolbox. (**Hint:** it's hidden as an option under the Gradient tool!) Click on the top area to fill it with black. You might have to do some clean-up work around the brush line by painting any unfilled areas with black.

NOTE | What is a Layer Mask, Anyway?

A layer mask determines what portions of an image can be seen or hidden, and uses opacity levels to achieve this from all the way on to all the way off. When painting in the layer mask, pure black represents all the way off, while pure white represents all the way on. If you were to paint with gray, a dark gray would create a mask that is almost transparent, and a light gray would create a mask that is almost opaque. Transparency is represented in Photoshop in terms of blacks and whites when working with layer masks.

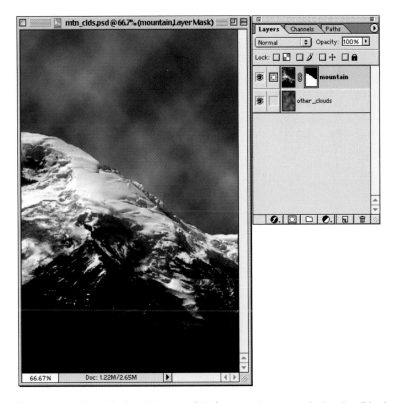

7. Option+click (Mac) or **Alt+click** (Win) on the **layer mask** thumbnail in the **Layers** palette to toggle the image layer back on. You'll now see through to the layer below, and the old sky will be masked out.

If you paint with white, you'll paint the old sky back in! That's the beauty of layer masks—the original image is always preserved. This is called non-destructive image editing—cool term, eh? Layer masks work identically in ImageReady, except you cannot view the mask in the document window. Bummer! We love the feedback of being able to look at the black and white mask, because it helps you see if you haven't painted a solid area where you intended.

8. Leave this file open for the next exercise.

 MOVIE | layer_mask.mov

To learn more about layer masks, or if the past exercise was confusing (masks can seem very strange if you're unaccustomed to them), check out **layer_mask.mov** from the **movies** folder on the **H•O•T CD-ROM**.

[PS]

9. ——————————Adjustment Layer

Adjustment layers allow you to make image adjustments that are non-destructive, preserving the original image just like layer masks do. They are great for changing contrast, hue, or color balance levels of an image. You'll learn how to implement them in this exercise.

1. Use the image from the last exercise, or open **mtn_clouds2.psd** from the **chap_04** folder you transferred to your hard drive.

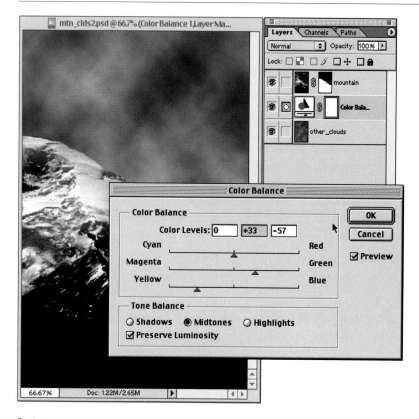

2. Select the **other_clouds** layer and click the black-and-white **New Fill** or **Adjustment Layer** icon at the bottom of the **Layers** palette to access the pop-up menu. Choose **Color Balance** from the pop-up menu. In the **Color Balance** dialog box, change the color levels, and watch the image change. Click **OK**.

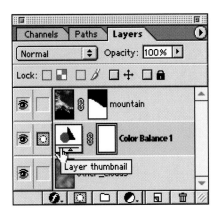

3. Notice the new **Color Balance 1** layer that appeared? You can reaccess the color balance settings at any point by double-clicking on the **layer** thumbnail on the left side of this layer.

4. Add a different **adjustment layer** to the **mountain** layer. Try **Levels, Hue, Saturation, Posterize**, and any others that make you curious. Once you've set an adjustment layer you can always turn it off to return to the original image.

Adjustment layers are recognized by ImageReady, but they cannot be created there. You can go back and forth between the two applications however, and the adjustment layers will not be disturbed or altered.

5. Close the file and move on to the next exercise.

IO._____Clipping Groups

You've probably seen type on the Web and elsewhere that contains a photographic image inside the letters. This technique can be achieved in Photoshop and ImageReady by using **clipping groups.** This technique consists of artwork that is used as a mask and content that goes into that mask. In this example, we're using type, but you can use other kinds of artwork for clipping groups, too.

1. Open **dinosaurs.psd** from your **chap_04** folder.

2. Move the **dinoset** layer above the type layer in the **Layers** palette by clicking and dragging it to the top position. This will temporarily obscure the type layer.

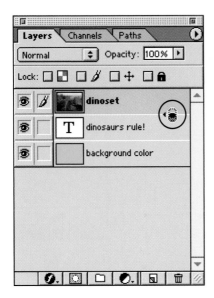

3. Hold down the **Option** (Mac) or **Alt** (Windows) key and move your cursor to the line that divides the **dinoset** and type layers. The cursor will change from a hand to the **clipping groups** icon. When your cursor is directly over the line, click, and the photograph will appear inside the type.

When you create a clipping group by clicking on the line that divides the layers, an arrow will appear to the left of the layer thumbnail, indicating that the clipping group is in effect.

4. Make sure that the **dinoset** layer is selected and that the **Move** tool from the Toolbox is active. Click on the screen, and notice that you can move the photograph independently from the type. Position it where you like it.

 MOVIE | **clipping_group.mov**

To learn more about setting up clipping groups, check out **clipping_group.mov** from the **movies** folder on the **H•O•T CD-ROM**.

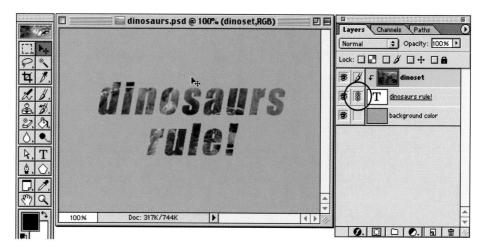

5. If you want to move the type and the photo together, select the **dinoset** layer and click on the **Link** region (circled above) in the type layer. Now if you use the **Move** tool to move the artwork, both items will move together.

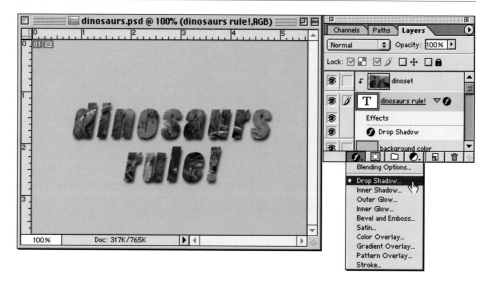

6. You can add **layer styles**, too. Click on the **type** layer and then click on the *f* icon at the bottom of the **Layers** palette to choose **Drop Shadow**. Sweet! Save and close this file.

This works identically in ImageReady. Because the type is editable, you can still change the font, the size, or the style even though the clipping group is in effect. This allows experimentation with numerous variations.

NOTE | Clipping Groups

A clipping group involves two or more layers. The artwork that will serve as the mask for the group needs to be on the layer below whatever it is masking. This is a great technique for inserting content inside a shape. In an earlier version of Photoshop, we used **Edit > Paste Into** to get this effect, but a clipping group is a much better method. It's better because it's more flexible—you can still move the layers above the dotted line or alter them, whereas the older Paste Into method could never be edited once it was pasted.

5.

Type

Options Bar Settings	Character Palette
Paragraph Palette	Warp Text	Jump To ImageReady
Rasterizing Text	Transforming Text

chap_05

Photoshop 6 / ImageReady 3
H•O•T CD-ROM

Text on the Web can be a touchy subject for professional designers, because HTML affords very little typographic control. Many Web designers avoid the limitations of HTML type by making artwork for type instead of relying on code. If you make GIF or JPEG files for the Web that contain typography, you're gonna love what Photoshop 6 and ImageReady 3 can do for you. Fortunately, this set of programs has unsurpassed typographic control.

This chapter covers the many aspects of type in Photoshop and ImageReady, including anti-aliasing, coloring, changing fonts, using transform tools on type, the new warping feature, and using paragraph text. Type is one of our favorite subjects, and many of the techniques found in this chapter are likely to add great visual appeal to the sites you design.

Differences in Type in Photoshop 6 and ImageReady 3

The differences in the way Photoshop and ImageReady handle type are minimal in the latest versions of these programs. A big change to Photoshop is that it now handles type more like ImageReady did in version 2, in that you type directly into your document and not inside a type dialog box. This offers much better creative control, because you can see what you're doing right away in relation to other objects on your screen. Working with type relies on some of the layer skills that you built up in the previous chapter. For example, selecting the right layer is essential when editing your type.

A small difference between Photoshop and ImageReady is that a tiny blue line appears under type in ImageReady. If you are an Adobe Illustrator user, this might be a familiar sight. You'll learn a shortcut key (**Command+H** on Macs or **Control+H** on Windows) to make this blue line disappear. One thing that you might not realize about type in Photoshop and ImageReady is that it is vector-based, not raster-based. This means that you can transform the type (scale, rotate or skew) without losing any fidelity. You'll get to try this soon enough, so it's time to get busy!

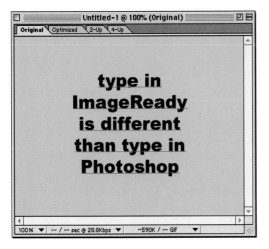

In ImageReady, a tiny blue line appears under editable text.

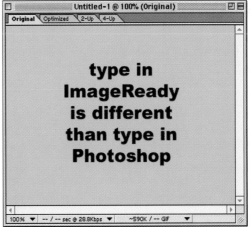

To make the blue line disappear, click off the type layer in the Layers palette or use the shortcut key Command+H (Mac) or Control+H (Windows).

[PS]

I. ——————————Type Options Bar

Type has changed for the better in the new version of Photoshop. The next few exercises will familiarize you with the new ways of working—editing on the screen and using the **Type Options** bar to access common settings. Follow along even if you've used these features in past versions of Photoshop. Enough things have changed in terms of how you edit type that even experienced Photoshop users will be on new turf for type basics.

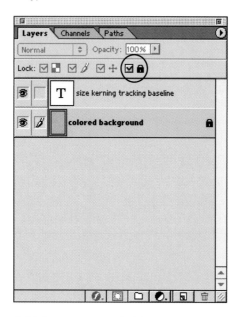

1. Make sure you are in Photoshop, and open **typebasics.psd** from the **chap_05** folder that you transferred to your hard drive from the **H.O.T CD-ROM**. If your **Layers** palette is not visible, choose **Window > Show Layers**. Select the layer **colored background**, and click the **Lock All** checkbox at the top of the **Layers** palette. This will make it impossible to move or edit the colored background layer, so you can focus on editing the type.

This Lock All feature is new to Photoshop 6 (and ImageReady 3), and it's a great technique to use when you don't want to accidentally move or edit a layer. When you check Lock All, you'll see a light gray checkmark next to all the locks, meaning that they all are activated. If you want to review what each of the locks does, turn back to Chapter 2, "Web Color."

Note: If you do not have Verdana or Georgia installed, other fonts will be substituted. You can download these fonts for free from the Microsoft Web site (http://www.microsoft.com/ typography/fontpack/default.htm) if you'd like, or work with whatever fonts are automatically substituted for you.

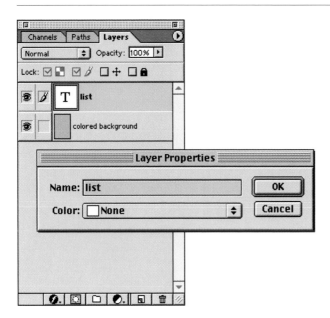

2. Notice that the type layer is named by what is actually typed on the screen? This is the default naming behavior of Photoshop. Sometimes it can be distracting, so we renamed the layer "list." In Photoshop 6, do this by **Option+double-clicking** (Mac) or **Alt+double-clicking** (Windows) on the type layer to open the **Layers Properties** dialog box. Rename the layer "**list**" and click **OK**.

We had an ulterior motive for asking you to change this layer's name. If anything annoys us about this version of Photoshop (and very little does!), it's this one new technique. Experienced Photoshop users are used to double-clicking on a layer to rename it. This is still the way you do it in ImageReady 3. For some unknown reason, you have to hold down the Option (Mac) or Alt (Windows) key to rename a layer in Photoshop 6. If you don't, you'll end up opening the Layer Style dialog box. You already ran into this issue in Chapter 4, "Layers on Steroids." We're forcing you to get practice doing this again, because if you don't know this new technique you'll be extremely frustrated when you want to rename a layer!

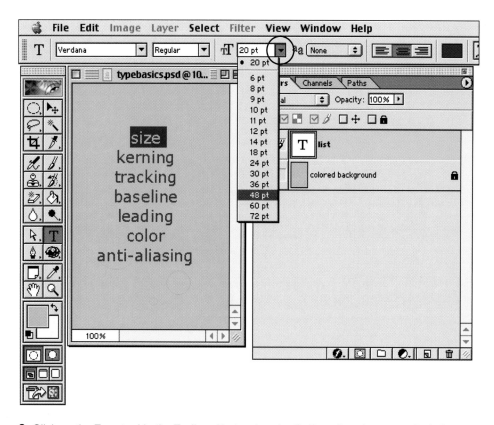

3. Click on the **Type** tool in the Toolbox. Notice that the **Options** bar changes to include settings for type? Click and drag your cursor across the word "size" on the screen (this is a new way of selecting type, and it might be awkward for you older Photoshop geezers), and click the arrow next to the Size field to select **48 pt** from the pop-up menu in the Options bar.

You should see the change appear on your screen. You can change the size of any character or word this way, even if it's within a paragraph.

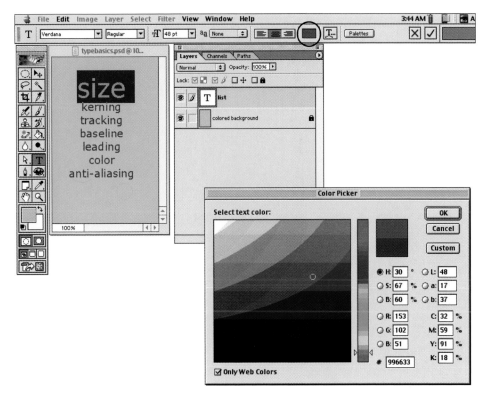

4. With the word "size" still selected, click in the **Color** field of the Options bar to access the **Color Picker**. Choose a **dark red** (or any other dark color other than what's already chosen) and click OK.

Notice that the color change is hard to see while the type is still selected? That's because the highlight on the type selection area causes the type color to reverse and be difficult to accurately see. There's a good trick to fix this problem. It's essential that the type is selected, or you can't edit it. First select the type (in this case, it's already selected); then use the shortcut key Command+H (Mac) or Control+H (Windows). This command key is easy for us to remember because H stands for "hide."

5. Using the **Command+H** (Mac) or **Control+H** (Windows) shortcut to hide the selected type, click on the **Color** field in the **Options** bar again, and change the type to a dark blue (or any other dark color). This time, you can see what you're picking! When you are finished picking a color, click **OK**.

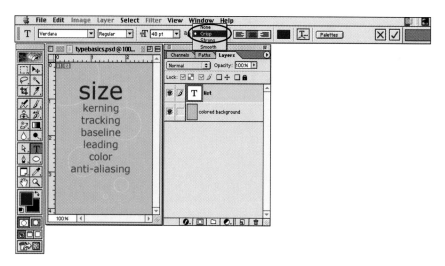

6. Click on the **pop-up** menu next to the **Anti-Alias** button on the **Options** bar, and choose from **Crisp**, **Strong** or **Smooth**.

Having this many choices for anti-aliasing is a great feature for Web work, because different levels of anti-aliasing work best depending on the font and size you are using. If you design for print, these issues are not as important because you would typically print your work at high resolution. Because the resolution of the Web is so low, you have to judge whether or not your type looks good on the screen. We usually choose None for type that is under 14 points, and we experiment with Crisp, Strong, and Smooth for larger type.

7. Experiment with other settings in the **Options** bar, like type orientation, font, and alignment, to familiarize yourself with all the type options found there. Leave the file open for the next exercise.

NOTE | What is Anti-Aliasing, Anyway?

Aliased

Anti-Aliased

Anti-aliasing is a term that refers to how the edges of artwork look. An anti-aliased edge is made up of colors that gradually blend into a neighboring color so that the edge looks less pixilated. In the context of this chapter, aliased type looks jaggy, while anti-aliased type looks smooth. Most of the time you'll choose to anti-alias the type in your Web graphics, though sometimes on very small point sizes aliased type is more readable.

2. ──────────Using the Character Palette

So far, you learned to work with the Options bar at the top of your screen. There are two other type-related palettes: **Character** and **Paragraph**. First, you'll get to try some of the Character settings. The Paragraph settings will be employed in a later exercise.

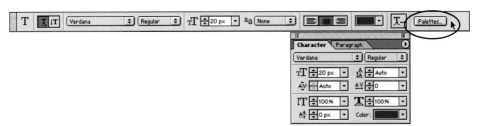

1. Click the **Palettes** button to bring forth the Character palette and Paragraph palette. Next, you'll work with some features found in the **Character** palette, but not found in the Options bar.

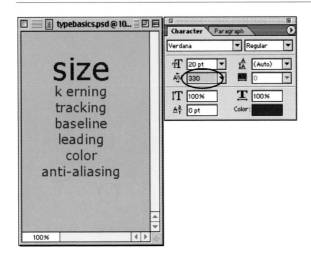

2. Position your cursor between the letters **k** and **e** in the word **kerning** and click so the insertion bar appears. Hold down the **Option** (Mac) or **Alt** (Windows) key and press the right or left arrow on your keyboard. Notice how the space between the two letters expands and contracts? You can also adjust the kerning in the **Character** palette. In the field for **kerning**, change the setting to **330** so your document and palette match the example above.

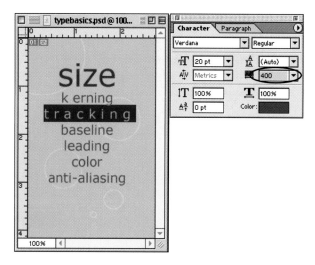

3. Select the word **tracking** in the document, and enter **400** in the **Tracking** field in the **Character** palette.

Notice how all the letters in the word expand. Kerning affects the space between two characters, while tracking affects the space between all the selected letters.

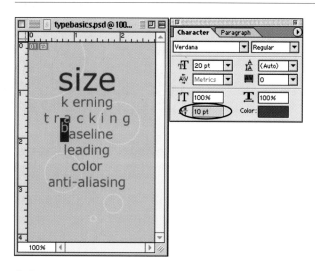

4. Select the letter **b** in **baseline** and enter **10** in the **Baseline** field.

Notice that the letter "b" moved above the baseline of the rest of the word? If you use a negative number, the letter will drop below the baseline. Baseline adjustments can be applied to entire words or individual characters.

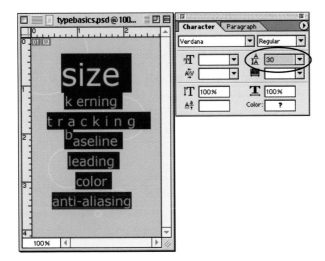

5. Select all the words in the list and enter **30** in the **Leading** field. When you're done, click off the type to deselect it.

Notice that all the lines of type expand so there is more vertical space between them?
Leading affects the space between each line of type. The term refers to the olden days of
typesetting, when foundries would use actual pieces of lead to physically separate each line
of type. We wonder if some old typesetters are turning in their graves watching this process?

6. Click the **checkmark** icon in the **Options** bar to accept the edits you made to the type layer. If you wanted to cancel the changes you'd made, you would click the **X** icon on the **Options** bar. Save and close this file.

The Character Palette

The Character palette contains many settings. This handy chart should provide a good reference for each feature.

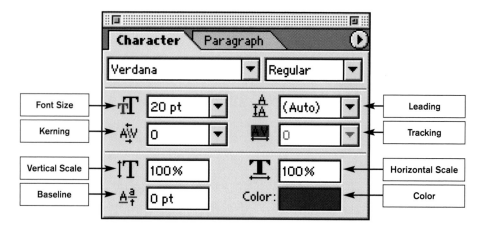

Character Settings	
Feature	**Function**
Font Size	Adjusts the size of type
Kerning	Adjusts the spacing between two individual characters
Vertical Scale	Distorts the type by scaling it on a vertical axis
Baseline	Adjusts the baseline of type to create subscript or superscript
Leading	Adjusts the amount of space between lines of type
Tracking	Adjusts the amount of space between all the characters in a word or paragraph (based on what is selected).
Horizontal Scale	Distorts the type by scaling it on a horizontal axis
Color	Changes the color of a character, word, or line of type (based on what is selected).

[PS]

3. _____Using the Paragraph Palette

The Paragraph settings are new to Photoshop 6, and they are fantastic for controlling the formatting of text. You can use these settings to reshape, rotate, indent, align, and justify type in paragraphs. You'll get to try these settings first hand in this exercise.

1. Open **paragraph.psd** from the **chap_05** folder of the **H.O.T CD-ROM** that you copied to your hard drive.

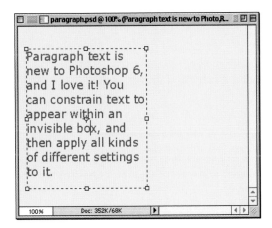

2. Using the **Type** tool from the Toolbox, click on the text. You'll notice that this activates a bounding box around the text.

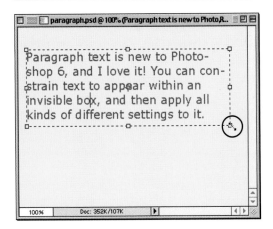

3. If you move your mouse over one of the corners of the bounding box, you'll see an arrow appear. If you click and drag with this arrow you can reshape the bounding box!

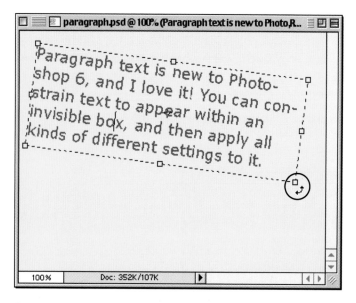

4. If you move your mouse outside one of the corners of the bounding box, you'll see the cursor change to a rotate symbol. Once you see the symbol change, click and drag to rotate the text.

5. Once you're happy with the rotation, click the **checkmark** icon in the **Options** bar. If you didn't like the rotation, you could click the **X** icon, and this would cancel the rotation.

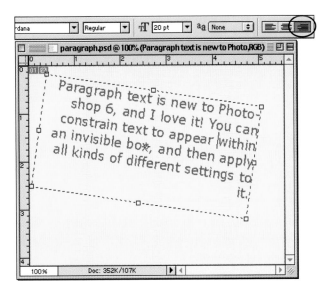

6. Using the **Type** tool from the Toolbox, select all the type by clicking inside the bounding box. Click on the **right align** icon on the **Options** bar to align the type to the right. You can use any of the alignment settings found on the Options bar with the paragraph text selected.

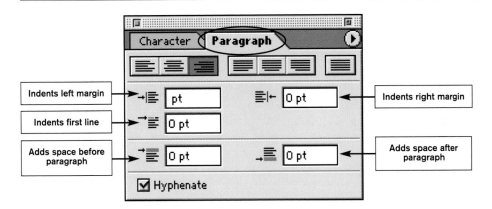

7. Click on the **Palette** button on the **Options** bar, and then click on the **Paragraph** tab to bring it forward and make it active.

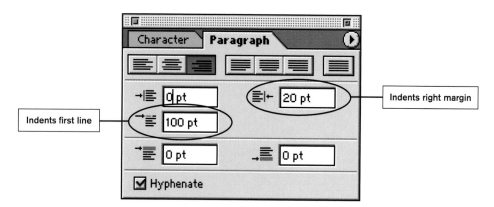

8. Enter **100 pt** into the indents **first line** field and **20 pt** into the **right margin** field in the Paragraph palette, and watch the paragraph type move around. Click on the **checkmark** icon in the **Options** bar to accept your settings.

You are probably wondering how to make this special kind of text in a bounding box. The next step will show you how.

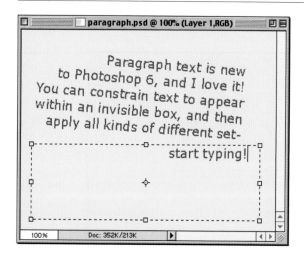

9. With the **Type** tool selected from the Toolbox, click and drag a new bounding box in which to type. Start typing, and your type will appear and become constrained by the shape of the box. Don't like the shape of the box? Move your mouse over one of the corners to drag it out to a new shape and the type will rewrap to fit the new shape. We're sure you'll agree that this new feature is pretty dang cool.

10. Save and close this file.

[PS]

4. ——————Warped Text

Another new feature in Photoshop is the ability to create warped text. This is an effect that we doubt you'll use often, but it's fun to learn, so you can take it for a test spin in this exercise.

1. Open the file **warpme.psd** from the **chap_05** folder that you copied from the **H.O.T CD-ROM** to your hard drive.

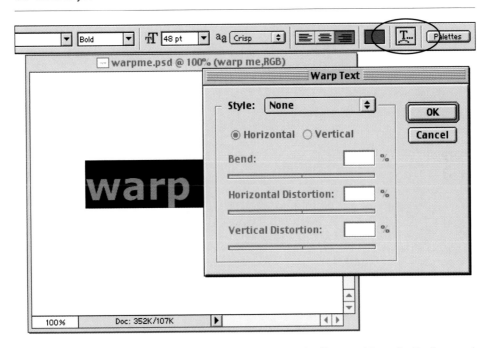

2. Select the type by clicking and dragging across it with the **Type** tool from the Toolbox, and click on the **Warp Text** tool on the **Options** bar.

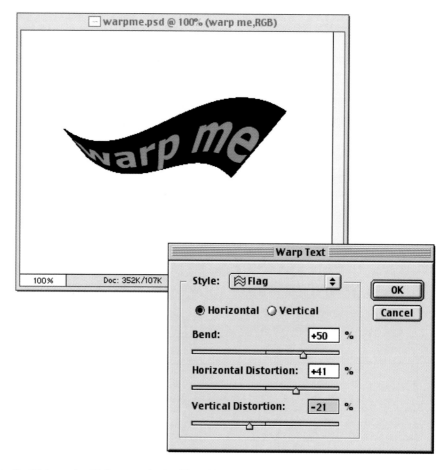

3. Click on the **Style** menu in the **Warp Text** dialog box, and choose **Flag**. Move the sliders and watch the type distort. When you like what you see, click **OK**. Woo Hoo! Go ahead and save the file.

Warped type can be edited and even undone after the file is saved. Try changing what the type says and notice how it keeps the warp effect. Try undoing the warp effect by choosing None from the Style menu. We suppose this is cool! OK, you might note some sarcasm here. We guess we think this is an interesting novelty effect, but one that could be easily abused. Have fun with this tool, but don't mistake its gimmick for a concept or high art.

4. If you'd like to experiment with **Warp** Text menu settings other than **Flag**, knock yourself out. When you're finished, save and close the file.

5. ————————Jump To ImageReady

ImageReady's text handling tools are very similar to Photoshop's, except that you cannot create paragraph text there. That doesn't mean that it isn't supported, however. Even though ImageReady can't create paragraph text, it can still display it and allow limited editing. You might wonder why anyone would care about seeing or editing paragraph text in ImageReady anyway? There are certain things, such as animation and rollovers that can only be accomplished in ImageReady. Sometimes you'll want to combine what you can only do in Photoshop (paragraph text) with what you can only do in ImageReady. You could quit Photoshop and launch ImageReady and open the file you just saved, or you could more easily use a neat shortcut, using the **Jump To** button in Photoshop which is preset to open ImageReady. This does require that you have enough RAM. If you don't, you can always quit Photoshop and open the file inside ImageReady instead.

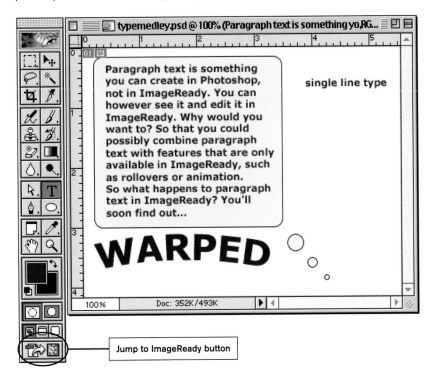

1. You should still be in Photoshop, but you're about to switch to ImageReady. Open **typemedley.psd** from the **chap_05** folder in Photoshop. This document contains single line type, paragraph type, and warped type. To see how this same document looks in ImageReady, press the **Jump To** button at the bottom of the **Photoshop Toolbox**. This will open the document inside ImageReady if you have enough RAM to open both programs. If not, simply open the file in ImageReady (after closing Photoshop).

Notice that the display of the type is different in ImageReady, in that it didn't have a blue underline in Photoshop or a bounding box. Remember that handy shortcut key for hiding selections, Command+H (Mac) or Control+H (Win)? If you try that now, the blue underline will go away. The only way to make the bounding box disappear is to deselect this layer by selecting a different layer in the Layers palette.

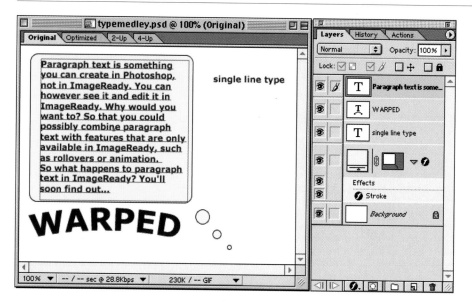

2. In ImageReady, select the **top** layer in the **Layers** palette. This is the layer on which the paragraph text resides. Notice the blue underline on all the text, and the bounding box around the text.

If you wanted to edit the paragraph text, you could. You could access the Paragraph palette by choosing Window > Show Paragraph, and you would find all the same settings that are in Photoshop.

3. Click on other type layers in the document and you will see blue lines under the text on those layers. This is the system that ImageReady uses to illustrate that a type layer is active.

4. Close the file. You won't be needing it for the next exercise.

The Jump To feature is very useful to go between these two applications, and has been improved in this version in that you don't have to worry about which program has updated the image. In your Web design workflow, we predict you will use the Jump To feature often, and without any trepidation.

[IR]

6. ——————————Rasterizing Type

It's wonderful that type is editable in ImageReady and Photoshop, because you can change your mind at any time. There are certain Filter effects, however, that cannot be applied to editable type. This exercise will show you how to rasterize type so a plug-in filter can be successfully used.

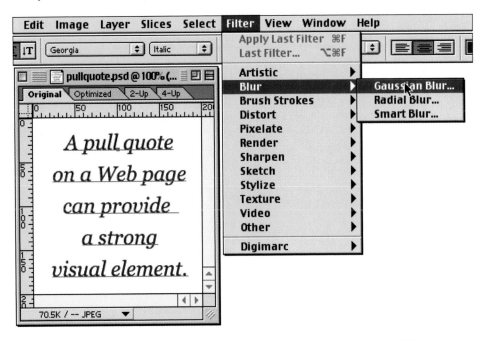

1. You should still be in ImageReady. Open **pullquote.psd** from the **chap_05** folder that you copied from the **H•O•T CD-ROM** to your hard drive. Choose **Filter > Blur > Gaussian Blur**.

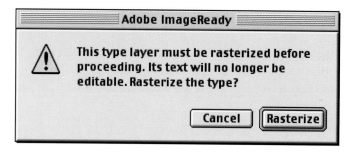

2. A dialog box will appear with a warning that the type must be rasterized before the Filter effect can be applied. Click **Rasterize** (Mac) or **Yes** (Windows) to render the layer as fixed pixels instead of editable type.

Choosing to render a type layer converts the type from editable text to non-editable text. It freezes the type into pixels, and it is no longer editable as type but is now fully editable as an image. This enables the features that are disabled when the type is editable.

3. In the **Gaussian Blur** dialog box, change the slider to adjust the amount of blur, and click **OK** when you're happy with the preview.

4. Choose **File > Save As...** and name it **pullquote2.psd**. Once the file is saved, close it because you won't be needing it again. Leave ImageReady open for the next exercise.

Note: This exercise would work identically in Photoshop 6. Saving the file as pullquote2.psd effectively saves a copy with your changes and leaves the original pullquote.psd untouched, so you can try this exercise in Photoshop if you want to.

[IR]

7. —————————Transforming Type

One of the most common things that you'll want to do with type is to change its size, rotate it, skew or distort it. You learned how to change type size using the Options bar, how to rotate using Paragraph text, and how to distort using the Warp text feature. There are some alternate ways to achieve some of these same functions using Transform features.

1. In ImageReady open the file **transform.psd** from the **chap_05** folder that you transferred to your hard drive from the **H.O.T CD-ROM**.

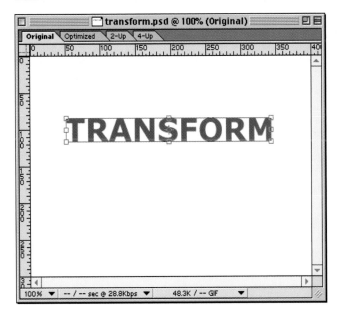

2. Select the type by clicking on the **Transform** type layer. Once it is selected, use the short-cut key **Command+T** (Mac) or **Control+T** (Win). This is the shortcut key for using the **Free Transform** feature, which allows you to scale or rotate. A bounding box should appear.

What is a Free Transform, you might well wonder? It means that you can scale or rotate the selection by any value (as in freedom of movement).

3. Click on one of the anchor points with your mouse and drag to transform your text in the direction that you want. The following chart describes your options when you manipulate objects using the Free Transform tool and your mouse.

Using Free Transform With Your Mouse	
Feature	**Function**
Stretch Vertically	Click top or bottom anchor point with your mouse, and drag
Stretch Horizontally	Click a side anchor point with your mouse and drag
Scale Uniformly	Hold Shift key down, click a corner point, and drag with your mouse
Rotate	Move your mouse outside one of the corners of your object. When the cursor turns into a rotate symbol, click and rotate the selection into place.

Don't be afraid to scale the type larger. Editable type in ImageReady and Photoshop is made of vectors, meaning that it is based on mathematical instruction rather than fixed pixels. Unless you've rasterized your type, if you scale it up in size its edges will still be crisp and beautiful. You can also transform rasterized artwork using the Free Transform feature, but your images will tend to get fuzzy if they are scaled larger.

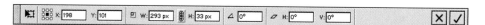

4. You can also transform objects using the **Options** bar. Enter values into any of the fields on the **Transform Options** bar, as shown in the illustration above. When you're satisfied with your transformations, press **Return** (Mac) or **Enter** (Win), or click the **checkmark** icon on the **Options** bar.

5. If you want to add distortion or perspective, you must first rasterize the type, as these effects are not available for editable type. Choose **Layer > Rasterize > Type**. Then choose **Edit > Transform > Distort** or **Edit > Transform Perspective**. Click and drag on the anchor points to achieve the Perspective or Distort transformations. Once you're satisfied with the result, click the **checkmark** on the **Options** bar, or press **Return** (Mac) or **Enter** (Win) on your keyboard.

---

6. Save and close the file. Congrats, you've completed another chapter and got another notch on your Photoshop belt :).

6.

Layer Styles

Shape Tools and Shape Layers	Set Up Button Artwork
Create Layer Styles	Save Custom Layer Styles
Apply Layer Styles	Work with Prebuilt Layer Styles

chap_06

Photoshop 6 / ImageReady 3
H·O·T CD-ROM

A **layer style** offers a combination of features that were available in previous releases (filter effects, layer effects, layer blending modes, layer opacity, and styles). Layer styles bring these features together in one feature to offer an efficient way to create almost unlimited variations of special effects.

Making button art is one of the most common tasks in Web graphics workflow. Many typical button designs include bevels, drop shadows and/or inset type effects. The layer styles feature in Photoshop 6 allows you to easily experiment with drop shadows, glows, bevels, and all kinds of other effects that are just a simple click away.

In older versions of Photoshop, blurs, glows, and other special effects were made with filters. Unfortunately, filter effects can't be edited once they are applied. You can always go back and change the color of a drop shadow or the height of a bevel that's applied as a layer style. Another great thing about layer styles is that they can be used over and over to make Web graphics that have a consistent look. A layer style created on one layer can be automatically reapplied with all its settings to other layers or files. This makes it easy to set up an efficient production process for your navigation buttons. You'll get to try layer styles in this chapter, and we're sure you'll find them easy to implement and fun to explore.

Bitmaps and Vectors

There are two new types of vector features in Photoshop 6 that have never before existed: the **shape drawing tools**, and **shape layers**. This chapter introduces you to these new tools, but before you get to them we felt an explanation was in order.

In the past, Photoshop has been exclusively known as a bitmap-editing program. Bitmap graphics are created pixel-by-pixel, as each pixel is assigned a specific color and location on the screen. Vectors, instead, are created as mathematical instructions. A bitmap circle is defined as a finite number of pixels that form that particular image. A vector circle is created as a mathematical instruction, for example "radius=100." You might have worked with vector programs in the past, such as Illustrator, CorelDraw, FreeHand, or Flash.

Photoshop documentation draws a distinction between "painting" and "drawing." In this context, painting means using bitmap/pixels and drawing means using objects/vectors. The Paintbrush tool in the Photoshop Toolbox will paint with pixels, while the Shape tool will draw with vector objects.

All this behind-the-scenes explanation helps you understand the difference, but in practical terms how and when are bitmaps superior to vectors, and how and when are vectors superior to bitmaps? Here's a chart that explains the pros and cons of each format:

Bitmap Versus Vector	
Bitmap	**Vector**
Continuous Tone: Bitmaps are best used to describe continuous tone content, such as photographs, glows, soft edges, blurs.	*Shapes:* Vectors are best used to describe graphic content, such as shapes, type, and images with sharp edges and solid fills.
Editing Bitmaps: Bitmaps are edited by changing the physical pixels.	*Editing Vectors:* Vectors are generally edited by manipulating points and handles around the object.

About the Shape Tools

The vector shape tools are new to Photoshop 6, and offer several advantages to drawing artwork from scratch or importing from other vector programs, such as Illustrator, FreeHand or CorelDraw. Shapes are object-oriented, meaning that you can select, resize, and move a shape. A shape's path can be edited after it's been drawn and attributes can be changed at any time (such as line weight, fill color, and fill style). Photoshop 6 supports libraries of custom shapes, making it easy to store logos and custom button artwork. Shapes are resolution-independent and maintain crisp edges when resized, printed to a PostScript printer, saved in a PDF file, or imported into a vector-based graphics application.

Here's a handy chart that describes the different types of shape tools:

Press on the
shape tool icon to
see its options.

Rectangle Tool	U	A
Rounded Rectangle Tool	U	B
Ellipse Tool	U	C
Polygon Tool	U	D
Line Tool	U	E
Custom Shape Tool	U	F

Shape Tool Functionality	
Tool Name	**Functionality**
A. Rectangle tool	Draws squares and rectangles.
B. Rounded Rectangle tool	Draws squares and rectangles with rounded corners. The radius of the rounded corner can be controlled via the Options bar.
C. Ellipse tool	Draws ellipses and circles.
D. Polygon tool	Draws multi-sided shapes. The number of sides can be set on the Options bar when this tool is active.
E. Line tool	Draws straight lines.
F. Custom Shape tool	Draws shapes that are stored in a library, accessed via the Options bar. You can create your own custom shapes and store them in the custom shape library.

Shape Layers

A shape layer is automatically created when you use any of the shape tools. This new type of layer combines a solid color layer (you learned about these in Chapter 4, "*Layers on Steroids*") with a clipping path. A clipping path is a type of vector object that operates as a mask, to hide or reveal contents of another layer. In a shape layer, the clipping path thumbnail is stored to the right of the solid color layer thumbnail. This combination of a solid color layer and a clipping path works in tandem to produce a shape layer. To change the color, you would double-click on the solid color side; to change the shape, you would click on the clipping path side. You'll learn to do both of these edits in the following steps.

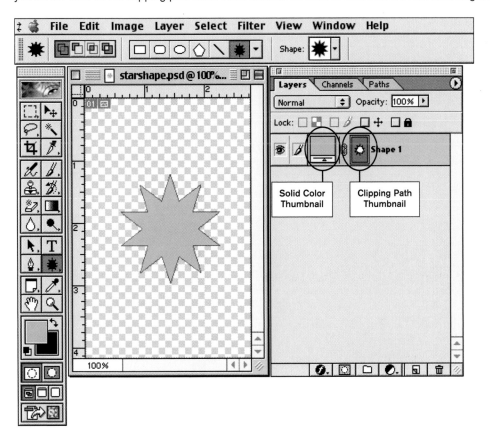

Double-clicking on the solid color thumbnail allows you to access the Color Picker to change the color of a shape layer. Clicking once on the clipping path thumbnail activates the visibility of the outline around the shape object. You'll learn how to edit the shape created by the clipping path in the following exercise.

[PS]

 I. —————————————Shape Tools and Shape Layers

You've read all about shapes and shape layers; now it's time to try them out on your own. In this exercise, you'll learn to edit the shape and color of a vector shape object. Woo-hoo!

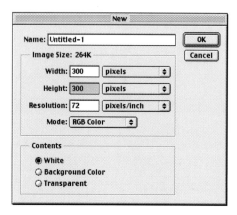

1. Choose **File > New** and enter the settings above. Click **OK**.

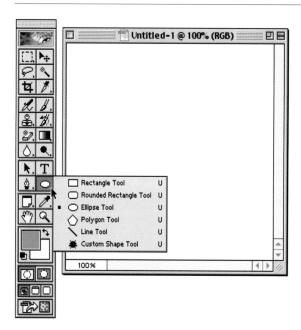

2. Select the **Ellipse** tool from the Toolbox. If it isn't visible, hold your mouse button down on the Toolbox as shown above to reveal the tool choices.

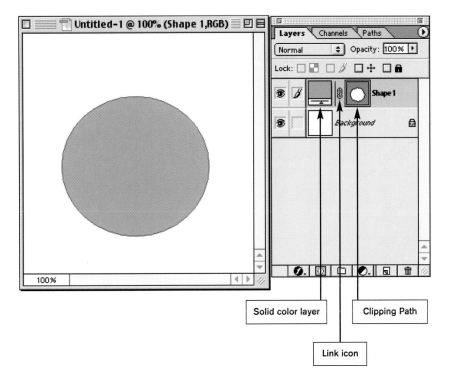

Solid color layer

Clipping Path

Link icon

3. Hold down the **Shift** key to constrain the ellipse shape to a circle, and drag out a circle on the screen. Notice that the **Shape 1** layer that's automatically created looks unusual in the **Layers** palette? (If the Layers palette isn't visible, choose Window > Show Layers.) The left thumbnail image on the Layers palette indicates that this is a solid color layer. The Link icon means that it's linked to the thumbnail to the right. The thumbnail on the right represents a clipping path for the solid color layer, and it is created with vectors (like a path created with the Pen tool).

4. Click on the **clipping path** thumbnail to deselect the vector edges of this shape. The vector outline can be toggled on and off by clicking on this thumbnail. Make sure the vector outline is visible for the next step. Look closely because the outline is pretty thin.

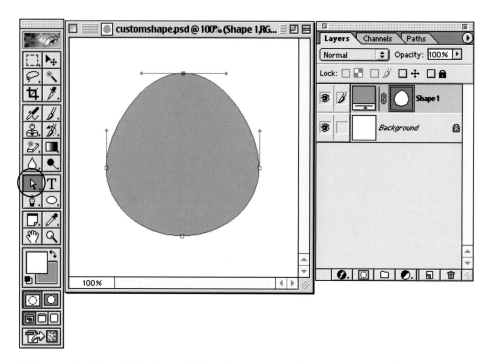

5. Locate the **Direct Selection** tool (the white arrow icon) from the Toolbox. (To find it, leave your mouse depressed over the path component selection tool.) Click on the vector outline of your circle. You will see handles appear. Move the handles to stretch the shape or change the curves, just like any vector shape from other programs.

6. Double-click on the solid color thumbnail to access the **Color Picker**. Choose a different color, and click **OK**. The color fill will change.

7. Experiment by dragging out some other custom shapes until you've fully explored this tool. When you're finished, save it as **customshape.psd** and close the file.

Artwork built with shape layers offers more flexibility than standard layers. Shape layers can be recolored and reshaped, and are perfect for buttons and Web graphics that involve primitive shapes. Shapes work identically in ImageReady, except the vectors can be edited only with the Transform commands.

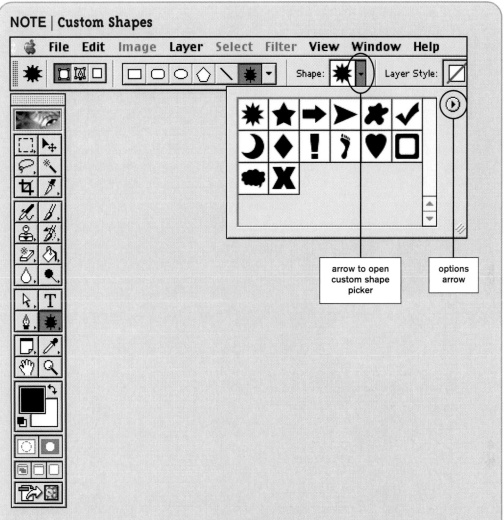

NOTE | Custom Shapes

arrow to open custom shape picker

options arrow

Photoshop includes a number of custom shapes to use with your Custom Shape tool. You can explore this library of shapes by clicking on the Custom Shape tool in the Toolbox or Options bar. Then click on the small arrow in the shape field on the Options bar to open the custom shape picker. Even better, you can make artwork for your own custom shapes to use over and over, and always have them available to you from within Photoshop. For now, however, you can work with the default custom shapes that ship with Photoshop. Hint: Look under the options arrow (circled above) for another custom shapes library (**Custom Shapes.csh**) that you can load.

[PS]

2. ——————————Creating Layer Styles

Next, you'll get to work with a file that contains button artwork that was created using a shape layer and an editable type layer. This artwork starts its life in black and white, and you'll get to work with layer styles to change its appearance. If you have never worked with layer styles before, you're bound to be quite enthralled. Layer styles have been around since Photoshop 5.0 (when they were called layer effects), but you might not know about them. They offer the ability to add common effects—such as drop shadows, glows, bevels, and colors—through an easy-to-access menu. Many of the types of effects available through layer styles used to require learning complicated steps and combining filters. These complicated steps and filters often resulted in changes that were set in stone, so that they were difficult, if not impossible, to edit at a later time. Layer styles, instead, are easy to use and easy to edit. You'll see soon enough, by trying out the following steps!

1. Open **button.psd** from the **chap_06** folder that you transferred to your hard drive from the **H•O•T CD-ROM**.

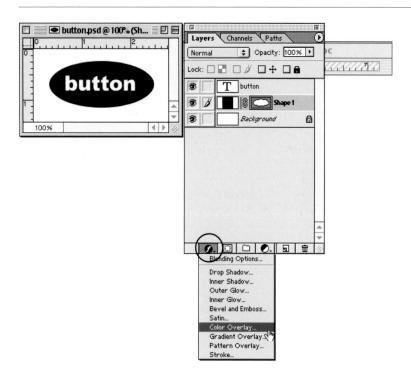

2. With the **Shape 1** layer selected, click the *f*-shaped layer style icon at the bottom of the **Layers** palette. Choose **Color Overlay…** from the drop-down menu.

This will cause the Layer Style dialog box to open.

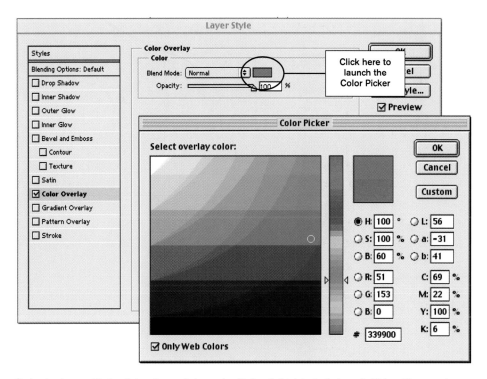

3. In the **Layer Style** dialog box, click on the **Color** field (circled above). This will open the **Color Picker**. Change the color from red (default) to a **dark green**. Click **OK** to close the **Color Picker**. Do not click OK in the Layer Style dialog box yet; you will need it open for the next step.

The Color Overlay layer style allows you to change the color of artwork on a layer. This is a very useful feature, because the color can be edited at any time, which is great for client changes or artistic changes you might impose on yourself.

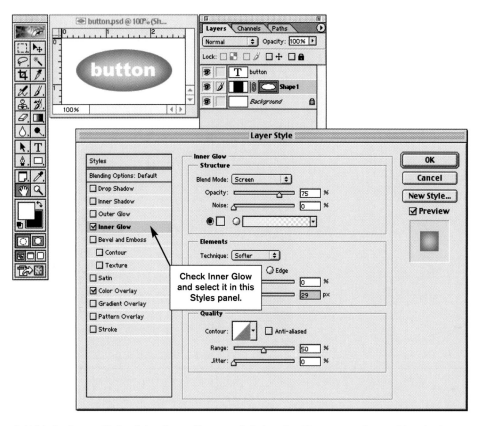

4. With the **Layer Style** dialog box still open, click the checkbox next to **Inner Glow** in the **Styles** panel. Select **Inner Glow** (by clicking on it) to activate the settings for this layer style. We changed the **Source** to **Center** and the size of the **Inner Glow**. Feel free to experiment with any of the settings. When you're finished exploring this dialog box, click **OK**.

You should see the changes appear on the button.psd document as you are making changes in the Layer Style dialog box. There are many strange new terms in the settings, such as choke, contour, and jitter. For a complete list of descriptions, turn to the chart at the end of this exercise.

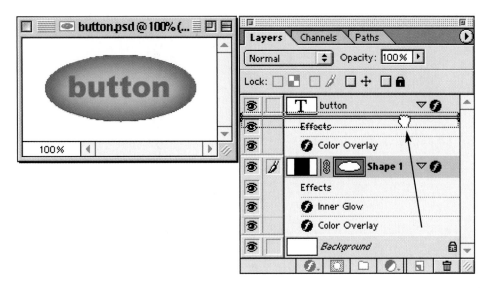

5. Drag the **Color Overlay** style from the **Shape 1** layer to the line below the **button** type layer, and release your mouse.

The text should turn green! You can copy any layer style to another layer by simply dragging it there. You can move multiple layer styles one at a time to another layer. This is a lot simpler than recreating the settings for each layer, eh?

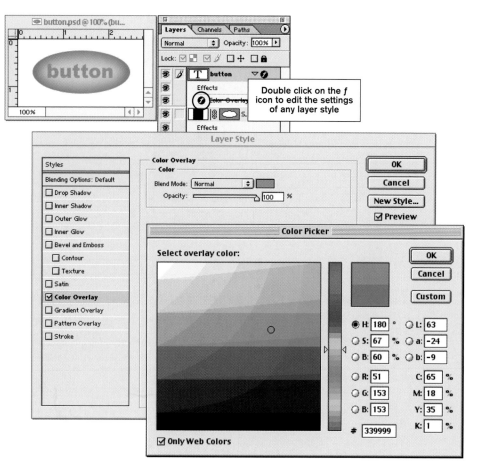

6. Double-click the *f* icon next to the **Color Overlay** layer style on the **button** type layer. The **Layer Style** dialog box will open. Click the green **Color** field to open the **Color Picker** and change the green to a **blue**. Once you've done so, click **OK** to close the **Color Picker** and **OK** again to close the **Layer Style** dialog box. The word **button** should now be blue.

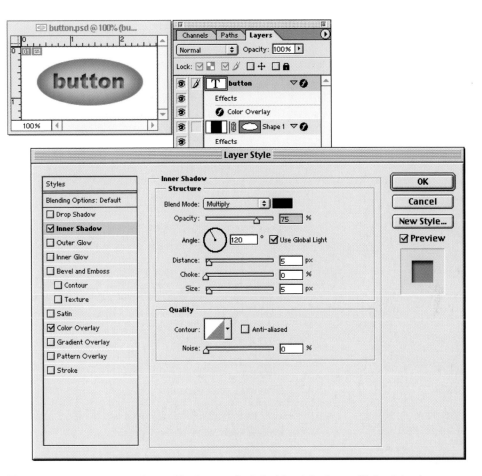

7. Put a checkmark next to **Inner Shadow** on the left side of the **Layer Style** dialog box to add an inner shadow layer style to the **button** text. Click on **Inner Shadow** in the **Layer Style** dialog box to display options for that layer style. Experiment with any of the settings, and click **OK** when you're ready. Leave this file open for the next exercise.

You can add new layer styles from the Layer Style dialog box, as you did here, or from the menu that drops down from the f icon on the Layers palette.

Layer Style Dialog Box

The Layer Style dialog box has enough settings to make anyone's head spin! As you try different layer styles (Drop Shadow, Inner Shadow, Outer Glow, Inner Glow, Bevel and Emboss, etc.), you'll see that this dialog box will change. Some of the terms are awfully alien, such as Spread, or Contour, or better yet . . . Gloss Contour! Here's a handy chart to refer to that describes what some of these weird terms actually mean.

Layer Style Terms	
Term	**Definition**
Blend Mode	Determines how the layer style blends with underlying layers. Uses all the standard Photoshop modes, such as Multiply, Screen, etc.
Opacity	Changes the opacity of the layer style only.
Color	Specifies the color of the layer style, such as the drop shadow or glow color.
Angle	Determines the lighting angle.
Spread/Choke	Determines the intensity of some effects, such as glows or strokes.
Noise	Adds dithering to soft edges.
Contour	Allows you to sculpt the ridges, valleys and bumps that are used in some effects, such as bevels and embosses.
Anti-Alias	Affects how the edges of an effect blend.
Depth	Affects the dimensional appearance of effects like bevel and emboss.
Gloss Contour	Adds a glossy, metal-like appearance to bevel or emboss.
Gradient	Allows you to select from a gradient editor.
Highlight or Shadow Mode	Determines the blending mode of a highlight or shadow, such as Multiply, Screen, etc.
Jitter	Varies the gradient color and opacity.
Layer Knocks Out Drop Shadow	Controls the drop shadow's visibility or invisibility on a semi-transparent layer.
Soften	Blurs the effect.

NOTE | Layer Styles are Non-Destructive

The beauty of layer styles is that they are non-destructive, meaning you can edit them at any time and the original document is never harmed. Try turning the eye icons of the layer styles on and off in the Layers palette. You'll see that with them turned off, the original black and white button art is still there! Be sure to turn them all back on for the next exercise, though. You'll need them turned on to learn how to make re-usable styles.

NOTE | Deleting a Layer Style

If you ever want to delete a layer style, simply drag it to the **Trash** icon on the Layers palette. If you want to throw away all the layer styles on a layer, drag the word **Effects** to the Trash, and all the sub-layers below it will go bye-bye at once.

[PS]

3. ─────────Saving a Custom Layer Style

Let's say that you were totally happy with the layer styles you applied to the file you just worked on. Wouldn't it be cool if you could save the layer style in a library so it could be applied to other layers or documents? Luckily, you can easily save a custom layer style for the future. This exercise shows you how.

1. You should be working in Photoshop, with **button.psd** still open from the previous exercise. Double-click on the **button** layer in the **Layers** palette to open the **Layer Style** dialog box.

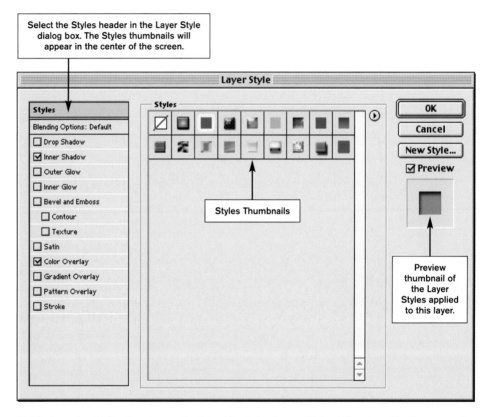

Select the Styles header in the Layer Style dialog box. The Styles thumbnails will appear in the center of the screen.

Styles Thumbnails

Preview thumbnail of the Layer Styles applied to this layer.

2. Click on the **Styles** header on the left side of the **Layer Style** dialog box. You'll see a collection of styles thumbnail icons appear in the center panel. Make sure the **Preview** box is checked, and you should see a thumbnail icon of the layer style you custom-created in the last exercise for the button type layer.

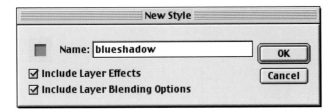

3. Click the **New Style...** button in the **Layer Style** dialog box. The **New Style** dialog box will open. Enter **blueshadow** in the **Name** field, and click **OK**.

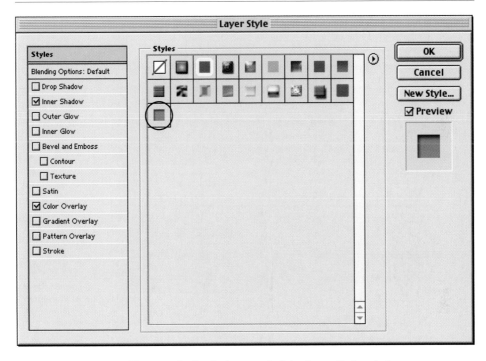

Your new layer style will appear in the Styles panel of the Layer Style window.

4. Click **OK** to close the **Layer Style** dialog box.

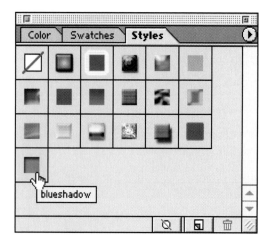

5. Choose **Window > Show Styles** to open the **Styles** palette. Drag the window by the lower right corner to stretch it larger. You should see a thumbnail of the style you just created! If you move your mouse over the thumbnail, the name **blueshadow** will appear.

Next, you'll learn an alternative way to make a style in Photoshop 6, right from the Styles palette.

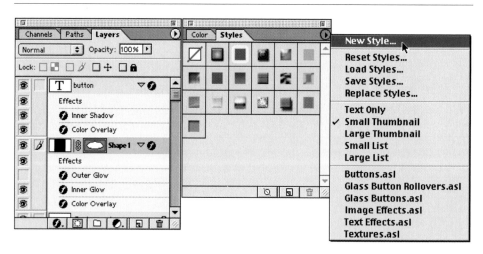

6. Select the **Shape 1** layer on the **Layers** palette. In the **Styles** palette, press the upper right arrow to choose **New Style...** from the pull-down menu. This will open the **New Style** dialog box. Name this style **button** and click **OK**.

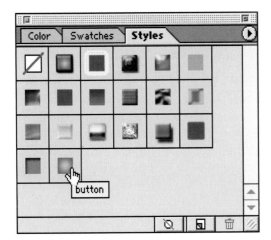

A thumbnail of the new style you just created will appear.

---

7. Save and close **button.psd**.

---

4. ————————————Applying Styles from the Styles Palette

Now that you've designed a button and created some custom layer styles, it's a snap to apply those layer styles to other artwork and quickly create a collection of buttons with a consistent appearance.

1. In Photoshop, open **buttons.psd** from the **Chap_06** files you transferred from the CD-ROM to your hard drive. (Note the plural: Be careful not to confuse **buttons.psd** with **button.psd** from the previous exercises!)

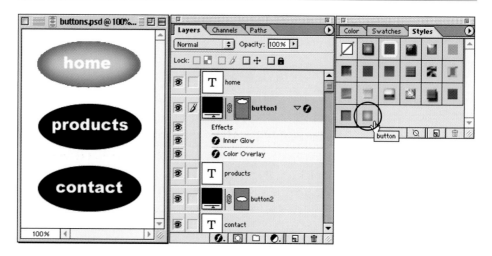

2. Select the **button1** layer, and press the **green** button thumbnail from the **Styles** palette. Voila, the button should magically change, and three layer styles should appear below as sub-layers to the **button1** layer.

3. Select the **button2** layer from the Layers palette and press the **green** button thumbnail from the Styles palette. Do the same for the **button3** layer.

You should now see three green buttons on your screen, and layer styles should be visible as sub-layers inside the Layers palette. Pretty simple and fast to make these buttons look identical, is it not?

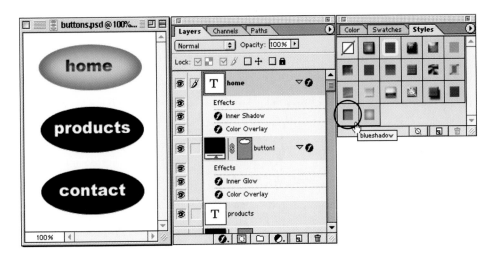

4. Select the **home** layer, and press the **blueshadow** thumbnail from the **Styles** palette. Repeat this process for the other type layers, **products** and **contact**.

See how fast and easy it is to create similar buttons using layer styles? Imagine how much you would love this feature if you had a zillion buttons on one screen that had to look consistent? OK, maybe not a zillion, but even if you had a few buttons that needed to quickly look the same, this feature would be your new best friend.

5. Save and close the file. Congrats, you've finished this chapter! Layer styles and styles are great workflow enhancers for developing Web graphics.

7.

Background Images

Size Relationships	Previewing Backgrounds	Saving Backgrounds
Magic Eraser	Seamless Backgrounds	Tile Maker Filter
Full-Screen Backgrounds	Directional Backgrounds

chap_07

Photoshop 6 / ImageReady 3
H·O·T CD-ROM

Designing for HTML is challenging because standard HTML is capable of displaying only two layers—a background layer and a foreground layer. By contrast, it's possible to work with unlimited layers in just about every digital design program we can think of, including Photoshop, InDesign, PageMaker, QuarkXPress, Illustrator, FreeHand, etc. Because HTML restricts you to only two layers, knowing how to create a variety of appearances for the background layer is particularly important. So in this chapter we've put a lot of effort into presenting numerous techniques for creating images that work well as Web page backgrounds.

You can work around the two-layer limitation by using style sheets instead of standard HTML. But this is a book about making Web artwork, not about writing code or using a Web page editor. For that reason, this chapter focuses on the challenges of and solutions for making effective background images that work with standard HTML. There are two core issues to think about when you're making a background image: the speed with which it will download, which involves optimization, and its appearance, which involves imaging techniques.

What Is a Background Image?

A background image appears in the background layer of a Web page. By default, it will repeat to fill the size of a browser window. The number of times that a background image will repeat (or tile, as it's also called) is dictated by the size of the original image and the size of the particular browser window in which it is being viewed at the moment. This means that a background image can appear differently on different monitors. The challenge is to design one piece of art that can look different on different monitors and still look good everywhere. Not easy! This chapter will offer some concrete examples and solutions to this common challenge.

Regardless of how many times a background image tiles in a browser window, it downloads to the viewer's computer only once. Each time the image appears on a Web page it is called out from the cache in the viewer's computer, rather than downloaded again. This means that as a designer, you can get a lot of mileage from a background tile. If you create a tile that is relatively small in file size, you can fill an entire browser window for a very small penalty in download time.

The other important property of a background image is that you can put other images on top of it. In fact, in standard HTML, a background image is the only kind of image on which you can place another item that's in a graphic format. So if you want an illustration, a photograph, or text you've made as a graphic to float on top of an image, you'll have to identify the underlying image as an HTML background, as you'll learn to do in this chapter.

A background image begins life no differently than any other GIF or JPEG. The thing that makes it a background is the HTML code inside the **BODY** tag. The HTML for a tiled background is simple. Here's the minimum code required to transform an image (**small.jpg** in this example) into a tiled background in an HTML document.

```
<HTML>
<BODY BACKGROUND="small.jpg">
</BODY>
</HTML>
```

NOTE | Vocabulary: Background Tile and Tiling

In this chapter, you'll run into the terms **tiling** and **background tile**, both of which we've used in a technical sense that we want to make sure you understand. **Tiling** refers to the horizontal and vertical repetition of an HTML background image in a Web browser. **Background tile** is used interchangeably with the term **background image** to mean a GIF or JPEG that repeats in an HTML background.

TIP | Design Tips for Readability

When you are creating artwork for background tiles, it's especially important to pay attention to contrast and value. Try to use either all dark values or all light values. If you combine darks and lights in a single background image, your background might look great on its own, but neither light nor dark type will work consistently against it, and your image won't read well.

light background

dark background

If you are wondering how to pick colors for backgrounds in relation to foreground type, here are some basic guidelines.

- *If you're using a light background, use dark type.*

- *If you're using a dark background, use light type.*

- *Avoid using a medium value for a background image, because neither light nor dark type will read well on top of it.*

- *Avoid using contrasting values in a background image, because they will interfere with type of any value.*

Background Image Sizes

Artwork that is used for a background image can be any dimension, large or small. The size of a background tile will determine the number of times its pattern will repeat inside a Web browser.

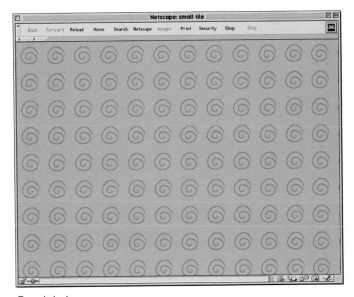

Small *Result in browser*

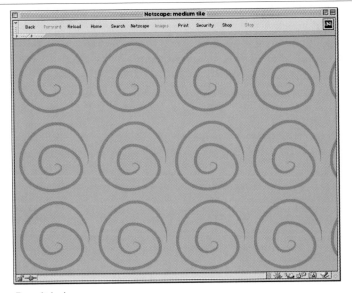

Medium *Result in browser*

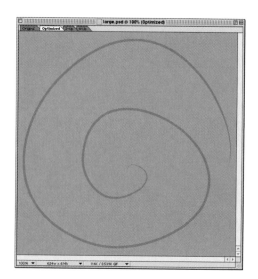

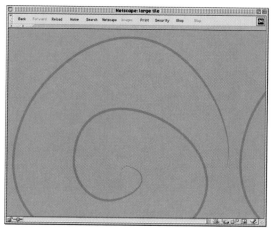

Large   *Result in browser*

As you can see in these examples, a background tile with larger dimensions is going to repeat less often than a smaller tile. A tile that measures 40 x 40 pixels will repeat 192 times (16 times across and 12 times down) in a 640 x 480 browser window. A tile that measures 320 x 240 pixels will repeat four times (2 times across and 2 times down) in a 640 x 480 browser window. You can create an image so large that it's only going to repeat once in a standard-size browser window. Basically, the size of the image you choose to make depends on the effect you want to create.

Enlarging the dimensions of a background tile will enlarge its file size as well. If you create a background tile that is 50K, it is going to add that much file size to your Web page and adversely affect download speed. (One formula we use, though it is not scientifically accurate or measurable, is that each kilobyte of file size represents one second of download time for the average viewer.) Therefore, it is just as important to practice good optimization skills with background images, as it is with other types of images.

A background image doesn't necessarily have to be big to look big. Later in this chapter, you'll learn how to make some very big-looking background tiles that are actually very small in dimensions and file size.

[IR]

I. ────────Defining, Editing, and Previewing a Background Image

Once you've created or opened an image in ImageReady, the program's **output settings** make it easy to define your image as a background image. You can then use the preview feature to see how the image will look in a browser as a tiled Web page background. In this exercise, you'll learn to define, edit, and preview artwork as a background image in ImageReady. You can also perform these functions in Photoshop from the Save For Web interface, but we prefer to make background images in ImageReady, because the Output and Preview settings are more accessible from ImageReady's main program interface.

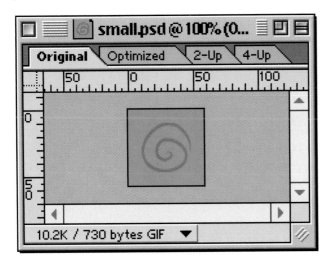

1. In ImageReady, open **small.psd** from the **chap_07** folder that you transferred to your hard drive from the **H•O•T CD-ROM**.

The first step in previewing an image as a background tile is to identify it as an HTML background, as you'll do in the next two steps. This lets ImageReady know that when you preview this image, you want to see it as a tiled background image, rather than as a single foreground image.

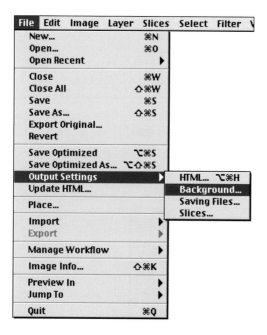

2. Choose **File > Output Settings > Background....** This will open the **Output Settings** dialog box to its **Background** settings.

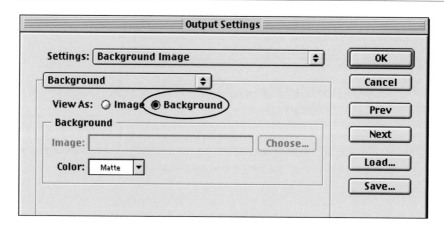

3. In the **Output Settings** dialog box, select **View As: Background**. Click **OK**.

If the View As field is not visible, choose Background from the pop-up menu below the Settings menu to access the Background options.

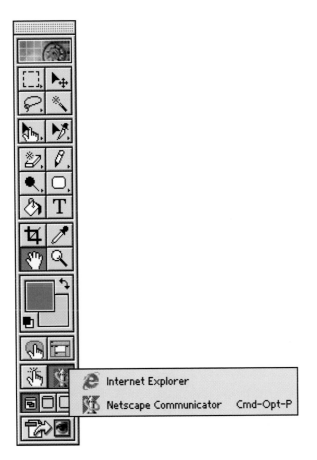

4. Click the **Preview in Default Browser** button in the Toolbox, and select the browser of your choice from the pop-up menu.

All browsers that were on your computer when you installed ImageReady should appear in the Preview in Default Browser pop-up menu. If you want to select another browser, choose File > Preview In> Other, and navigate to the file in the browser's application folder that launches that browser.

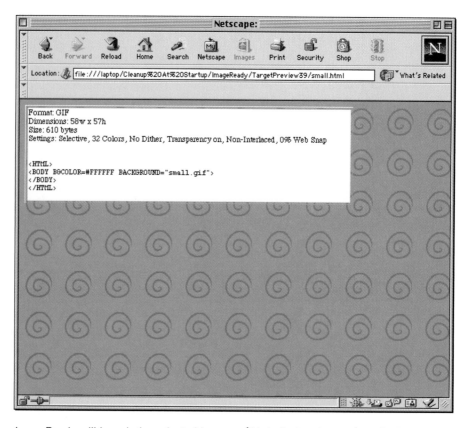

ImageReady will launch the selected browser (if it isn't already open), and will display a preview of this document as a repeating background image. Notice that the preview includes a white text box that contains details about how the image was optimized, as well as the HTML used to define this image as a background. In the next exercise, you'll learn how to have ImageReady write this file as a final HTML document that will not include the text box that appears in this preview.

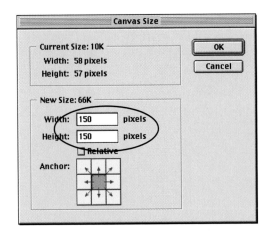

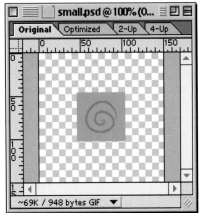

5. The size and content of this image affect its appearance in a browser. Return to ImageReady. Choose **Image > Canvas Size…**. Set the canvas size to **150** pixels by **150** pixels, make sure the center square in the **Anchor** diagram is selected, and click **OK**. This will change the size of the canvas around the image to be larger than the image itself.

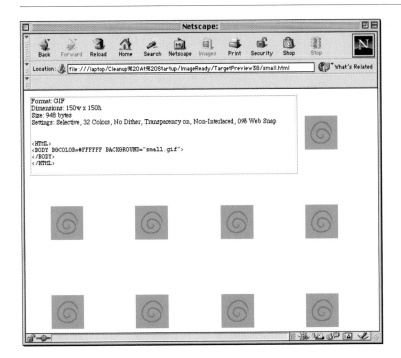

6. Click the **Preview in Default Browser** button, and choose a browser again to see how this change in dimensions will affect the appearance of the tiled background.

Notice that in the browser, the areas of the exposed canvas that were transparent appear as a white background around the spirals. That's because ImageReady will substitute a white color for any transparent pixels unless you specify otherwise. In order to change the color of the areas around the spirals, you'll need to fill in the transparent pixels with another color.

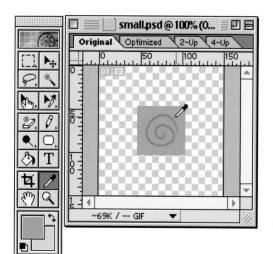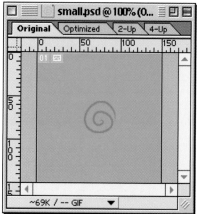

7. To fill the transparent pixels with the same green that is already in the image, select the **Eyedropper** tool from the ImageReady Toolbox, and click on the **green** in the document to sample that color. Select the **Background** layer from the **Layers** palette (if it's not visible, choose Window > Show Layers). Press **Option+Delete** (Mac) or **Alt+Backspace** (Windows) to fill the entire background layer with green.

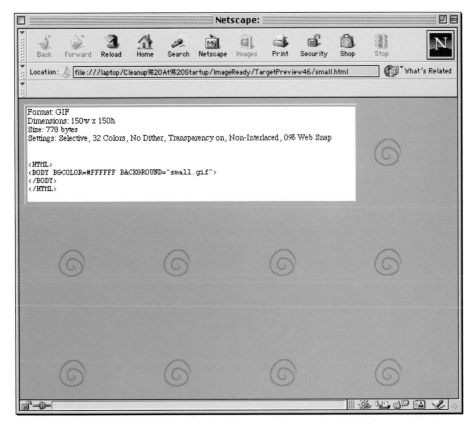

8. Click the **Preview in Default Browser** button, and select a browser of your choice to see how the change will affect the repeating background image. The spirals should now be on a green field.

9. Return to ImageReady, choose **File > Save**, and leave the file open for the next exercise.

It's great that ImageReady previews the image as a background so easily. This allows you to try different dimensions, color treatments, or other image qualities before you commit to the design of your background tile.

[IR]

2. ——————————Saving a Background Image

In this exercise, you'll learn to save a background image as a final document, instead of just previewing it from ImageReady as you did in the last exercise. When you're working on your own Web projects, this is what you'll do when you've finished experimenting with the look of your background tile. The image will still be in Photoshop format, so you'll need to optimize it in order for it to function properly on the Web. The resulting GIF file will be no different than any other GIF image. The only thing that will make it a background image is the code inside the HTML file that tells the browser to display that GIF as a background image. Fortunately, ImageReady saves images and the necessary HTML code to make this happen! Alternatively, you could save just the optimized image without HTML, bring the resulting GIF into the HTML editor of your choice, and code it as a background tile in the HTML editor.

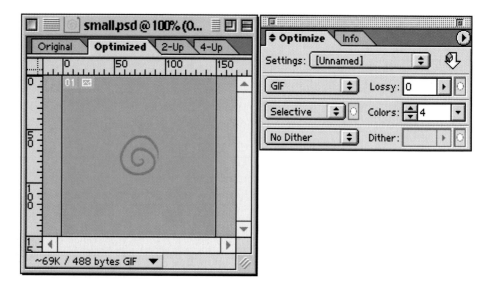

1. With **small.psd** still open from the last exercise, click on the **Optimized** tab in the document window. If the **Optimize** palette isn't open, choose **Window > Show Optimize**. Match your **Optimize** settings to the ones shown above.

Because the image is composed of flat colors, it is going to look and compress best as a GIF.

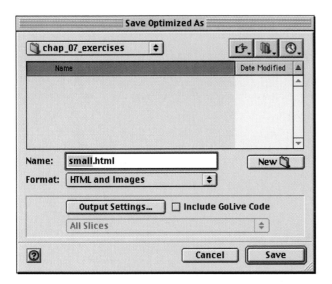

2. Choose **File > Save Optimized As....** In the dialog box, choose **HTML and Images** from the **Format** menu (Mac) or **Save as type** menu (Windows). Click the **new folder** icon, and create a new folder called **chap_07_exercises**. Click **Save**.

When ImageReady saves the file, it will generate a GIF (small.gif), as well as an HTML document (small.html) containing the BODY BACKGROUND tag that identifies this GIF as a background image. ImageReady will know to include this tag in the HTML code it writes, because you designated this image as a background image in Step 3 of the previous exercise.

When you save the file, the Name field defaults to the name of your original image file with the extension .html. You can rename the HTML file, along with the accompanying GIF if you like, or keep their default names. Navigate to the "chap_07_exercises" folder to see the image and HTML file that were just generated. Next, you'll get to check out the final results by opening the newly-created HTML document in a browser.

NOTE | Save HTML or Not?

We never use the HTML file that ImageReady generates for background images, because we prefer to use an HTML editor like GoLive or Dreamweaver to assemble Web pages. That's usually because we like to put foreground images on top of background images and position them wherever we want, which the HTML allows with much more control than ImageReady. The only reason we save the image and the HTML is so that we can view the background image without the white preview text readout.

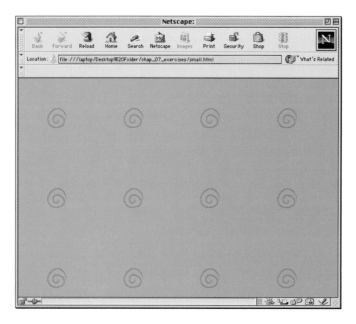

3. Double-click on the HTML file ImageReady just created (**small.html)** in the **chap_07_exer-cises** folder to open that file in your computer's default browser. If you prefer to view the file in a different browser, launch that browser, choose **File > Open**, and navigate to **small.html** on your hard drive.

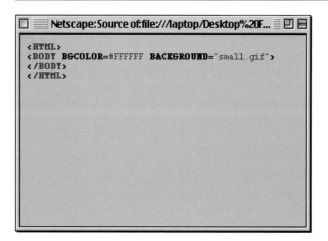

4. If you choose **View > Page Source** (Netscape Navigator) or **View > Source** (Internet Explorer), you will see the HTML code that ImageReady generated. Return to ImageReady, and save and close the source file, **small.psd**.

[IR]

3. ——————Recoloring Background Image Artwork

In this exercise, you will learn one way to recolor a black and white image in ImageReady. You'll also learn how to use the custom Swatches palette, color.aco, to select colors with similar values. Once you have learned this basic procedure, you can experiment with various combinations of colors to see the impact of choosing colors with similar or contrasting values. You will need to have the custom Swatch palette color.aco loaded to do this exercise, so if you haven't already done so, follow the instructions in Chapter 2, *"Web Color,"* Exercise 7.

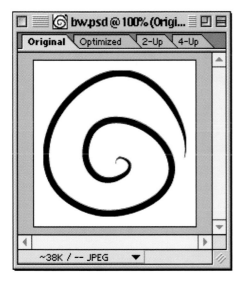

1. Open **bw.psd** from the **chap_07** folder you copied to your hard drive from the CD-ROM.

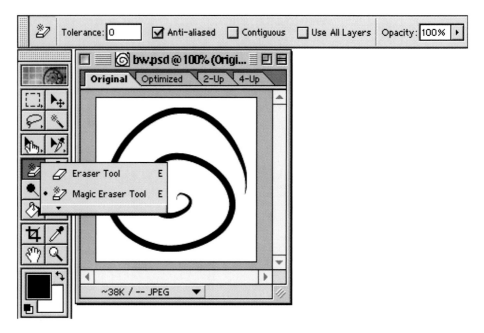

2. Select the **Magic Eraser** tool. If it's not visible in the Toolbox, press your mouse on the Eraser tool until a pop-up menu of choices appears, and select the Magic Eraser (which has a little cluster of dots on its upper left). In the **Options** bar, match the settings you see above, **Tolerance: 0**, and **Anti-aliased**.

Photoshop also has a Magic Eraser tool, which works the same way as ImageReady's Magic Eraser tool.

TIP | What Does Tolerance Mean?

The **Magic Eraser**, like a number of tools in Photoshop and ImageReady, contains a setting for **tolerance**. This setting determines how the Magic Eraser tool selects and acts
upon pixels that are defined by whatever spot you sample. That range of color values is
narrower if you set the tolerance to a low number, and wider if you set the tolerance to a
high number. For example, when you click somewhere in an image, the tool notes the
color value at that point, and erases all pixels in the image whose color values are within
a specified range of that color value. The image you are working with in this exercise
contains just a few colors (white, black, and some grays). We set the tolerance of the
Magic Eraser to **0**, because we wanted the tool to erase only a narrow range of pixels
(those that were pure white). If instead, we were trying to erase a more complex image
with more colors to subtract, we would have set the tolerance to a higher value.

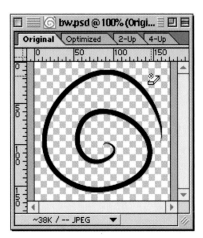

3. Click anywhere on the **white background**, and the all the white pixels in the background will be deleted, leaving transparent pixels.

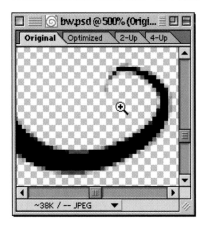

4. Select the **Zoom** tool from the Toolbox, and click on the image several times to magnify the image so you can examine it close up. (The letter **Z** is the shortcut key for accessing the Zoom tool at the bottom right of the ImageReady Toolbox.) You'll see that the edge of the black spiral shape is anti-aliased (filled with partially transparent pixels that gradually fade to transparency). That's going to help you keep a smooth edge when you recolor the image. To zoom back out to a view of 100%, hold down the **Option** (Mac) or **Alt** (Windows) key and click on the image several times with the **Zoom** tool. **Tip:** If you need a refresher on anti-aliasing, revisit Chapter 5, *"Type."*

A useful shortcut for zooming back out to 100% magnification is to double-click the Zoom tool in the Toolbox.

5. With the white background out of the picture, it's easy to add some color to just the spiral. Select **Layer 1** in the **Layers** palette, and check the **Lock transparent pixels** box.

Checking Lock transparent pixels will protect all the transparent pixels in the image, so that when you fill the layer with a new color in a subsequent step, ImageReady will fill only the layer's image area—the spiral—and will preserve the transparent areas.

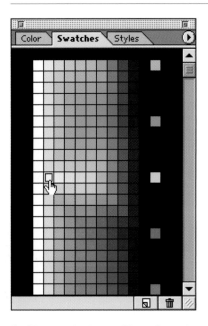

6. Choose **Window > Show Swatches** to bring up the **Swatches** palette. You should still have the **color.aco** custom swatches loaded from Chapter 2, *"Web Color."* If not, turn back to Chapter 2 for instructions. This swatch is arranged by color value, with the lighter values on the left and the darker values on the right. Click on a color with a light value (from a vertical row on the left side of the swatch) to select it.

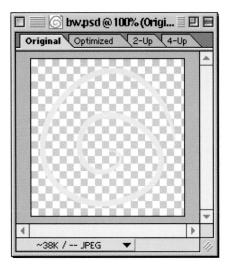

7. Next press **Option+Delete** (Mac) or **Alt+Delete** (Windows) to fill the spiral with the color you selected.

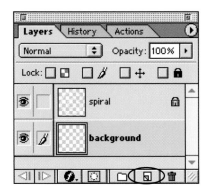

8. Click on the **new layer** icon at the bottom of the **Layers** palette to add a new layer. Double-click on the new layer to rename it. In the **Layer Options** dialog box, name this layer **background** and click **OK**. Then double-click on **Layer 1**, rename it **spiral**, and click **OK**. Drag the **background** layer below the **spiral** layer in the **Layers** palette. As soon as you see a heavy, dark line below the **spiral** layer, release your mouse, and the **background** layer should end up below it.

In previous chapters you learned that the procedure for renaming a layer in Photoshop 6 has changed. But it is still done the old, familiar way in ImageReady 3—by double-clicking the layer to open the Layer Options window.

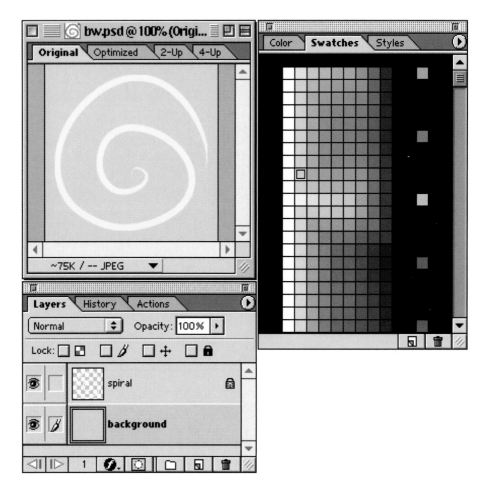

9. Select the **background** layer. Make sure that the **Lock transparent pixels** box in the **Layers** palette is not checked. Select another color from the same vertical row in the **Swatches** palette, and press **Option+Delete** (Mac) or **Alt+Delete** (Windows) to fill the **background** layer with the second color. Your image's background will be filled with the color you selected.

The reason we suggested you choose another color from the same vertical row in the Swatches palette was because it will have a similar value (lightness or darkness) to the color of the spiral. This swatch set is organized by lights and darks, so that colors selected from the same vertical row will have similar values.

Note: You didn't need to check Lock transparent pixels *in Step 9 because your goal was to fill all the transparent pixels of the background layer with a color. This lock feature is only useful when you want to change the color of just active pixels in a layer, as you did in a previous step. In fact, if you check Lock transparent pixels for a layer that has no active pixels, such as this one, the feature will actually prevent you from filling the layer with color. For more information on Lock transparent pixels, revisit Chapter 2, "Web Color," where it was first introduced.*

10. Save and **close** this document, and leave ImageReady open.

Now that you've learned this coloring procedure, you can experiment with different color combinations. It's easy to make color changes when you work in layers, isn't it? As you can see, the colors we selected in this exercise are extremely close in value, and that makes the pattern effect very subtle. By value, we mean that the colors are of similar lightness. Value is the measurement of light or dark color. If you want, you can preview this image in your Web browser to get a better idea of how this particular color combination performs inside a background tile. If you don't remember how to preview an image as a background image, revisit Exercise 1 in this chapter.

NOTE | Eraser Tools in ImageReady

Standard Eraser

Magic Eraser

There are two eraser tools in ImageReady—the standard **Eraser** and the **Magic Eraser**. The standard Eraser subtracts color based on whatever areas of an image you click and drag over. The Magic Eraser is a better choice when you want to subtract areas of your image based on color, as in this last exercise. It would have been pretty tricky to erase all the white away from the black with the standard Eraser; hence the need for some "magic."

[IR]

4. ——————————Seamless Background Tiles

The background images you've created so far have produced patterns that very obviously repeat when previewed in a browser. In the following exercises, you'll learn how to use ImageReady's **Offset** filter to create the illusion of a seamless (non-repeating) background.

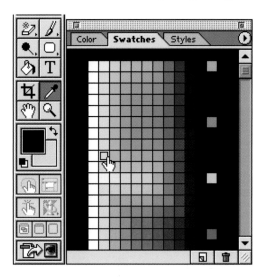

1. In ImageReady, **Option+click** (Mac) or **Alt+click** (Windows) on a color in the **Swatches** palette to select a background color for a tile.

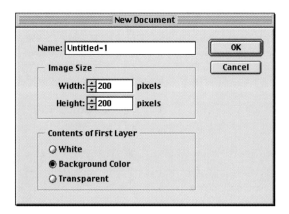

2. Create a new document that is **200 x 200** pixels. This is just a recommended size; you can make the canvas larger or smaller if you like. Select **Background Color** as the contents of first layer. Leave the file untitled for now. Click **OK**.

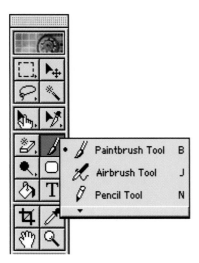

3. Select the **Paintbrush** tool from the Toolbox. If it is not visible, click the **Pencil** or **Airbrush** tool (whichever is showing in the Toolbox), and choose the **Paintbrush** tool from the pop-up menu.

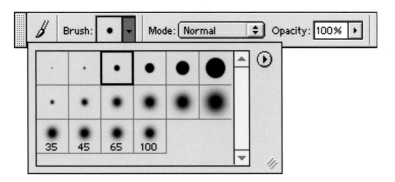

4. Select a hard-edged or soft-edged brush from the pop-up **Brushes** palette, which is accessible from the **Options** bar in ImageReady 3 and Photoshop 6.

The change in location of the Brushes palette is another new feature experienced users may find frustrating at first. We think you'll like this feature once you get used to it, because it guarantees consistent access to the frequently used Brushes palette, so that you don't have to think about whether it's visible or has been moved.

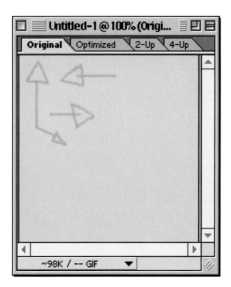

5. Select a foreground color with a value similar to the background color from the **Swatches** palette, and draw an image on the **Background** layer of your canvas. Make sure that you do not draw to the very edge of the canvas, and that your image does not touch the edge of the document window. We intentionally draw the artwork in one corner, so that we can easily see where we last drew shapes as we apply the Offset filter.

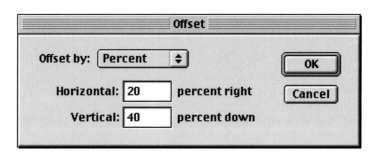

6. Choose **Filter > Other > Offset...**. In the **Offset** dialog box, enter **Horizontal: 20** and **Vertical: 40**. Click **OK**.

We usually pick irregular values other than the defaults (which are 50 x 50 percent) in order to create a non-symmetrical background. Because a seamless tile should look organic and not predictable, it is better to use irregular numeric values so the offset is less predictable.

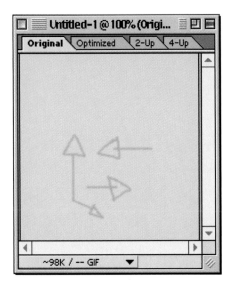

The Offset filter shifts your original image to the right and down, and wraps it so that part of your image will drop off one edge of the screen and appear at the opposite edge.

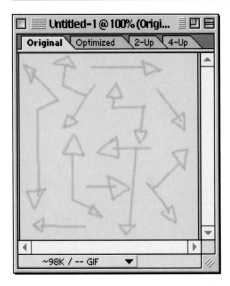

7. Continue to draw inside the blank areas of the image.

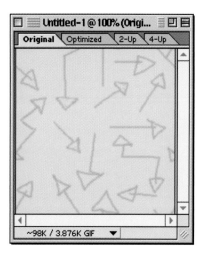

8. Press **Command+F** (Mac) or **Control+F** (Windows) to apply the **Offset** filter again.

Note: This keyboard shortcut will reapply whichever filter you last applied. This will again shift the pixels and wrap them around the image, opening some blank area on the canvas. Continue to draw, filling in the blank areas without touching the edge of your canvas.

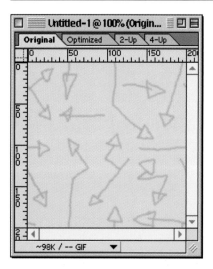

Notice that there is no large unfilled area in this image.

9. Press **Command+F** (Mac) or **Control+F** (Windows) to apply the **Offset** filter again. You may need to repeat the Offset filter process several times until no large areas of background color are visible.

10. To see what this image looks like in the browser, you must first identify it as an HTML Background. As you did in Exercise 1, choose **File > Output Settings > Background...**, then select **View As: Background** and click **OK**.

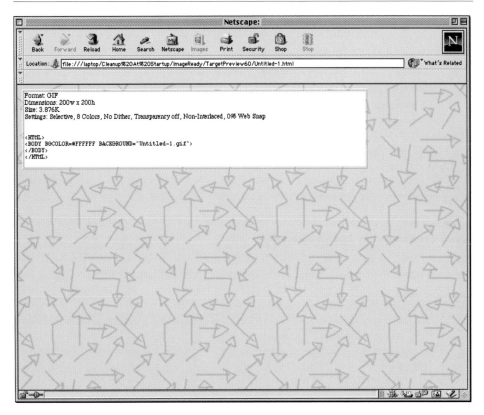

11. Next, click the **Preview in Default Browser** button on the ImageReady Toolbox to preview your tiling image in a browser. Notice that it's hard to tell where the smaller background image begins or ends? That is the power of this technique!

12. Return to ImageReady and choose **File > Save As** to save the original file. Name the file **tilebg.psd** and save it inside your **chap_07_exercises** folder.

It's always a good idea to save both a Photoshop document (.psd) and an optimized graphic, so that you can go back to the original Photoshop document to re-edit the image if you have to.

13. With the **Optimized** tab selected in the document window, check the **Optimize** palette to make sure the controls are set to **GIF** and the number of colors is low. These are the best settings for this image because it is made up of flat colors and is not continuous tone like a photograph. If you need a refresher on how to make the smallest possible GIF, revisit Chapter 3, *"Optimization."*

14. Choose **File > Save Optimized As...** to save the optimized file as a GIF. Choose **Images Only** if you plan to use an HTML editing program, instead of ImageReady, to write the code to make your image tile in an HTML background. The application will offer to name it **tilebg.gif** for you. Click **Save**, and close the file.

MOVIE | offset.mov

To learn more about how to use the **Offset** filter to create a seamless background image, check out **offset.mov** from the **movies** folder on the **H•O•T CD-ROM**.

Save Options in ImageReady

There are many different Save options in ImageReady. Here's a handy chart that explains them.

Save Options	
Function	**Result**
Save Optimized	Saves the file with its current optimization settings and file name.
Save Optimized As...	Saves the file with its current optimization settings and enables you to change the file name. It can also overwrite an old file if you save it with the same name.
Update HTML...	Allows you to overwrite HTML that ImageReady generated. You will get to try this out in Chapter 15, *"Importing/Exporting."*
Save	Saves the file as a .psd.
Save As...	Saves the file as a .psd and enables you to change the name. It can also overwrite an old file if you save it with the same name.
Export Original	Offers other file format options, such as Amiga IFF, BMP, PCX, PICT, Pixar, QuickTime Movie, Targa, and TIFF. **Note:** Photoshop has no Export Original option. To save a file in another format from Photoshop, choose File > Save As.

5. ——————————Copying and Pasting with Offset

There's another way to create a seamless background tile in ImageReady. In this exercise, you'll apply the Offset filter after you've copied and pasted existing artwork into a new document. This exercise, like the preceding exercise, could be done in Photoshop, but is easier in ImageReady where the Output and Preview settings are accessible from the regular Toolbox.

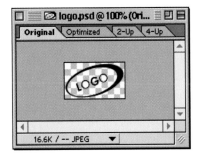

1. Open **logo.psd** from the **chap_07** folder you copied to your hard drive from the **H•O•T CD-ROM**.

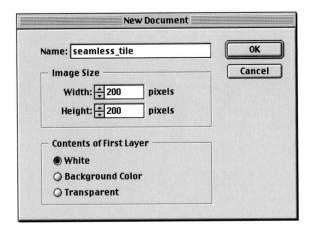

2. Choose **File > New** and create a new document that is **200 x 200** pixels against a white background. Type **seamless_tile** into the **Name** field and click **OK**.

When you try this on your own without our canned artwork, you can make the canvas larger or smaller if you like. The key is to make this document larger than the artwork you're using as the repeating pattern (which in the case of our exercise file, logo.psd, is 78 x 45 pixels). The relationship between the size of the tile you're creating and the size of the source artwork will determine the spacing of the logo on the background tile.

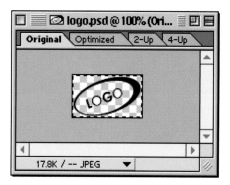

3. Click **logo.psd** to make that file active. Then press **Command+A** (Mac) or **Control+A** (Windows) to select the entire image area.

4. Press **Command+C** (Mac) or **Control+C** (Windows) to copy the logo. Click on your new, empty document **seamless_tile.psd** to make it active, and then press **Command+V** (Mac) or **Control+V** (Windows) to paste the logo into the new document.

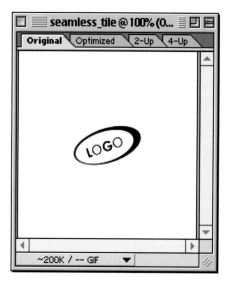

The logo appears in the center of the document. Whenever you paste an element into a document, ImageReady automatically centers it. With the logo in place, you're ready to apply the Offset filter.

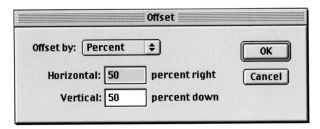

5. Choose **Filter > Other > Offset....** In the **Offset** dialog box that appears, match the settings to what you see above, and click **OK**.

In this instance, you will be making a symmetrical repeating tile, so leaving the default settings at 50 percent by 50 percent is desirable.

 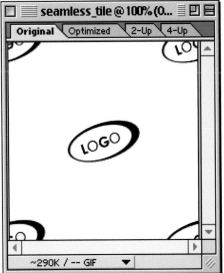

6. The logo looks like it's split into four quarters, which are now positioned at the four corners of the tile. Press **Command+V** (Mac) or **Control+V** (Windows) again to paste another copy of the logo into the center.

7. Choose **File > Output Settings > Background** to identify this image as an HTML background, then select **View As: Background** and click **OK**.

Now you're ready to preview your seamless background tile in a browser to see the results of your labor.

8. Click the **Preview in Default Browser** button in the Toolbox, and select a browser.

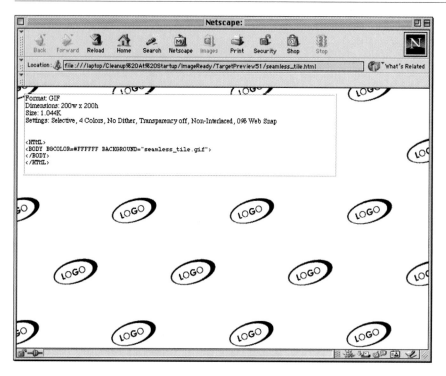

Here are the results of the preview. The first logo you pasted, which was offset by 50 percent and split to the four corners of the tile using the Offset filter, is flawlessly reassembled in the browser window when the image is tiled as a background.

This background effect is very symmetrical and formal. Each repeat of the logo is an equal distance from all the others. That's because you started with a square image, pasted both logos to the document's center, and set both the Horizontal and Vertical offset values to 50 percent. You can also use the Offset filter to create less symmetrical effects by adjusting the offset percentages.

Now that you've previewed this document, you can go back and experiment with adjusting the Offset filter settings or try doing the exercise over with a tile of smaller or larger dimensions. You could also recolor the logo or the background, using the techniques you learned in Exercise 3.

9. When you're finished playing, save the file. See if you can remember how to save it as both a .gif and a .psd.

Tip: *Use File > Save Optimized As... and File > Save. When you've saved the file, close it because it won't be needed again in this chapter.*

Ways to Access the Offset Filter in ImageReady

You might have noticed that there are three different ways to access the Offset filter in ImageReady. Here's a chart to explain the differences.

Offset Filter in ImageReady	
Option	**Result**
Filter > Other > Offset...	This is the way to access the Offset filter the first time you apply it to an image, or when you are reapplying it and you want to enter new settings.
Filter > Apply Offset...	This is another way to reapply the Offset filter with an opportunity to change its settings.
Filter > Offset	This is the way to access the Offset filter when you want to reapply it with the same settings as before.

NOTE | The Offset Filter in Photoshop

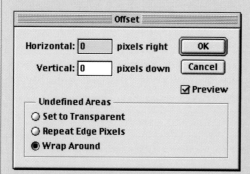

If you want to use the **Offset** filter in Photoshop, it can be accessed by choosing **Filter > Other > Offset**. Photoshop uses a slightly different interface than ImageReady for the Offset filter. It doesn't have a percent option and it offers nonwraparound options (such as **Set to Background** and **Repeat Edge Pixels**). You can make seamless tiles in Photoshop using the **Wrap Around** setting. The major drawback to creating background images in Photoshop is that they cannot be identified as HTML backgrounds nor previewed in the browser from the main program interface. To do either of those operations, you have to be in the Save For Web interface, which involves extra steps.

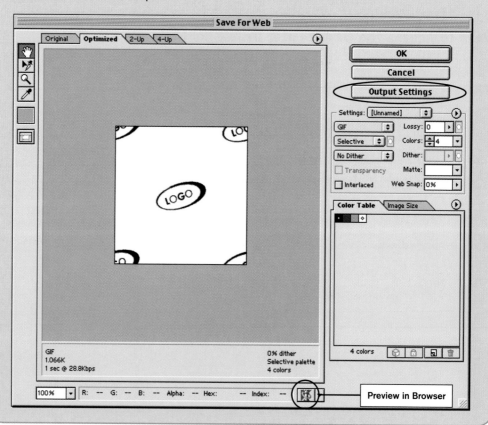

[IR]

6. _____Seamless Photographic Background Images

Seamless background images are not limited to graphics. With ImageReady's **Tile Maker** filter, photographs can be the source of perfect seamless background images too. This filter overlaps and blends the edges of an image, which creates a convincing seamless pattern effect. Consider this approach if you are looking for ways to incorporate photographic backgrounds into your Web design while keeping file sizes down. This technique works best with abstract images because they are least likely to reveal easily discernible repeating patterns. This exercise only works in ImageReady; Photoshop does not have a Tile Maker filter.

1. In ImageReady, open **grass.psd** from the **chap_07** folder you copied to your hard drive.

2. Choose **File > Output Settings > Background....** In the **Output Settings** dialog box, set **View As** to **Background,** then click **OK.**

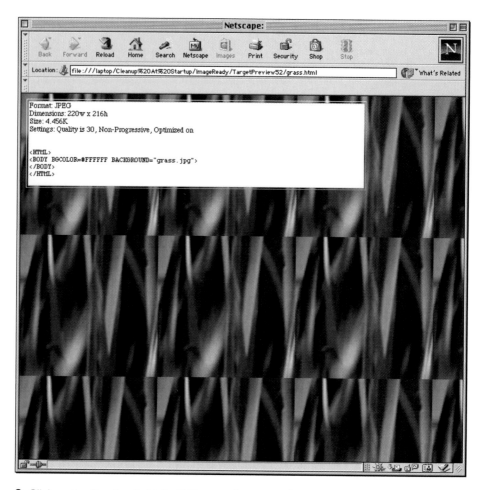

3. Click on the **Preview in Default Browser** button, and select a browser .

Notice the obvious edges from the seams of the source image? The Tile Maker filter will fix those in a snap.

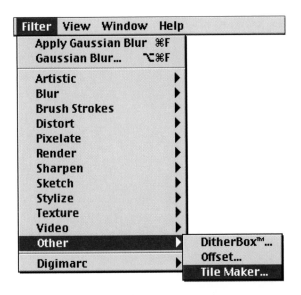

4. Return to ImageReady and choose **Filter > Other > Tile Maker....**

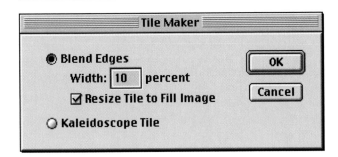

5. The **Tile Maker** dialog box will appear. Match the default settings you see above: **Blend Edges** selected, **Width: 10** percent, and **Resize Tile to Fill Image** checked. Click **OK**.

Tip: *Kaleidoscope Tile can also give you some beautiful abstract effects, so you might want to experiment with it later.*

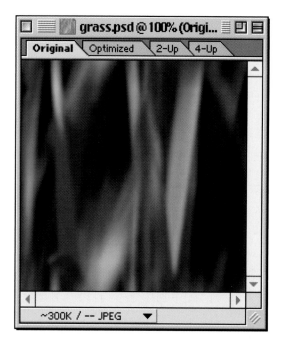

Here's what the image will look like after you apply the filter. You can see it's a little magnified, but the true difference is easier to see when you preview it.

6. Click the **Preview in Default Browser** button again.

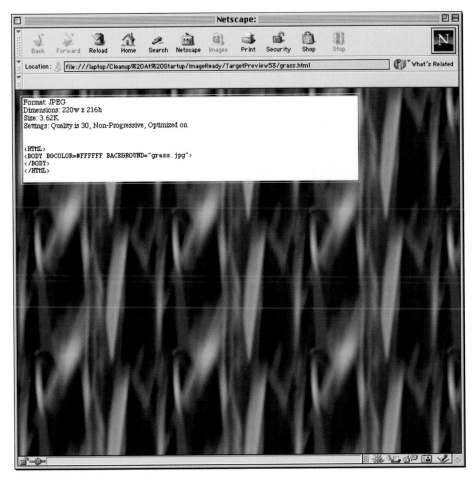

```
Format: JPEG
Dimensions: 220w x 216h
Size: 3.62K
Settings: Quality is 30, Non-Progressive, Optimized on

<HTML>
<BODY BGCOLOR=#FFFFFF BACKGROUND="grass.jpg">
</BODY>
</HTML>
```

In a browser, the background has become a little softer and the edge blending has hidden the sharp edges where the grass blades run off the image.

Tip: If you want to preview just the background without the HTML information box displayed, generate an HTML document by choosing File > Save Optimized As..., and in the Save Optimized As dialog box choose Save HTML and Images from the drop-down Format menu (Mac) or Save as type menu (Windows). If you need a refresher on saving and previewing, revisit Exercise 2.

Although this image is attractive and has no seams, it contains too much contrast to read with text over it. The next step will show you one of our favorite methods for modifying an image's brightness and hue.

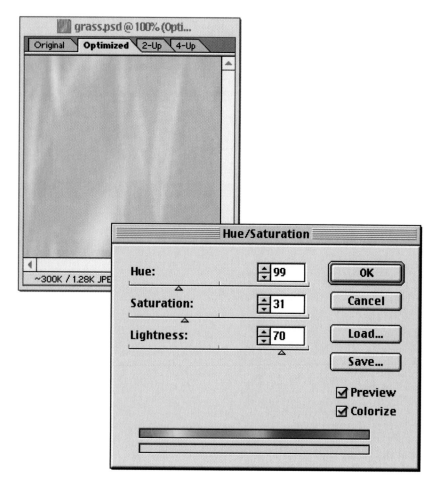

7. In ImageReady, choose **Image > Adjust > Hue/Saturation....** Try the settings that you see here or pick some you like better. If **Colorize** is checked, the image will appear mono-chromatic, rather than full color. You can uncheck it if you want to retain the natural colors of the image. Click **OK**.

```
Format: JPEG
Dimensions: 220w x 216h
Size: 1.28K
Settings: Quality is 30, Non-Progressive, Optimized on

<HTML>
<BODY BGCOLOR=#FFFFFF BACKGROUND="grass.jpg">
</BODY>
</HTML>
```

8. Optimize as a JPEG, and click the **Preview in Default Browser** button to preview the results. This background image would be much easier to work with than the unadjusted version if you were trying to layer it with readable text.

9. Close the file. If you want to save it, revisit the previous exercises that have described how to save original and optimized background images. Keep ImageReady open for the next exercise.

7. _____Full-Screen Graphic Background Images

Using a full-screen graphic as a background image can produce an impressive effect. If optimized properly, a full-screen graphic doesn't have to be too large to download efficiently, particularly if you limit your colors and use large areas of flat color. We recommend that you make all your full-screen background images at least **1024 x 768**, even if you are designing your site to work at a smaller resolution. This will avoid the problem of a background image that's intended to fill an entire screen repeating itself in a browser window that's bigger than the dimensions of the graphic. It's important that the background looks good when viewed at all sizes, from **640 x 480**, to **800 x 600**, all the way up to **1024 x 768** (and for some target audiences even beyond that).

Feature film directors face this problem when they shoot a wide-screen film that will also come out on video. Most directors try to frame their shots to look good in both the wide-screen theatrical screen size and your home TV. You can use the same idea to design a flexible full-screen graphic background that looks good in a variety of browser windows.

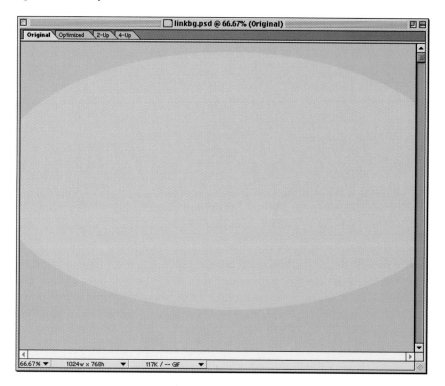

1. This exercise can be done in ImageReady or Photoshop, but because most of our background exercises are done in ImageReady, we'll stick with that program here. So in ImageReady, open **linkbg.psd** from the **chap_07** folder you copied to your hard drive.

This is the background image from the Links page of our lynda.com Web site. It's a big file—1024 x 768 pixels—but when optimized as a GIF with four colors its file size is less than 4K. Images with large areas of solid colors like this optimize unbelievably well. Download speed won't be an issue with an image like this. The issue will be how this graphic will look on different viewers' browsers when cropped by their different resolutions.

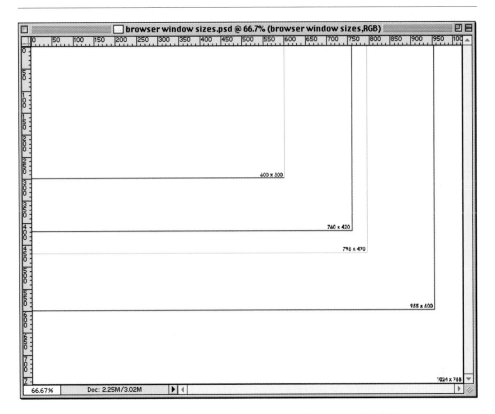

2. Open **browserwindowsizes.psd** from the **chap_07** folder on your hard drive.

This .psd file can be used as an overlay for full-screen background images. Its measurements are an approximation of how much your viewers will be able to see at different resolutions. It will help you to understand how the image will appear to different viewers, depending on the resolution to which a viewer's computer system is set. For example, a viewer whose system is set to 640 x 480 pixels will see only that portion of the background image (and any foreground elements you place on top of it) that fits within the box at the upper left of browserwindowsizes.psd that is marked 640 x 480.

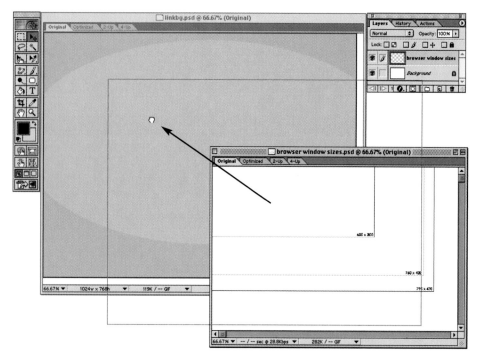

3. Select the **Move** tool from the Toolbox, make sure the layer labeled **browser window sizes** is selected, and click and drag that layer from the **browserwindowsizes.psd** file into the open **linkbg.psd**.

4. Align the upper-left corner of the layers, using the **Move** tool and the arrow keys on your keyboard. These are rather large images, so you might want to zoom in to fine-tune the alignment.

Tip: To get the two aligned just so, you might want to go back and forth between the letters Z and V (the Zoom tool and the Move tool). Remember that to zoom back out, you'll need to hold down the Option (Mac) or Alt (Windows) key and click on the image again. We move this overlay document into our full-screen background images all the time at lynda.com to visualize how background images will look at different sizes.

 MOVIE | dragginglayer.mov

To learn more about how to drag a layer from one document into another, check out **dragginglayer.mov** from the movies folder on the H•O•T CD-ROM.

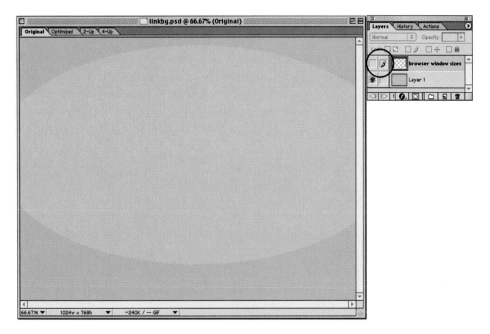

5. When you're ready to create a GIF of the background image, be sure to turn the **browser window sizes** layer off by toggling off the **Eye** icon on that layer in the **Layers** palette. You don't want this layer to become part of the final optimized image, because it is just a design guide.

If you need a refresher on how to optimize this image as a GIF, revisit Chapter 3.

6. Close both files.

The point of this exercise was to show you how to use an overlay to visualize how a large image would look in smaller browsers. You don't actually want to publish the graphic with the overlay; it's there for your reference only. Feel free to steal this overlay and use it to design all your large background images. We find it useful, and we hope you do too.

[IR]

8. _____Large-Screen Photographic Background Images

Full-screen backgrounds are not limited to flat color graphics, like the one used in the last exercise. If you optimize a large photograph carefully, you can use it as a full-screen background. The key is to compress the photograph so that it's small enough to download at a reasonable speed on most browsers. This exercise will allow you to explore some of the optimization options for large-screen photographic images.

1. In ImageReady, open **purpleorange.psd** from the **chap_07** folder on your hard drive. Click on the **Optimize** palette, and choose the **JPEG** format. With the settings above, we were able to reduce the image size to around 33K.

Tip: If you recall, there are a few other ways to make a photograph smaller. One thing that would make a photograph smaller in file size would be to reduce its contrast and saturation using ImageReady image adjustments. This would offer the added benefit of making it easier to read text placed on top of the photographic background. Be sure to click back on the Original tab before making these adjustments. If you're in the Optimized tab, the program will slow down because it will try to optimize the image with each change you make.

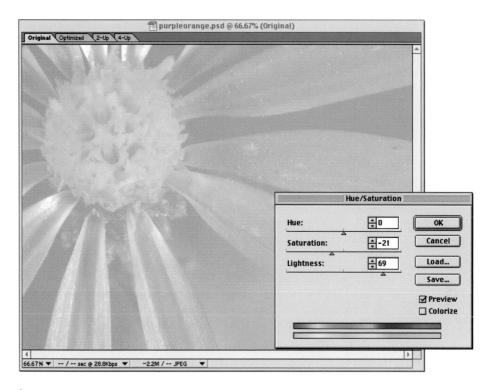

2. Choose **Image > Adjust > Hue/Saturation....** Match the settings shown above or experiment with your own. Click **OK** when you're happy with the results.

3. Click on the **Optimized** tab again, where you can check the **File Size Information** field to see if the file size got smaller. The changes we made brought the image down to 13K.

4. When you are ready to preview the image, choose **File > Output Settings > Background...**, click **View As: Background**, and click **OK**. Then click the **Preview in Default Browser** button. Once you're happy with the results, you can choose to **Save Optimized As...**, which will save a JPEG version of this document, or **Save**, which will save a .psd file. Either way, close the file.

[IR]

9.————————Directional Tiles

A wonderful trick that's widely used on the Web is to make what are called directional tiles—graphics that are narrow and tall or wide and short before you preview them, but that expand into full-screen images when repeated as background images. You can create the illusion of a big full-screen graphic background with a tiny tile. A tall, skinny directional tile like the one below will repeat from left to right across the browser window and create a background of broad horizontal stripes.

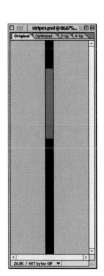
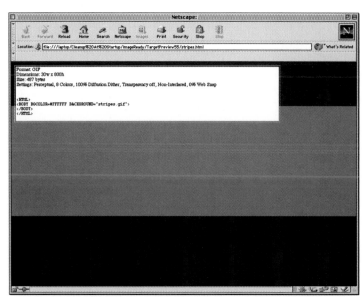

1. Open **stripes.psd** from the **chap_07** folder on your hard drive, and identify it as an HTML background (choose File > Output Settings > Background..., choose View As: Background, and click OK). Click the **Preview in Default Browser** button, and select a browser. Notice the effect of the long and narrow tile—it repeats in a horizontal fashion.

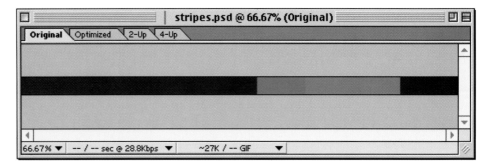

2. Return to ImageReady and rotate the artwork by choosing **Image > Rotate Canvas > 90°CW**.

The CW stands for clockwise, so this will rotate the image to the right. CCW stands for counter-clockwise.

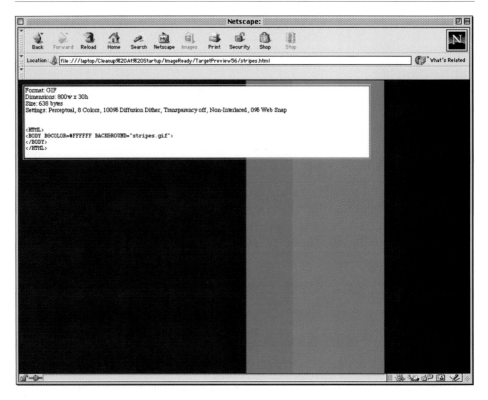

3. Click the **Preview in Default Browser** icon one more time, and select a browser from the list.

This ought to give you an idea of how these directional tiles work. Try changing the image inside this graphic, and watch the results. Fill it with a different color scheme or select and fill a new area for a new stripe. The sky's the limit, now that you know how images repeat inside browsers and you have ImageReady's great preview options at your disposal!

4. Save and close the file. You've finished another chapter, folks!

Transparent GIFs

Problems with GIF Transparency	Transparency Terminology
Creating and Previewing Transparency	Fixing Bad Edges
Pitfalls of Backgrounds	Saving Transparent GIFs
Transparent Layers

chap_08

Photoshop 6 / ImageReady 3
H•O•T CD-ROM

By default, all images made on the computer are in the shape of a rectangle or square. This is the reason you see so many rectangular graphics on the Web, causing many sites to have a similar look. We refer to this in our classes as "rectangle-itis." You can eliminate rectangle-itis in your designs by using the GIF transparency techniques covered in this chapter.

At the moment, GIF is the only format in wide use for the Web that supports transparency. Unfortunately, GIF transparency settings are very limited and can produce an unwanted halo around a graphic. As you'll see, both Photoshop and ImageReady have excellent tools for countering the problems that are inherent to transparency in the GIF format. This chapter's exercises are designed to help you master these tools.

Problems with GIF Transparency

Any time you create artwork in Photoshop or ImageReady that contains soft edges (like a drop shadow, a glow, a feathered edge, or an anti-aliased edge), you are using what is called 8-bit or 256-level transparency. This kind of transparency is built into Photoshop, and it means that the program can create many different levels of partially transparent pixels at the edges of your graphic. Edges are given a smooth and natural appearance with 8-bit transparency, making artwork in shapes other than rectangles look so natural that you would never even give it much thought.

Photoshop anti-aliased edge.

Photoshop glow.

Photoshop and ImageReady use up to 256 levels of opacity when layering artwork. This makes anti-aliased edges, glows, and other soft edges look natural.

Sadly, the GIF file format supports only 1-bit masking, rather than the more sophisticated 8-bit masking of the original artwork. And 1-bit masking does not support partially transparent pixels. Instead, each pixel in an image with 1-bit masking is either fully transparent or fully opaque (either on or off). This limitation of 1-bit masking is the cause of the unattractive halo (sometimes called a fringe or matte) of colored pixels that you may have seen around some images on the Web. You'll learn how to control this problem in the following exercises.

GIF anti-aliased edge.   *GIF glow edge.*

The GIF file format is limited to 1-bit masking. Notice the halos around the edges of these transparent GIFs when they are displayed against a colored HTML background. You'll learn why this happens and how to fix it in this chapter. Yay!

What Is Anti-Aliasing?

The term **anti-alias** describes an edge of a graphic that blends into a surrounding color. The advantage of anti-aliasing is that it hides the otherwise jagged nature of color transitions in computer-based artwork. Most computer graphics programs offer the ability to anti-alias. In Photoshop and ImageReady there's an anti-aliasing option available for most of the graphics-creation tools, including the selection tools, the Type tool, and the brushes and erasers.

An anti-aliased edge.

A blurry graphic uses anti-aliasing too.

An aliased edge.

How to Recognize a Transparent Layer

In order to create transparent GIF files in Photoshop or ImageReady, you must first create your artwork on, or convert it to, a transparent layer. How can you tell if your document is using a transparent layer? The checkerboard pattern in Photoshop or ImageReady is the visual cue to let you know that transparent pixels are present.

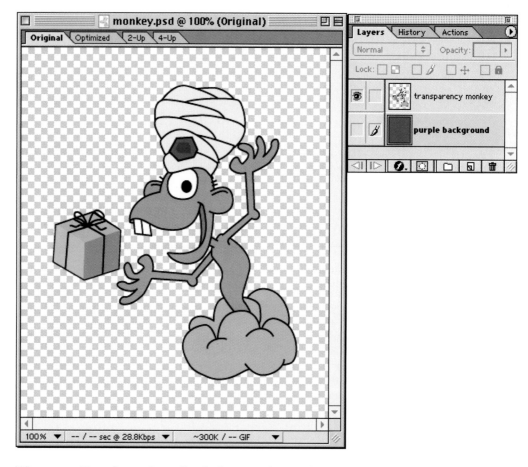

Whenever a Photoshop or ImageReady document is stored on a transparent layer, you will see a checkerboard pattern in the background. If you have other layers turned on that prevent you from seeing the checkerboard background, turn them off before you save the image as a transparent GIF. You'll find this process described in detail in this chapter.

Transparency, Masks, and GIFs

Here's a helpful chart to explain some of the terminology used in this chapter.

Transparency Terminology	
Term	**Definition**
Mask	A mask hides parts of an image from being visible. In the case of a transparent GIF file, the mask is what hides the transparent areas of the image, but the mask itself is not visible to the end user.
Transparent	The checkerboard pattern on a Photoshop layer indicates that a mask is in effect. When you draw a shape on a new layer in Photoshop, an invisible mask (called the *transparency channel*) is invoked.
Transparent GIF	A transparent GIF includes an invisible mask and is displayed by the Web browser in shapes other than squares or rectangles. This chapter shows you how to mask out parts of GIF images.
GIF	A GIF can be transparent or not. To make it transparent, you simply turn on the *Transparency* setting in the Photoshop Save For Web dialog box or the ImageReady Optimize palette.

[IR]

 I. ——————————**Creating and Previewing GIF Transparency**

You can create transparent GIF files in either Photoshop or ImageReady. We've chosen to show this process first in ImageReady, because you can define background and foreground images and preview the results in a browser more readily from ImageReady than from Photoshop's Save For Web interface. This first exercise will teach you how to set GIF transparency and how to preview the results in a browser.

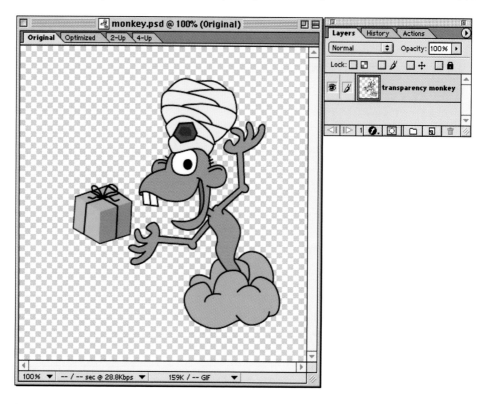

1. Open **monkey.psd** from the **chap_08** folder that you copied to your hard drive from the **H•O•T CD-ROM**.

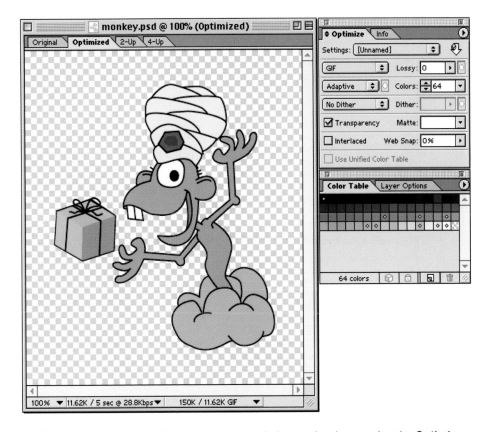

2. Click on the **Optimized** tab in the document window, and make sure that the **Optimize** and **Color Table** palettes are visible. If either palette is not visible, choose **Window > Show Optimize** or **Window > Show Color Table** to open it.

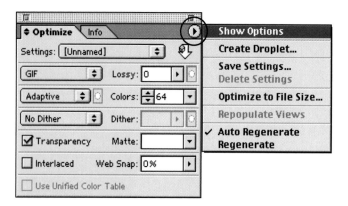

3. In the **Optimize** palette, match the compression settings to what you see in this example: **GIF**, **Adaptive**, **Colors: 64**, **No Dither**. Make sure that you can see the **Transparency** checkbox on the palette, and that it is checked.

Tip: If you don't see the Transparency checkbox, expand the Optimize palette to display all its options by clicking on its upper-right arrow and choosing Show Options.

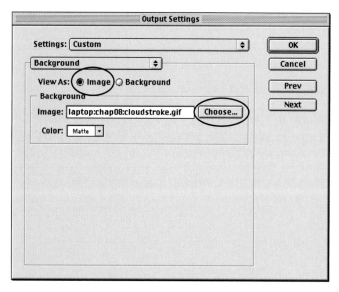

4. Choose **File > Output Settings > Background....** In the **Output Settings** dialog box that appears, choose **View As: Image**.

This lets ImageReady know that when you preview this image, you want to see it displayed as a foreground image.

5. Click the **Choose** button in the **Output Settings** dialog box, and navigate to the **chap_08** folder you copied to your desktop from the **H•O•T CD-ROM**. Select **cloudstroke.gif,** and click **Open**. You will be returned to the **Output Settings** dialog box, where the path name to the file should appear inside the Background Image field. Click **OK**.

This tells ImageReady that when you preview your transparent foreground image, you want cloudstroke.gif to appear behind it as a background image.

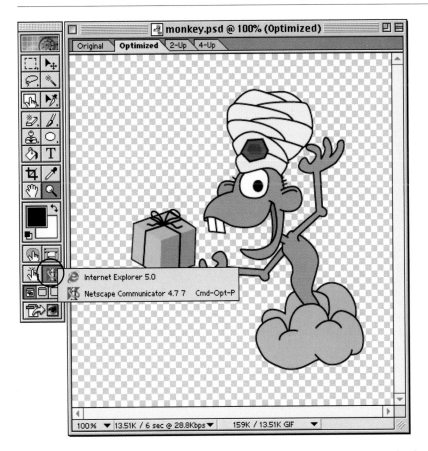

6. Click and hold the **Preview in Default Browser** button in the Toolbox, and select a browser from the pop-up menu.

The Preview in Default Browser button is a new tool in ImageReady 3. From its pop-up menu you can set any of the Web browsers installed in your computer as a default browser for previewing your ImageReady files in progress.

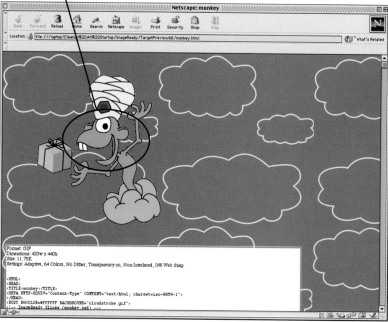

The browser will open and display the monkey image on top of the background image you selected in Step 5. You can see that the transparency settings are working, but notice the white fringe around the edges of the monkey. You'll learn to eliminate that problem in the next exercise.

Tip: The white box with HTML text is a product of the preview. To see the page without the text box in a browser, you would have to choose File > Save Optimized As, save the images and the HTML, and open the HTML file in a Web browser. You learned how to do this in Chapter 7, "Background Images." You may want to revisit it for a refresher on saving HTML.

7. Return to ImageReady, and leave this document open for the next exercise.

[IR]

2. ——————————Fixing Bad Edges

In the last exercise, you learned to specify transparency in the GIF optimization settings and to preview the results against a patterned background. This resulted in an unwanted edge that is commonly referred to as a fringe, halo, or matte. This exercise shows you how to eliminate this unwanted edge, so that the resulting preview will look good.

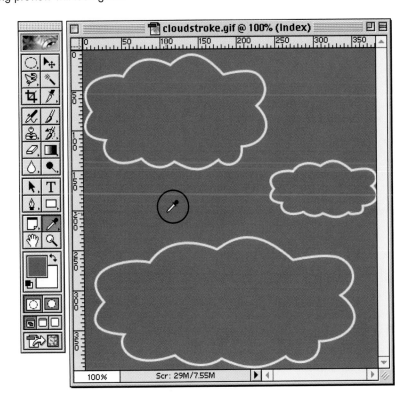

1. In ImageReady, with the **monkey.psd** file still open, choose **File > Open,** and browse to **cloudstroke.gif** in the **chap_08** folder on your hard drive. Select the **Eyedropper** tool from the Toolbox, and click on the magenta background in **cloudstroke.gif**. This will cause the same magenta color to appear in the Foreground Color swatch in the Toolbox.

The reason we asked you to sample the color from cloudstroke.gif is so that you could specify it easily as the matte color for your transparent GIF. You'll learn how to do this in the next step, but it's important first to get the color into the Foreground Color swatch.

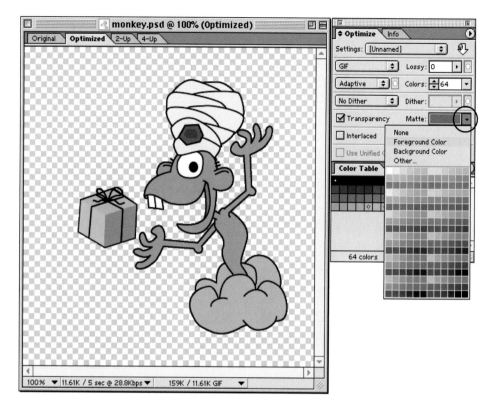

2. Switch to the **monkey.psd** image, which you should still have open from the last exercise. (If it's hidden behind other windows on your screen, choose Window > monkey.psd.) Make sure the **Optimized** tab in the document window is selected. In the **Optimize** palette, click on the **down-pointing arrow** to the right of the **Matte** field to open a pop-up color menu. Choose **Foreground Color** from the pop-up menu.

The same magenta color that you just put in the Foreground Color swatch of the Toolbox will appear in the Matte field of the Optimize palette. Look closely at the edge of the monkey image on the screen, and you should see that the same magenta color now appears under the anti-aliased edge of the graphic.

 MOVIE | setting_mattecolor.mov

To learn more about setting matte color, check out **setting_mattecolor.mov** inside the **movies** folder you transferred to your hard drive from the **H•O•T CD-ROM**.

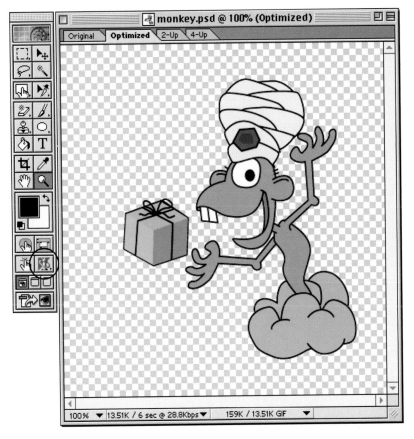

3. Check this out in a browser by clicking the **Preview in Default Browser** button in the Toolbox.

Clicking the Preview in Default Browser button, instead of selecting a browser from its pop-up menu as you did before, will open your file in the default browser you set in the last exercise.

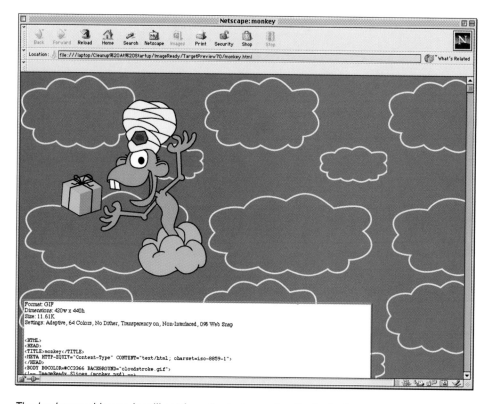

The background image is still set from the last exercise. So in the browser you will see the foreground monkey image laid over the cloudstroke.gif background again, except that this time you won't see a distracting white halo around the monkey. Instead, the monkey image will have a magenta matte around the edge that blends in with the background. With a fine-toothed background pattern like this, even though the background is busy, the matte color produces a nice, clean edge.

---

4. Return to ImageReady, and leave **monkey.psd** open for the next exercise. You won't need **cloudstroke.gif**, so close it.

[IR]

3. ——————Adding a Drop Shadow Over a Fine-Toothed Background

Changing the matte color to match the color in the background image did the trick of eliminating the unattractive halo on a simple, anti-aliased foreground image. What if the edge of your foreground image contains a very soft edge, like a drop shadow or a glow? As you'll see in this exercise, the matching technique you just learned can camouflage even a soft drop shadow, as long as you place it over a certain kind of background image—one that has a fine-toothed pattern (as opposed to a pattern with big bold elements).

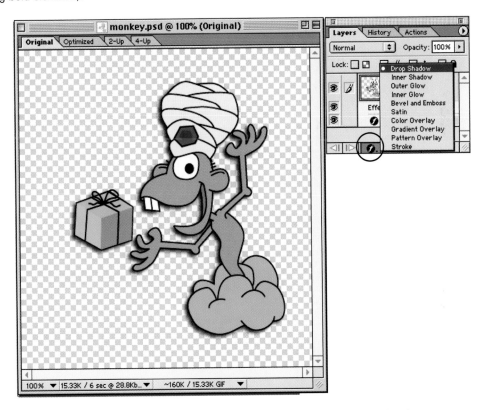

1. With **monkey.psd** still open in ImageReady, click on the **Original** tab of the document window. In the **Layers** palette, you can add a drop shadow layer effect to this image by clicking on the **layer effect (f) icon** and choosing **Drop Shadow** from the pop-up menu. You can leave this layer effect at its default settings in the Drop Shadow Options palette for this exercise.

Tip: Again, we recommend that you edit images when you're in the Original tab of the document window. Otherwise ImageReady tries to optimize the graphic as you're editing it, which slows things down. When you're in the Original tab it's also possible to perform editing tasks (such as drawing or typing) that are not allowed when the document is set to the Optimized tab.

2. Click on the **Optimized** tab of the document window. The image will appear with a gangly magenta border around it because of the matte color you assigned to it in the last exercise.

Although the image looks extremely yucky here, it will look just fine against the background image in a browser, which you'll get to preview in the next step.

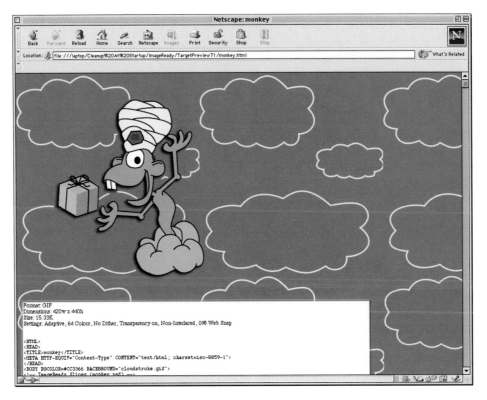

3. Click the **Preview in Default Browser** button in the Toolbox to check this out in a browser.

If you look closely, you can see the magenta matte showing in spots. Regardless, it sure beats having unwanted colored edges around the entire image.

---

4. Return to ImageReady and leave the file open. Don't worry about saving it just yet. The next exercise will show you a situation in which the technique you just learned won't work.

---

4. ————————The Pitfalls of Broad Backgrounds

The reason the magenta matte worked so well in the previous exercises is that the specified background image had a fine-toothed pattern that contained the same magenta you assigned as the matte color. This technique does not work in every scenario, as you'll see when you switch to a background image with a broad pattern in this exercise.

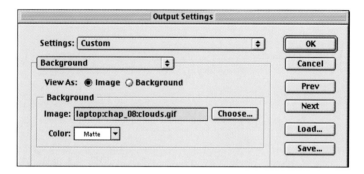

1. With **monkey.psd** open, choose **File > Output Settings > Background…**. In the **Output Settings** dialog box, click **Choose,** and select **clouds.gif** from the **chap_08** folder you copied to your hard drive. Click **Open.** Back in the **Output Settings** dialog box, click **OK.**

2. Preview this in a browser by clicking the **Preview in Default Browser** button in the Toolbox. Ugh… the results are not pretty.

*This is a case when matching the matte to the background image will not work, because
the areas of different colors in the background image are too broad and the color changes
between them too extreme. When you set the matte to magenta, it shows up in the white
areas, as you can see in this exercise. If you changed the matte color to white, it would
show up against the magenta areas of the background. The best solution is to remove the
soft edges created by the drop shadow effect and the anti-aliasing of the graphic, and also
to remove the matte altogether, creating a hard-edged, aliased, non-matted image, as you'll
do in the next steps.*

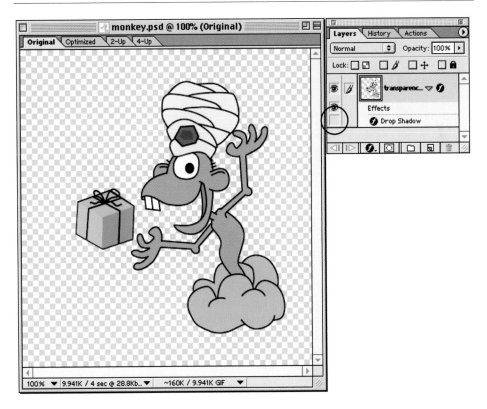

3. Return to ImageReady, and click on the **Original** tab. Turn off the layer effect that you added
in the last exercise by clicking on the **Eye** icon to the left of that effect in the **Layers** palette.

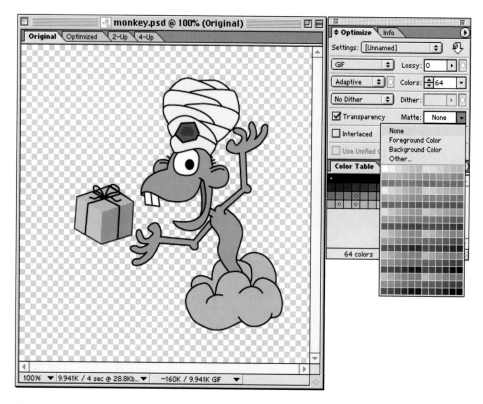

4. In the **Optimize** palette, click on the **down-pointing arrow** to the right of the **Matte** field, and choose **None** from the pop-up menu.

This will remove all the anti-aliasing from the outside edge of the monkey graphic. The nice thing about using Matte: None *is that it removes anti-aliasing only from the outer edges of the graphic. Any anti-aliasing that exists in the interior of the image (like the anti-aliasing around the black pupil of the monkey's eye) is preserved.*

5. Preview the image in a browser. It doesn't look so bad anymore, but it doesn't contain the drop shadow either.

Actually, there is nothing you can do to save the drop shadow except to use a different background, like the fine-toothed pattern you used before. On broad backgrounds you can't use any matte color because the illusion will be broken over the changing colored image. This is a limitation of the GIF file format, rather than a flaw in ImageReady or Photoshop.

6. Return to ImageReady and keep the same image open.

5. —————————Saving Transparent Images

So far, you've learned how to create a transparent GIF image and how to preview it over different background images, but you haven't yet learned how to save a transparent GIF, alone or with its corresponding background. This exercise will focus on saving techniques in ImageReady.

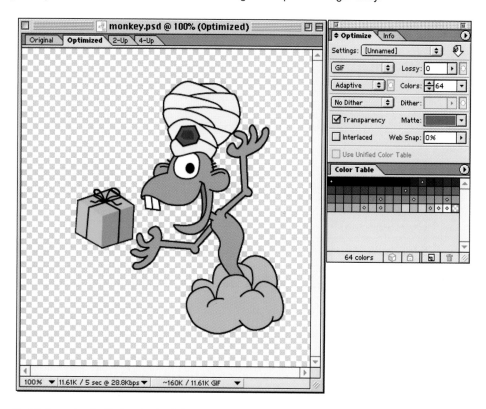

1. Click on the **Optimized** tab of the **monkey.psd** document window. Check the **Optimize** palette to ensure that the optimize and transparency settings are configured the way you want them to be. Assume that the monkey is going to appear against a broad background, like the one in the previous exercise. Remembering what you've learned about different kinds of backgrounds, set the **Matte** field to **None**.

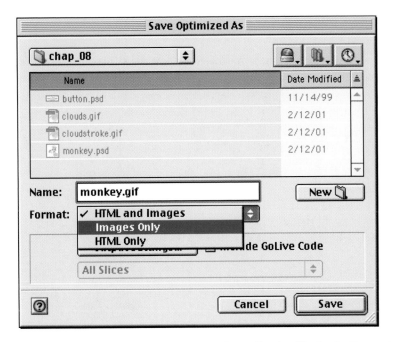

2. Choose **File > Save Optimized As…**. ImageReady will take the first part of the file name from the original image and will insert the **.gif** extension at the end of the file name (**monkey.gif**). Click on the pop-up menu in the **Format** field (Mac) or the **Save as type** field (Windows), and choose **Images Only**. Navigate to the **chap_08** folder on your hard drive, and click **Save**.

Note: The GIF file you are saving will carry all of the settings that are in the Optimize palette. If you want to save the HTML, which specifies the background image as well, choose HTML and Images from the Format (Mac) or Save as type (Windows) pop-up menu. This choice depends on whether you would like ImageReady to build your page, or whether you prefer to build pages within an HTML editor such as GoLive, Front Page, or Dreamweaver. Either way, click the Save button.

3. Close the **monkey.psd** file.

[PS]

6. ————————————Transparency in Photoshop

We mentioned earlier in the chapter that a transparent GIF can be made in Photoshop or in ImageReady, but that we prefer to do this kind of work in ImageReady because it's easier to access its background and preview settings. As you might now realize, being able to quickly preview the transparent foreground image against a background image is a very useful feature, because seeing the preview will help you determine which matte technique to use. Still, there are times when it will be more convenient to work inside Photoshop. So this next exercise will teach you how to create transparent GIFs there.

1. Open Photoshop. Choose **File > Open**, and navigate to **monkey.psd** inside the **chap_08** folder on your hard drive.

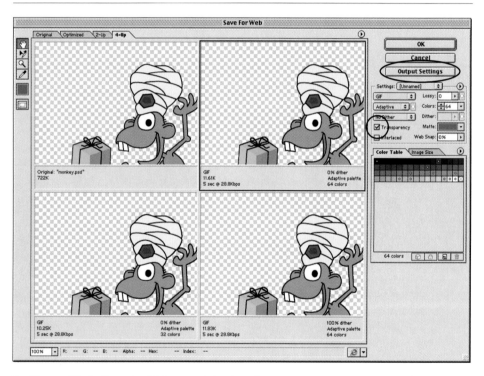

2. Choose **File > Save for Web...**, and the file will open inside the **Save For Web** dialog box. If you are not in the 4-Up view, as shown above, click on the **4-Up** tab so you can compare optimization settings. Make sure that **Transparency** is checked and that you've selected the preview that has your preferred optimization settings.

3. Click the **arrow** to the right of the **Matte** field in the **Save For Web** dialog box, and you'll see that you have menu choices similar to those you had in ImageReady, except that there is no color swatch. To pick a color, choose **Other...** from this pop-up menu. In the **Color Picker** that opens, choose a magenta color (or type **CC3366** into the **Hexadecimal Value** field at the bottom of the Color Picker), and click **OK** to exit the Color Picker.

4. Still in the **Save For Web** dialog box, click the **Output Settings** button. This will open the Output Settings dialog box.

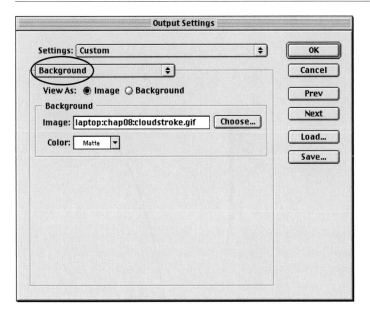

5. In the **Output Settings** dialog box, click on the pop-up menu below the **Settings** field and choose **Background** from the menu. This will cause the **Background** options to appear in this dialog box.

6. Choose **View As: Image**. Click the **Choose** button to the right of the **Image** field, browse to **cloudstroke.gif** in the **chap_08** folder on your hard drive, and click **Open**. In the **Output Settings** dialog box, click **OK**.

This lets Photoshop know that you want the monkey image to be viewed in the foreground, over the tiling background image cloudstroke.gif.

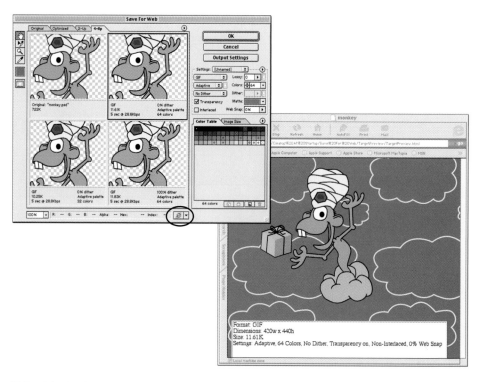

7. Back in the **Save For Web** dialog box, click the **Preview in Browser** button. This will open the Photoshop default browser, so you can preview your transparent GIF on top of the background image you specified in the last step.

8. Return to the **Save For Web** dialog box. If you were satisfied with the browser preview, click **OK**. This will open the Save Optimized As... dialog box.

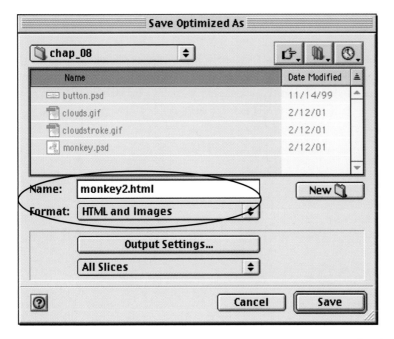

9. In the **Save Optimized As...** dialog box, click on the **Format** field (Mac) or the **Save as type** field (Windows), and choose **HTML and Images**. Change the **Name** field to **monkey2.html**, navigate to the **chap_08** folder on your hard drive, and click **Save**.

Photoshop will save a transparent GIF called monkey2.gif, *as well as the HTML file* monkey2.html *that identifies the background image. If you'd rather build your Web page and add a background manually in an HTML editor, choose* Images Only *from the Format menu, and change the Name field to* monkey2.gif. *This is a personal choice that depends on the workflow you prefer.*

10. That's all there is to creating a transparent GIF in Photoshop! Close the file.

Note: *Photoshop 6 has an Assistant that will walk you through the steps of creating a transparent GIF, but we don't recommend using it because it doesn't allow you to set or preview a background image. You'll have a lot more control over creating and saving your transparent GIFs in Photoshop if you follow the steps you've learned in this exercise. If you just have to have a look at the Assistant, go to the Photoshop Help menu and choose Export Transparent Image....*

[PS]

7. ——————————————Transparent Layer Versus Transparent GIF

Although you've worked on **monkey.psd** in this chapter, you might not realize that it was created on a Photoshop transparent layer before you made it into a transparent GIF. Why is this important for you to know? Because as we mentioned earlier, it's impossible to create a transparent GIF unless your original artwork contains transparent areas. In this exercise you'll practice turning off layers so you can access a file's transparent layers before saving it as a transparent GIF.

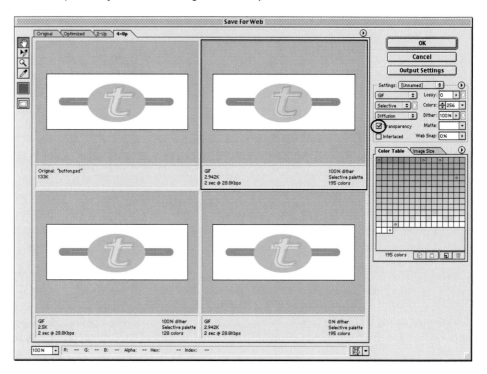

1. In Photoshop, open **button.psd** from the **chap_08** folder on your hard drive. Choose **File > Save for Web...** and select one of the **4-Up** views with the GIF format. Click the **Transparency** checkbox on and off.

Notice that nothing happens. You cannot create a transparent GIF from a document that doesn't display any Photoshop layer transparency. Photoshop and ImageReady look at the document in a flattened state, even if it contains a lot of layers, as this one does. It's essential that the Photoshop layer transparency (indicated by a checkerboard pattern) be visible. Even though the layers containing the artwork in this image have transparency, Photoshop cannot access the necessary information because the background layer is turned on in the Layers palette. The next step will show you what to do.

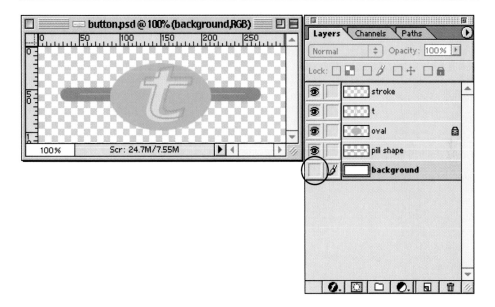

2. Click **Cancel** to return to the document window. In the **Layers** palette (Window > Show Layers), turn off the visibility of the background layer by clicking its **Eye** icon off. Now you will see the checkerboard pattern that indicates Photoshop layer transparency. Choose **File > Save for Web...** again.

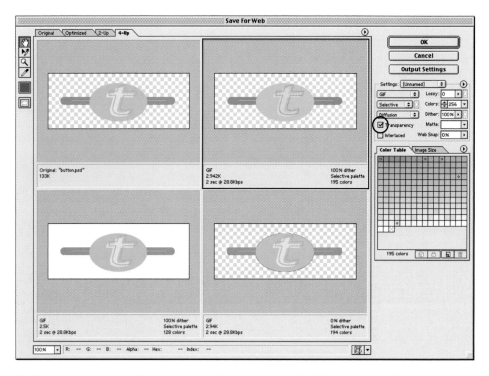

3. Now when you put a checkmark in the **Transparency** checkbox, you should see the previews of the transparent GIF change. Play around with this for a while. Select different **Matte** colors and watch the edge color change.

---

4. Click **OK** when you've arrived at the settings you like, and save the optimized file. Close the **.psd** file without saving it.

Congratulations! You are now prepared to create transparent GIFs against a variety of backgrounds in ImageReady and Photoshop.

Offset Problems in Browsers

You might wonder, why the fuss with all this transparency stuff? Couldn't you simply make a fore-ground image with the background image incorporated and position it over the same background image? Unfortunately, due to constraints within the HTML authoring language, foreground and back-ground images don't line up in browsers, You'd end up with an unwanted offset, as shown below.

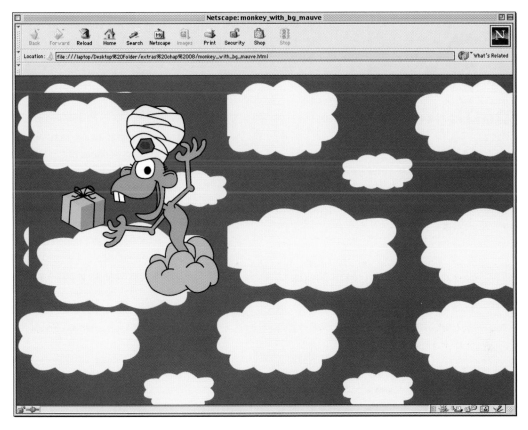

You can't forgo making a foreground GIF transparent, because if you just place the foreground and background images together, they don't necessarily line up in browsers. You can do much better than this by using the methods described in this chapter.

9.
Image Maps

chap_09

Photoshop 6 / ImageReady 3
H•O•T CD-ROM

Most buttons and navigation bars on the Web are composed of individual images that link to individual URLs. An image map is called for when you want a single image to link to multiple URLs, such as a map of the United States in which each state is linked to a different URL.

In the past, image maps were not made in image editors but in HTML editors or standalone image map-editing software. ImageReady makes it easy to create image maps without the need for other applications. Although it isn't possible to make an image map in Photoshop, if you make and save an image map in ImageReady, and later open that document in Photoshop, it will retain the image map information until you return to ImageReady.

Server-Side or Client-Side Image Maps?

There are two types of image maps—server-side and client-side. In the early days of the Web, it was only possible to create server-side image maps. When Netscape 2.0 was released, the ability to work with client-side image maps was introduced.

What do those terms mean? Anything that is server-side resides on the Web server and is accessed through a CGI (**C**ommon **G**ateway **I**nterchange). A CGI is a type of script that can be written in Perl, C++, AppleScript, or other programming languages. CGI scripts reside on the Web server. Typically, most Internet service providers supply their subscribers with a CGI script that can activate server-side image maps. It's then a matter of linking to the script and uploading a map definition file that should also be stored on the Web server. To further muddle the issue, there are two types of Web servers— those that follow the conventions of CERN (**C**onseil **E**uropéen pour la **R**echerche **N**ucléaire—where Tim Berners-Lee conducted research at the time the Web was being developed) and those that follow the NCSA (**N**ational **C**enter for **S**upercomputing **A**pplications) conventions. If you decide to create a server-side image map, you will need to check with your Web-hosting company to see if they are CERN or NCSA compliant.

Sound complicated? It is, in fact, much more complicated to create a server-side image map than a client-side image map. Calling something "client-side" means that it is performed on the client. What is a client? Why, it's a Web browser, silly. You mean you weren't born knowing that? Don't fret, neither was anyone else. The Web browser that you use on your hard drive is your very own Web client. Bet you never thought of it that way, but now you can have two kinds of clients in your life—those who pay the bills, and those that display your Web pages!

The deal is that a client-side image map is performed by the browser and doesn't involve the server at all. Client-side image maps are always easier to work with because you don't have to fuss with CGI scripts, map definition files, and knowing what kind of Web server your hosting company uses.

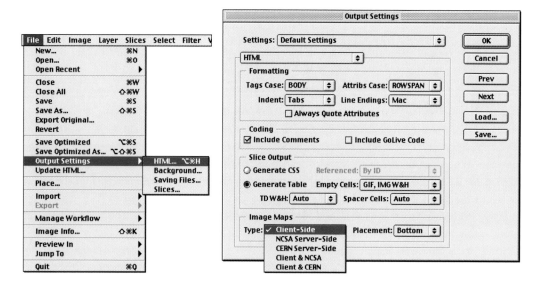

Most Web sites today use only a client-side image map, and that's what this chapter will cover. If you want to create a server-side image map in place of or in addition to a client-side image map, here's how: With your artwork open in ImageReady, choose **File > Output Settings > HTML**. This will open the HTML options panel of the **Output Settings** dialog box, where you can change the **Image Maps Type** setting to reflect your choice. The default is **Client-Side**, so if that's what you plan to create, you won't need to change this setting. If your choice includes a server-side image map, ImageReady will create a separate map definition file for you, in addition to an HTML file and an image file.

What Does an Image Map Look Like?

The HTML for a client-side image map contains **MAP** and **USEMAP** tags, as well as all the coordinates for the image map regions. The coordinates plot the dimensions and location of the "hot spots" in an image map.

What's a hot spot? It's an area on a Web page that triggers a link. Clicking inside a hot spot will activate a link to another page. Moving a cursor over a hot spot will change the cursor to a hand, which may be the only indication a viewer has that a particular spot is hot.

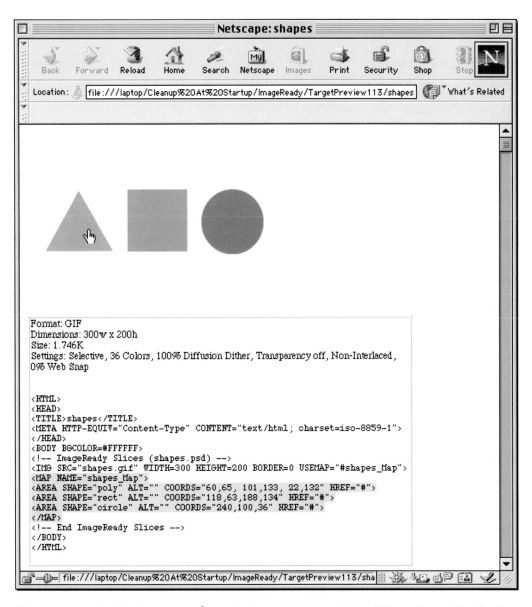

```
Format: GIF
Dimensions: 300w x 200h
Size: 1.746K
Settings: Selective, 36 Colors, 100% Diffusion Dither, Transparency off, Non-Interlaced,
0% Web Snap


<HTML>
<HEAD>
<TITLE>shapes</TITLE>
<META HTTP-EQUIV="Content-Type" CONTENT="text/html; charset=iso-8859-1">
</HEAD>
<BODY BGCOLOR=#FFFFFF>
<!-- ImageReady Slices (shapes.psd) -->
<IMG SRC="shapes.gif" WIDTH=300 HEIGHT=200 BORDER=0 USEMAP="#shapes_Map">
<MAP NAME="shapes_Map">
<AREA SHAPE="poly" ALT="" COORDS="60,65, 101,133, 22,132" HREF="#">
<AREA SHAPE="rect" ALT="" COORDS="118,63,188,134" HREF="#">
<AREA SHAPE="circle" ALT="" COORDS="240,100,36" HREF="#">
</MAP>
<!-- End ImageReady Slices -->
</BODY>
</HTML>
```

This is an example of an image map (on a single graphic that contains all three shapes—the triangle, square, and circle), and of the HTML code for an image map that ImageReady will write. Notice that in the code there are three types of **AREA SHAPE** *elements—***POLY** *(polygon),* **RECT** *(rectangle), and* **CIRCLE.** *After those, you'll see a listing for* **COORDS** *(coordinates), followed by a lot of comma-separated numbers. Those numbers describe the coordinates of the hot regions around each shape.*

[IR]

I. ——————————— Making an Image Map with Drawing Tools

Making image maps is a snap in ImageReady 3. There are two ways to create image maps in the latest release of the program—by hand with the new image map drawing tools, and automatically with the layer-based image map features.

In this exercise you'll learn how easy it is to create and modify an image map with the image map drawing tools. This is the method to use when you want to create multiple links from artwork that is on a single Photoshop layer. The image map drawing tools are also useful when you want to create an image map hot spot that's complex in shape, because this method gives you lots of control over the form and location of a hot spot.

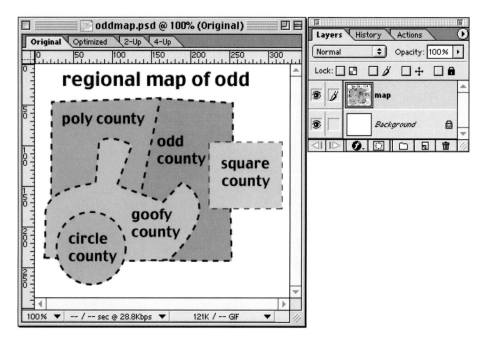

1. In ImageReady, open **oddmap.psd** from the **chap_09** folder you copied to your hard disk from the **H•O•T CD-ROM**.

Notice that all of the artwork in this image is on a single layer. When this is the case, the image map drawing tools are the ideal method for creating an image map and its hot spots. If the artwork were separated onto individual layers, you'd have the option of using either this method or the layer-based method of creating an image map (which you'll learn in the next exercise).

2. In the ImageReady Toolbox, click on the **Image Map Select** tool (or whichever image map drawing tool is in the foreground in your Toolbox), and move your mouse to the small **arrow** at the bottom of the tools pop-up menu. When you release the mouse, you'll see a breakaway menu that contains all of the image map drawing tools. Move the breakaway menu to a convenient place on your screen, so you'll have easy access to all of the drawing tools.

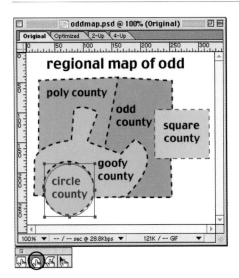

3. In the breakaway menu, click on the **Circle Image Map** tool. Then click and drag over the **circle county** graphic in the document to create a circular image map hot spot. **Tip:** To draw a circular hot spot from the center out, hold down the Option (Mac) or Alt (Windows) key while dragging out the shape.

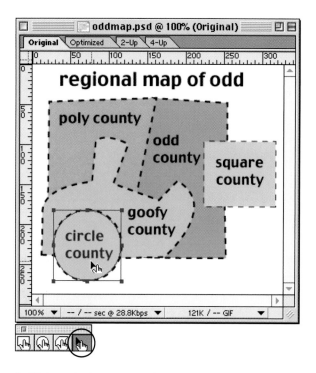

4. Click on the **Image Map Select** tool in the breakaway menu. Click inside of the hot spot you just drew, and move it into position on top of the **circle county** graphic. **Tip:** You can use the arrow keys on your keyboard to nudge the hot spot into place.

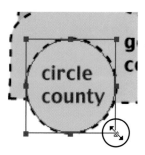

5. You can modify the shape of the hot spot you've drawn if it doesn't quite match the shape of the artwork. With the **Image Map Select** tool still selected, move your cursor over one of the corners or outside borders of the hot spot until the cursor changes to a double-pointed arrow. Drag to modify the shape of the hot spot to fit the underlying artwork.

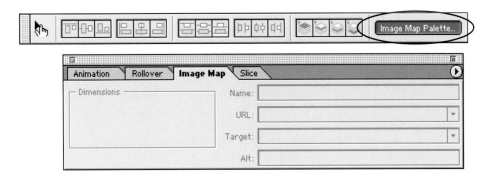

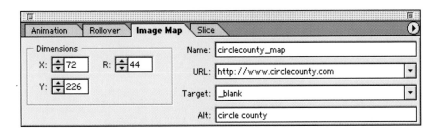

6. Click the **Image Map Palette** button on the **Options** bar to access the **Image Map** palette.

The Image Map Palette button is a handy way to make the Image Map palette visible. Another way to do that is to choose Window > Show Image Map. Remember that the Options bar is context sensitive, so it will display the Image Map Palette button only when you've chosen the Image Map Select tool.

7. In the **URL** field of the **Image Map** palette, enter a URL of your choice. It can be an external URL to a page in another site (like **http://www.circlecounty.com**) or an internal URL to a page that will be in the same site as your image map (**circle.html**, for example).

> ## NOTE | External Versus Internal URLs
>
> If you are linking to a Web site other than the one where this document will be uploaded, you must include the entire **http://www** header information. If, however, you were uploading this image map to lynda.com and wanted to link to classes.html, you wouldn't need the **http://www** header information. The link to an outside URL is called an external link, and the link to the interior URL is called an internal link. If you are going to use internal links, it's really important to know the exact directory structure of your site. Here are some examples.
>
> - *If you stored the HTML file for this image map inside the same folder as the HTML pages to which it linked, you could specify the URL like this:* **classes.html**
>
> - *If you stored this image map inside an **images** folder and the HTML to which it linked inside an independent folder named **html**, you would specify the URL like this:* **../html/classes.html**
>
> - *If you stored this image map inside an **images** folder and the HTML to which it linked inside a folder named **html** that was inside the **images** folder, you would specify the URL like this:* **html/classes.html**
>
> Many HTML editors, including GoLive and Dreamweaver, have site-management features that help you manage these links. It's easiest to link to an external URL because you don't have to know the location of the file and how it relates to the location of the image map. If you plan to link to internal pages, it might be best to set the actual links inside your HTML editor.

8. In the **Name** field of the **Image Map** palette, type **circlecounty_map** instead of the default map name that appears there. **Tip:** Avoid using spaces when you name an image map. A good substitute is an underscore or a hyphen.

Naming an image map is optional, but you'll find that a meaningful name will make it easier to find a particular image map in the code if you ever need to.

9. Choose **_blank** from the **Target** menu in the **Image Map** palette.

Choosing _blank as the target instructs a Web browser to open the page to which you've linked in a separate browser window. You don't have to specify a target if you don't want to. If you don't choose a target, by default the page you linked to in the Image Map palette will show up in the same Web browser window as the page that contains the image map.

10. Enter **circle county** in the **Alt** field of the **Image Map** palette,

Entering alt text in the Image Map palette is also optional. Alt text is a way to give informa-tion about your graphics to viewers who can't see the graphics (either because they've turned image-viewing off in the browser or because they are visually disabled). It's OK to use spaces and special characters in alt tags, as they do not follow the strict naming con-ventions required in HTML file names.

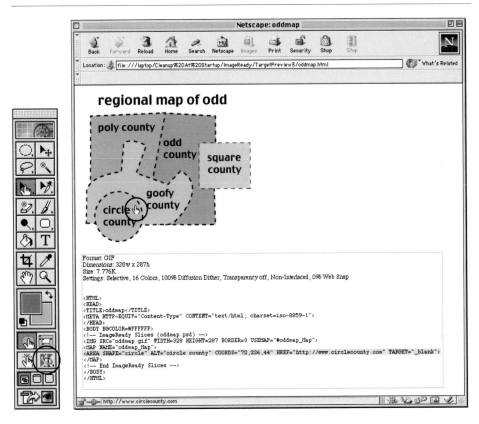

11. Click the **Preview in Default Browser** button in the ImageReady Toolbox to preview your image map in a Web browser. Move your cursor over the **circle county** graphic in the browser, and notice that the cursor changes to a hand, indicating that this is a hot spot.

In the code, notice that there is a line that reads: **<AREA SHAPE="circle" ALT="circle county" COORDS="72,226,44" HREF="http://www.circlecounty.com" TARGET="_blank">**. *This is telling the browser to recognize an image map hot spot in the shape of a circle, with the coordinates of 72, 226, 44, to link it to the index page of the circlecounty.com Web site, and to display that page in a separate browser window.*

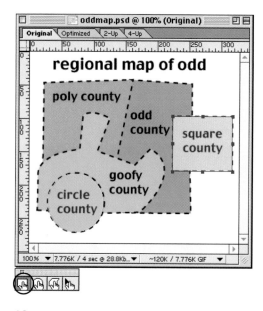

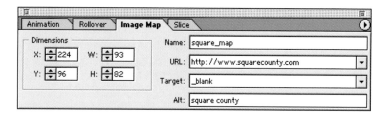

12. Back in ImageReady, select the **Rectangle Image Map** tool from the breakaway menu. Click and drag over the **square county** graphic to create another hot spot. **Tip:** Hold down the Shift key while drawing with the Rectangle Image Map tool if you want to create a perfectly square hot spot.

13. In the **Image Map** palette (Window > Show Image Map), enter an external or internal URL of your choice, enter **square_map** in the **Name** field, and, if you like, choose _**blank** in the **Target** field and enter **square county** in the **Alt** field.

14. Click the **Preview in Default Browser** button. In the browser, move your cursor around the artwork, noticing that there are now two hot regions—circle county and square county— over which the cursor changes to a hand.

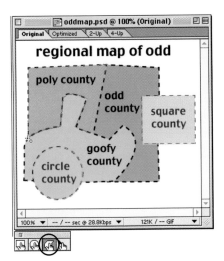

15. Return to ImageReady and select the **Polygon Image Map** tool from the breakaway menu. Click on one corner of the **poly county** graphic, and move your cursor around the border of it, clicking whenever you need to create a contour. This will make a hot spot that matches the irregular shape of poly county. When you've gone all the way around poly county, move the cursor over the spot where you first clicked. When the cursor changes to a small circle, click to close the path.

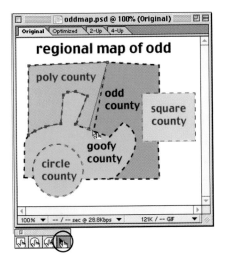

16. To adjust a leg of the polygon you drew, click on the **Image Map Select** tool in the breakaway menu. Then click on one of the square points of the polygon, and drag the leg into position.

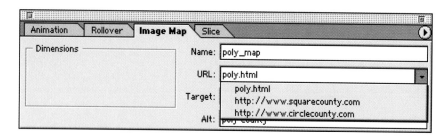

17. In the **Image Map** palette, enter **poly_map** into the **Name** field. Click on the small **arrow** next to the **URL** field to display a menu of all the URLs you've entered so far. You can choose a URL from that convenient list or type another URL into the field. Set **Target** to **_blank**, and enter **poly county** in the **Alt** field. Click the **Preview in Default Browser** button again to test this hot spot. When you move the cursor over **poly county** in the browser, the hand symbol should appear.

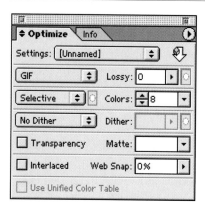

18. In ImageReady, click on the **Optimize** tab and choose optimization settings (**GIF, Selective, Colors: 8, No Dither**) in the **Optimize** palette. If you need help with this, refer to Chapter 3, "*Optimization*." **Tip:** Although GIF is the preferred format in this case due to the flat, graphic nature of the image, you can also make an image map on a JPEG.

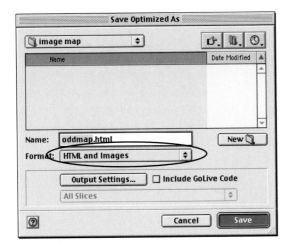

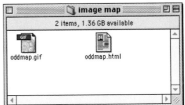

19. Choose **File > Save Optimized As...**. In the **Save Optimized As** dialog box, make sure that the **Format** field (Mac) or the **Save as type** field (Windows) is set to **HTML and Images**. Navigate to your desktop, click the **New Folder** button, and name the new folder **image map**. Click **Save**. Go out to the desktop and open the **image map** folder to see the two files that ImageReady created—a GIF file called **oddmap.gif** and an HTML file called **oddmap.html**.

It's important to tell ImageReady to create an HTML file along with the image file, because the image map instructions are not part of the image; they are stored separately in the accompanying HTML file. In this case, oddmap.gif *is just like any other GIF file. The only thing that makes it an image map is the code that is stored in* oddmap.html, *which tells Web browsers the coordinates of the linked regions.*

20. Save and close ***oddmap.psd***. The image map content will be stored with the Photoshop document, even though it will not be visible unless viewed from within ImageReady.

[IR]

2. _____Making an Image Map from Layers

There's another way to make image maps in ImageReady that is even easier than using the drawing tools. You can have ImageReady automatically create hot spots for you based on the shape of your layered artwork. In the past, creating an image map involved manually tracing around the regions of the image to which you wanted to assign a URL. What's revolutionary about the layer-based approach is that you don't have to do any drawing or positioning of the image map. The program does it for you! The key to making layer-based image maps is having the individual pieces of your artwork separated onto different transparent layers. If you've done that, ImageReady is smart enough to know where the regions of each layer are. Creating an image map this way is as simple as clicking on a layer and making a menu choice.

One of the neat things about a layer-based image map is that it will move with the layer of artwork on which it was created. This is the method to use when you want the flexibility to move artwork around after making an image map, without having to redraw the hot spots after every move. You'll see what we mean as you work through this exercise.

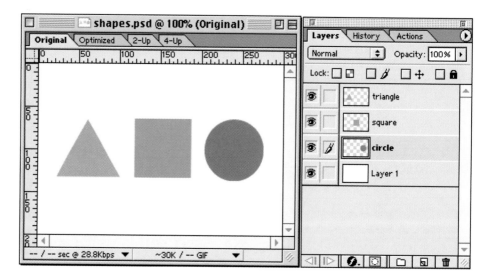

1. Open **shapes.psd** in the **chap_09** folder you transferred to your hard disk from the **H•O•T CD-ROM**.

Notice that each piece of artwork in this image—the triangle, the square, and the circle—is on a separate layer, and that each of those layers has a checkerboard pattern (which, as you learned in Chapter 8, means that there are transparent pixels on those layers). This is important, because ImageReady can make an image map from a layer only if there is transparency on that layer.

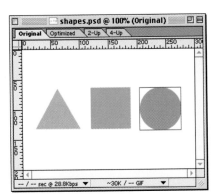

2. In the **Layers** palette, **Control+click** (Mac) or **right-click** (Windows) on the layer named **circle.** (If the Layers palette isn't visible, choose Window > Show Layers). Choose **New Layer Based Image Map Area** from the pop-up menu that appears.

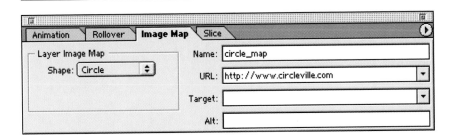

3. Click the **Image Map** tab. (If you don't see it, choose Window > Show Image Map.) With the **circle** layer still selected in the **Layers** palette, click on the **Shape** field and choose **Circle** from the pop-up menu.

By default, layer-based image maps are rectangular. Choosing circle *or* polygon *in the Shape field may result in a closer fit between the shape of an image map hot spot and the shape of certain artwork. The better the fit, the easier it is for a viewer to locate the hot spot in a Web browser, using the artwork as a clue.*

4. In the **Name** field of the **Image Map** palette, enter **circle_map** instead of the default image map name that appears there.

5. In the **URL** field of the **Image Map** palette, enter **http://www.circleville.com**, or the URL of your choice. **Note:** If you are not online when you test the preview or final file, the link to the URL you specified will not work. In this example, **http://www.circleville.com** is a fictitious URL, so it probably won't work even if you are online (unless someone has registered that domain name since this book was published).

You can add a target window or alt text in the Image Map palette, if you choose.

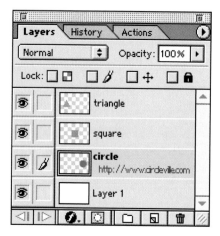

6. Press **Return** (Mac) or **Enter** (Windows) to see that a URL has been listed inside the circle layer on the Layers palette. This indicates that ImageReady has stored image map information with this layer.

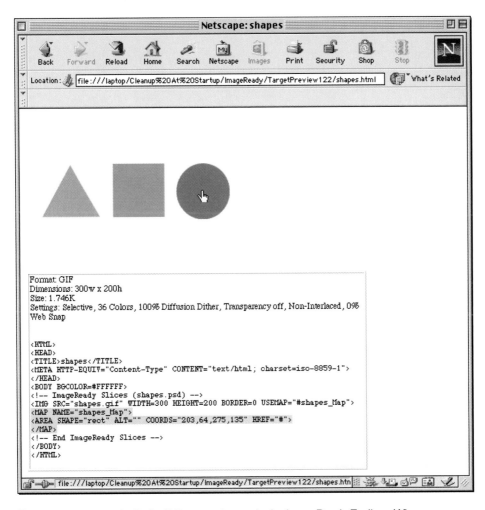

7. Click the **Preview in Default Browser** button in the ImageReady Toolbox. When you place your cursor over the circle shape previewed in the browser, the telltale hand will appear, indicating that this is a link.

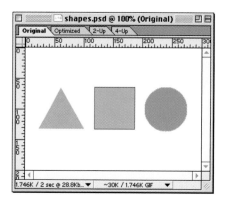

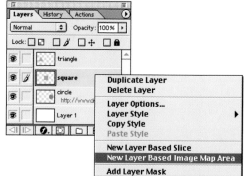

8. Return to ImageReady. **Control+click** (Mac) or **right-click** (Windows) the layer named **square** in the **Layers** palette. Choose **New Layer Based Image Map Area** from the pop-up menu that appears.

Notice that the image map defaults to a square shape, so you don't need to change it in the Image Map palette to match the shape of the square artwork on this layer.

9. In the **Image Map** palette, enter **square_map** in the **Name** field, and **http://www.squaresville.com** in the **URL** field. Add a target and alt text if you'd like.

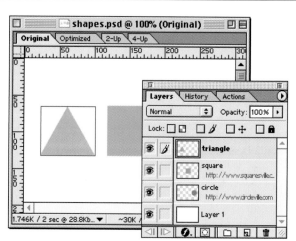

10. Select the layer named **triangle** in the **Layers** palette. From the **Layer** menu at the top of the screen, choose **Layer > New Layer Based Image Map Area**.

This is another way to create a layer-based image map. It's an alternative to using the pop-up menu from the Layers palette, as you did in Steps 2 and 8 of this exercise.

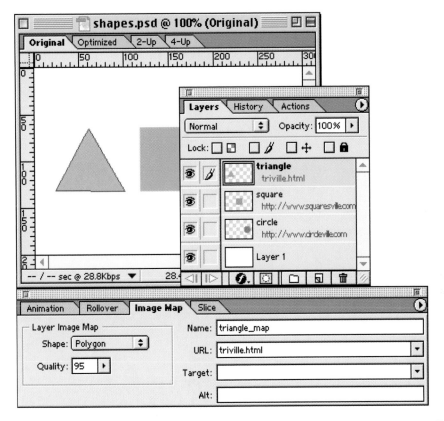

11. In the **Image Map** palette, change the **Shape** to **Polygon** and the **Quality** to **95.** Enter **triangle_map** as the map **Name**, and type in a different URL. Press **Return** (Mac) or **Enter** (Windows) to see feedback on the URL name in the triangle layer of the Layers palette.

*The quality setting affects how tightly the polygon-shaped image map will hug the underlying artwork. The higher the tolerance, the closer the match between those shapes. **Tip:** You won't always want the quality to be at its highest setting, because in some cases (like complex shapes or text) that will produce hot regions that are too narrow for practical use.*

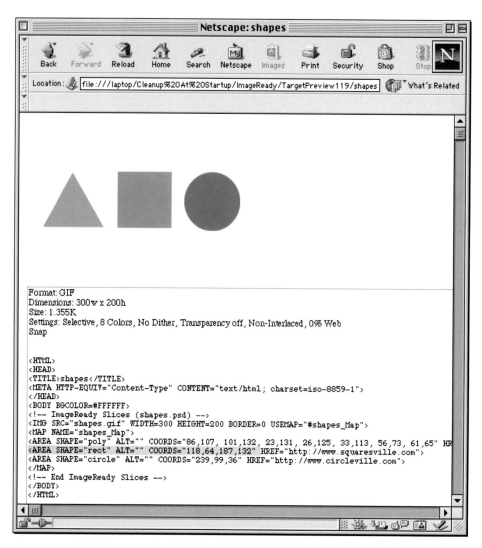

12. Click the **Preview in Default Browser** button. In the browser preview, move your cursor over each of the three graphics to see the cursor change to a hand. If you are online, you can even test the links and they should work, assuming that you entered real URLs. Notice the coordinates of the rectangular hot spot—118, 64, 187, 132. You'll want to compare them to another set of image map coordinates when you get to Step 13 in a moment.

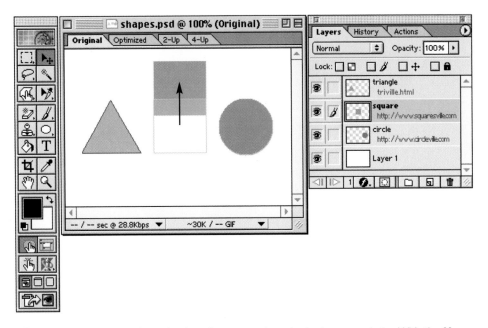

13. Return to ImageReady, and select the **square** layer in the **Layers** palette. With the **Move** tool from the Toolbox, click in the document window and drag to move the artwork on the square layer. Notice that the thin blue outline of the rectangular image map moves with the underlying artwork.

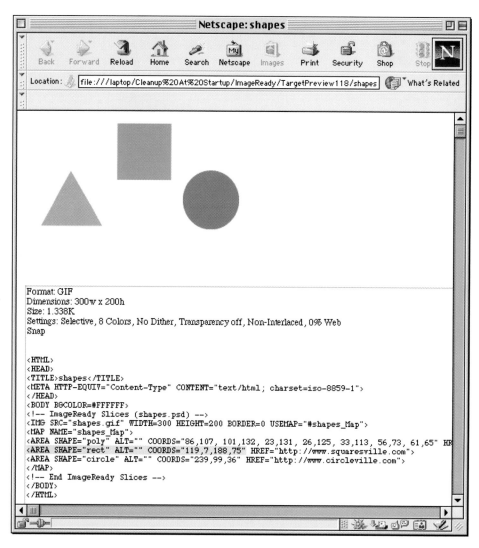

14. Click the **Preview in Default Browser** button again, and notice that the coordinates of the rectangular-shaped hot spot have changed to reflect the move (in the case of our illustration, the new coordinates are 119, 7, 188, 75, but yours may be different depending on where you moved the square), proving that this layer-based image map really did move with the underlying artwork.

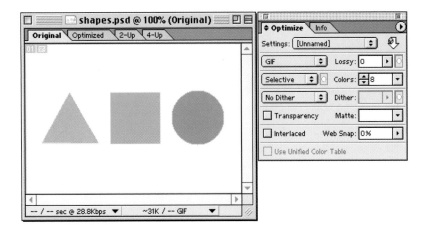

15. So far, you have only previewed the image map. Return to ImageReady to save a final version. Select the **square** layer in the **Layers** palette, and with the **Move** tool, drag the square artwork (with its hot spot) back into line with the other graphics. Select the **Slice Select** tool from the Toolbox, and click anywhere in the image. Click the **Optimized** tab, and create appropriate settings for the whole image inside the **Optimize** palette. (We chose **GIF**, **Selective**, **No Dither**, **Colors: 8**.) If the Optimize palette is not visible, choose Window > Show Optimize to display it.

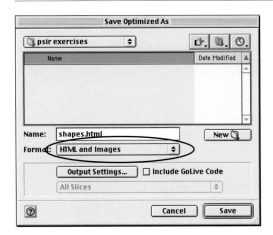

16. Choose **File > Save Optimized As…**, make sure you choose **HTML and Images** as the **Format** (Mac) or **Save as type** (Windows) setting, and click **Save**. ImageReady will save a GIF file called **shapes.gif** and an HTML file called **shapes.html** that contains the image map code.

17. Choose **File > Save**, and leave **shapes.psd** open for the next exercise.

[IR]

3. ——————————Making an Image Map to Fit Text

Making an image map to fit text or other complex shapes can be tricky. In this exercise, you'll learn how to create practical image maps for text with the image map drawing tools. You'll also see that you can use both of the image map creation methods you've learned—the tool-based method and the layer-based method—together on a single image. This is often the best solution when you're working with hybrid images that contain images with graphics and text.

1. The file **shapes.psd** should be open in ImageReady from the last exercise, in which you created layer-based image maps for the graphics in this document.

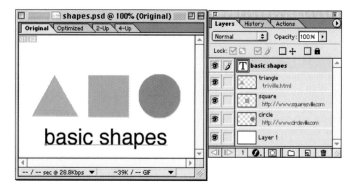

2. Select the **Type** tool from the Toolbox. In the Options bar, choose **Helvetica** or **Arial** as the font and **36 px** as the font size. Click in the document and type the words **basic shapes**. This will add a separate type layer to the document.

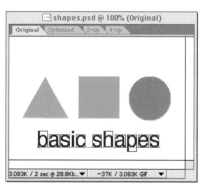
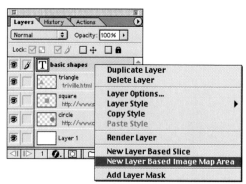

3. **Control+click** (Mac) or **right-click** (Windows) on the **basic shapes** type layer in the **Layers** palette. From the drop-down menu that appears, choose **New Layer Based Image Map Area**. This will apply a layer-based image map with rectangular hot spots to the type.

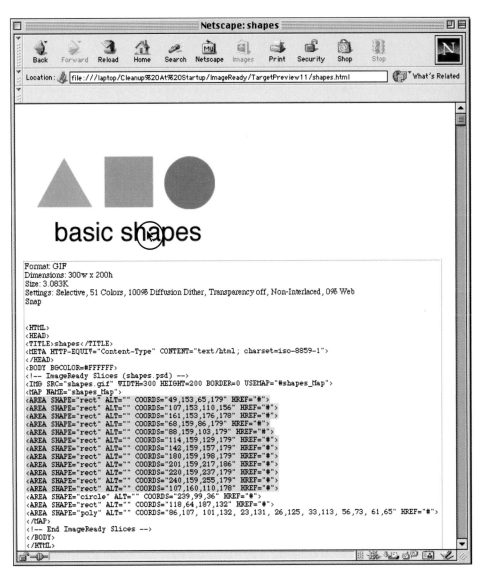

4. Click the **Preview in Default Browser** button in the ImageReady Toolbox. In the browser, move your cursor over the type. Notice that there are some areas of type over which the cursor does not change to a hand, making it difficult to discover just where to click to activate a link.

Notice the many lines of code and image map coordinates that were generated by the layer-based image map. Programmers usually try to avoid creating unnecessarily complex code, which is difficult to read and can contribute to the file size of a Web page.

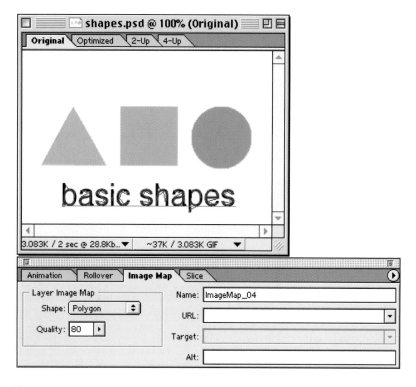

5. Back in ImageReady, with the **basic shapes** type layer still selected in the **Layers** palette, go to the **Image Map** palette, and change the **Shape** field from Rectangle to **Polygon**. Leave the **Quality** setting at its default level for now.

Changing to the Polygon shape will cause the hot spots around the letters to cinch in even tighter to the text. This is not the result you want, as you'll see when you preview in a browser in the next step.

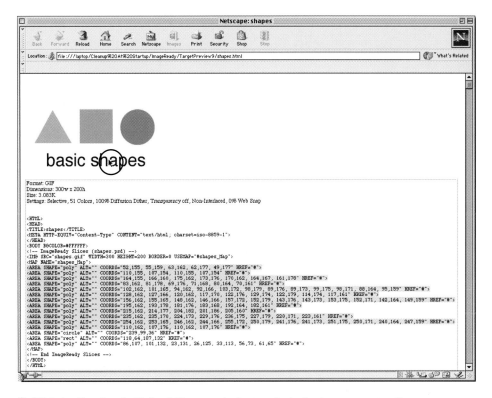

6. Click the **Preview in Default Browser** button again. In the browser, move the mouse over the type. Notice that the hot region for the type is even more difficult to find, and there are even more image map coordinates in the code than when you used rectangular layer-based hot spots (as in Steps 3 and 4 of this exercise).

As the last few steps show, a layer-based image map is not ideal when the underlying art-work consists of complex shapes, like multiple letters on a type layer. The tighter the hot spots fit the letters, the more difficult it can be for a viewer to find the link regions.

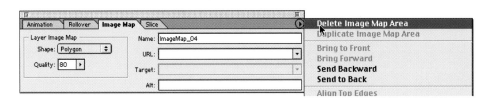

7. In ImageReady, delete the layer-based image map you created by clicking the **arrow** on the right of the **Image Map** palette and choosing **Delete Image Map Area** from the drop-down menu that appears.

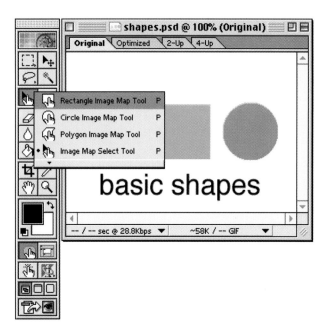

8. Click on the **Image Map Drawing** tool that is displayed in your ImageReady Toolbox, and select the **Rectangle Image Map** tool from the drop-down tools menu. **Note:** If the break-away tools menu is still on your desktop from a previous exercise in this chapter, go ahead and select the Rectangle Image Map tool from that menu.

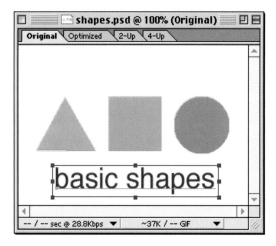

9. Click and drag to draw a rectangular hot spot around the text in the document.

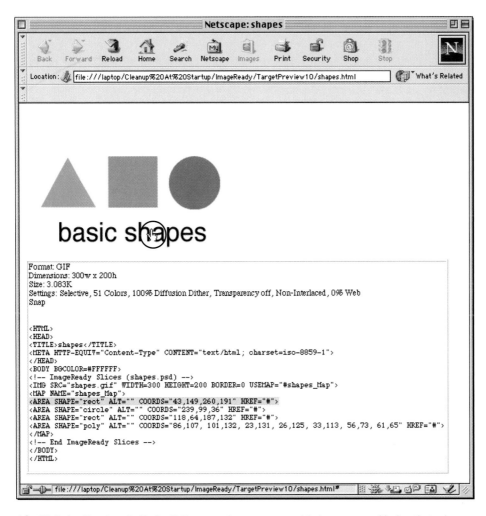

10. Click the **Preview in Default Browser** button to test this image map. Notice that when you move your cursor over the text in the browser window, it is easy to find the hot spot, which is now one contiguous area. Also notice that the code for this tools-based image map is much simpler than the code for the layer-based image maps that you made and previewed earlier in this exercise.

11. Return to ImageReady, select **File > Save**, and leave **shapes.psd** open for the next exercise.

[IR/PS]

4. ────────────**Jumping to Photoshop with an Image Map**

In the introduction to this chapter, we mentioned that Photoshop honors image map information from ImageReady even though it cannot display it. In this exercise you'll see this for yourself.

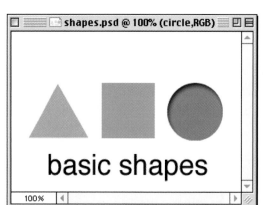

1. With **shapes.psd** open from the last exercise, click the **Jump To** button at the bottom of the ImageReady Toolbox. This will open the same document in Photoshop. In Photoshop, select the **circle** layer in the **Layers** palette, and click the **layer effect** icon (the *f* symbol) at the bottom of the palette. Choose the **Inner Shadow** layer effect from the drop-down menu that appears. In the **Layer Styles** dialog box that opens, click **OK**.

An inner shadow will appear on the circle graphic, and an f-shaped layer effect icon will appear on the circle layer in the Layers palette. But you won't see any of the image map information while the document is open in Photoshop.

2. Click the **Jump To** button at the bottom of the Photoshop Toolbox to reopen the modified document in ImageReady.

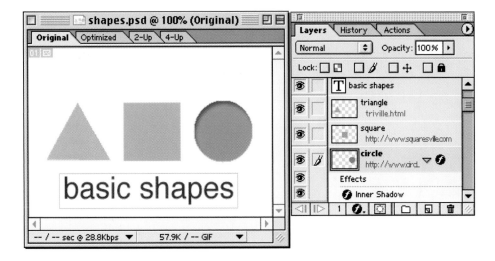

You should now be back in ImageReady, and the changes you made to the document in Photoshop should appear. Notice that the image map information that was not visible in Photoshop is still intact inside ImageReady. Told you so! You can edit freely between these two programs, and even though Photoshop does not directly support image maps, they will still be honored.

You can Preview, Save Optimized, and/or Save now by practicing what you've learned in the other exercises in this chapter.

3. Close the file when you're finished, and remain in ImageReady for Chapter 10, "*Slicing.*"

10.
Slicing

What Are Slices?	Slice Types	Slicing and Selecting
Slice Preferences	Optimizing Slices
Previewing and Saving Slices	Slice Options

chap_10

Photoshop 6 / ImageReady 3
H•O•T CD-ROM

Being able to slice a document is new to Photoshop 6. Slicing offers the ability to cut apart a single image into multiple images in order to reassemble them inside an HTML table. You might wonder why anyone would want to do such a thing. For starters, you can optimize different parts of an image with different compression settings and file formats in order to reduce the file size. You'll learn to do that in this chapter. Later chapters will show other uses for slices, such as producing rollovers and animations and setting parts of a sliced document to contain HTML links for graphical buttons.

Slicing is simple and complex at the same time. It's easy to cut apart the image, but managing all the resulting files takes practice and the ability to go under the hood to set HTML preferences. This chapter walks you through a slicing example that will help you learn the nuances of making slices and generating table code from Photoshop. You can create slices in ImageReady as well, and you'll learn how to do so in Chapter 11, "*Rollovers*."

What Are Slices?

Slices are the result of cutting up an image into multiple pieces. A single document is sliced into smaller pieces, and those pieces are reassembled to look like a single image again using an HTML table.

When you create slices in Photoshop and save the optimized file, the program generates multiple images (one for each slice) and HTML table code. The table allows the browser to assemble all the separate images seamlessly so they look like one document again.

```
Netscape: Source of: file:///laptop/Desktop%20Folder/slices/pink.html

<HTML>
<HEAD>
<TITLE>pink</TITLE>
<META HTTP-EQUIV="Content-Type" CONTENT="text/html; charset=iso-8859-1">
</HEAD>
<BODY BGCOLOR=#33CC33>
<!-- ImageReady Slices (pink.psd) -->
<TABLE WIDTH=432 BORDER=0 CELLPADDING=0 CELLSPACING=0>
        <TR>
                <TD>
                        <IMG SRC="images/pink.gif" WIDTH=161 HEIGHT=263></TD>
                <TD>
                        <IMG SRC="images/sky.jpg" WIDTH=271 HEIGHT=263></TD>
        </TR>
</TABLE>
<!-- End ImageReady Slices -->
</BODY>
</HTML>
```

The source code that ImageReady generated once an image was cut apart into slices and viewed in Netscape.

In the following exercises, you'll have Photoshop cut a document into several pieces and reassemble them inside an HTML table. The program's settings will affect how the code is written and how the slices are named and saved.

Slice Types

Once you start to make slices, Photoshop will display clues that show what type of slice each is. **User slices**, which are the slices you draw yourself, have bright blue numbers and icons and are surrounded by solid lines. **Auto slices**, which are the slices that Photoshop generates to fill in all the regions where you haven't drawn a slice, have gray numbers and icons and are bordered by dotted lines. You may have noticed that different slices have different-looking icons. You'll learn about the different kinds of slice icons and what they mean in Chapter 11, "*Rollovers*."

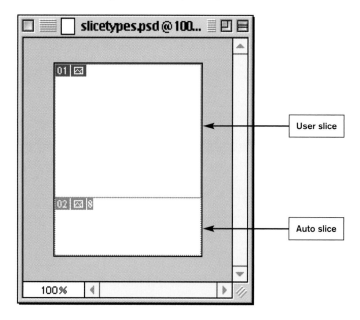

This example shows the different-colored icons and different styles of lines that identify auto slices and user slices.

[PS]

I. —————————Slicing and Selecting

When slicing artwork manually in Photoshop, you will use two tools—**Slice** and **Slice Select**. This first exercise will demonstrate how to slice up an image using these two tools. Why would you cut this image into slices? You'll see how creating different optimization settings for the right and left sides of this image will not only reduce the file size, but will also make the graphics look better. You'll learn to slice in this exercise and to optimize in the next.

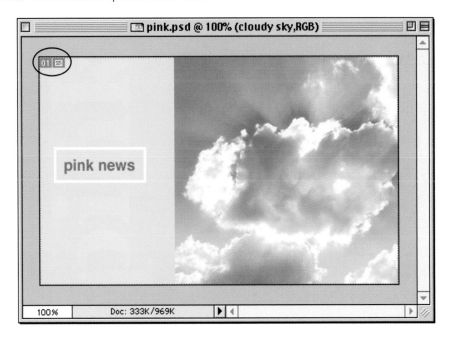

1. In Photoshop, open **pink.psd** from the **chap_10** folder you transferred to your hard drive from the **H•O•T CD-ROM**.

You may see the slice number 01 and a slice icon in the top left corner of the image, because Photoshop automatically treats every newly opened document as if it had one all-inclusive slice. If you don't see the slice number and icon, it's because slice visibility is turned off in your copy of Photoshop. To turn it on, choose View > Show > Slices.

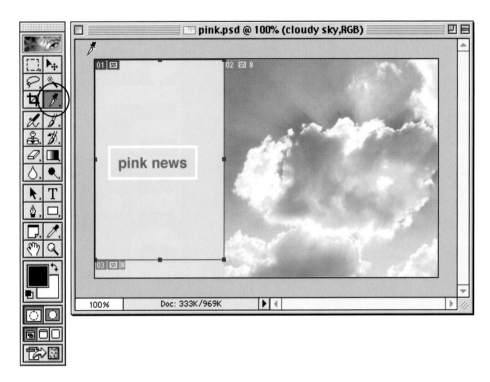

2. Select the **Slice** tool, which is new to Photoshop's Toolbox, and drag a slice around the pink region of the image, stopping short of the bottom to match what you see in the figure above.

Tip: You'll find it easier to draw this slice if you first click and drag the bottom right corner of the document to show the gray area of the canvas. Then you can start drawing this slice from the gray area so that you're sure to include the outside edges of the graphic.

Notice that the slice you drew has been marked with bright blue icons and a solid line, while other slices have appeared without you even defining them. Photoshop creates slices for all the areas the user doesn't define, so that all of the areas are divided into slices. The slices you create (the bright blue slices) are called user slices, and the rest are called auto slices.

*Why are all those slices numbered, you ask? When ImageReady creates the user slices and the auto slices, it keeps track of them by assigning numbers to them. **Important note:** Your numbers might not perfectly match the ones shown here if you do not slice your document identically. If that's the case, you should still be able to do the exercise, but realize that your numbered slices might be different from those we describe.*

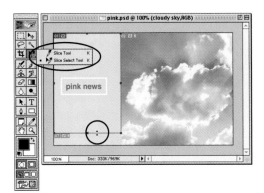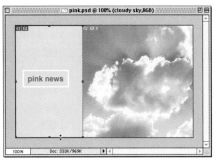

3. In the Toolbox, click and hold the **Slice** tool, and choose the **Slice Select** tool from the pop-up menu that appears. Move your cursor over the bottom border of the slice you just drew (slice 01 in this illustration) until the cursor changes to a double-pointed arrow. Click and drag down to the bottom of the image. Photoshop will adjust the border of slice 01 and will redraw all the slices to look like the illustration on the right.

Slice Select is the tool to use for making all kinds of adjustments to your user slices. With this tool, you can move a slice by clicking inside the slice and dragging. You can delete a slice by clicking inside the slice and pressing the Delete key on your keyboard. You can select multiple slices by Shift+clicking on more than one slice. A common mistake is to try to make these changes using the standard Move tool. Whoops! The Move tool affects the image, but not the slice.

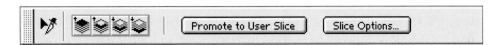

If you want to adjust an auto slice, you first have to change it into a user slice. Using the Slice Select tool, click inside the slice and click the Promote to User Slice button that will appear on the options bar. Then you'll be able to use the Slice Select tool to resize, move, or even delete the slice.

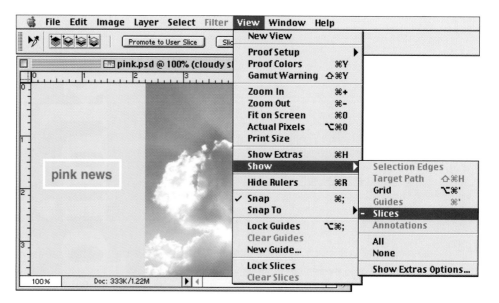

4. You might be wondering if there's a way to turn slices off so you can see the image without the interference of slice borders and icons. You can toggle the preview of slices on and off by choosing **View > Show > Slices**. When you're finished trying this command, leave slices toggled on so you'll be able to see them for the rest of this exercise.

As long as Slices are toggled on in the View > Show menu, another way to turn slice visibility on and off is with the View > Show Extras command, or with the shortcut key Command+H (Mac) or Control+H (Windows). The slice visibility toggles are hard to find in Photoshop 6. In the next chapter, you'll see that it's easier to turn Slices on and off in ImageReady 3, because that program has Show and Hide Slices buttons right in the Toolbox.

5. Save and leave this file open for the next exercise.

NOTE | Slice Preferences

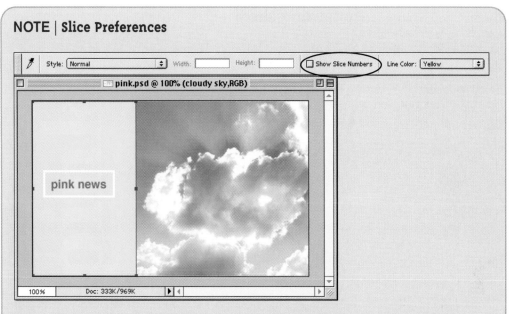

If you want to preview slices without seeing the numbers for each slice, click on the **Slice** tool and uncheck the **Show Slice Numbers** box on the options bar. You can also change the line color of slices and set slices to draw to a fixed size on the Slice tool options bar.

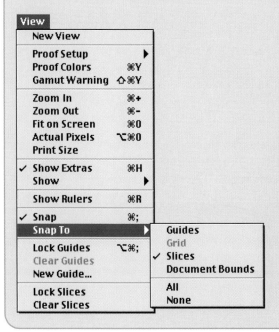

You can also choose to have your slices snap to the edges of other slices. You'll find that this helps align slices and avoid overlap. Turn this feature on and off by choosing **View > Snap To > Slices**.

You might like to have rulers showing as you draw your slices. Choose **View > Show Rulers**, and make sure you set your ruler preferences to pixels if you haven't already done so (**Edit > Preferences > Units and Rulers... > Rulers: Pixels**).

[PS]

2. ———————————Optimizing Slices

One reason to cut apart a document is to optimize different sections appropriately. The image you sliced in the last exercise has areas of solid color that would compress better as GIF, as well as areas of continuous-tone photographic content that would compress better as JPEG. In this exercise, you'll apply different optimization settings to these areas to get the best overall file size and quality. This is where slicing comes in really handy.

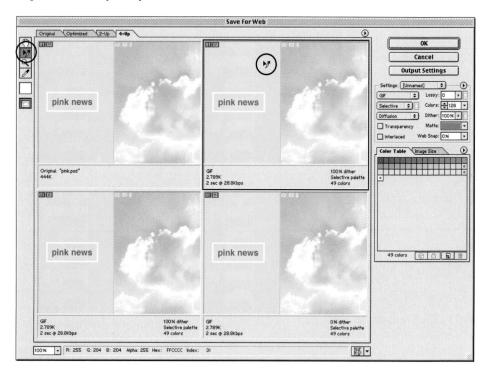

1. With **pink.psd** still open from the last exercise, choose **File > Save for Web…**. In the **Save For Web** dialog box, select the **4-Up** tab. Click on the **Slice Select** tool on the left of the dialog box, and select the **pink news** slice (slice 01) in one of the image previews.

Don't be confused by the fact that there are two Slice Select tools in Photoshop 6. You'll use the one in the main interface to adjust the size and position of slices, as you did in the last exercise. You'll use the one in the Save For Web dialog box to select slices for optimizing, as in this exercise.

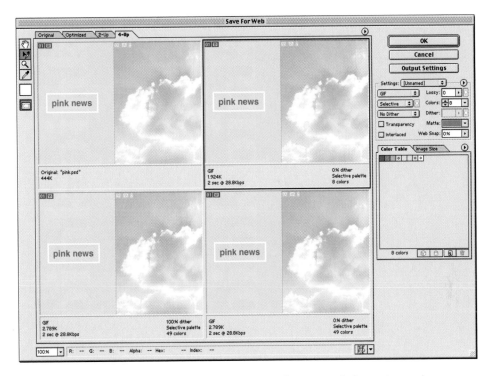

2. Change the **Optimize** settings for the **pink news** slice to match those shown above (**GIF, Selective, Colors: 8, No Dither**). The area of the image covered by this slice is best optimized as a GIF because it's composed of solid colors.

Note: *Notice the readout at the bottom of the preview? It's showing the file size for just this particular optimized slice—1.924K. Your optimization results might differ from ours in the figure above because you might have drawn slices that are different sizes than ours.*

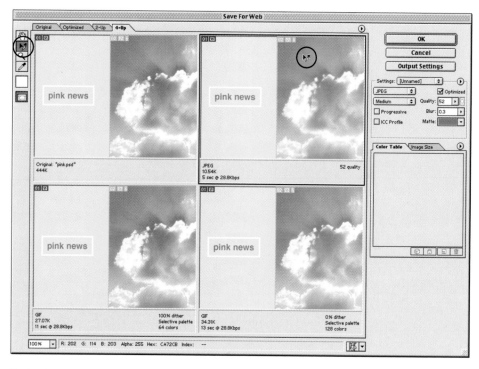

3. Again using the **Slice Select** tool from the **Save For Web** dialog box, select the **sky** slice (slice 02 in the figure above) in your image preview. The area affected by this slice is a continuous-tone photograph, best optimized as a JPEG. Change the settings for this slice to those you see above (**JPEG, Quality: 52, Blur: 0.3**).

Notice that these settings reduce the sky area of the image to around 10.54K. (Your number may be different if you drew your slices differently than ours.) The optimized file size of the entire document is the total of the two individually optimized slices (which comes to just over 12K). If you had optimized the entire image as either a GIF or a JPEG, the overall file size and quality would not have been as good.

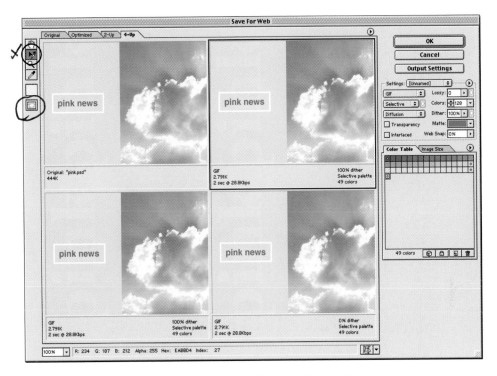

4. Toggle off the **Slices Visibility** button in the **Save For Web** dialog box to check the appearance of the image at the settings you've chosen. We toggle this button frequently so we can double-check optimization settings, because when slice visibility is on, auto slices (like the sky slice in this image) appear slightly discolored.

You learned in the last exercise that there is no Slice Visibility button in the main Photoshop interface—only hidden menu commands for turning off slice visibility. At least there's a button for this purpose in the Save For Web window to help when you're optimizing slices.

Slicing an image creates foreground images. Next you're going to set a background color for a Web page that matches the pink color in the pink news *slice.*

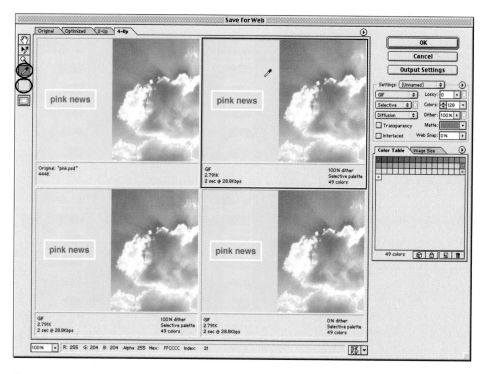

5. Make sure slice visibility is still toggled off, so you can get a clear view of all the colors in the image from which to make your background color choice. Choose the **Eyedropper** tool from the **Save For Web** dialog box, and click on the deep pink color on the left of your image preview. That pink color will appear inside the Eyedropper Color swatch in the Save For Web dialog box. You can toggle slice visibility back on.

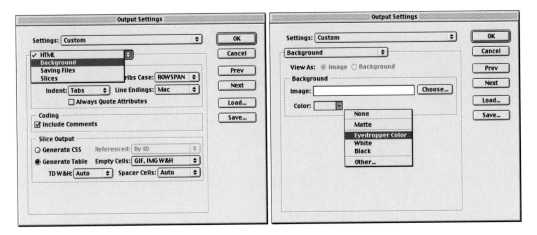

6. Click the **Output Settings** button in the **Save For Web** dialog box. From the second pop-up menu in the **Output Settings** dialog box, choose **Background** to display options for setting the HTML background of a page. Click the black arrow next to the **Color** field, and choose **Eyedropper Color** from that pop-up menu. Click **OK**.

7. Leave this file open in the **Save For Web** dialog box for the next exercise, in which you will learn the nuances of previewing and saving a sliced document in Photoshop.

[PS]

3. ———————————Previewing and Saving Slices

It's not enough to slice and optimize, you've also got to save the slices and the resulting HTML. This next exercise will cover previewing and saving.

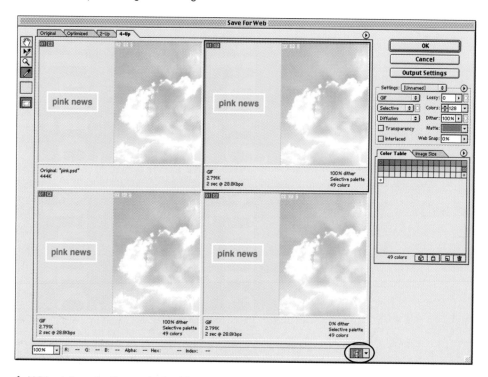

1. With **pink.psd** still open in the Photoshop **Save For Web** dialog box from the last exercise, preview what you've done so far by clicking the **Preview in** button at the bottom of the dialog box.

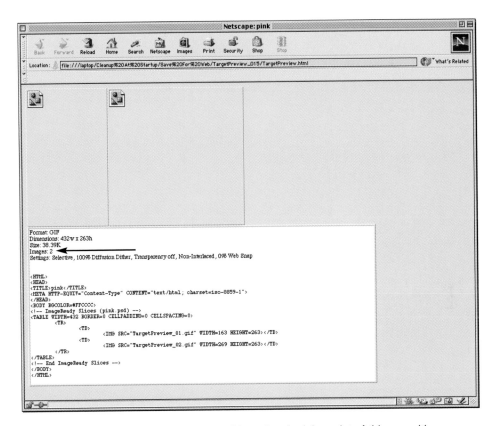

If it takes a while to preview, don't worry. Photoshop is doing a lot of things—writing an HTML table, cutting apart images, and optimizing each one according to your specifications. You couldn't do it any faster yourself if you tried! As the preview loads into the browser, you'll be able to briefly see the slices loading into the HTML table. Once the file is finished loading, the regions of the table should be totally invisible. Notice that the HTML in the preview references two images. These are the result of the two slices you made in the single image you started with.

2. Previewing is a great way to test the slices, but it doesn't save a permanent record of any of the hard work you've done. It's time to do some real saving now. Return to Photoshop's open **Save For Web** dialog box, and click **OK**. This will open the **Save Optimized As** dialog box.

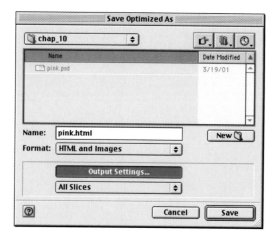

3. Click the **Output Settings** button in the **Save Optimized As** dialog box.

This is another way to get to the Output Settings dialog box. In the last exercise, you opened the same Output Settings dialog box from the Save For Web dialog box.

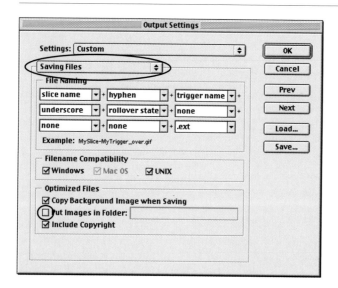

4. From the second pop-up menu in the **Output Settings** dialog box, choose **Saving Files**, and uncheck **Put Images in Folder**, as circled above. This will change the output settings so that the HTML file you save will be stored with your images in one folder. We're suggesting you make this change because you'll be looking closely at how the files get saved in this exercise, and it's easier to see how everything works together if all the files (images and HTML) are in one single folder.

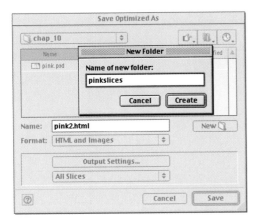

5. Next, it's time to save the actual slices and HTML. Click **OK** in the **Output Settings** dialog box to be returned to the **Save Optimized As** window. Make sure **HTML and Images** is selected in the **Format** field (Mac) or the **Save as Type** field (Windows). It's important to save the results into a separate folder because otherwise it's really messy—files will be scattered about your hard drive!

- **Mac:** Click on the **New Folder** button. Name the new folder **pinkslices**, and click on the **Create** button and then the **Save** button.

- **Windows:** Click on the **yellow folder** icon to make a new folder. Name the folder **pinkslices**, and double-click it so that it opens. Click on the **Save** button, and all the files will populate the new folder you just created.

6. Navigate to your hard drive to open the **pinkslices** folder you just made. You'll see the fruit of Photoshop's labor—a folder filled with two image files and one HTML file. Not bad for a few seconds' work!

Notice that one of the documents is a GIF and one is a JPEG. If you'll recall, you gave Slice 01 a GIF setting and Slice 02 a JPEG setting in the Save For Web dialog box. When you're done admiring your handiwork, return to Photoshop to save a copy of the .psd document with its slices.

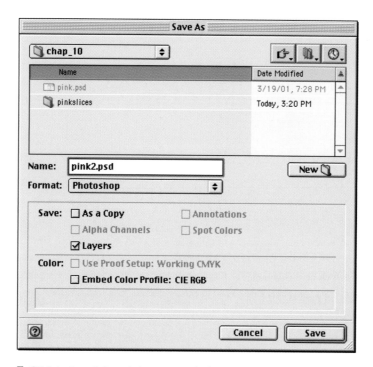

7. Click in the **pink.psd** document window and choose **File > Save As...**. In the **Save As** dialog box, name this copy **pink2.psd**, and click **Save**. Leave **pink2.psd** open for the next exercise.

When you choose Save As... you have the opportunity to make a copy of the .psd document—either by renaming the file, as you did here, or by checking the Save: As a Copy checkbox. Now you'll have two versions of the file—the unsliced version and the sliced version. You don't always want to keep two versions of your .psd documents, but we often do when we make a significant change, in case we want to revert quickly back to the original. It's important to note that Photoshop saves all the slice information when you save a file in the .psd format.

[PS]

4. —————————Using Slice Options

Slice options offer a means to manage the way slices are named when they are saved in Photoshop. In this exercise, you will learn to name and set **alt** text for the critical image files inside a document that contains slices. Alt text is what the end users will see if their images are turned off. As an added bonus in Internet Explorer, a speech balloon appears if you hover over an object that contains alt text.

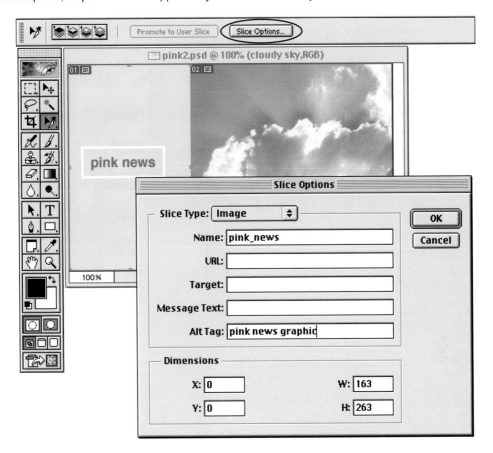

1. The document **pink2.psd** should be open in Photoshop from the last exercise. Choose the **Slice Select** tool from the Toolbox, and select **Slice 01** in the document. Click the **Slice Options** button on the **Options** bar to open the **Slice Options** dialog box.

2. In the **Slice Options** dialog box, change the **Name** of the selected slice from its default, **pink_01**, to **pink_news**.

Tip: It's important not to use any spaces in the name for the file, or you might have problems with broken images once you upload this file to a live Web server. You can use an underscore if you want to simulate a space.

3. Type **pink news graphic** into the **Alt Tag** field, and click **OK**. Notice that you can include spaces in **alt** text.

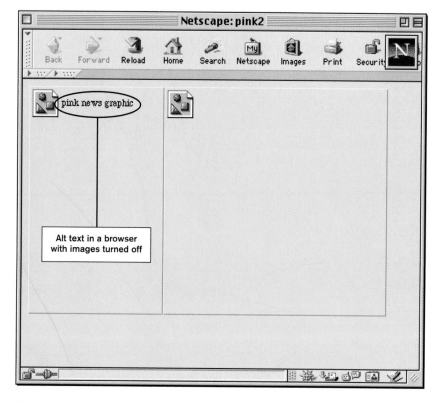

Alt text shows in a browser if the end user turns off images in the browser's Preferences or is accessing a Web page with a text-only browser. Some people turn their images off when they surf the Web to speed up downloading. Sight-impaired visitors to your site might have an automatic reader machine to "read" the alt text to them because they can't see the graphics. Alt text should not be added for every single slice, just for the critical information that would be needed if someone were viewing this page without images.

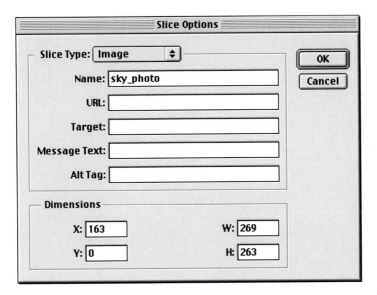

4. Using the **Slice Select** tool, click on **Slice 02**. Click on the **Slice Options** button on the options bar to open the **Slice Options** dialog box. Enter **sky_photo** into the **Name** field. Click **OK**.

If your slice numbers are different than what we've shown here, just enter the correct names into the Name field, and your document will be just fine. You might also want to add an appropriate alt tag for the sky slice. Man, you are now the ultimate slicing machine!

5. Choose **File > Save for Web...**. Your optimization settings should still be there from previous exercises, so just click **OK**.

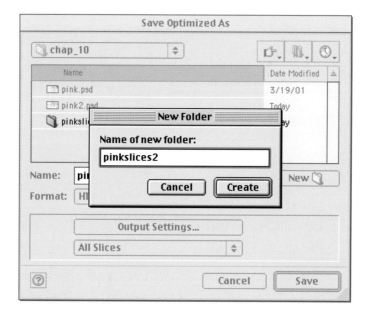

6. In the **Save Optimized As** window that opens, make sure **HTML and Images** is selected in the **Format** field (Mac) or the **Save as type** field (Windows). Make a new folder called **pinkslices2**. Once again, this prevents the files from being scattered about your hard drive.

- **Mac:** Click on the **New Folder** button. Name the new folder **pinkslices2**, and click on the **Create** button and then the **Save** button.

- **Windows:** Click on the yellow folder icon to make a new folder. Name the folder **pinkslices 2**, and double-click it so that it opens. Click on the **Save** button, and all the files will populate the new folder you just created.

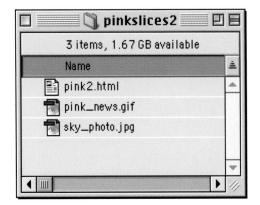

7. Return to your hard drive to look at the contents of the **pinkslices2** folder. This time, the images are named in a way that suggests what they contain, so you don't have to memorize which numbered slice relates to which image.

This chapter is a wrap. Slices were used in this chapter for optimization purposes, but in future chapters you'll get to use them for rollovers and animation. Since Photoshop doesn't offer rollover or animation features, most of your future slicing practice will happen in ImageReady.

II.

Rollovers

| Single Button Rollovers | Rollovers in User-Slices |

| Image Map-Based Rollovers |

| Layer Visibility Rollovers | Multi-Event Remote Rollovers |

| Optimizing Multiple Rollovers | Saving Rollovers |

chap_11

Photoshop 6 / ImageReady 3
H•O•T CD-ROM

A rollover is triggered when an end-user's mouse interacts with an element that has been programmed to change using JavaScript. Normally, you would need to know how to program JavaScript or how to use an HTML editor such as GoLive, Dreamweaver, or FrontPage to create rollovers. What's great is that ImageReady not only lets you create the graphics for rollovers, but it then writes the code for them, so you don't have to learn a line of code if you don't want to.

Although you can work with .psd files that originated from Photoshop, you can't program rollovers in it. ImageReady is the tool of choice for creating rollovers. For this reason, all the exercises in this chapter take place in ImageReady, not Photoshop.

In this chapter, you'll learn how to make remote rollovers, and how to trigger several events with one rollover. You will also have another chance to work with styles, layer effects, and image maps. This is where all the skills you've learned so far culminate in some pretty exciting results. This is a long, meaty chapter. Dig in, and prepare to be challenged (in a good way, of course!).

Slice Symbols

Most of the rollovers you make in this chapter and the next will be based on slices. Photoshop and ImageReady display icons, called **slice symbols**, which identify the type of slice that you've created. Take a minute to familiarize yourself with the various slice symbols and what they mean.

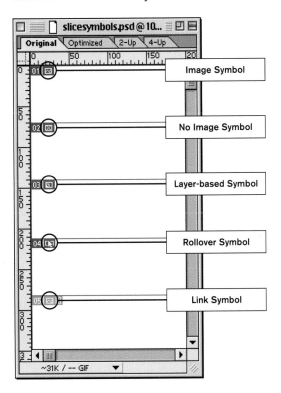

This figure shows all the different slice symbols: An Image symbol identifies a slice that contains a single image; a No Image symbol is for a slice that contains no images at all; a Layer-based symbol is for a slice that is made with the layer-based slicing method (which you'll learn about in Chapter 12, "Layer-Based Rollovers"); a Rollover symbol identifies a slice that contains rollover images; and a Link symbol is for a slice that's linked to other slices for purposes of optimization. You'll run into all of these slice symbols as you work through the exercises in the next two chapters.

Notice that there are no special symbols for user slices and auto slices, which are broad categories of slices. (Remember from Chapter 10, "Slicing," that user slices are those you draw yourself, and auto slices are those Photoshop or ImageReady creates automatically to fill in the gaps.) It's possible to distinguish these categories of slices by the color of the slice numbers and symbols they contain blue for user slices, and gray for auto slices.

[IR]

I. ————————Single-Button Rollover without Slicing

This first exercise will introduce you to the basic principles of making rollovers. Rollovers are defined with what ImageReady calls "states." For example, the **Normal** state is the way the rollover looks before a viewer's mouse moves over the rollover graphic, and the **Over** state is the way it looks while the mouse moves over it. Starting simple, with a single button, you'll learn how to create two rollover states. You'll give the Over state a different appearance from the Normal state by using the **Styles** palette, though you could also use layer effects or different artwork to design the Over state.

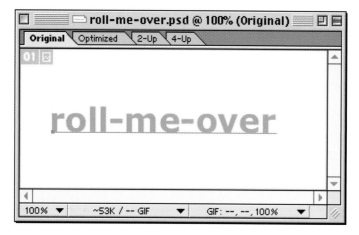

1. Make sure you are in ImageReady. As stated in the introduction to this chapter, it's not possible to program rollovers in Photoshop. Open **roll-me-over.psd** from the **chap_11** folder you transferred to your hard drive from the **H.O.T CD-ROM**.

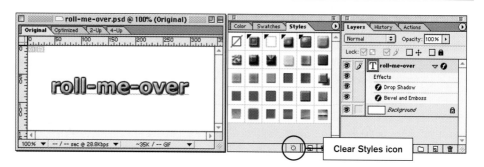

2. Add a style to the **roll-me-over** layer. If the **Styles** and **Layers** palettes aren't open, you will find them under the **Window** menu. Then, select the **roll-me-over** layer in the **Layers** palette, and click on a style in the **Styles** palette.

It doesn't matter which style you choose or whether you customize it. Settle on a look and feel for your rollover's first state (the Normal state) and then move on to the next step. In case you're wondering, in the illustration above we used the Outline Bevel style.

If you're curious about the contents of the style you applied, twirl down the arrow next to the f symbol in the roll-me-over layer to see which layer effects are contained in that style. The style that we used (Outline Bevel) contains Drop Shadow, Bevel, and Emboss layer effects.

***Tip:** If you apply a style and then change your mind about using it, click the clear styles icon at the bottom of the Styles palette, which is a new feature in ImageReady 3.*

3. Choose **Window > Show Rollover** to view the **Rollover** palette. You'll see a thumbnail of the **Normal** state in the palette. Click on the **New Rollover State** icon at the bottom of the palette to create an **Over** state.

When you make a new state in ImageReady, it duplicates the previous state. The Normal state and the Over state thumbnails should look identical in the Rollover palette at this point.

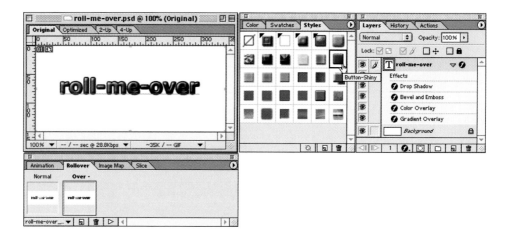

4. Notice that the **Over** state is selected, which you can tell from the thin black outline around that state in the **Rollover** palette. Make sure the **roll-me-over** layer is still selected in the **Layers** palette. Apply a different style than you applied to the Normal state by clicking on a style in the **Styles** palette. (We chose the **Button-Shiny** style for the Over state in this illustration.)

As you do this, you are creating the graphic for the Over state. If you click back and forth between the Normal and the Over states you'll see that ImageReady memorizes which styles you put on each state.

Tip: *There are a couple of other methods for applying a style to a graphic in ImageReady. With the Over state selected, you could drag the style from the Styles palette onto the roll-me-over layer in the Layers palette, or you could drag it from the Styles palette directly onto the roll-me-over artwork in the document. It's more fun to drag a style than to click on it, so try this out! All three techniques work equally well, so you can choose whichever method you prefer.*

5. Click on the **Optimized** tab of the document. Open the **Optimize** palette (**Window > Show Optimize**), and change the settings to whichever type of compression is best for both states of the rollover you just made.

See if you can figure out which is better, GIF or JPEG. Try lowering the number of colors to reduce the file size as a GIF, or lowering the quality or adding some blur to reduce the file size as a JPEG. The object is to make the smallest possible graphic that still looks good, and because we don't know what styles you used, we have no way to instruct you on exactly how to do this. Hey, it's good practice for the real world once you've finished this book! If you need to refresh your memory on how to optimize graphics in ImageReady, revisit Chapter 3, "Optimization."

Note: *Whichever compression method you use will be applied to both states of the rollover. Sadly, you cannot choose different optimization settings for individual rollover states. Sometimes one state would be better compressed as a GIF than as a JPEG or vice versa, but you have to settle on one choice for all states of the rollover.*

Rollover Preview button

6. Click the **Rollover Preview** button in the Toolbox, and move your mouse in and out of the document window to preview both states of the rollover in ImageReady. (Or click back and forth between the **Normal** and **Over** states in the **Rollover** palette.) Check that both states of the rollover look good with the compression settings you chose.

Note: The Rollover Preview button is new to ImageReady 3! It's a nice addition because you used to have to leave ImageReady to preview rollovers in a browser.

7. Click the **Preview in Default Browser** button in the Toolbox. In the browser, move your mouse over the graphic, and you'll see your rollover in action. Scroll down the browser window and check out all the code ImageReady wrote in order to achieve this effect. Impressive, whether or not you know how to write JavaScript!

You'll learn how to save a rollover later in the chapter, and then you won't have the HTML text showing in a white text box in your browser. This is just a by-product of previewing the rollover from ImageReady.

Notice that the graphic changes before your mouse moves directly over it in the browser? That's because the rollover was based on a slice that includes the entire ImageReady document. If you don't define a slice yourself, ImageReady automatically generates one big slice around the entire document and bases any rollover you make on that big slice (because a rollover must always be based on a slice or an image map region). This can cause the sensitive rollover region to be much bigger than the rollover graphic—a problem you'll learn how to solve in the next exercise.

---

8. Return to ImageReady, and leave **roll-me-over.psd** open for the next exercise. Don't save just yet.

Tip: In this exercise, you created different looks for the Normal and Over states of the rollover by applying different styles to each state. Another way to change the look of the artwork between the two states would have been to apply a style to the Normal state and modify that same style in the Over state, by changing some of the layer options settings for the layer effects that make up that style.

[IR]

2. ———————————Slice Before You Rollover!

The last exercise yielded impressive results with little effort. The only criticism might be that the graphic changed before the mouse reached it. To fix this you could trim the ImageReady document to the size of the graphic; but that only works when there is nothing in the document except the single rollover graphic. There is a better solution, which works even when there is more to your document than a single graphic (like a navigation bar of multiple rollover buttons, or an entire page mock-up). You can make a slice around the graphic, and base the rollover on that slice, which is what you'll do in this exercise.

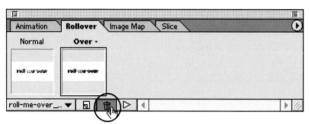
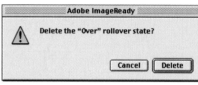

1. Roll-me-over.psd should still be open in ImageReady. Make sure the **Original** tab is selected in the document window. Delete the rollover you made in the last exercise by clicking on the **Over** state in the **Rollover** palette and clicking the **Trash Can** icon at the bottom. At the prompt click **Delete** (Mac) or **Yes** (Windows).

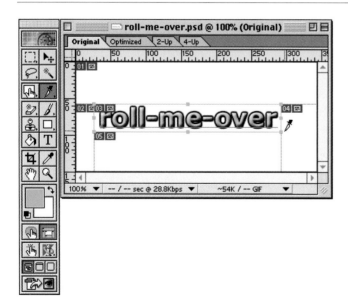

2. Click on the **Slice** tool in the Toolbox, and draw a slice tightly around the artwork.

3. Check that the slice you just drew (the **roll-me-over** slice) is still selected , which is indicated by a yellow border and resizing handles. Click the **New Rollover State** icon in the **Rollover** palette to generate an **Over** state. Again, this process will simply duplicate the Normal state.

If for any reason the roll-me-over slice has become deselected, press on the Slice tool in the Toolbox and choose the Slice Select tool from the pop-up menu. Then click on the roll-me-over slice in the document to select it.

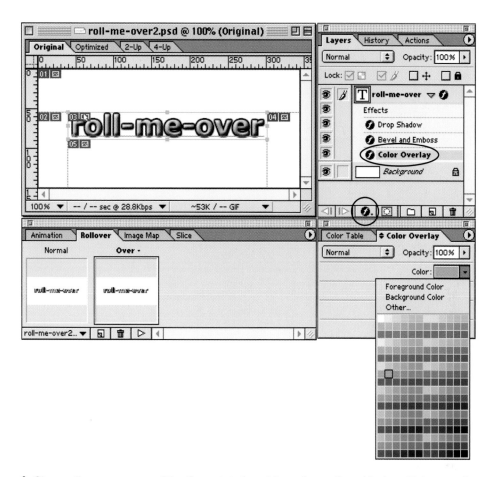

4. Change the appearance of the **Over** state by adding a layer effect this time. Make sure the **Over** state is selected in the **Rollover** palette. In the **Layers** palette, select the **roll-me-over** layer, press the *f* icon at the bottom of the palette, and choose **Color Overlay** from the pop-up menu of layer effects. If you want to change the color of the effect from the default red, select the **Color Overlay** sublayer in the **Layers** palette. In the **Color Overlay** palette that opens, press the arrow next to the **Color** field and click on a color swatch.

Tip: The Color Overlay layer effect is a handy way to change the color of a graphic from one rollover state to another without having to make an entirely new graphic.

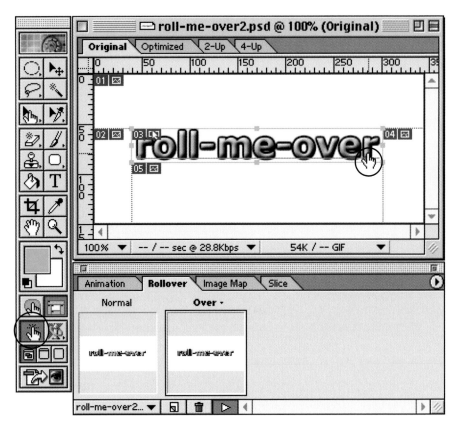

5. Click the **Rollover Preview** button in the Toolbox, and move your mouse into the **roll-me-over** slice in the document window to test the rollover.

Notice that the graphic doesn't change until you move the mouse right into the roll-me-over slice? That's because this rollover is based on the narrow slice you drew, rather than on the entire document like the rollover in the last exercise.

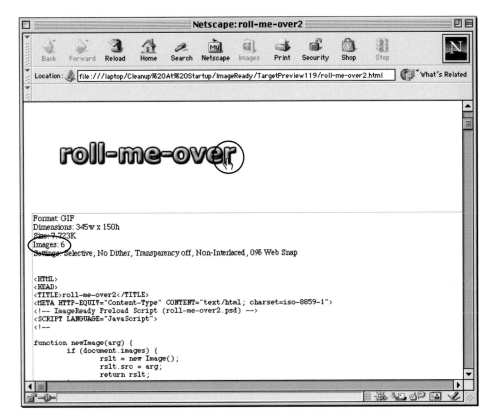

6. Click the **Preview in Default Browser** button, and move your mouse over the graphic in the browser. The color doesn't change until your mouse is right next to the artwork, which is the way you want it to behave! The HTML code in the browser preview gives you some useful information about the rollover. It shows that it took six images to make this rollover from the ImageReady document. ImageReady made one image from each of the two rollover states in the roll-me-over slice, plus one image from each of the four neighboring slices.

7. Return to ImageReady, and close **roll-me-over.psd** without saving.

[IR]

3. —————————————Setting No-Image Slices

Every time you create or modify a user slice, ImageReady is right behind you generating and rearranging auto slices to fill in the gaps of the HTML table it will build. ImageReady will make individual images from each of the user slices and auto slices in a document unless you tell it not to. You can save file size and user download time by designating some slices as **No Image** slices. In this exercise you'll learn how and when to make No Image slices.

1. In ImageReady, open **roll-no-image.psd** from the **Chap_11** folder on your hard drive.

2. Select the **Slice** tool, and draw a slice around the **green** button. If your slice is a little off, take the **Slice Select** tool and resize or move the slice to fit the button.

It doesn't matter which layer is selected when you draw a slice. Slices drill down through all layers of a document.

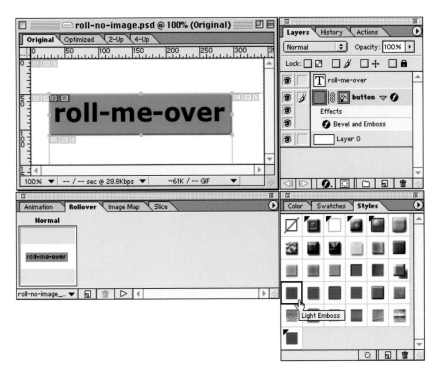

3. Select the **button** layer in the **Layers** palette. Choose **Window > Show Styles**, and click on the **Light Emboss** style in the **Styles** palette to create a pushed up look for the **Normal** state of the button.

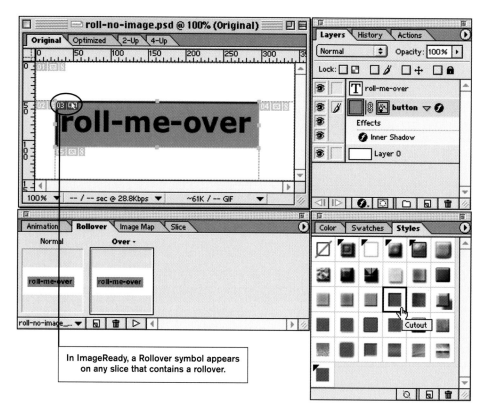

In ImageReady, a Rollover symbol appears on any slice that contains a rollover.

4. Make sure there's a yellow border around the **button** slice, which tells you that slice is selected. (If there isn't, click on that slice with the Slice Select tool.) Click on the **New Rollover State** icon in the **Rollover** palette to create an **Over** state. With the **button** layer still selected in the **Layers** palette, click on the **Cut Out** style in the **Styles** palette to give the **Over** state of the button a pushed down look.

Did you notice that the Slice symbol in the button slice changed from an Image symbol to a Rollover symbol as soon as you added the Over state? This is a visual indicator that ImageReady provides to identify the nature of each slice. It can be helpful to know the significance of this icon, so you can easily recognize when an ImageReady document contains a rollover or multiple rollovers.

5. Notice the **auto slices** (the slices with the gray icons) that ImageReady generated? Select any one of them with the **Slice Select** tool. In the **Optimize** palette (Window > Show Optimize), press the small **arrow** next to the **Matte** field, and choose a **dark color** from the pop-up menu.

The matte color you choose for any of the auto slices will become the page background color in the HTML that ImageReady writes. If you look closely, you'll see that all of the auto slices have a Link symbol. The Link symbol means that these slices are linked for purposes of optimization, so that setting the matte color in the Optimize palette for one auto slice sets the same matte color for all the auto slices.

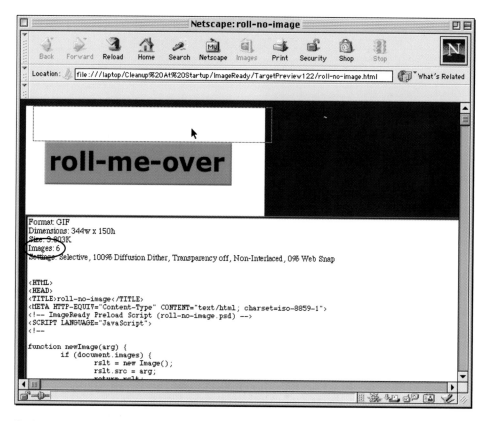

6. Click the **Preview in Default Browser** button. Notice that the page background color is the matte color you chose in the last step.

You may be wondering why there are white areas around the button. These are images made from the auto slices in your document. You can see in the HTML code that ImageReady made a total of six images—two from the rollover states in the button slice and one each from the surrounding auto slices. Because you don't want the white color from the auto slices, and you do want to minimize the number of images your viewer has to download, it's better to create auto slices as No Image slices, as you'll learn to do in the next step.

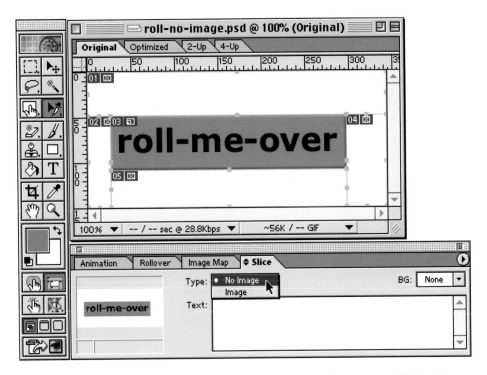

7. Back in ImageReady, choose the **Slice Select** tool. Hold the **Shift** key and click inside each of the auto slices to select them all at once. Choose **Window > Show Slice** to bring the **Slice** palette to the foreground. In the **Slice** palette, choose **No Image** from the **Type** pop-up menu.

This will change all of the auto slices from Image *slices (which is the default for any slice) to* No Image *slices. In the HTML that ImageReady writes, each No Image slice will become an empty table cell held open by a small, transparent GIF (instead of a table cell filled with a large, opaque image).*

Notice that the slices you converted to No Image now have blue, rather than gray slice numbers and slice symbols? That's because they were automatically promoted from auto slices to user slices when you set them to No Image.

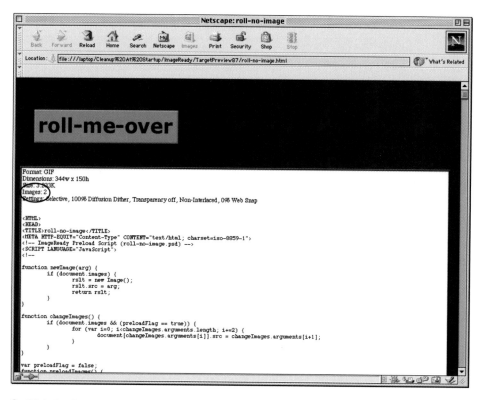

8. Click the **Preview in Default Browser** button. Now you can see straight through to the Web page background, because you've eliminated the solid images around the button.

The HTML code, which you see in the white text box, confirms that you now have only two images (the rollover images made from the button slice). Previously, you had six images before you set the auto slices to No Image (the rollover images plus the surrounding white images).

NOTE | When to Set Slices to No Image

The upshot is that you should consider setting a slice to *No Image* if the slice contains no artwork or color that you want to show up on your Web page. However, if your ImageReady document includes a background pattern, you won't want to use this technique because the pattern will drop out. In general, the more No Image slices you have, the faster your Web page will download and the happier your viewers will be.

---

9. Leave this file open in ImageReady for the next exercise. Don't save it yet. That's what the next exercise is all about.

[IR]

4. —————————Saving a Rollover

Saving a rollover is similar to saving a transparent GIF, and you already know how to do that. The one big difference is that when you save a rollover, you must save not only its images, but its HTML code too. A rollover is nothing more than multiple static images unless it retains the HTML code that contains the JavaScript that makes the rollover work. This exercise will demonstrate that, as well as explain some of the nuances of saving rollovers in the Optimize interface.

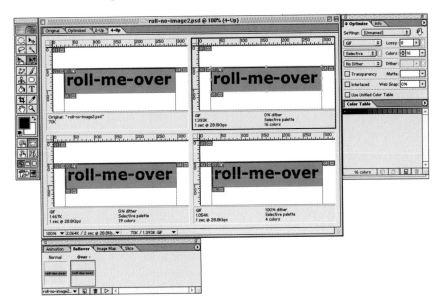

1. The document **roll-no-image.psd** should be open from the last exercise. Before you save, optimize the Image slices. (In this document there's only one Image slice left, because you changed all the other slices to No Image in the last exercise.) Click on the **Optimized, 2-Up,** or **4-Up** tab in the document window, and choose **Window > Show Optimize** to bring the **Optimize** palette forward. Using the **Slice Select** tool, select the **button** slice in any of the document previews. Choose settings in the **Optimize** palette that are similar to those in the illustration above.

You learned in the last exercise that the optimization settings you apply to a rollover slice also apply to the graphics in all states of the rollover. Click back and forth between the Normal and Over states in the Rollover palette to make sure the optimization settings you've chosen look OK in both states of this rollover.

Tip: You'll have a better view of the artwork you're optimizing if you temporarily turn off slice visibility. Click the Toggle Slices Visibility button (or just press the letter Q on your keyboard), which lets you toggle between hiding and showing slices.

2. With the **button** slice selected, bring the **Slice** palette to the foreground (Window > Show Slice), and type **button** in the **Name** field.

As you learned in Chapter 10, "Slicing," It's a good idea to give your image slices meaning-ful names so that you can recognize the resulting images later on when you're building a Web site. If you don't, ImageReady automatically gives each image a name that starts with the prefix of the .psd file from which it was made. This can result in long, unrecognizable file names, particularly when you're making rollover graphics. (See the following section for more information on how ImageReady automatically names rollover graphics.)

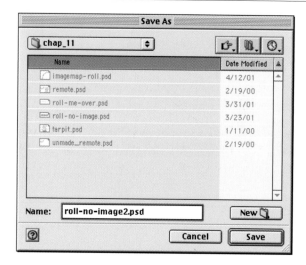

3. Choose **File > Save As...** and name the file **roll-no-image2.psd**. Navigate to the **chap_11** folder that you transferred to your hard drive from the **H·O·T CD-ROM**, and click **Save**.

Saving the modified file as a .psd ensures that you can access the layers and styles settings. You haven't saved this file for the Web yet, but you've saved it as a .psd file, which you'll be happy to have in the event a client asks you to change something or you ever want to edit parts of it again. Files saved in GIF or JPEG format don't store the slices, rollover states, layer and styles information, and other editable items that are stored in the .psd format. It's important to save a master .psd file and the necessary GIFs and JPEGs, in addition to HTML, when you're working on projects, so all your bases are covered.

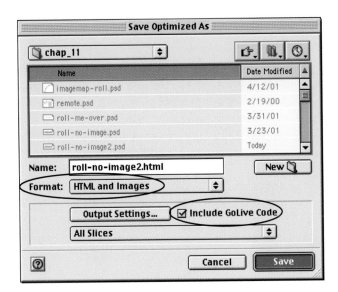

4. Choose **File > Save Optimized As...** and leave the suggested name, **roll-no-image2.html**, in the **Name** field. ImageReady will offer to name it for you that way, because by default the application bases the name of the HTML document it generates on the name of the corresponding .psd file.

If you hadn't named your Image slices, the images also would get saved with roll-no-image2 as part of their names. By default, the images will go into an automatically created new folder called images. Read the following section, "Output Settings for Saving Rollovers," to understand how to eliminate the images folder if you want to.

---

5. Still in the **Save Optimized As** window, make sure that **HTML and Images** is selected in the **Format** (Mac) or **Save as type** (Windows) field. This tells ImageReady to create and save not only the rollover images, but also an HTML file that contains the JavaScript that makes the rollovers function.

---

6. If you plan to use GoLive as your HTML editor, put a checkmark in the **Include GoLive Code** box. If you plan to use Dreamweaver or some other HTML editor, leave this box unchecked.

Either way, the code will work just fine in any browser. It's just that if you check this box, GoLive will recognize the code ImageReady writes as its own, making it possible to copy and paste rollovers that you save out of ImageReady from one HTML page to another in GoLive. There's great information about getting rollovers into an HTML editor in Chapter 15, "Importing/Exporting." Don't skip ahead just yet though. There are important and challenging tasks to complete first ;-).

---

7. Click **Save** in the **Save Optimized As** window.

You may have to wait a second while ImageReady does the following work for you: creates an individual image for each of the rollover states in the button slice, makes a small transparent spacer.gif for the No Image slices, writes an HTML file that contains JavaScript to make the rollover work, and generates a table to hold the images in place.

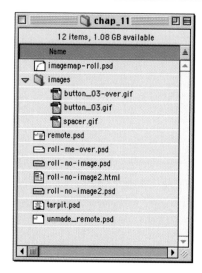

8. To see what ImageReady made for you, go to the **chap_11** folder on your hard drive. You should see a master, editable Photoshop file (**roll-no-image2.psd**), a working HTML document (**roll-no-image2.html**), and an **images** folder with images in Web-ready format (**button.gif**, **button-over.gif**, and **spacer.gif**). Notice that the rollover images carry the name of the slice from which they were made?

The HTML file and associated images could be brought into any HTML editor to be integrated into a Web site, or opened directly in a browser.

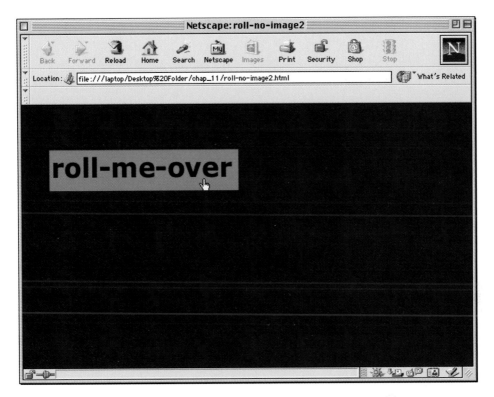

9. Click on **roll-no-image2.html** to open the file in a Web browser. Move your mouse over the graphic to see the rollover work. Congratulations! You've finished making and saving a simple rollover button.

Notice that you don't see the white box of HTML code like you did when you previewed in a browser from ImageReady? Sometimes we use File > Save Optimized As...just so that we can see the rollover in a browser without the white box. If you want to view the HTML code that ImageReady wrote, click View > Page Source (Netscape Navigator) or View > Source (Internet Explorer).

10. Close the file, as you won't need it again for this chapter.

The next section describes the settings for rollovers in much more detail.

Output Settings for Saving Rollovers

When ImageReady writes the code and graphics for a rollover, it uses standard, default settings for how the files are named and formatted. There might be times when you'll want to change the way ImageReady writes the files for a rollover. If so, you will want to visit the Output Settings for saving files. To do this, with a file open, choose **File > Output Settings > Saving Files....** Another way to reach this same dialog box is to click the **Output Settings...** button in the **Save Optimized As** window, and choose **Saving Files** from the second popup menu in the **Output Settings** dialog box.

It's important to realize that naming rollover graphics is a lot trickier than naming a single image. For one thing, as you learned earlier in this chapter, every ImageReady document contains one default slice. Later in this chapter you will learn to make much more complex rollovers that contain many slices. Also, consider that when a rollover is made, two graphics, at minimum, have to be generated— the Normal and Over states. There are all kinds of factors that contribute to naming each image that is saved, including the name of the slice, the name of the rollover state, and the number of the slice that is triggering the rollover event.

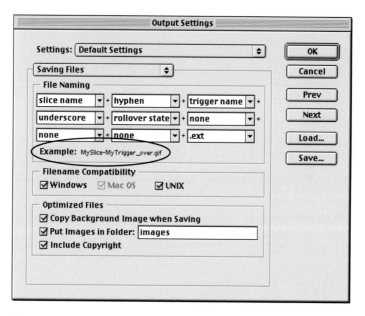

The settings in the Saving Files/Output Settings refer to how ImageReady names the image files made from your rollovers. Notice that each one of the File Naming settings, such as what's currently set to **slice name, hyphen, trigger name, underscore,** etc., is a similar pop-up menu? Some of the pop-up menus are set to none. If we had named a slice and created an Over state for a rollover, the current File Naming settings would create a name like that shown in the **Example** area (circled above)— **MySlice-MyTrigger_over.gif**.

✓	**slice name**
	rollover state **rollover abbr.**
	trigger name **trigger no.**
	doc. name
	slice no. (1, 2, 3 …) **slice no. (01, 02, 03 …)** **slice no. (a, b, c …)** **slice no. (A, B, C …)**
	mmddyy (date) **mmdd (date)** **yyyymmdd (date)** **yymmdd (date)** **yyddmm (date)** **ddmmyy (date)** **ddmm (date)**
	underscore **hyphen** **space**
	none

If you wanted to change the format for ImageReady's automatic file naming, you would change the pop-up menus to choose a different combination of formatting options. These options are explained in a chart below. You can actually click on each item on the pop-up menu to change its setting. This chart should help you understand what these settings mean.

File Naming Options	
Setting	**Description**
slice name	If you have given the slice a name in the *Slice* palette, then each graphic in that slice will be saved with that name, such as *button.gif*, and *button-over.gif*.
rollover state	Each graphic will be saved with the name of its state, such as *button-over.gif*.
rollover abbr.	Each graphic will be saved with the name of its state, but in abbreviated form, such as *button-o.gif*.
trigger name	A remote rollover is triggered by a slice that is different than the slice in which the rollover appears. This choice lists the name that was assigned to that trigger slice in the *Slices* palette.
	continues on next page

File Naming Options *continued*	
Setting	**Description**
trigger no.	Same as above, only the trigger slice number would be used instead of the trigger slice name.
slice no. (I, 2, 3…)	Each graphic will be saved with the number of its slice, such as *button-1.gif.*
slice no. (01, 02, 03…)	Each graphic will be saved with the number of its slice in double digits, such as *button-01.gif.*
slice no. (A, B, C…)	Each graphic will be saved with a slice letter, such as *button-A.gif.*
document entry	The graphics will be saved with the prefix of the original .psd file, such as *roll-me-over2.gif, and roll-me-over2-over.gif.*
mmddyy (date)	The graphics will be saved with the date, starting with the month, day, and then the year, such as *button-110100.gif.*
mmdd (date)	The graphics will be saved with the date, starting with the month and then the day, such as *button-1101.gif.*
yyyymmdd (date)	The graphics will be saved with the date, starting with the year, month, then day, such as *button-20001101.gif.*
yymmdd (date)	The graphics will be saved with the date, starting with the year, then month and day, such as *button-001101.gif.*
yyddmm (date)	The graphics will be saved with the date, starting with the year, then day and month, such as *button-000111.gif.*
ddmmyy (date)	The graphics will be saved with the date, starting with the day, then month and year, such as *button-011100.gif.*
underscore	An underscore will be placed between items before and after this element, such as *button_01.gif.*
hyphen	A hyphen will be placed between items before and after this element, such as *button-01.gif.*
space	A space will be placed between items before and after this element, such as *button 01.gif.* We don't recommend this because it might cause broken links on some Web servers.
none	If you don't want any of the selections available, choose *none.*

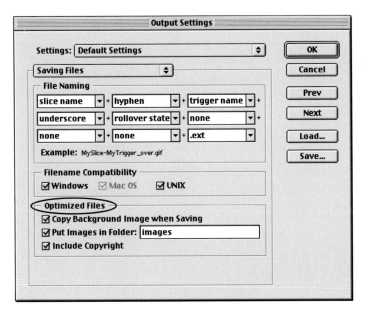

There are several settings in the **Optimized Files** section of the Saving Files/Output Settings dialog box. Their definitions are listed in the chart below. It should help you understand what these settings mean.

File Optimization Options	
Setting	**Description**
Copy background image	If this box is checked and you've specified an external file as a background, that file will be copied to the folder of final images for your rollover graphics.
Put images in subfolder	Because rollovers can often produce numerous image files, it is a good idea to put the images in a subfolder just to keep things organized. You can change the default name of that subfolder, "images," by typing in a name of your choice. If you uncheck this setting, the images and HTML will not be separated.
Embed copyright	This setting will embed a copyright into a comment tag in the HTML.

MOVIE | outputsettings.mov

To learn more about the ImageReady Output Settings for saving rollovers, watch the **outputsettings.mov** located in the **movies** folder on the **H•O•T CD-ROM**.

[IR]

5. ——————————Image Map-Based Rollovers

The rollovers you've made so far have been based on slices. You can usually do a pretty good job of matching the shape of the rollover region to the underlying graphics by defining a slice before you program the rollover, like you did in Exercise 2 earlier in this chapter. However, when you have irregularly-shaped artwork, this technique doesn't always work. A bad fit between a rectangular slice and non-rectangular artwork will cause the rollover to happen before the viewer's mouse reaches the artwork, and if you're making multiple rollovers, it can result in lots of extra slices and complicated HTML tables.

You can fix this problem by using an image map, instead of slices, to contour the shape of the rollover regions to the shape of the artwork. In this exercise, you'll learn to make multiple, image map-based rollovers in a document with irregularly-shaped artwork, and to save the entire image map as a single Web-ready image.

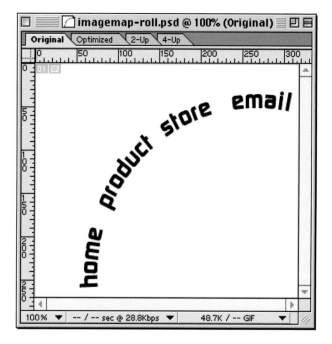

1. Open **imagemap-roll.psd** from **chap_11** on your hard drive.

Note: If you look at the Layers palette, you'll see that each of the graphics in this document was created on a separate layer. This will make it easy to create a separate rollover from each. It's good to plan ahead, putting your important pieces of artwork on separate layers, particularly when you think you'll be making multiple rollovers.

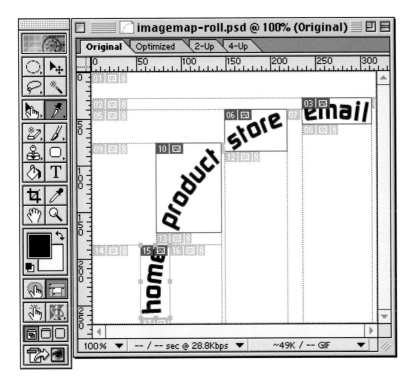

2. Select the **Slice** tool, and draw slices around each of the words **home**, **product**, **store**, and **email.**

Notice that ImageReady had to create lots of auto slices to fill in the gaps around the four user slices you drew? This arrangement of slices will make a pretty complex HTML table.

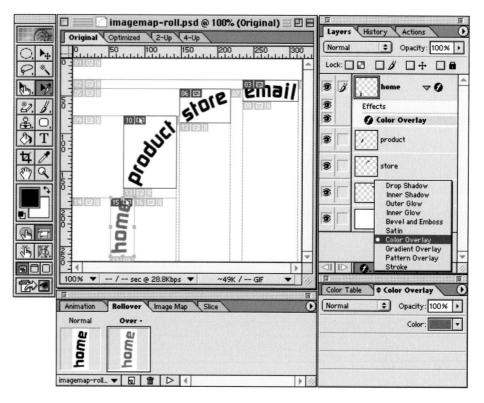

3. Select the **home** slice with the **Slice Select** tool, and create a new **Over** state in the **Rollover** palette. In the **Layers** palette, select the **home** layer, and add a **Color Overlay** layer effect for the **Over** state of the first rollover.

4. Select the **product** slice, and create a new **Over** state. Select the **product** layer, and add a **Color Overlay** effect. Repeat this step with the **store** slice and then the **email** slice, using the corresponding layers.

This will create multiple rollovers, each of which could be linked to a different URL.

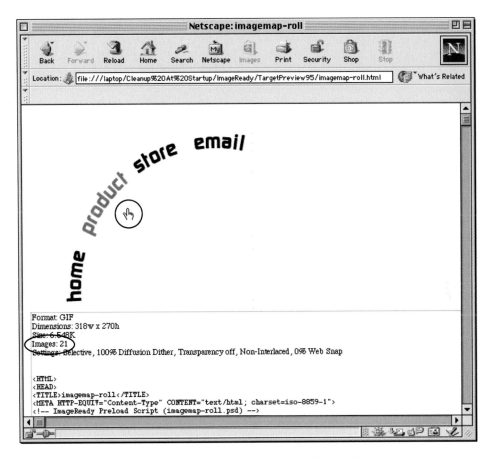

5. Click the **Preview in Default Browser icon** to test the rollovers. Notice that the **product** and **store** graphics change color when the mouse is far away from the corresponding graphic?

Also, see the large number of images (around 21 depending on how you drew your slices) that ImageReady generated to create these simple rollovers? You could reduce the number of images by setting the empty slices to No Image, but there would still be a pretty complex table to download.

6. Return to ImageReady, and delete all the slices, along with the rollovers, by choosing **Slices > Delete All**.

Next, you'll try basing the same rollovers on an image map with multiple hot spots, rather than on slices, to get a better fit between the rollover regions and the underlying artwork.

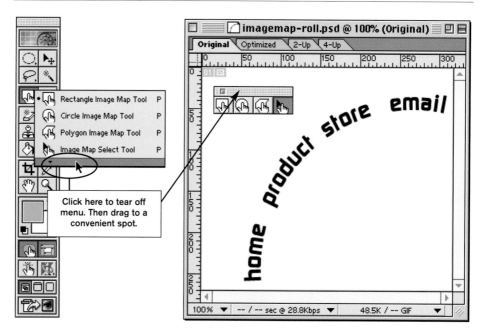

7. Click and hold whichever **Image Map** tool is showing in your Toolbox to see all the **Image Map** drawing tools. Click near the small **black arrow** at the bottom of the pop-up menu to tear off a menu of **Image Map** drawing tools. Click the **title bar** of the tear-off menu, and drag the menu to a convenient spot.

Tip: Any ImageReady tool that has a black arrow at the bottom has a tear-off menu. These are handy because they display related tools and can be placed anywhere on your screen. Photoshop does not have tear-off menus.

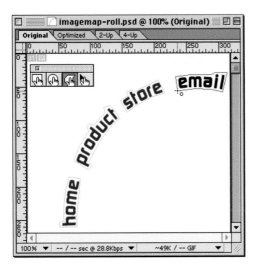

8. Select the **Polygon Image Map** tool from the tear-off menu. Click around the **home** graphic, creating a path with anchor points. Close the path by clicking on the hollow circle that appears when you get back to the first point. Now repeat this step on the **product**, **store**, and **email** graphics to make multiple hot spots.

9. To change the shape of any of the hot spots you've drawn, select the **Image Map Select** tool from the tear-off menu. Click on an anchor point in a hot spot and drag. To delete a hot spot, click on the hot spot with the **Image Map Select** tool, and press the **Delete** key on your keyboard.

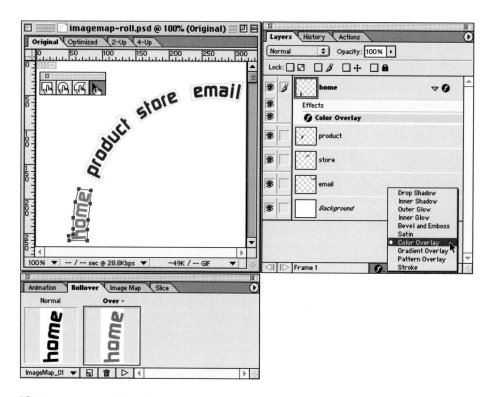

10. Now create a rollover in each of your hot spots. With the **Image Map Select** tool, click on the **home** hot spot. Click the **New Rollover State** icon in the **Rollover** palette. In the **Layers** palette, select the **home** layer, click the *f* icon, and choose **Color Overlay** from the pop-up menu of layer effects. Repeat this step on the **product**, **store**, and **email** graphics to create four separate rollovers.

11. Preview in a **browser** and notice that the hand icon doesn't appear until your cursor is directly over each area that was defined as a hot spot. Told ya an image map would do the trick.

According to the HTML in the browser preview, there are fewer images now (five images) than there were when you based the rollovers on layer-based slices (21 images). That's because each time the mouse moves over any of the hot spots in an image map, the entire document changes, rather than just the part of the image map that's under the hot spot. Sometimes this may result in a larger overall file size when you use an image map than when you use slices, which is a trade-off you should evaluate on a case-by-case basis.

Warning: *In some versions of Internet Explorer, you may find that clicking on a rollover region leaves a blue ring around the hot spot. Don't worry, this is not because you did anything wrong. Unfortunately, it has to do with how Internet Explorer displays image maps. Sad, but true.*

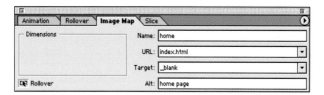

12. Return to ImageReady, and open the **Image Map** palette (Window > Show Image Map). Using the **Image Map Select** tool, select the **home** hot spot, and give it a name in the **Name** field of the **Image Map** palette. This is also where you can insert a link to an external URL (like **http://www.mystore.com**) or to an internal URL (like *index.html*), although you may prefer to do this in your HTML authoring program. Choose **_blank** in the **Target** field if you want the linked-to file to open in a separate browser window. Add some **Alt** text if you like. You can review Chapter 9, "*Image Maps*," for more detailed information about naming files, external versus internal URLs, targeting, and Alt text. Repeat this step on the **product** and **store** hot spots.

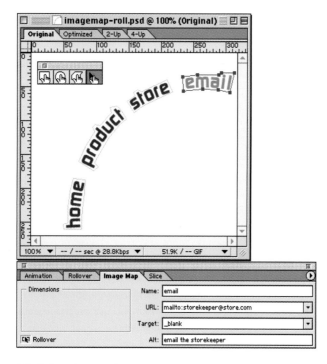

13. Select the **email** hot spot with the **Image Map Select** tool. In the **URL** field of the **Slice** palette, type **mailto: storekeeper@mystore.com** to create a link to an email address. Fill in the other fields as you did for the other rollover graphics.

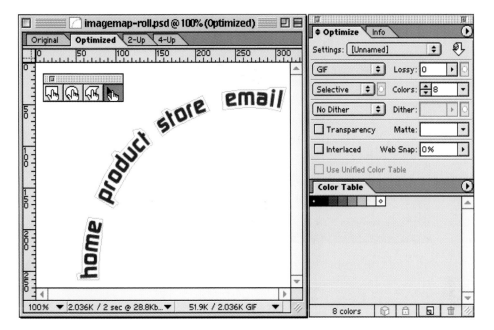

14. Click the **Optimized**, **2-Up**, or **4-Up** tab, and choose optimization settings for the entire document in the **Optimize** palette.

The optimization settings you choose will apply to the whole image map document, includ-ing the rollover states of each hot spot. If you were using slices, rather than an image map as the basis for your rollover, you'd have to optimize each slice (or group of linked slices) separately.

15. Choose **File > Save As...**, and save the .psd file with its image map information as **imagemap-roll2.psd**. Choose **File > Save Optimized As...**, create a new folder in your **chap_11** folder called **imap**, and save the Web-ready versions of the image and the HTML that contains the JavaScript that will make the rollovers work. The procedure for saving rollovers based on an image map is the same as for saving rollovers based on slices. Refer to Exercise 4 if you need a refresher on saving rollovers. Close **imagemap-roll2.psd**.

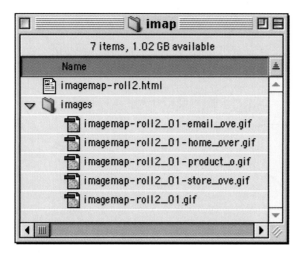

15. Open the **imap** folder you just created on your hard drive. Notice that it contains an HTML file and five image files—one for the Normal state, and one for the Over state of each of the four rollovers.

There are only five image files for these four rollovers because when you base multiple rollovers on an image map, the entire image changes in the Over state.

[IR]

6. ——————Single-Button Rollover with Layer Visibility

You've made all the rollovers in this chapter so far by using styles and layer effects to change the appearance of each state. This next exercise will show you how to create a rollover by showing or hiding layers instead of using styles or layer effects.

1. Open **tarpit.psd** from the **chap_11** folder on your hard drive.

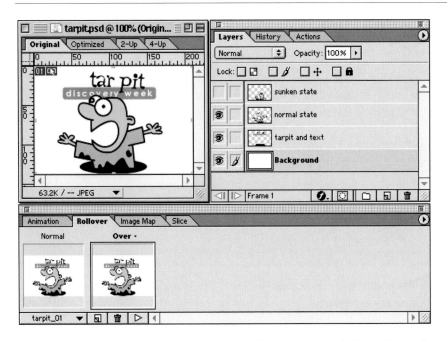

2. Click on the **New Rollover State** icon in the **Rollover** palette to duplicate the previous state.

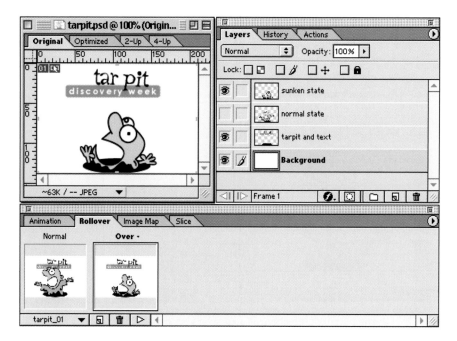

3. With the **Over** state selected in the **Rollover** palette, turn off the **Visibility** Eye icon for the **Normal state** layer and turn on the **Eye** icon for the **Sunken state** layer. Leave the **tarpit and text** layer icon turned on.

Notice how ImageReady has memorized which eye icons were turned on and off for both the Normal and the Over state? Go back and forth between the two in the Rollover palette and you'll see what we mean.

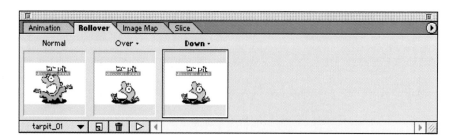

4. Again, click on the **New Rollover State** icon, this time to make a third state that is automatically called **Down**.

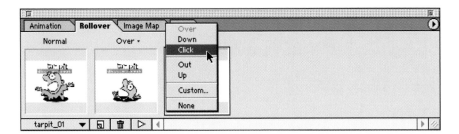

5. Put your mouse over the word **Down** and click to access a pop-up menu. Choose **Click**.

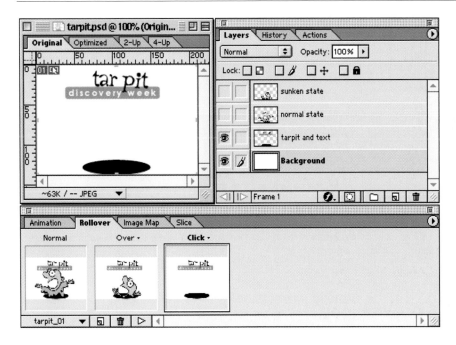

6. Turn off the **Eye** icon for the **sunken state** layer. Only the two bottom layers should be visible.

7. Preview your work in a browser, roll your mouse over the image, and click your mouse on it.

Way to go! You just made a multiple rollover that included a Normal, Over, and Click state. This exercise demonstrated an alternate way to make rollovers—set up the different states on different Photoshop layers and use the Rollover palette to memorize which layers were on or off.

8. Close this file. You can save it if you want. Just follow the steps in Exercise 4, "Saving a Rollover."

What JavaScript States Are Allowed In ImageReady?

When you are specifying a rollover state in ImageReady, you are invoking a JavaScript call. Now that you see there are more than just the Normal and Over states for rollovers, here's a handy chart to describe what the possible states are.

JavaScript Rollover States in ImageReady	
Rollover State	**Definition**
Normal	When the page loads into the browser.
Over	When the mouse enters the slice or image map region.
Down	When the mouse is depressed inside the slice or image map region.
Click	When the mouse is depressed and released inside the slice or image map region. Older versions of Netscape don't support the Down state, so some developers prefer to use Click, which is supported.
Out	When the mouse leaves the slice or image map region. If there is no defined Out state, the document will automatically return to the Normal state.
Up	When the mouse is released inside the slice or image map region. If there is no defined Up state, the slice will return to the Over state when the mouse is released.
Custom	When a custom-programmed event occurs. Available to hand coders who want to write their own JavaScript event to add to the HTML.
None	This is a placeholder for when you want to experiment with different states but don't want to assign a real one yet. It's not supported by browsers.

[IR]

7. ───────────Remote Rollovers

All the ways you've made rollovers so far in this chapter have resulted in one type of rollover, in which an image swaps itself for another image. The next type you'll learn to make is a **remote rollover**, in which multiple pieces of artwork change when the mouse enters a specified region. This exercise is going to combine what you learned in Chapter 10, "*Slicing*," with the layer visibility-based rollovers and style-based rollovers you've learned about in this chapter. Whew—that's a mouthful. You'll soon see, however, that you can put all these strange new terms to use in the process of making a useful and complex remote rollover!

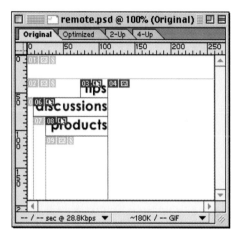

1. Before you get going, it might be nice to visualize what you are about to build. In ImageReady, open **remote.psd**, which we've sliced up for you and filled with pre-programmed rollovers. If you don't see the slices, click the **Toggle Slices Visibility** button in the Toolbox.

2. Preview this file in a browser of your choice. Roll your mouse over the words "**tips**," "**discussions**," and "**products**."

See how each word changes color to red and that additional information appears to the right? This is what we meant when we said that multiple pieces of artwork change at once in a remote rollover. A rollover, in this case, is triggering a change in other slices. This is very impressive!

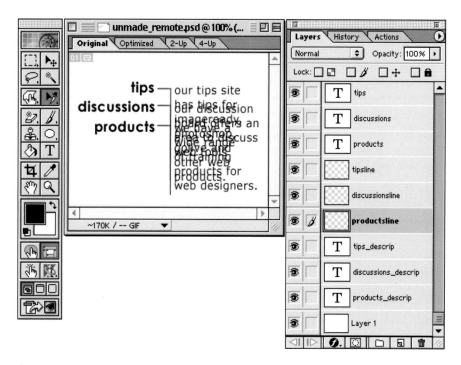

3. Return to ImageReady, close this file, and open **unmade_remote.psd** from the **chap_11** folder you copied to your hard drive. Turn all the **layers** on in the document so you can see what's on all of them at one time. We usually do this so we can see how to slice the artwork properly. **Tip:** You can click one eye icon on, leave your mouse depressed and drag over the rest to turn them all on in a more easy fashion than clicking them individually.

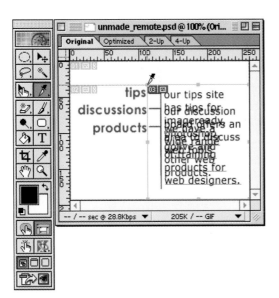

4. Using the **Slice** tool, drag a slice around an area that encompasses all the line and description images.

Tip: If you make a mistake or want to adjust the boundaries of the slice, use the slice select tool, as you learned how to do in Chapter 10, "Slicing."

5. Next, drag slices around the words "**tips**," "**discussions**," and "**products**."

Tip: When working with multiple slices and rollovers, it's very important that you make all your slices before you begin creating the rollovers. That's because it's much harder to change your mind to add a slice later after you've set up rollovers.

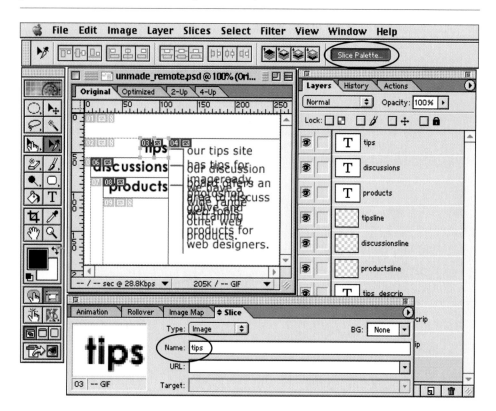

6. Bring the **Slice** palette to the foreground by clicking on the **Slice** tab (or by selecting the Slice Select tool and clicking the **Slice Palette** button on the **Options** bar). With the **Slice Select** tool, click the slice you just created around the word **tips**, and enter **tips** in the **Name** field of the **Slice** palette. Repeat this with each of the slices you created, naming them respectively: **discussions**, **products**, and **descriptions**. As you've learned, naming each region is important so that the resulting files will be named in a recognizable way.

 MOVIE | naming_slices.mov

To learn more about naming slices, check out **naming_slices.mov** from the **movies** folder on the **H•O•T CD-ROM**.

Now that you've named the slices, you're ready to set up the rollovers. The first thing to do is to imagine how this series of images should look in the **Normal** state, before anyone has moved his or her mouse over the words. The object of this exercise is to make these three words–**tips**, **discussions**, and **products**–visible first.

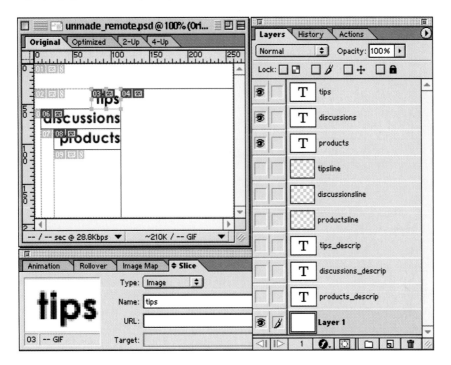

7. Turn off the layers named **tipsline**, **discussionsline**, **productline**, **tips_descrip**, **discussions_descrip**, and **products_descrip**, so that only the words **tips**, **discussions**, and **products**, and the white background on **Layer 1** are visible.

NOTE | Slices and Layers

You might wonder which layer should be selected while you are slicing. It actually does not matter. Slices "drill" through each layer that's turned on in the document. The only time it matters which layer is selected is when you're adding a layer effect or editing a specific layer. You do not need to select a layer to turn its visibility on or to slice through it.

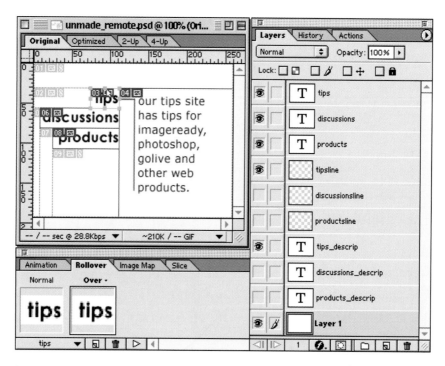

8. With the **Slice Select** tool, select the **tips** slice. Click on the **Rollover** tab, and then click on the **New Rollover State** icon.

9. Turn on the **Eyes** for **tipsline** and **tips_descrip**.

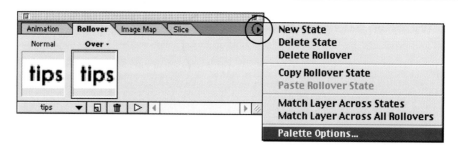

Notice how the Rollover palette doesn't display a big enough preview for you to see the changes that you just made on the Over state? You can change this so you can view the whole document with the pop-up menu.

10. Click the **Rollover** palette's upper-right arrow to select **Palette Options....**

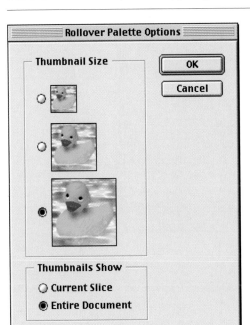

11. In the **Rollover Palette Options** window that opens, click on the **large thumbnail** icon and on the **Entire Document** radio button, then click **OK**.

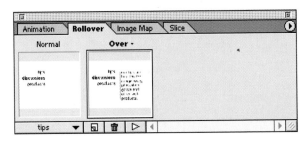

With the Rollover Palette Options set to show the largest icon and the entire document, the Over state offers much better feedback.

Next, you need to change the word "**tips**" so it lights up in red.

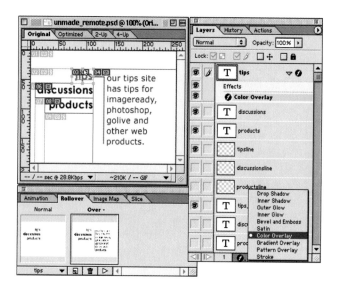

12. Select the **tips** layer in the **Layers** palette. Click on the *f*-shaped **layer effect** icon at the bottom of the palette and select **Color Overlay**. The type will turn red in the Over state but remain black in the Normal state.

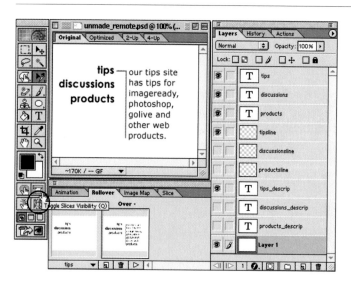

13. If you want to see how things look without the slices showing (which can be very distracting at times) click on the **Toggle Slices Visibility** button at the bottom of the Toolbox, or press your keyboard's letter **Q**. Try clicking on the **Normal** and **Over** states with visibility off so you can more easily see the results of your labor so far.

14. Be sure to click the **Toggle Slices Visibility** button again to turn slices on before the next step, so you can select a new slice and continue programming this remote rollover.

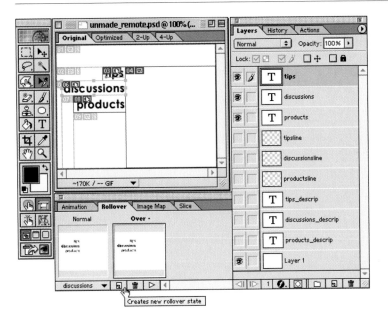

15. Select the slice that contains the word **discussions**. Notice that there is no Over state set yet. Click the **New Rollover State** icon to create an **Over** state for that slice.

Did you notice that when you selected the discussions slice you could no longer see the rollovers you'd added to the tips slice? Click back onto the slice that contains the word tips and you'll see that the work you just did wasn't lost. It was associated with the tips slice, and wasn't visible when you selected the discussions slice because every slice in a document can possess its own distinct set of rollover states. Be sure to reselect the discussions slice before moving on.

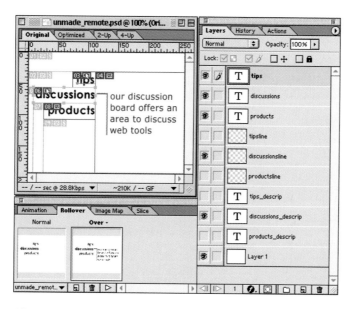

16. Turn on **layer visibility** for the layers **discussionsline** and **discussions_descrip**.

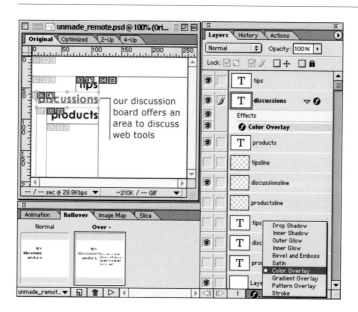

17. In the **Layers** palette, select the **discussions** layer and click on the *f*-shaped **Layer effect** icon to select **Color Overlay** from the pop-up menu. The word **discussions** should turn red in the document window.

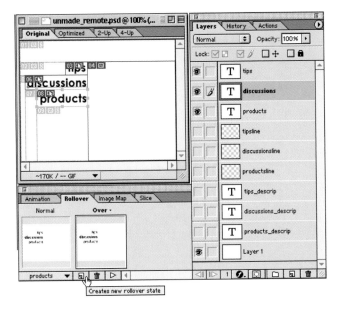

Creates new rollover state

18. Select the **products** slice. Click the **New Rollover state** icon at the bottom of the
Rollover palette to create an **Over** state.

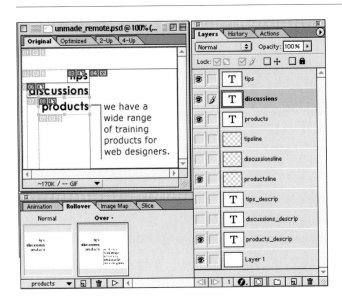

19. Turn on **Visibility** for the layers **productsline** and **products_descrip**.

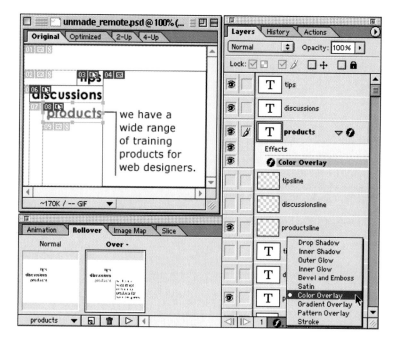

20. Now, select the **products** layer and click on the **Layer effect** icon at the bottom of the **Layers** palette to choose **Color Overlay** from the pop-up menu. The word **products** should turn red in the document window.

---

21. Preview all this work in a browser. Your remote rollover file should function identically to what you previewed at the beginning of this exercise.

Not only did you program a remote rollover, but you combined techniques from other chapters and exercises as well, including layer visibility and layer effects. The slices were key to creating multiple rollovers inside a single document.

 MOVIE | remote_roll.mov

To learn more about making a remote rollover, as shown in this exercise, check out **remote_roll.mov** from the **movies** folder on the **H•O•T CD-ROM**.

---

22. Return to ImageReady and leave this document open. Don't save just yet. You'll learn the nuances of saving this file in the next exercise.

[IR]

8. ——————Saving Complicated Rollovers

You've already learned to save rollovers and sliced documents. The last exercise you completed contained both rollover graphics and slices. Even though you've already learned to save a rollover, this example is more complicated than the first time you did this. It never hurts to review the process, especially when saving rollovers is such a new practice to most Photoshop and ImageReady users.

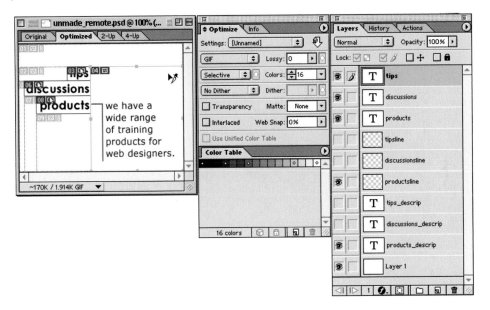

1. Before saving, you'll optimize each slice in the document. With **unmade_remote.psd** still open from the previous exercise, click the **Optimized, 2-Up,** or **4-Up** tab. Using the **Slice Select** tool, click the **descriptions** slice, and turn on the **Visibility** icons for any of the "description" layers and "line" layers (at least one of each) so you can see a sample of what you're optimizing. Choose optimization settings similar to those in the figure above.

The same optimization settings will apply to all of the description and line graphics in all of the rollover states. This is because, as you learned earlier in this chapter, compression settings for rollovers apply to a slice, and not to a particular layer, rollover state, or graphic. You may want to turn the Eye icons on and off next to all of the description and line layers (tips_descrip, discussions_descrip, products_descrip, tipsline, discussionsline, and productsline) in the Layers palette to make sure that all of the description graphics look good at the compression settings you chose. (They ought to, because they were all made the same way.)

You may wonder why we didn't ask you to optimize this slice as a transparent GIF, by checking the Transparency box and setting the matte color for this slice in the Optimize palette. Yes, you could optimize the Image slices in this file as transparent GIFs, but we didn't because they would be more difficult to see in these illustrations and there would be no noticeable file size savings. If, however, you wanted to place this example over a complex background image, you could easily turn all the slices to transparent GIFs.

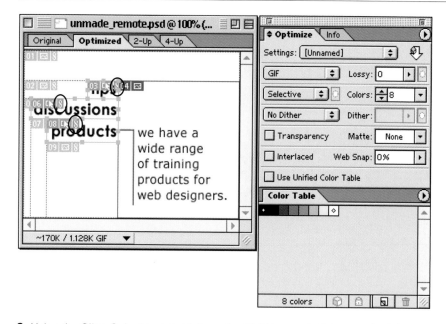

2. Using the **Slice Select** tool, hold down the **Shift** key and click on each of the slices with single words—the **tips** slice, the **discussions** slice, and the **products** slice—to select all of these slices at once. Then choose **Slices > Link Slices**. The color of the slice numbers and symbols in all of the selected slices will change, and a **Link** symbol will appear in each selected slice.

3. Click on any one of the linked slices, and set the **Optimization** controls like those in the figure above. Those same settings will be applied automatically to all of the linked slices.

We chose to link these slices because the graphics are similar in all the slices, and therefore are likely to require the same compression.

You can have more than one group of linked slices in an image. If you were to link another group of slices, they would share slice numbers and symbols of a different color than the first group of linked slices.

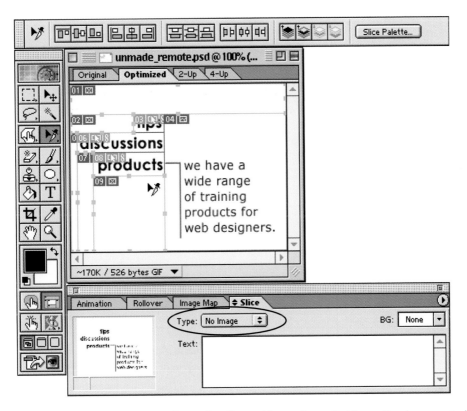

4. Don't forget about the auto slices—the slices with gray icons that ImageReady generated. Using the **Slice Select** tool, click on the **Slice Palette** button on the options bar to bring that palette forward. Hold the **Shift** key while clicking on each of the auto slices to select them all at once. Then press the **Type** button in the **Slice** palette, and change it to **No Image**. This will set all of the auto slices to No Image slices, and promote them to user slices (with blue icons instead of gray).

This approach works best for this file. It's better than optimizing each of the auto slices as full-size GIFs, because that would increase the number of images involved and take a toll on total file size. See Exercise 4 above to review what you've learned about when to set slices to No Image slices.

5. Now that you're done preparing your file, it's time to save it. Choose **File > Save As...** and name this file **remote2.psd**. Navigate to save it in your **chap_11** folder. Saving a .psd master document will allow you to make a change in the future because, as you've learned, only a .psd file can store all the slicing and layer information.

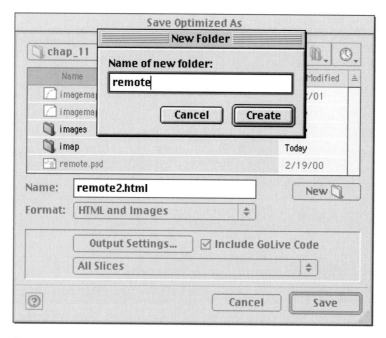

6. Choose **File > Save Optimized As...** and create a new folder called **remote**. On the Mac, click on the **New Folder** icon, name the new folder **remote**, and click **Create**. In Windows, click on the yellow **New Folder** icon and name the new folder **remote**. Then double-click to open the **remote** folder.

7. In the **Save Optimized As** window, make sure **Format** (Mac) or **Save as type** (Windows) is set to **HTML and Images**, put a checkmark next to **Include GoLive Code** if you're a GoLive user, and make sure **All Slices** is chosen. Leave the name as suggested, **remote2.html**, and click **Save**.

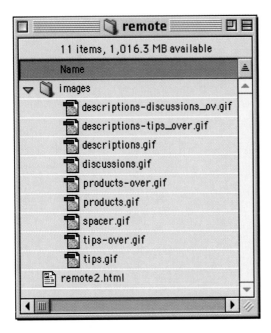

8. Look on your hard drive to ensure that you did actually create a folder called **remote** and that it contains the HTML file and a folder called **images,** full of rollover images with recognizable names.

---

9. Return to ImageReady and close the file.

Are you curious why ImageReady wrote all those separate images and HTML? A rollover, by nature, has to generate an image for every single state and slice. If there is a Normal, Over, and Click state in one slice, ImageReady needs to generate three separate images. The HTML contains the JavaScript that makes the rollover work.

You might wonder why we asked you to make a folder called remote. If you don't make a separate folder, all the pieces of the rollover will still work but if you save it to a folder that already contains files, then the HTML and images will mix in with your other files, making it difficult to keep your files organized.

That's it for this chapter. We suggest you go right on to the next chapter, which builds on what you've learned here, and shows you how to use a couple of terrific new features in ImageReady 3—layer-based slicing and rollover styles.

12.

Layer-Based Rollovers

| Layer-based Rollovers | Rollover Styles |
| Navigation Bar Rollovers |

chap_12

Photoshop 6 / ImageReady 3
H•O•T CD-ROM

Layer-based slicing and rollover styles are
two new features in ImageReady 3. Using
layer-based slicing is very practical when
you're making rollovers, because a layer-
based slice is more "intelligent" than a
manually drawn user slice. A layer-
based slice will automatically move
and resize itself with the artwork
on your rollover states, and it's the
only kind of slicing that supports
rollover styles.

Rollover styles are a great new
way to streamline the production of
rollover buttons. This special kind of
style memorizes and lets you reapply
the rollover JavaScript code as well
as the appearance of all of the states
in a rollover. In this chapter, you'll learn
how and when to use layer-based slicing
and rollover styles, and you'll use these new
features to make a navigation bar of rollover
buttons from scratch. All of the exercises in this
chapter are shown in ImageReady for the simple
reason that ImageReady is the only program in which
you can make rollover styles from layer-based slices.

What is a Layer-Based Slice?

In Chapter 10, "*Slicing*," you learned how to draw user slices manually using the **Slice** tool. In this chapter, you'll learn an alternative method of slicing, layer-based slicing (which is a way of automatically creating a slice based on the size of artwork on a layer). One reason this feature is particularly useful for making rollovers is that a layer-based slice will expand so that it's big enough to cover the artwork in all rollover states. This can minimize the number of images that ImageReady has to make to create a rollover, as you'll learn about in the following exercise.

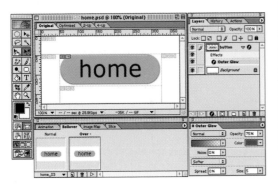
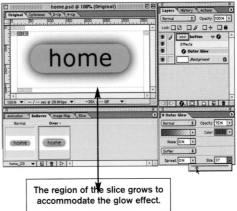

The region of the slice grows to accommodate the glow effect.

When a glow is added to a layer-based slice, the slice automatically expands to include the glow (or any other effect that extends beyond the shape of the original object). This is useful because it creates fewer slices in the resulting HTML, which will download faster for the end user.

[IR]

I. ——————————Creating a Layer-Based Slice with a Rollover

Creating a layer-based slice is fairly simple. This exercise shows you how to create this type of slice, and demonstrates how this "intelligent" slice will grow when the artwork expands or changes.

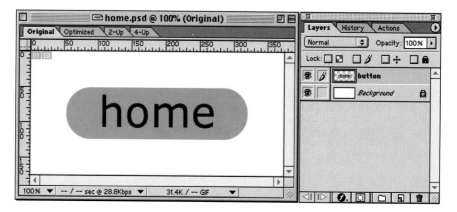

1. Open **home.psd** from the **chap_12** folder you copied from the **H•O•T CD-ROM** to your hard drive.

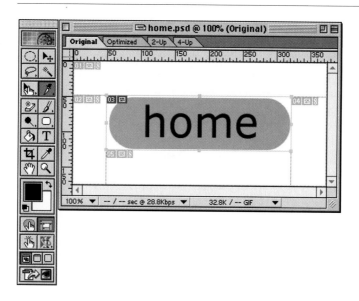

2. Select the **Slice** tool from the Toolbox, and manually draw a slice that fits tight around the button.

If you don't see any slices, click the Toggle Slices Visibility button in the Toolbox.

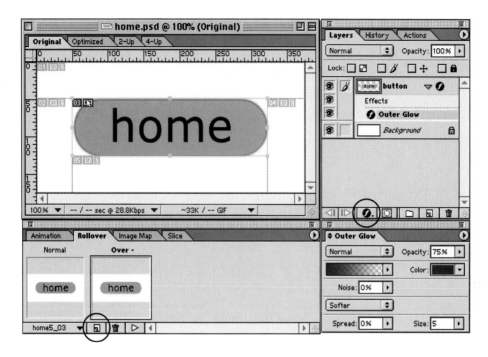

3. Check that there's a yellow border around the **home** slice, indicating that it is selected. (If it isn't, click on it with the Slice Select tool, which you'll find hidden behind the Slice tool.) Click on the **New Rollover State** icon in the **Rollover** palette to create an **Over** state. Select the **button** layer in the **Layers** palette, click the **f** icon at the bottom of the Layers palette, and choose **Outer Glow** from the pop-up menu of **layer effects**. In the **Outer Glow** palette (Window > Show Layer Options/Style), choose a dark color from the **Color** dropdown menu, and change the **Blending Mode** to **Normal** to make the Outer Glow more visible.

You've just added an Outer Glow layer effect to the Over state of the button, using the techniques you learned in Chapter 11, "Rollovers."

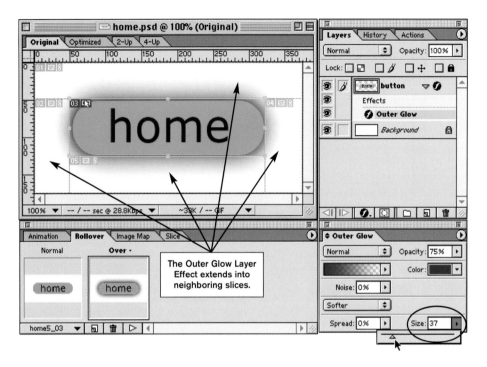

The Outer Glow Layer Effect extends into neighboring slices.

4. In the **Outer Glow** palette, move the **Size** slider to **37**.

*Notice that the enlarged Outer Glow bleeds over the edges of the **home** slice into each of the neighboring slices? You'll see the consequence of this in the next step.*

5. Click the **Preview in Default Browser** button to test your rollover. Take a look at the HTML in the browser preview, which tells you that ImageReady will create **10** images to make this simple rollover.

The reason ImageReady will make so many rollover images is that the Outer Glow extends into five different slices. (ImageReady will make two rollover images for each of those five slices.) If you'd used layer-based, rather than manual slicing, the Outer Glow would be contained inside one slice, so that you'd end up with fewer rollover images for your viewers to download, as you'll see in the following steps.

Tip: *If you see bands in the glow when you preview in a browser, it's because you haven't yet optimized the slices of the document in ImageReady. We suggest that you ignore the banding for now, and continue on with these exercises. If you were to save this document, you would optimize each slice first, as you learned to do in Exercise 8 in Chapter 11, "Rollovers."*

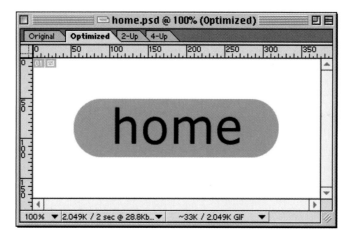

6. Select the **home** slice using the **Slice Select** tool, and press the **Delete** key on your keyboard.

Deleting the home slice will also delete the rollover in that slice and the auto slices, because they were all based on the home slice.

7. Turn off the **Visibility** icon (the eye) on the **Background** layer so that only the **button** layer is visible. The checkerboard pattern tells you that there are transparent pixels on the button layer, which means that you can create a layer-based slice from this layer. Click the **Visibility** icon again to turn the **Background** layer back on.

A layer-based slice can only be made on a layer that contains transparent pixels.

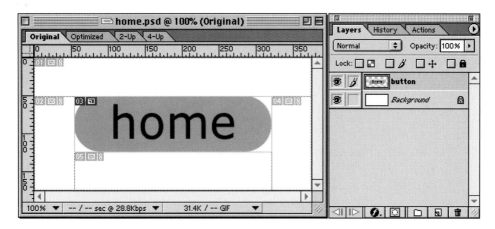

8. Select the **button** layer in the **Layers** palette, and choose **Layer > New Layer Based Slice**.

That's all you have to do to get ImageReady to automatically create a layer-based slice. Notice that the slice cinches in tightly around the pixels of artwork on the layer on which it's based.

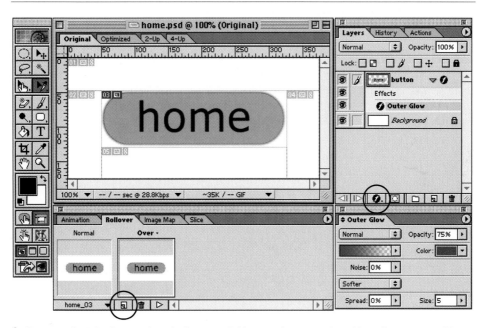

9. Repeat all of the instructions in **Step 3** of this exercise to again add an **Over** state with an **Outer Glow** layer effect to the **home** slice.

Rollovers are always created the same way, regardless of whether the underlying slice is a layer-based slice or a user slice drawn with the Slice tool.

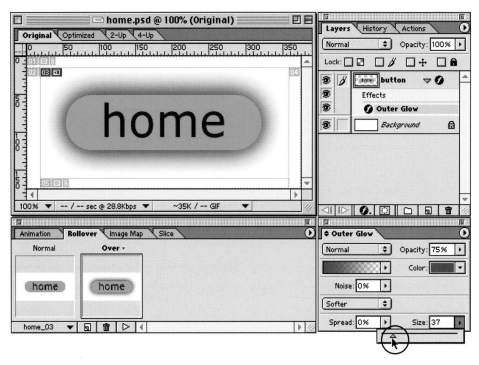

10. Increase the **Size** slider in the **Outer Glow** palette to **37** to make the glow bigger. Notice that as you do, the borders of the **home** slice expand to fit the enlarged glow that's on the Over state.

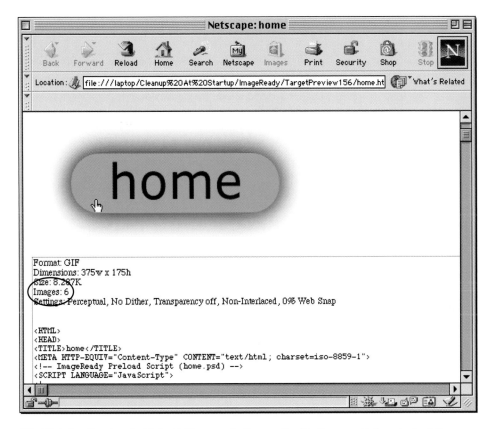

11. Click the **Preview in Default Browser** button on the Toolbox, and take a look at the HTML code in the browser preview. It tells you that this time ImageReady will create only six images to make the same rollover that required ten images when you sliced manually.

This is one of the big advantages of using layer-based slices for rollovers. The ability of a layer-based slice to automatically expand to fit the artwork in all states of a rollover can result in fewer rollover images, which means less download time at the viewers' end.

12. Return to ImageReady, choose **File > Save**, and leave this document open for the next exercise.

[IR]

2. ———————Moving a Rollover in a Layer-Based Slice

Another reason layer-based slicing is useful when you're making rollovers is that a layer-based slice will move with the underlying artwork. This means that you can change the position of your rollover artwork or align it with other graphics without having to reslice the document or reprogram its rollovers.

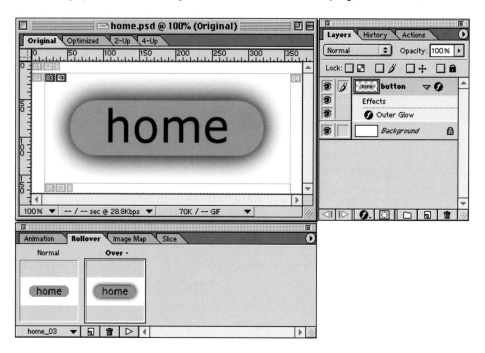

1. With **home.psd** open in ImageReady from the last exercise, make sure that the **button** layer is still selected in the **Layers** palette.

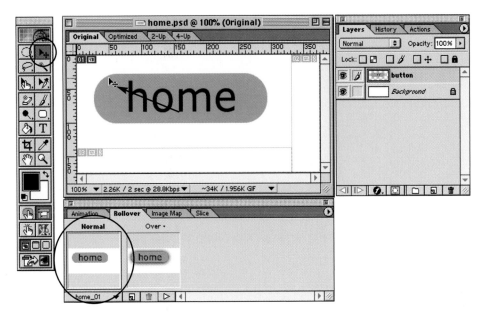

2. Select the **Normal** state of the rollover in the **Rollover** palette. Select the **Move** tool in the Toolbox, click anywhere in the document, and drag to move the artwork on the **button** layer. Did you see that the **home** slice moved with the artwork?

Be sure to use the regular Move tool, not the Slice Select tool, to move the artwork.

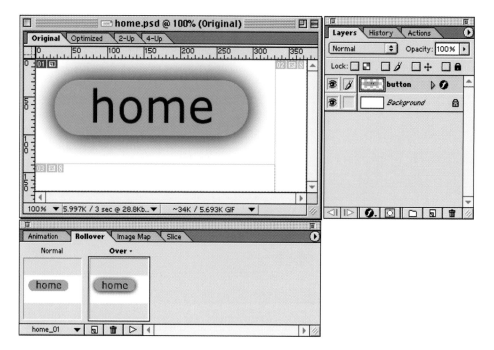

3. Click on the **Over** state in the **Rollover** palette. Notice that the artwork on the Over state moved along with the artwork on the Normal state.

This means that you can move the artwork on all rollover states together, which is an incredibly useful feature!

4. Click the **Preview in Default Browser** button to test the repositioned rollover in a browser. Move your mouse over the button graphic to see that it is in the same position on both states of the rollover. This would not be the case if you used a user slice, because that form of slice doesn't respond to the size or shape of the sliced artwork.

What this means is that you have lots of flexibility to reposition your artwork even after you've created a rollover. You can move all of your rollover graphics together, and you can do so without having to reslice the document and reprogram the rollovers. This only works if your rollover is made in a layer-based slice. It's another important reason that we recommend using the layer-based slicing method when you're slicing for the purpose of making rollovers.

In order to get the artwork on all rollover states to move with a layer-based slice, you must select the Normal state of the rollover before moving any artwork, as you did in Step 2. There may be times when you don't want the artwork on all states to move together. For example, you may want a graphic to appear to be offset when the mouse moves over it in a browser. The next few steps show how to move the artwork on just one state of a layer-based slice.

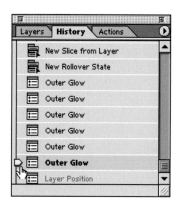

5. Bring the **History** palette to the foreground by clicking its tab or choosing **Window > Show History**. Move the slider up to the history state just above the **Layer Position** state. This will put all of the artwork back as it was before you moved the graphics on the **button** layer.

6. This time select the **Over** state in the **Rollover** palette. Select the **Move** tool from the Toolbox, and click and drag the artwork.

 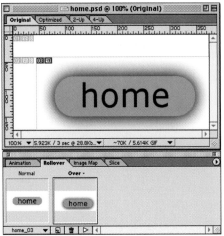

7. Click back and forth between the **Normal** and **Over** states in the **Rollover** palette. Notice that the artwork on the Over state moved with the slice, but the artwork on the Normal state stayed where it was? That's because you did not have the Normal state selected when you made the move.

8. Click the **Preview in Default Browser** button. Move your mouse over the graphic in the browser, and notice that it appears to move.

9. Return to ImageReady, choose **File > Save**, and leave this document open for the next exercise.

[IR]

3. ─────────── Promoting a Layer-Based Slice

What makes layer-based slices special is that they automatically fit the shape of your artwork, and expand and move with the artwork, as you've seen. However, there may be times you'll want to override the automatic behavior of a layer-based slice because you actually want the slice shape to be different than the shape of the artwork. To do that, you'll have to change the nature of the slice from a layer-based slice to a user slice.

1. The file **home.psd** should still be open from the last exercise. Select the **Slice Select** tool, click on one of the borders of the **home** slice and try to drag it. Nothing happens!

One disadvantage of a layer-based slice is that you cannot reshape its borders or move the slice without the underlying artwork, as you can do with a user slice.

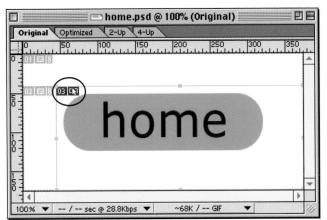

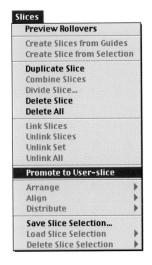

2. Make sure the **home** slice is selected. Then choose **Slices > Promote to User-slice**. Notice that the Slice Symbol in the home slice changed to a regular Rollover symbol, indicating that the slice is no longer layer-based.

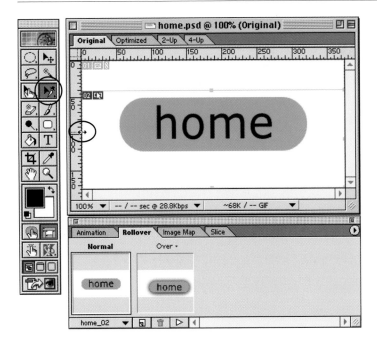

3. Using the **Slice Select** tool, click on the left border of the **home** slice, and drag it all the way to the left of the document.

Now that the home *slice is no longer layer-based, you can adjust it just like a slice you might have drawn with the Slice tool. By changing its size, you've eliminated an extra auto slice, which is a smart move because it minimizes the number of slices viewers have to download, and simplifies the HTML table.*

Keep in mind that once you promote a layer-based slice, it will no longer expand or move with the underlying artwork.

4. You're finally done with **home.psd**. Close it, saving your changes if you like.

Tip: If you were going to use this rollover in a Web site, you would choose File > Save to save the .psd file with its slicing and rollover information. Then you'd optimize each slice in the image, and you'd choose File > Save Optimized As to save the Web-ready images and HTML, all as you learned to do in Chapter 11, "Rollovers."

4. ———————————Creating Navigation Bar Artwork in Layers

Navigation bars are one of the most common uses for rollovers. Because a rollover graphic gives the visitor to your Web site great feedback about which images contain links, its popularity for this purpose is understandable. However, of all the types of rollovers you'll learn to make in ImageReady, this will be the most challenging. In this exercise, you will learn the benefits of naming and duplicating layers for the purpose of building a navigation bar. Later exercises will walk you through the other steps to building a navigation bar with rollovers.

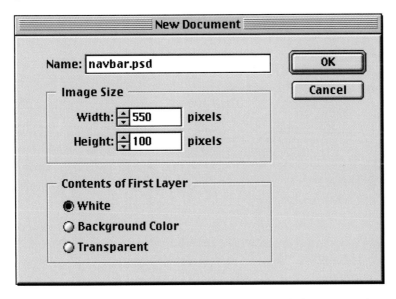

1. Choose **File > New** and create a new document with the same settings and name as you see above. Click **OK**.

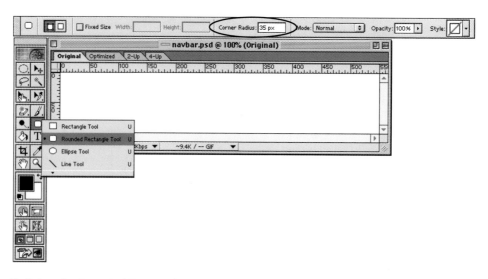

2. Select the **Rounded Rectangle** tool from the ImageReady Toolbox. If you don't see this tool, hold your mouse down on the Rectangle or Ellipse tool to display the fly-out menu of Shape tools, and choose the Rounded Rectangle tool from that menu. In the **Options bar**, type **35** in the **Corner Radius** field. This is going to make a more rounded rectangle shape than the default radius provides.

The Rectangle, Rounded Rectangle, and Ellipse shape tools are perfect for making Web buttons. The Shape tools in ImageReady are similar to those in Photoshop, which you learned about in Chapter 6, "Layer Styles," except that ImageReady has no Polygon or Custom shape tools.

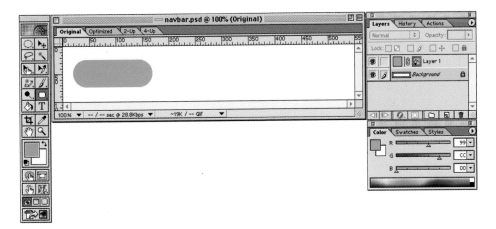

3. Select a **color** of your liking before you draw the shape. As you can see above, the color will be dictated by whatever color is in the foreground color swatch on the Toolbox. If you don't like the color you chose, you can always practice the coloring skills that you built in Chapter 2, *"Web Color."* Drag out a **rounded rectangle** shape in the document window. Make the size similar to what you see on the screen above. **Note:** Don't worry about aligning this shape yet.

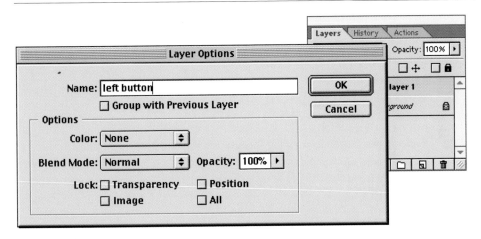

4. Double-click **Layer 1** to rename it **left button** and click **OK. Tip:** When you work with multiple layers, you will find that naming your layers makes it much easier to navigate around the document.

In ImageReady 3 you still name layers by double-clicking on the layer, even though in Photoshop 6 the procedure for naming layers requires a keyboard shortcut (Option+double-click (Mac) or Alt+double-click (Win)).

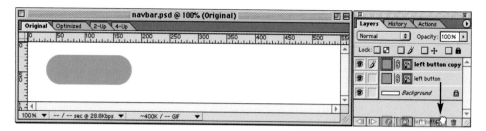

5. Drag the **left button** layer onto the **New Layer** icon at the bottom of the **Layers** palette. This will make a copy.

Note: The copy will only show in the Layers palette. It will not be visible in the document because it is in the exact same location as the original layer from which it was copied. You will move it to a new location in the next step.

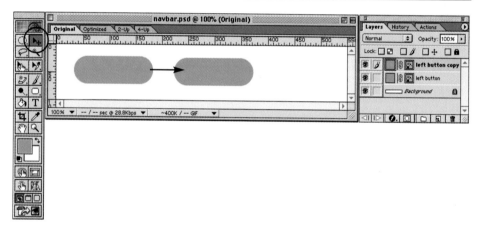

6. Select the **Move** tool from the Toolbox (the shortcut is the letter **V**), and position it over the **button** shape. Click and drag to the right, and you'll see the copy move away from the original. **Note:** You still don't have to worry about alignment. You'll get to that in a future exercise.

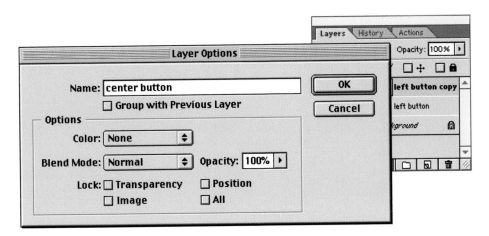

7. Double-click the **left button copy** layer to rename it **center button**.

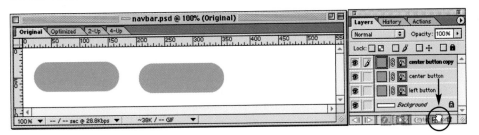

8. Drag the **center button** layer onto the **New Layer** icon at the bottom of the **Layers** palette. This will make a copy, which, again, won't be visible in the document window because it is hidden behind the original from which it was copied—in this case, the **center button** layer.

9. The **Move** tool should still be selected, so just click and drag the second button over to the right. You'll see the **center button copy** appear to the right of the **center button** original.

TIP | Using the Shift Key with the Move Tool

You can constrain the artwork to be moved in a straight line on a parallel path if you use the Shift key when you click and drag with the Move tool.

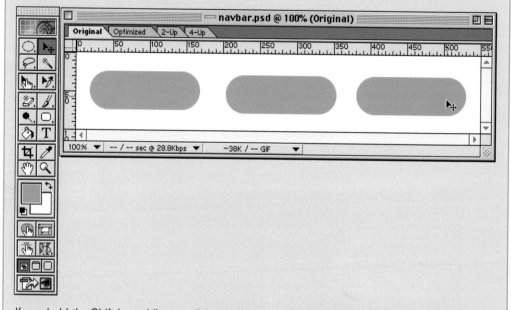

If you hold the Shift key while you click and drag to move the copy, it will be constrained to align horizontally.

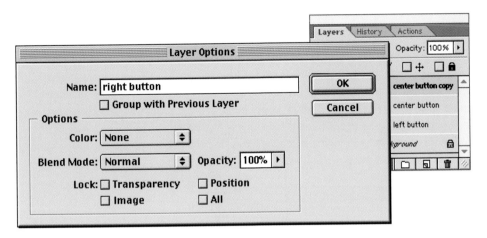

10. Double-click the **center button copy** layer and rename it **right button**.

11. Choose **File > Save**. Leave this document open for the next exercise.

NOTE | Why Duplicate Layers?

When you are making navigation bars, you will most likely want all your buttons to be the same size. You could have dragged out the rounded rectangle shape three times on your screen to make three distinct layers. Instead, this last exercise walked you through the steps of duplicating the layers. You might wonder why.

By duplicating the layers, you ensure that they are the same size. There are other methods to ensure this, such as setting a **Fixed Size** for the **Rounded Rectangle** tool in the Options bar. We prefer the method you learned here, which was to duplicate each layer.

[IR]

5. ——————————Aligning Layers

You learned how to link and align layers in Photoshop back in Chapter 4, "*Layers on Steroids*." This exercise is an opportunity for you to review and practice what you learned there. Learning to align layers is actually a pretty tricky thing. We predict that you might find this exercise frustrating. There's a movie to guide you on this one, (**align_layers.mov**), and you might want to watch it before you start the exercise. It's easier to understand some things if you see them performed than if they're explained with mere words. But before you watch the movie, recall that aligning layers involves learning to use the Link function of the Layers palette.

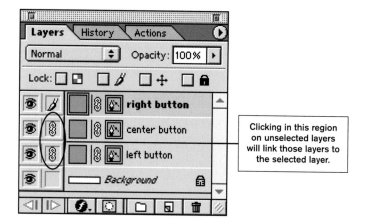

Clicking in this region on unselected layers will link those layers to the selected layer.

1. With the **right button** layer of **navbar.psd** still selected from the end of the last exercise, click inside the **Link** region of the **Layers** palette on the **center button** and **left button** layers. This causes the unselected layers (center button and left button) to be linked to the right button layer. To get 100 percent clear on what we mean, try selecting the Move tool and moving any of these layers on your screen. You'll see that they move together because they are linked.

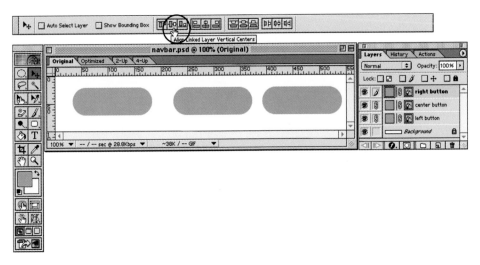

2. With the **Move** tool selected, click the **Align Vertical Centers** button on the **Options** bar (or choose Layer > Align Linked > Vertical Center). You'll see that all the layers align so they are at one horizontal level. One of the benefits to using the Layers palette's Link function is this powerful alignment function.

If you used the Shift key when you moved the buttons in the last exercise, as we suggested, you won't see an effect here because your buttons are already perfectly aligned horizontally.

Now that you've aligned all of the button shapes horizontally, it would be nice to align them so they have equal distance between them, wouldn't it? The following steps show you how.

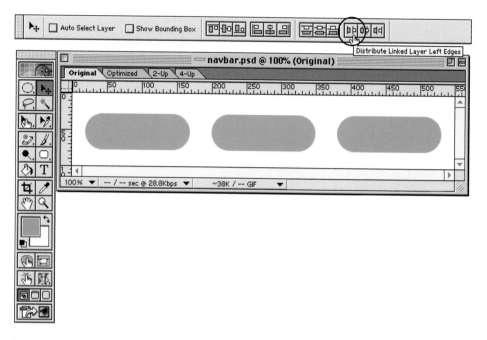

3. With the **Move** tool still selected, click the **Distribute Left Edges** button on the **Options** bar (or choose Layer > Distribute Linked > Left). This will perfectly distribute all the buttons. **Tip:** You can use the Move tool to move the block of three buttons around the screen to put them wherever you want, because they are linked.

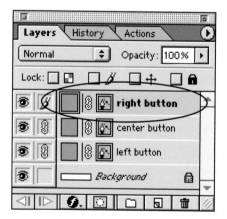

4. Now it's time to add some words for the buttons. Make sure you select the top layer in the **Layers** palette (**right button**) before adding the type. This will ensure that the type you add for the button will be above the other layers, which will become important later for alignment reasons.

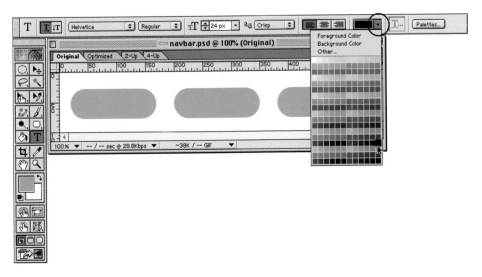

5. Select the **Type** tool from the Toolbox (the shortcut is the letter **T**). Click on the arrow next to the **Color** field on the **Options** bar, and choose a color for the type. (**Hint:** Pick a dark color if your button is a light color and vice versa.)

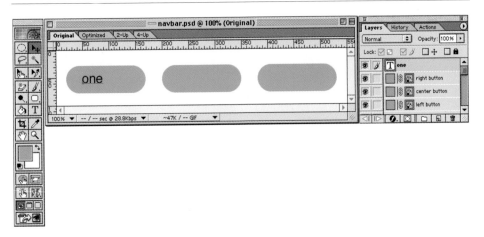

6. Click inside the **left button** graphic and type the word **one**. A new layer labeled **one** should appear at the top of the **Layers** palette. Switch to the **Move** tool, and ImageReady's blue editable text underline will appear under the word **one**. Now the type is selected so that it can be moved. **Note:** Unfortunately, ImageReady puts a blue underline on type when it is selected. You can turn this off by selecting another layer, or with the shortcut Command+H (Mac) or Control+H (Win).

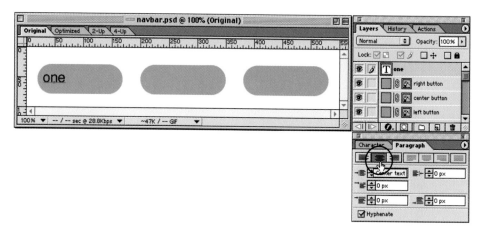

7. Open the **Paragraph** palette (Window > Show Paragraph). Click the **Center Text** button, as circled above. This will likely cause the type on your screen to look offset to the button, but that's OK, because you'll learn to fix that in a minute.

If you look closely, you'll see that clicking the Center Text button in the Paragraph palette moved the small blue anchor point under the word one *to the center of that word. This sets up the centering that you'll do in the next few steps.*

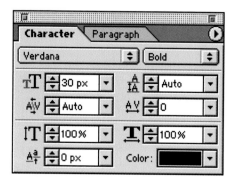

8. Click on the **Character** tab, and pick a different font and font size if you want.

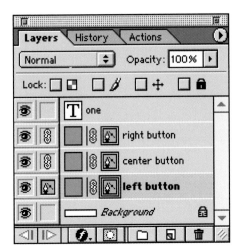

9. Click on the **left button** layer to select it. Notice that it is still linked to the **center button** as well as to the **right button** layers.

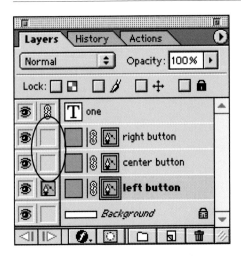

10. Click in the **Link** regions of the **center button** and **right button** layers to turn off those **Link** icons. Click in the **Link** region of the editable type layer named **one**. This links the **one** type layer to the **left button** layer.

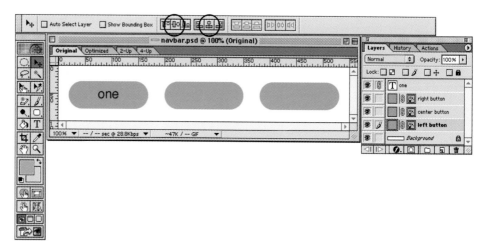

11. With the **Move** tool selected, click the **Align Horizontal Centers** button, and then click the **Align Vertical Centers** button (or choose Layer > Align Linked > Horizontal Center and then choose Layer > Align Linked > Vertical Center). This should perfectly align the **left button** and the word **one** to each other without disturbing the alignment you set in earlier steps.

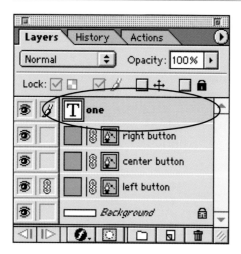

12. Make sure you select the top layer in the **Layers** palette (**one**) before adding more type. This will ensure that the type you add for the other two buttons will be placed at the top of the layer stack.

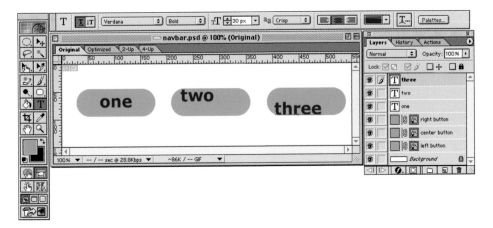

13. With the **Type** tool, click on the **center button** in the document window, and type the word **two**. Click twice on the **right button** in the document window (once to deselect the type you just created and again to type the word **three**).

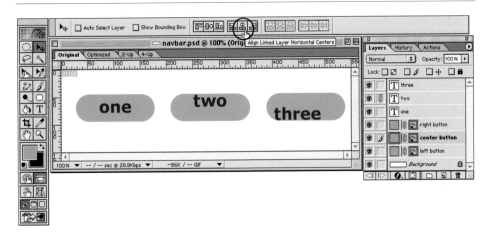

14. In the **Layers** palette select the **center button** layer, and then click on the Link region for type layer **two**. Select the **Move** tool in the Toolbox. In the **Options** bar, click the **Align Horizontal Centers** button.

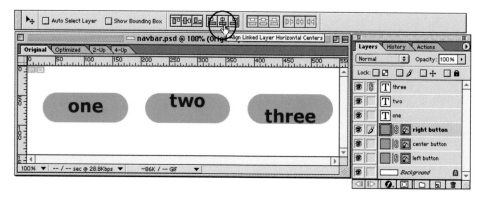

15. Select the **right button** layer, and click on the **Link** region for type layer **three**. Again click the **Align Horizontal Centers** button.

Now each piece of type is centered on its button horizontally (left to right). In the next step you'll align all the pieces of type to each other vertically (by their bottoms).

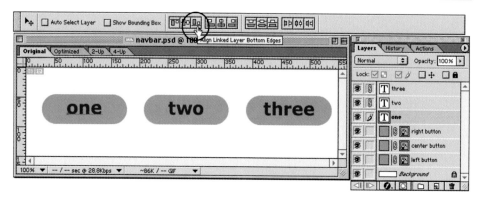

16. Click on the **one** layer in the **Layers** palette. Notice that the **Link** icon on the **left button** layer is still turned on? Click it to turn it off. Then click inside the **Link** regions on the **two** and **three** layers to link those layers to the **one** layer. With the **Move** tool selected, click the **Align Bottom Edges** button on the **Options** bar. Congratulations! It's not easy to align so many different elements.

17. Save the document and leave it open for the next exercise.

MOVIE | align_layers.mov

To learn more about using alignment features, check out **align_layers.mov** from the **movies** folder on the **H•O•T CD-ROM**.

What is a Rollover Style?

Rollover styles are new to ImageReady 3, and are much more powerful than simple styles that you learned about in Chapter 6, "*Layer Styles*." A rollover style contains the settings for multiple states in a rollover graphic, the JavaScript that creates the rollover, and will automatically create a layer-based slice around artwork to which it's applied. You'll learn to apply and create rollover styles in the next exercises.

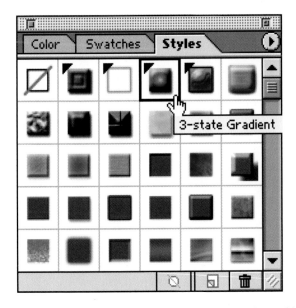

Rollover styles are represented in the Styles palette with a black triangle in the top left corner of the icon.

6. ———————————Using Rollover Styles

Now that you've made the artwork for your navigation bar, your next job is to make each of its buttons into a rollover. This used to require a lot of repetitive work; but ImageReady 3 has a new feature (rollover styles) that makes it quick and easy to produce a whole series of similar-looking rollover buttons. ImageReady ships with a few pre-made rollover styles. This exercise will show you how to apply rollover styles to artwork, and how quick and easy they are for creating a functioning rollover-based navigation bar. When you apply a rollover style, it will automatically create a layer-based slice, create multiple rollover states, apply different styles to each rollover state, and attach the JavaScript code to each button. Don't trust our word; try it out in this exercise. We think you'll be very impressed with this new useful feature!

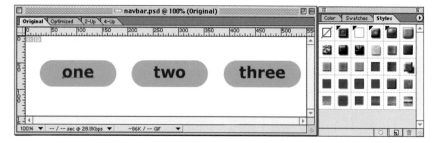

1. The file **navbar.psd** should be open from the last exercise. Bring the **Styles** palette to the foreground, by clicking on its tab or choosing **Window > Show Styles**.

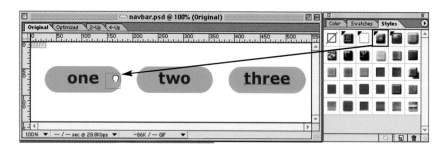

2. Click on one of the pre-built **rollover style** icons (one of the icons with a black triangle) in the **Styles** palette, and drag it directly onto the **left button** graphic in the document window. That's all you have to do to apply a rollover style to any artwork that's isolated on its own layer. It doesn't matter which layer is selected in the Layers palette when you apply a rollover style this way.

Tip: Be careful not to release your mouse too close to the word one *in the graphic, or you'll end up applying the rollover style to that text rather than to the button.*

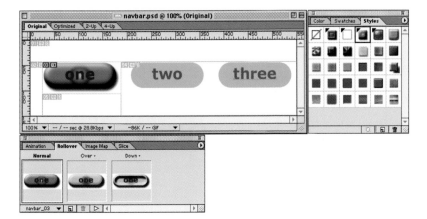

3. Notice that when you dragged the rollover style to the **left button**, ImageReady generated a layer-based slice around that graphic? With that slice selected, open the **Rollover** palette (Window > Show Rollover) and notice that this button now has multiple rollover states, each with a different appearance.

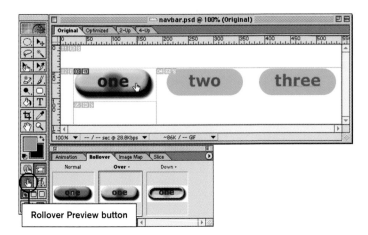

Rollover Preview button

4. To test the rollover, click the **Rollover Preview** button on the Toolbox, move your mouse over the **left button** in the document window, and then hold the mouse down on that button (if the rollover style you picked included a Down state).

The rollover works, because when you apply a rollover style ImageReady automatically writes the necessary JavaScript.

TIP | Changing Your Rollover Palette Views

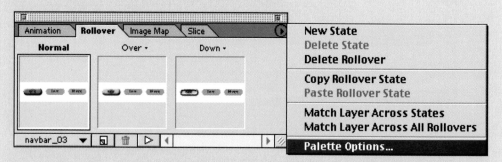

If you did the exercises in the previous chapter, you probably changed your palette settings, in which case all three buttons are visible in each of the states of your **Rollover** palette. For the purposes of this exercise you might want to change your **Rollover** palette settings back to the way they were originally, so that you only see one button per state. To do that, click on the arrow on the top right of the **Rollover** palette, and choose **Palette Options...**

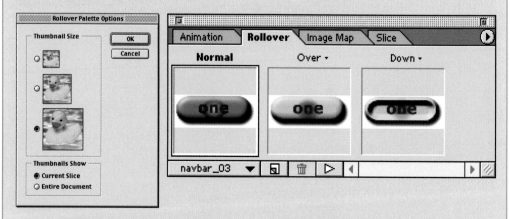

In the **Rollover Palette Options** dialog box, click on **Current Slice**, and then click **OK**. Your **Rollover** palette should now display only the artwork in the slice that's currently selected.

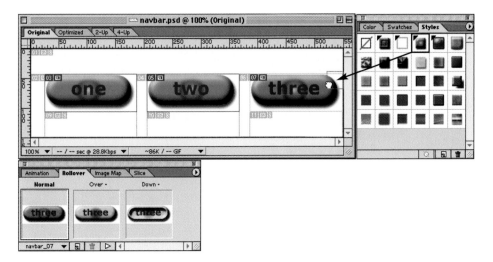

5. Drag the same rollover style you applied to the **left button** from the Styles palette onto the **center button** in the document window. Then drag that rollover style onto the **right button**. Notice that ImageReady created a layer-based slice around each of these buttons, and made each into a rollover with multiple states?

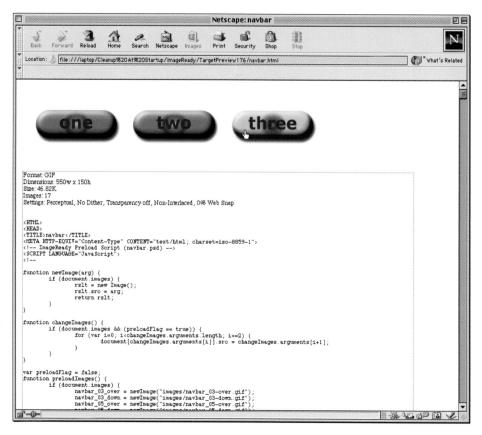

6. Click the **Preview in Default Browser** icon on the Toolbox. In the browser, test your rollovers and take a look at all the JavaScript ImageReady wrote when you applied the rollover style to your buttons. See how easy it is to produce a whole navigation bar of similar rollover buttons using rollover styles? We think this artwork is a little goofy and not terribly practical. That's OK, because you'll get to make your own custom rollover style soon enough!

Tip: If you see bands of color on your buttons in the browser, it's because you haven't yet optimized the button slices. Don't worry about it for purposes of this exercise, because you won't be saving this document for the Web.

7. Return to ImageReady, and close this file without saving the changes.

7. —————————— Creating a Custom Rollover Style

Now that you know what a rollover style is and how easy it is to use, you're ready to create and apply your own custom-designed rollover style. In this exercise, you'll create a rollover style by making a layer-based slice around one of the buttons in your navigation bar, and generating a rollover in that slice using layer effects. You already know how to do all that. The only thing that's new in this exercise is learning how to save the appearance and JavaScript programming of your rollover as a rollover style in the Styles palette. You're going to love how easy this is!

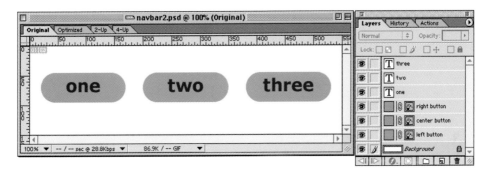

1. Open **navbar2.psd** from the **chap_12** folder you copied to your hard drive.

This document is identical to the file you would have created if you'd followed all of the steps in Exercises 4 and 5. In case you didn't, we made a fresh document for you to work with here.

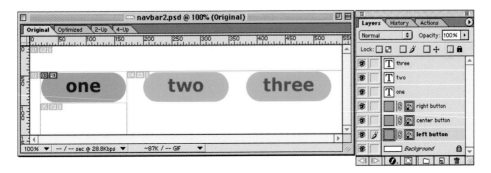

2. Select the **left button** layer in the **Layers** palette. Create a layer-based slice around the **left button** graphic on that layer by choosing **Layer > New Layer Based Slice**.

Note: It's crucial that you use layer-based slicing, rather than the Slice tool, for this step. That's because you're making a rollover style, which can be created only from a layer-based slice.

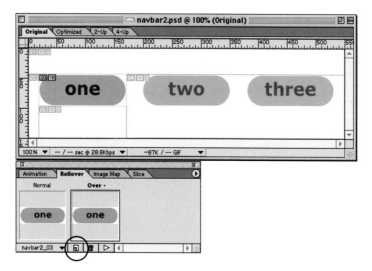

3. Bring the **Rollover** palette to the foreground by clicking its tab or choosing **Window >
Show Rollover**. With the **left button** slice selected, click on the **New Rollover State** icon
at the bottom of the Rollover palette to create an **Over** state for that slice.

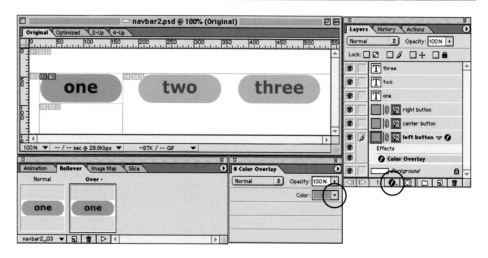

4. Make sure the **left button** slice and the **Over** state are both still selected. Select the **left
button** layer in the **Layers** palette. Click on the *f* icon at the bottom of the Layers palette, and
select Color Overlay from the pop-up menu of layer effects. Change the red default color of
the effect by pressing the arrow next to the **Color** field in the **Color Overlay** palette (Window >
Show Layer Options/Styles) and choosing a new color from the drop-down color palette.

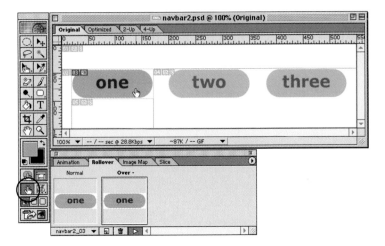

5. Click the **Rollover Preview** button in the Toolbox, and move your mouse over the **left button** to check that the rollover works.

Now comes the new part. In the next few steps you'll create a rollover style that memorizes the appearance of both states of this rollover along with the JavaScript programming that makes the rollover work.

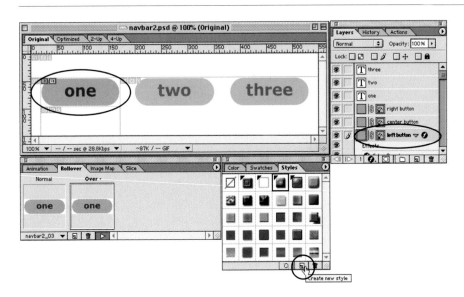

6. Make sure the **left button** slice is still selected. If it's not, click on it with the **Slice Select** tool. Select the **left button** layer in the **Layers** palette. Click the **Create new style** button at the bottom of the **Styles** palette.

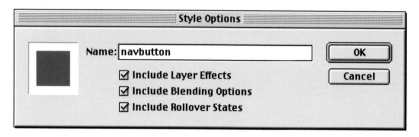

7. In the **Style Options** dialog box that opens, type **navbutton** in the **Name** field. Make sure that there is a checkmark in all three of the checkboxes, and click **OK**. If you don't check **Include Rollover States**, your rollover style will not function.

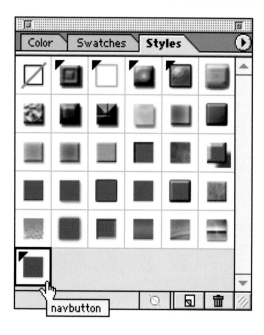

A new rollover style icon will appear in the Styles palette. The black triangle in the upper left corner of the icon indicates that this is a rollover style rather than a regular Style. Move your mouse over the icon to see the name you gave this rollover style (navbutton). This rollover style will show up in your Styles palette even if you close this file or quit the program, and it will remain there until you reset or replace this Styles palette.

8. Save the file, and leave it open for the next exercise.

[IR]

8. ————————Applying Your Rollover Style to Your Buttons

Now you'll see how easy it is to make all the buttons in your navigation bar into rollovers by applying the rollover style you just made to each remaining button. You don't even have to slice the other buttons first, because the rollover style does that job for you.

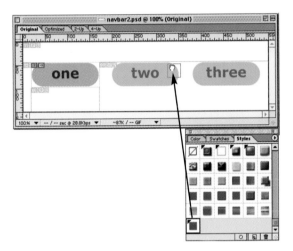

1. Click the **navbutton** rollover style you just made in the **Styles** palette, and drag it onto the **center button** graphic in the document window. Release your mouse anywhere over the **center button**, except on top of the word **two**. **Note:** It doesn't matter which layer is selected in the Layers palette, which slice is selected in the document, or which state is selected in the Rollover palette when you apply a style this way.

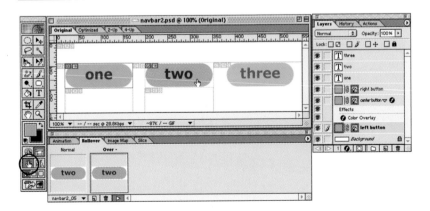

2. Click the **Rollover Preview** button and move your mouse over the **center button** to see the rollover work on this button.

Notice that applying the rollover style created an Over state in the Rollover palette, added a Color Overlay layer effect to the center button layer to change the appearance of the rollover in the Over state, and even created a layer-based slice around the center button graphic. Behind the scenes, ImageReady also wrote the JavaScript that makes this rollover button work. Think of all the work this saved you!

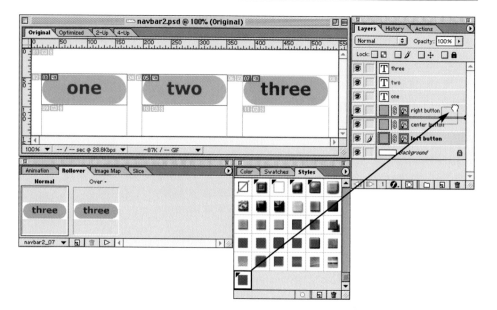

3. Drag the **navbutton** rollover style from the **Styles** palette onto the **right button** layer in the **Layers** palette. This is just an alternative way to apply a rollover style. It caused ImageReady to create a slice around the right button, generate an Over state for the right button, and change the appearance of that button on the Over state.

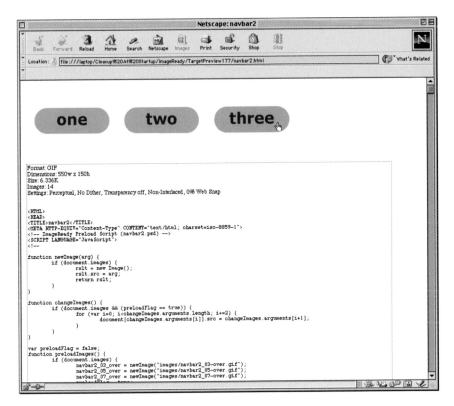

4. Click the **Preview in Browser** button on the Toolbox. In the browser, move your mouse over each of the navigation buttons to see that they all work. Look at all the JavaScript that ImageReady wrote to create these rollover buttons automatically from your rollover style.

MOVIE | multiple_roll.mov

To learn more about making a navigation bar rollover, shown in this last exercise, check out **multiple_roll.mov** from the **movies** folder on the **H•O•T CD-ROM**.

---

5. Return to ImageReady, and choose **File > Save** to save the file with all its slicing and rollover information. Close this file.

If you want to use this navigation bar on a Web page, then follow the instructions in Exercise 8 in Chapter 11, "Rollovers," to optimize each slice and save the rollover images and HTML.

You should be proud; this was a challenging chapter and you made it through alive. ;-)

13.
Animated GIFs

Frame-by-Frame	Setting Speed and Looping
Optimizing and Saving	Transparent Animated GIFs	Tweening
Reversing and Looping Frames	Animated GIF Rollovers
Designing Entire Interfaces

---

chap_13

Photoshop 6 / ImageReady 3
H•O•T CD-ROM

One of the coolest things about authoring for the Web is that you can include animation, which is something that print publishing obviously can't offer. It's likely that this is the first design medium you've ever worked in that supports animation, and that it's new to you. If that's the case, you're very lucky that you get to learn on such great tools as Photoshop and ImageReady. If you've done animation before, you'll still be grateful for these tools, but you likely had to learn on systems that were much more difficult.

Although animation appears to move when seen on a computer screen, that movement is actually created from a series of still images. The GIF format is popular for Web animation because it can contain a series of static images and display them one after the other in sequence, much like a slide show. It's also popular because it is backwards compatible with older browsers.

Although you can prepare images for animation in Photoshop, the only place that you can write animated GIFs is inside ImageReady. For this reason, all the exercises in this chapter take place in ImageReady.

Animation Terms

If you are new to creating animation in ImageReady, here are some illustrations to help familiarize you with several new terms and interface elements.

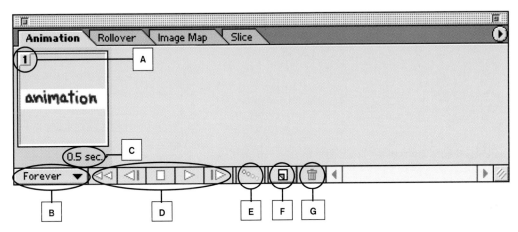

Animation palette: You'll create animations in ImageReady by using the Animation palette. **A:** This displays the frame number. **B:** Here is where you set how many times the animation plays. **C:** Here is where you set the delay of each frame. **D:** These are the playback controls. **E:** The Tween button tells ImageReady to automatically generate intermediate frames between keyframes you create. **F:** The New Frame icon creates a new frame by duplicating the selected frame. **G:** Use the Delete Frame icon to delete a frame.

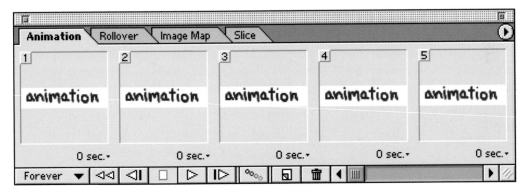

Frames: ImageReady's Animation palette numbers frames sequentially. A single frame indicates that the image is static, but two or more different frames displayed in sequence will create the illusion of movement.

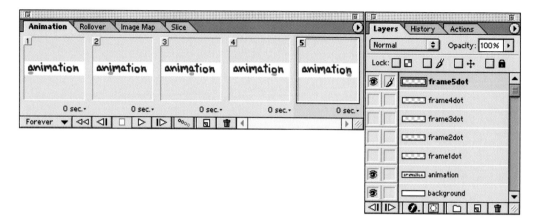

Frame-by-Frame Animation: *You create this kind of animation by turning on and off different layers over a series of frames.*

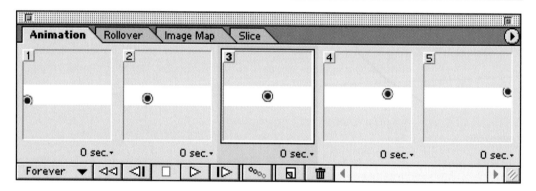

Position Tween: *You create a tween in ImageReady by taking two different frames (called keyframes) and applying the Tween command, which creates additional frames between the keyframes automatically. When you apply a position tween, one layer of artwork changes position over a number of frames.*

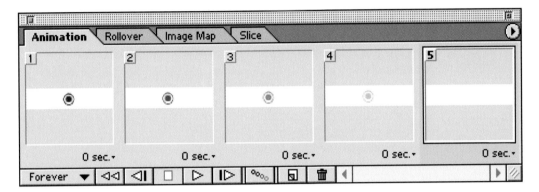

Opacity Tween: *You can apply an opacity tween to a layer of artwork to change its opacity over a number of frames.*

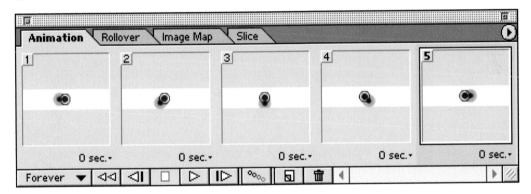

Layer Effect Tween: *You can apply a layer effect to a layer of artwork and then tween that effect so that it changes over a number of frames.*

Animated GIF Format

The GIF file format supports animation, but the JPEG format does not. A Web browser treats an animated GIF file no differently than a static GIF file, except that an animated GIF displays multiple images in a sequence, much like a slide show, instead of a single image. Because different frames can contain different timings, one frame can hold for a few seconds, and other frames can display in much less time.

Animated GIF files do not require browser plug-ins, which means they are accessible to all Web browsers (with the exception of text-only or 1.0 browsers). The HTML code for inserting an animated GIF is no different than that for a static GIF, so working with these animation files requires no extra programming expertise. Animated GIF files can be instructed to loop (or repeat endlessly), to only play once, or to play a specific number of times. The number of repeats is stored in the file itself, not in the HTML code.

Compression Challenges

The animated GIF format uses the same principles of compression that apply to static GIF images. Large areas of solid color compress better than areas with a lot of noise or detail. If you do use photographic-style images in an animated GIF, be sure to add **lossy** compression. It will make a substantial difference in file savings.

Animated GIFs will always be larger than static GIFs. ImageReady has two animation compression features—**Bounding Box** and **Redundant Pixel Removal** (that are turned on by default. What this means is that ImageReady will add file size only for the areas that have changed in your animation. If you have a photographic background, and the only thing that changes is some lettering that fades up over it, the photographic area will only be written once to the file, limiting the total file size. If you change every pixel of an animation, as in the animated slide show example in Exercise 10 below, the Bounding Box and Redundant Pixel Removal features won't be able to help keep the file size down.

When you compress an animated GIF, keep in mind that the file will stream in, meaning that frames will appear before the entire file has finished loading. For this reason, we usually divide the file size by the number of frames, and that makes us feel a lot better about big file sizes. For example, if we have a 100K animated GIF file that is 10 frames long, in reality each frame is only 10K, which makes us feel more at ease about publishing such a big file to the Web.

Controlling the Timing of Animated GIFs

Animation is time based, meaning that it depends on time passing as well as its artwork changing. If you alter artwork very slowly in an animation, it doesn't appear to move, but to sit for a long time and then change. If you change artwork very quickly, it appears to have more fluid movement.

Sometimes slide-show style animation is what you'll want, and other times you'll want to make movement happen more quickly. The GIF format supports delays between frames, which allows for the timing to change within a single animation file.

Video and film animation are also time-based mediums, with one key difference from animated GIFs. They play back at specific frame rates (30 frames per second for video, 24 frames per second for film). Unfortunately, animated GIF files may play back at different speeds depending on the computer upon which they are viewed. A slow Mac or PC (386, 486, 030, 040, or Power PC) will play an animation much more slowly than a new G4 or Pentium III. There's no controlling that the animation you author will play back at different speeds on different processors. The only suggestion we can make is that you view your work on an older machine if you can, before you publish it to the Web. This isn't always possible or practical, and the truth is that most people don't have a lot of old computers lying around to test with. It doesn't stop anyone from publishing animation, but it does mean that you might be surprised when you view your work on older machines.

Animation Aesthetics

Animation is going to draw your end-user's eye much more than a static image. Make sure that the subject matter you pick for animation is worthy of more attention than other images on your screen. We've seen Web pages contain so much animation that it distracts from the important content rather than enhances it. Good uses for animation might include ad banners, making certain words move so they stand out, diagrams brought to life, slide shows of photographs, or cartoon characters. You'll learn how to do some of these different kinds of animation in this chapter.

[IR]

I. ———————————————Frame-by-Frame Animation with Layers

This exercise walks you through the process of establishing frame-by-frame animation by turning layers on and off.

ImageReady can work with existing files made in Photoshop, or with artwork you create in ImageReady. It is important to note, however, that Photoshop 6 cannot write animated GIF files, which is why this entire chapter takes place in ImageReady.

1. In ImageReady, open **animation_finished.psd** from the **chap_13** folder that you transferred to your hard drive from the **H•O•T CD-ROM**.

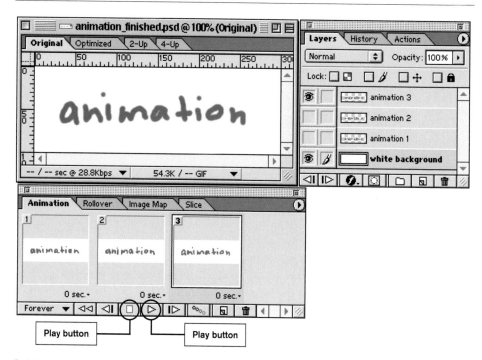

2. Make sure the **Animation** and **Layers** palettes are open (Window > Show Animation and Window > Show Layers). Click the **Play** button at the bottom of the **Animation** palette to watch the animation play inside the document window. You should see the letters in the word **animation** dance on the screen. Click the **Stop** button once you've watched the animation.

MOVIE | framebyframe.mov

To learn more about Exercise 1, *"Frame-By-Frame Animation with Layers,"* check out **framebyframe.mov** from the **movies** folder on the **H•O•T CD-ROM**.

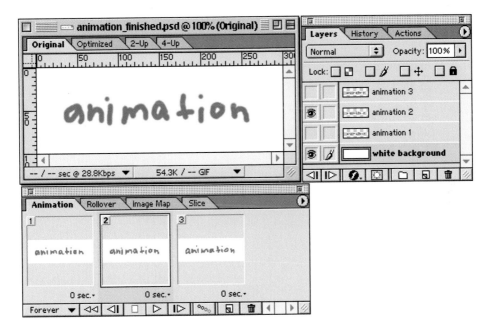

3. Select each frame in the **Animation** palette, and notice that as you do, the **Visibility** icons (the **Eye** icons) on different layers in the Layers palette turn on and off.

This animation was created by writing the word animation *three times, on three different layers. The layers were then selectively turned on and off in each frame of the animation. You will learn how to build this file in the following steps.*

4. Close **animation_finished.psd**, and do not save if prompted.

5. Open **animation.psd** from the **chap_13** folder. It contains only a single frame in the Animation palette.

To make this document into an animation the Animation palette must contain at least two frames with different content in each one. One way to achieve this is to turn the visibility of different layers on and off between frames, as you just witnessed. You will learn to create new frames and turn layers on and off in the following steps.

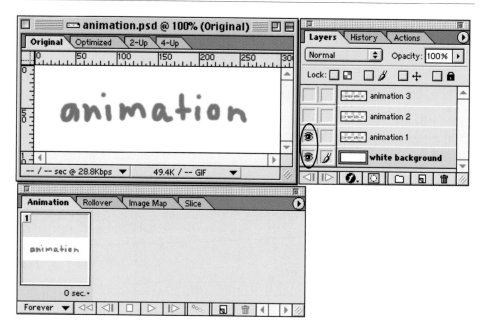

6. On the first frame make sure that there is an **Eye** icon next to the **animation 1** and **white background** layers, so that those layers are visible.

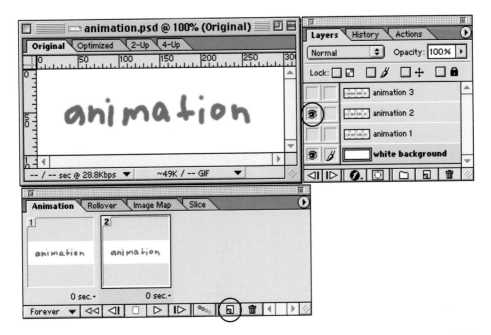

7. Click the **New Frame** icon at the bottom of the **Animation** palette to create **frame 2**, which will be a duplicate of **frame 1**. Make sure **frame 2** is selected in the **Animation** palette. In the **Layers** palette turn off the visibility of the layer **animation 1** by clicking its **Eye** icon off, and turn on the visibility of the layer **animation 2** by clicking its Eye icon on. Leave the layer **white background** turned on.

It does not matter which layer is selected in the Layers palette when you are turning layer visibility on or off with the Eye icons. ImageReady and Photoshop allow you to turn layers on and off without selecting a particular layer.

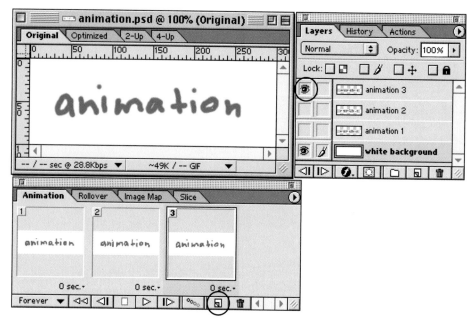

8. Click the **New Frame** icon on the **Animation** palette again to create a third frame. This duplicates the second frame until you make a change, such as turning on or off a different layer. With **frame 3** selected, turn off **animation 2** and turn on **animation 3** in the **Layers** palette. Leave the layer **white background** turned on.

---

9. Click the **Play** button on the **Animation** palette to watch your work. Click **Stop** when you're through admiring it.

---

10. Choose **File > Save** and leave the file open for the next exercise.

You might be surprised at how easy it was to set up your first animation in ImageReady. Animated GIFs have never been easier to make as far as we're concerned!

[IR]

2. —————————**Setting the Speed and Looping**

This exercise focuses on how to slow down the speed and change the looping from a **Forever** setting, like the one you just played and stopped, to a specific number of repeats.

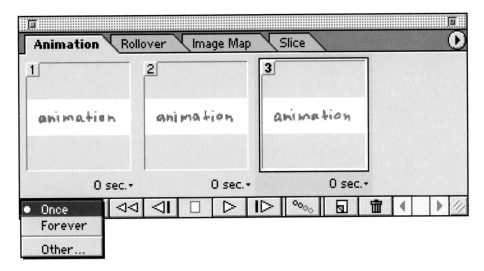

1. With **animation.psd** open from the last exercise, play the animation again by clicking the **Play** button on the **Animation** palette. Notice that it loops indefinitely? Click and hold down on the **Forever** pop-up menu at the bottom left of the **Animation** palette. Change it to **Once**, and press **Play** again. The animation should only play once. Return the setting to **Forever** once you've explored this setting.

Tip: If you want the animation to play more than once but less than forever, choose the Other... setting and enter the number of repeats you prefer. This particular animation will look best if it loops forever, but now you know how to change the looping if you want to for future animation projects.

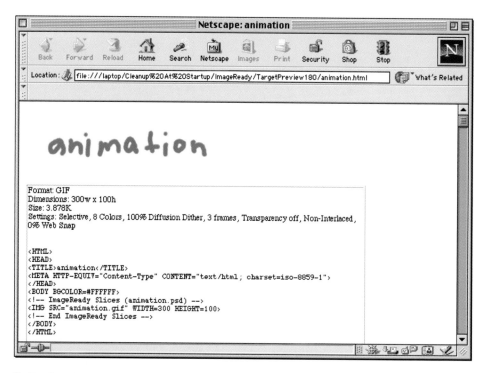

2. Preview this in a browser by clicking the **Preview in Default Browser** button in the ImageReady Toolbox. Notice that the animation plays much faster than it did when you previewed it by pressing Play. That's because ImageReady builds the animation as it plays back, while the browser plays the animated GIF that is already built. You'll notice that the animation plays too fast in the browser. Return to ImageReady to slow down the pacing.

It's impossible to estimate the speed of the animation unless you preview it in a browser. In most cases, this one included, the animation plays much faster in the browser than it does in ImageReady. For this reason, it's always important to view the animation in a browser before you finalize your speed settings. However, even in your browser you can't tell the true speed of the animation, because that depends in part on the speed of the processor in each viewer's computer.

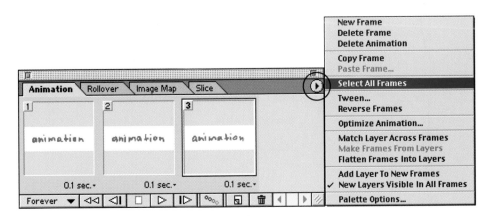

3. Click the upper-right arrow in the **Animation** palette and choose **Select All Frames**.

Don't be confused by the fact that all the frames don't have a black border. The blue high-lighting that's now around all the frames indicates that they are all selected.

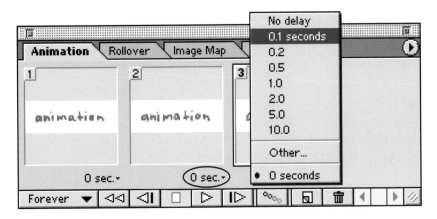

4. Click and hold down on any of the frame delay settings that currently read **0 sec**. From the pop-up menu choose **0.1 seconds**. All the frames should change at once.

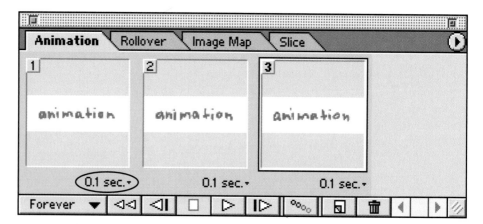

5. All of the frames should now appear with the **0.1 sec.** timing in the pop-up menu. Preview in the browser (**Preview in Default Browser** button) to see how the timing of the animation slowed down a little. **Tip:** You can change the rate of individual frames if you want, or change all of them at once by selecting all the frames first, as you did here.

6. Leave the document open for the next exercise. Don't save yet. You'll focus on saving an animated GIF in the following exercise.

3. ——————Optimizing and Saving an Animated GIF

Has all of this seemed too simple so far? It's easy to create and edit animation in ImageReady. Perhaps you are thinking that there must be something more to it? Nope. The only thing left to do is to optimize this animation and save it as a GIF. You'll see that there is little difference between saving an animated GIF and saving just a plain old static GIF.

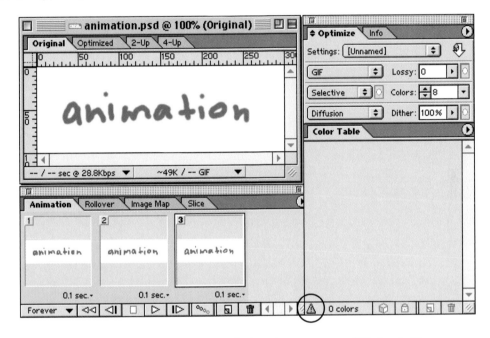

1. Make sure that the **Optimize** and **Color Table** palettes are open (Window > Show Optimize). Note that there may be nothing in the Color Table, and the warning symbol may appear at the bottom left of this palette. These signs are there to alert you that this document has never been optimized. Switch to the **Optimized** tab in the document window, and the warning symbol will disappear.

> ## NOTE | Animation Must Be Saved as GIF
>
> When creating animation, it's essential that you use the GIF setting instead of JPEG. There is no such thing as an animated JPEG. If you do use JPEG or PNG, in the browser you'll see only the first frame of the document and the animation won't play.

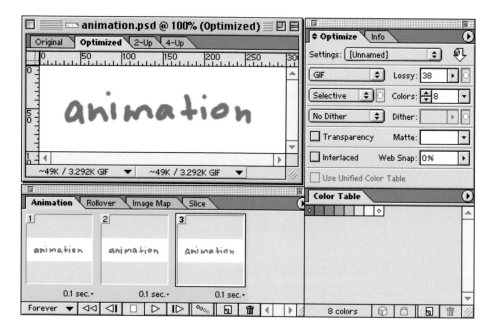

2. Go ahead and experiment with changing the settings in the **Optimize** palette.

The optimization settings you apply to one frame apply to all the frames in your animation. So if you've used very different artwork on different frames, it's a good idea to click through the frames in the Animation palette to check that the optimization settings you've chosen look good on all frames. This isn't an issue with this particular file, because the artwork on each frame is so similar.

Notice that we have set Lossy to 38. Lossy compression will often help animated GIFs (as well as static GIFs) get much smaller since this new compression feature was introduced back in ImageReady 2.

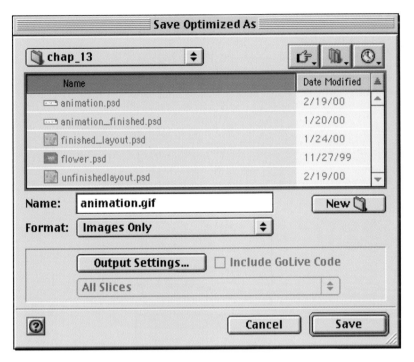

3. Choose **File > Save Optimized As…**, and you'll be prompted to save this as **animation.gif**. You do not need to save HTML in this instance, just choose **Images Only** in the **Format** field. Click **Save**. That's all there is to it.

You might wonder why we suggested that you save the images (but not HTML) in this instance. An animated GIF file knows to function properly with or without the accompanying HTML. You can insert this animated GIF into an HTML editor just as you would insert any static GIF. The GIF file format can display multiple frames with or without the accompanying HTML. You can even load an animated GIF directly into a browser without having any HTML. Try it, if you'd like. In Netscape Navigator–choose File > Open > Page, or in Internet Explorer, choose File > Open File, and navigate to animation.gif, or simply drag and drop animation.gif into an open browser window. How does the browser know to display this file as an animation? The browser recognizes an animated GIF if more than one frame has been saved in the file.

4. Choose **File > Save** to save **animation.psd**, and keep it open for the next exercise.

4. ————————Making a Transparent Animated GIF

What if you want to make a transparent animated GIF? The process is almost identical to making a transparent static GIF, with a few other issues thrown into the mix, like how to effect a change throughout an entire animation by using the **Match Layers Across Frames** setting. This exercise lets you practice this technique.

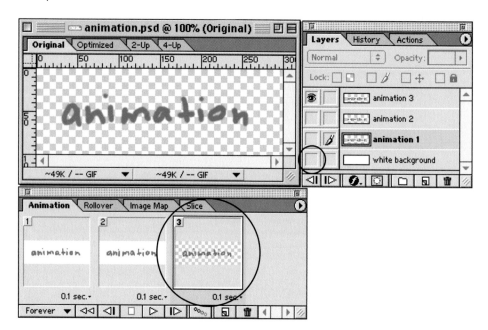

1. With **animation.psd** still open from the last exercise, turn off the **Eye** icon for **white background** in the **Layers** palette. Click on the **Original** tab, and you should see a checkerboard background inside the document window. This indicates a transparent GIF.

If you look carefully at the Animation palette, you will see that this change was only made for the frame that was selected, which means that ImageReady doesn't yet know that you want this change to occur throughout the entire animation. You'll remedy that next.

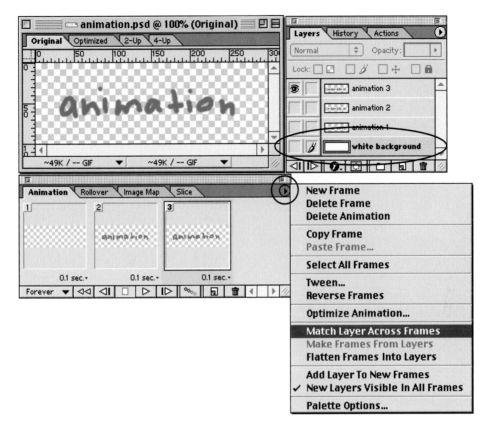

2. Select the **white background** layer inside the **Layers** palette. Click on the upper-right arrow in the **Animation** palette, and choose **Match Layer Across Frames** from the pop-up menu. After you make this change, you'll see that all the frames have a transparent background.

When using the Match Layer Across Frames feature, it's essential that the layer you are matching is selected inside the Layers palette.

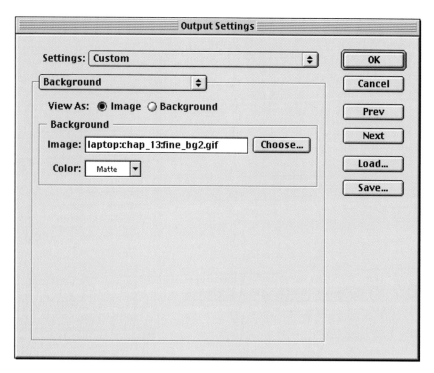

3. Choose **File > Output Settings > Background…**, and click on **Choose** to select **fine_bg2.gif** from the **chap_13** folder. Click **Open** and then **OK**.

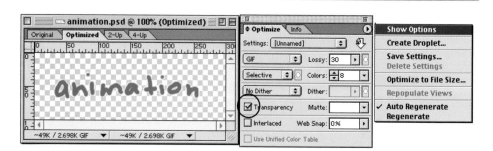

4. Click on the **Optimized** tab of the document window to check the optimization settings. Make sure the **Optimize** and **Color Table** palettes are open. Make sure that **Transparency** is checked in the Optimize palette. If you cannot see the Transparency checkbox, click on the upper-right arrow in the palette and choose **Show Options**.

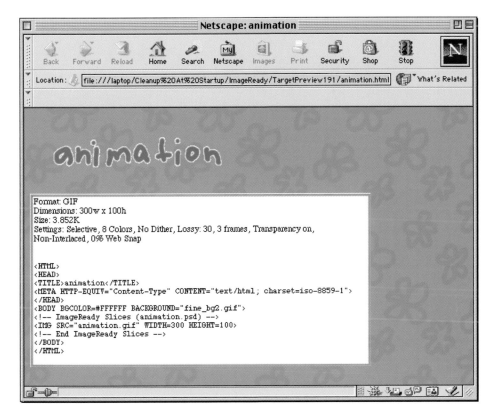

```
Netscape: animation

Back  Forward  Reload  Home  Search  Netscape  Images  Print  Security  Shop  Stop    N

Location: file:///laptop/Cleanup%20At%20Startup/ImageReady/TargetPreview191/animation.html    What's Related


animation


Format: GIF
Dimensions: 300w x 100h
Size: 3.852K
Settings: Selective, 8 Colors, No Dither, Lossy: 30, 3 frames, Transparency on,
Non-Interlaced, 0% Web Snap


<HTML>
<HEAD>
<TITLE>animation</TITLE>
<META HTTP-EQUIV="Content-Type" CONTENT="text/html; charset=iso-8859-1">
</HEAD>
<BODY BGCOLOR=#FFFFFF BACKGROUND="fine_bg2.gif">
<!-- ImageReady Slices (animation.psd) -->
<IMG SRC="animation.gif" WIDTH=300 HEIGHT=100>
<!-- End ImageReady Slices -->
</BODY>
</HTML>
```

5. Preview this in a browser by clicking the **Preview in Default Browser** button in the Toolbox. The file should appear over the background image.

There's that unattractive white edge again, which you might remember from making transparent GIFs in Chapter 8, "Transparent GIFs." The next step will show you how to fix the problem.

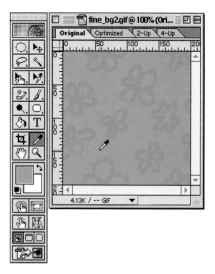

6. Return to ImageReady, choose **File > Open**, and navigate to **fine_bg2.gif** in the **chap_13** folder. Use the **Eyedropper** tool from the Toolbox to capture the color from this image. Go back to **animation.psd**. (You can either click on it to make it active, or choose Window > animation.psd.)

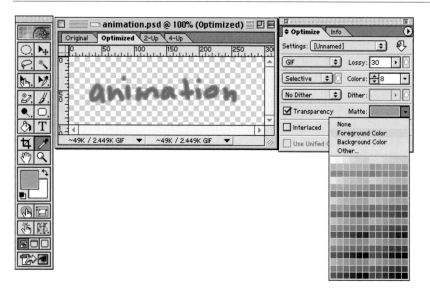

7. In the **Optimize** palette, click on the arrow to the right of the **Matte** field and choose **Foreground Color** from the pop-up menu. Changes in the **Optimize** palette apply to all the frames in the animation.

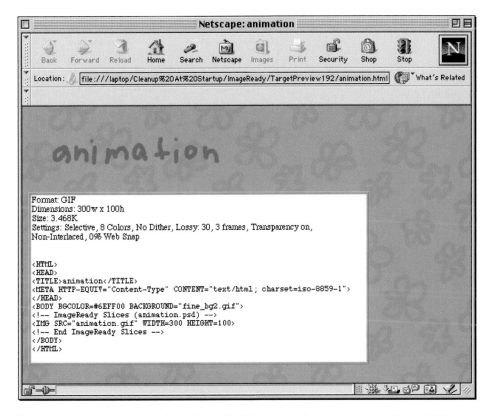

8. Preview in the browser again and you should see a perfect transparent animated GIF.

If you need help running through this process, revisit Chapter 8, "Transparent GIFs," to jog your memory. Making an animated transparent GIF has the same challenges as making a static transparent GIF. It's our hope that you can now transfer the skills you built in Chapter 8 to this new application of the same principles.

9. Save **animation.psd** and close it. Close **fine_bg2.gif**.

[IR]

5. ————————Tweening with Opacity

So far, you've been making animations by turning on and off layer visibility. This is one way to do it, but ImageReady has a few other tricks up its sleeve. This next exercise will introduce you to the **Tween** feature.

1. Open **flower.psd** from the **chap_13** folder.

2. Make sure that the **flower** layer is selected in the **Layers** palette; then enter **Opacity: 1%**. The word **flower** should disappear.

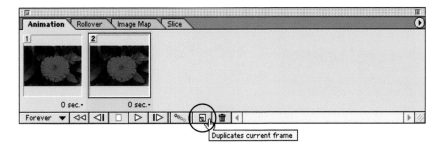

Duplicates current frame

3. Click the **New Frame** icon at the bottom of the **Animation** palette.

This will create a second frame with the exact settings that were in frame 1. To create another Opacity setting, which you need for the tween, you'll change frame 2 in the next step.

Frame 1 and frame 2 are the keyframes for this animation. When you tween later in this exercise, ImageReady will generate intermediate frames between these keyframes.

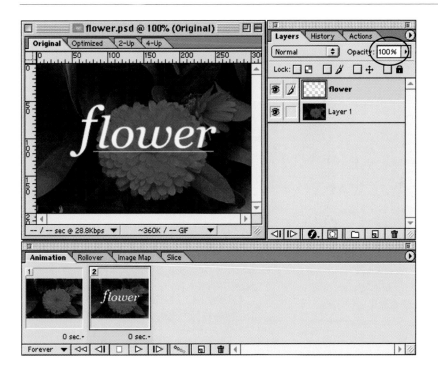

4. The new **frame 2** you just created will be highlighted, so any changes you make will apply to it. Select the **flower** layer in the **Layers** palette and enter **Opacity: 100%**. This should make the word **flower** visible in **frame 2**.

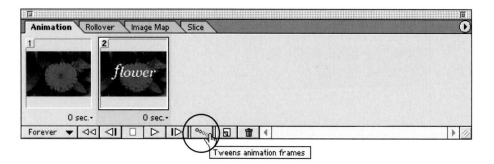

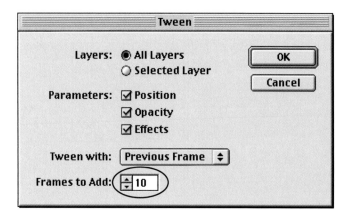

5. Click the **Tween** button on the **Animation** palette.

The Tween button is a new shortcut in ImageReady 3. Another way to tween is to press the arrow on the upper right of the Animation palette and choose Tween... from the pop-up menu.

6. When the **Tween** dialog box appears, enter **Frames to Add: 10**. Make sure there is a checkmark next to the **Opacity** parameter, because opacity is the quality you want to tween. Click **OK**.

The default is for all three of the parameters—Position, Opacity, and Effects—to be checked in the Tween dialog box. We usually leave it that way, so we don't have to think about which box to check each time.

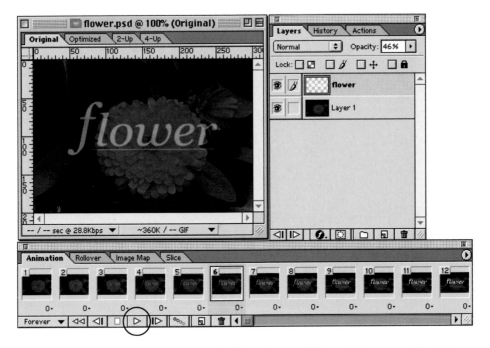

7. Click **Play** to test the animation. You should see the word **flower** fade up over the photographic background. Click **Stop**.

This particular animation might look best if it only plays once. Do you remember how to change the Forever setting? If not, revisit Exercise 2 in this chapter.

8. Click on any frame, click on the **Optimized** tab in the document window, and change the settings in the **Optimize** palette to match those in this figure. Click the **Preview in Default Browser** button to preview the animation in a browser.

Although it's convenient to preview your animation in ImageReady, don't forget to test this file in a browser as well. That's because you'll always get the best indication of speed in the browser, not in ImageReady.

We asked you to optimize because otherwise ImageReady will use the optimization settings from the last image that you worked on, which will make it difficult to see this animation in a browser. But don't get too worried about how you optimize this image. This exercise was created to familiarize you with tweening; other exercises in this chapter cover optimization techniques for animated GIF files.

9. Save and leave the file open for the next exercise.

MOVIE | tweening_opacity.mov

To learn more about Exercise 5, "Tweening with Opacity," check out **tweening_opacity.mov** from the **movies** folder on the **H·O·T CD-ROM**.

[IR]

6. ———————Selecting, Duplicating, and Reversing Frames

What if you wanted to make the words fade up, then hold, then fade out? This type of change is not only possible to do in ImageReady, it's easy once you know the steps.

1. With **flower.psd** still open from the previous exercise, click on **frame 1** in the **Animation** palette. Hold your **Shift** key down and click the last frame. All the frames should be selected.

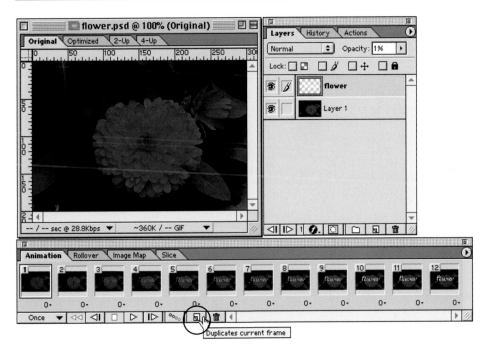

2. With all the frames selected, click on the **New Frame** icon at the bottom of the **Animation** palette. This duplicates all the selected frames and appends them to the end of the frames that were already there.

Tip: This technique offers a fast way to copy and paste. There's another way to do this in ImageReady 3. With all the frames selected, you can click the arrow at the upper right of the Animation palette, and choose Copy Frames from the pop-up menu. Then click on the last frame (frame 12), press the same arrow again, and choose Paste Frames. In the Paste Frames dialog box that appears, choose Paste After Selection, and click OK.

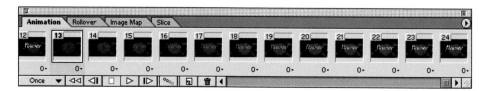

3. Use the **scroll bar** at the bottom of the **Animation** palette, and you'll see that the 12 frames you copied were just pasted at the end of the animation sequence (as frames 13–24). They should already be selected.

Note: *If you accidentally click off of these frames and deselect them, you can use the Shift+click method to reselect them. Click frame 13, hold your Shift key down, and click frame 24. This selects all the frames that you just duplicated.*

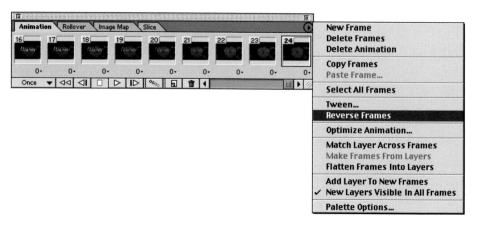

4. Click the upper-right arrow again and choose **Reverse Frames**. This puts all the selected frames in the reverse order.

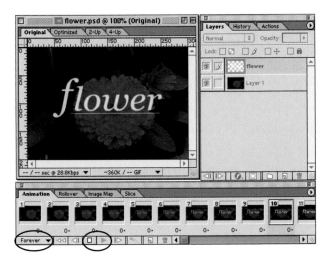

5. Change the **Once** setting to **Forever** and click **Play**. You should see the animation fade up and down. Click **Stop** when you're through admiring your handiwork.

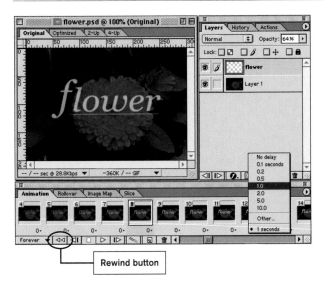

Rewind button

6. Click on **frame 12** and change the timing of that frame to **1.0** second, as shown above. Rewind the animation by clicking on the **Rewind** button at the bottom of the **Animation** palette. Click **Play** to watch the result of this change. The animation should now stop and hold in the middle and then continue to play. When you're finished watching, click the **Stop** button.

You can change the timing of all the frames, like you did in Exercise 2, or you can change the timing of individual frames.

7. Save and leave the file open for the next exercise.

This exercise taught you how to set the number of repeats with which an animation will play. You learned to create a loop by selecting, duplicating, and reversing frames, and how to set delays on individual frames.

 MOVIE | reversing.mov

To learn more about Exercise 6, "*Selecting, Duplicating, and Reversing Frames,*" check out **reversing.mov** from the **movies** folder on the **H•O•T CD-ROM**.

Different Ways to Duplicate Frames

In Exercise 6, you learned to duplicate a series of frames that were selected by clicking on the **New Frame** icon. Before you duplicate frames, you must first select them. You can select frames by holding down the Shift key, or you can use the upper-right arrow to choose **Select All Frames** from the pop-up menu. There are a few different ways to duplicate frames, and this chart outlines them.

Methods for Duplicating Frames	
Method	**Results**
From the Animation palette, select frames and click on the **New Frame** icon.	Duplicates the frames and appends them to the end of your animation.
Click on the upper-right arrow of the Animation palette to access the **Copy Frames** and **Paste Frames** features.	This is the method to use for copying animation from one document to another—ImageReady copies all the appropriate artwork to the target document. You'll also use this method when you want to append the copied frames someplace other than at the end of your animation. The *Paste Frames dialog box* gives you the choice of pasting before or after frames you've selected, or of replacing selected frames, all without creating additional layers. Replacing frames might be good if you had, let's say, an animation of a logo in one .psd file that you wanted to transfer to an ad banner that was being built inside a different .psd file. Another option in the Paste Frames dialog box *is Paste Over Selection*, which not only replaces the selected frame, but also creates additional layers in the Layers palette.

[IR]

7. ──────────Tweening a Tweened Sequence

You can also tween an animation more than once. This is useful in the event that you change your mind about a tween setting, such as the number of frames between keyframes.

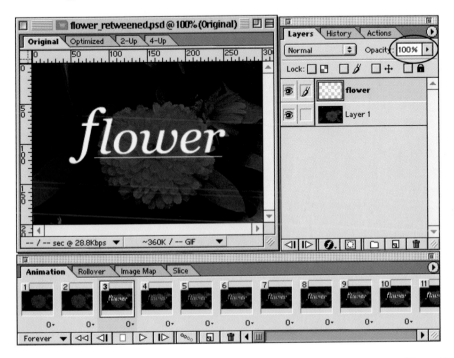

1. In **flower.psd**, be sure that the **flower** layer is selected in the **Layers** palette. Next, click on frame 3 in the **Animation** palette to select it. In the **Layers** palette on the **flower** layer enter Opacity: 100%.

 MOVIE | tweening_a_tween.mov

To learn more about Exercise 7, "*Tweening a Tweened Sequence*," check out **tweening_a_tween.mov** from the **movies** folder on the **H•O•T CD-ROM**.

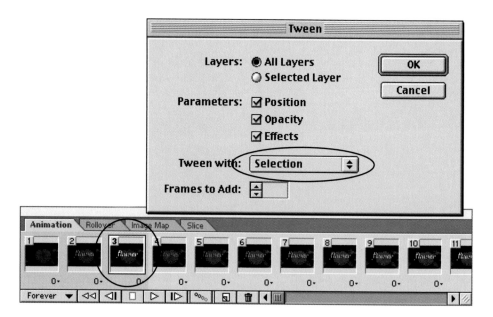

2. With **frame 3** selected, hold your shift key and click on **frame 1** to select **frames 1-3**. Click the upper-right arrow of the Animation palette to choose **Tween....** Click **OK**. Notice that you are not given the option to choose the number of frames but that the Tween with setting is on Selection. That's because you selected multiple frames before you selected the Tween... option.

Tip: The Tween button doesn't work when you're trying to tween a selection of frames. You have to use the method described in this step.

3. Play the animation or preview it in a browser. You'll see a short fade up at the beginning and an abrupt change in opacity as a result of the changes you made.

If you don't see the animation when you preview in a browser, it's because you didn't optimize the file in the last exercise. Try increasing the number of colors in the Optimize palette to fix the problem..

ImageReady allows you to tween either by defining a selection or defining a number of frames to insert between two keyframes.

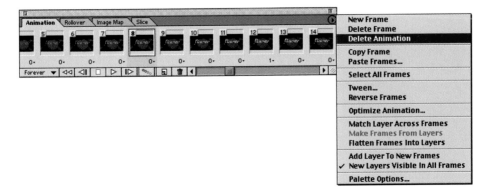

4. You've completed this exercise and don't need to save this document. In fact, the next exercise will require this same file without any animation. Delete the animation in **flower.psd** by clicking the upper-right arrow of the **Animation** palette and selecting **Delete Animation**. When prompted, click **Delete** (Mac) or **Yes** (Windows). This will leave the layers intact in the Layers palette, but delete all the frames in the Animation palette.

5. Leave this file open for the next exercise.

[IR]

8. ——————————Tweening with Position

So far, you've learned to create animations two different ways. Exercise 1 showed you how to create animation by turning on and off layers on different frames. Exercise 5 introduced you to creating animation by using the Tween setting and adjusting opacity between frames. There are two other types of tween parameters you can work with—**Position** and **Effects**. This exercise will show you how to tween with position. ImageReady will memorize the position of a layer between two frames, and those two stored positions can be tweened. You'll see how in this exercise.

1. With **flower.psd** still open from the last exercise, make sure the **flower** layer is selected in the **Layers** palette and that **Opacity** is **100%**.

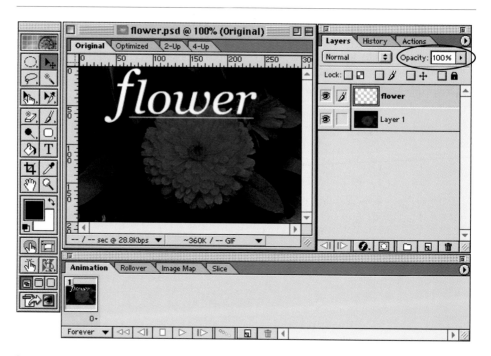

2. Using the **Move** tool from the **Toolbox**, click and drag inside the document window to move the lettering to the top.

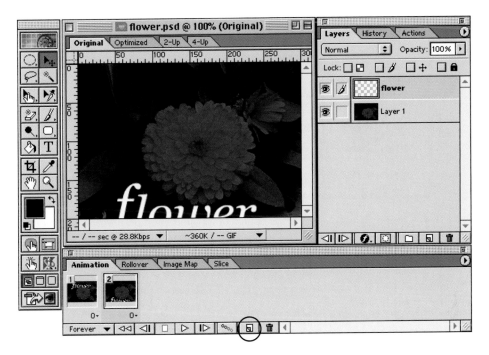

3. Click on the **New Frame** icon at the bottom of the **Animation** palette. With the second frame selected, move the lettering to the bottom of the document window using the **Move** tool. It's even OK to position the artwork so that it goes off the edge. **Tip:** If you're having trouble moving the artwork off the edge, try using the arrow keys to move the artwork instead of clicking and dragging. To do this, you must have the Move tool selected.

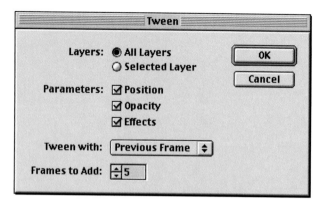

4. Click the **Tween** button at the bottom of the **Animation** palette. Enter **Frames to Add: 5**. Make sure there's a checkmark next to **Position**. Click **OK**.

5. Preview the results. You've just learned to create an animation by letting ImageReady tween between two different positions on the screen.

If you aren't pleased by what you see, you can go back and select any frame and make adjustments with the Move tool; but the main point is that you have now learned how to tween with position changes.

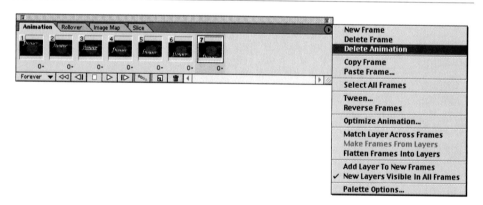

6. You won't need this animation for the next exercise, so go ahead and delete it by clicking the upper-right arrow of the **Animation** palette and choosing **Delete Animation**. When prompted, click **Delete** (Mac) or **Yes** (Windows). Leave the document open for the next exercise.

9. _____Tweening with Effects

ImageReady can also tween effects using **styles** or **layer effects**. This next exercise will walk you through the process.

1. In **flower.psd**, which should still be open from the last exercise, select the **flower** layer in the **Layers** palette. Use the **Move** tool to move the word **flower** back to the center of the document window.

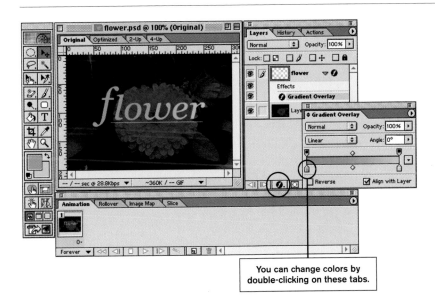

You can change colors by double-clicking on these tabs.

2. In the **Layers** palette, click the **Add Layer Effect** icon at the bottom of that palette, and choose **Gradient Overlay** from the pop-up menu. In the **Gradient Overlay** palette, enter **0** in the **Angle** field. (If you don't see the Gradient Overlay palette, choose Window > Show Layer Options/Style).

Notice how the Gradient Overlay layer effect pulls colors from the foreground and background colors in the ImageReady Toolbox? That's why the colors of your gradient might not be the same as those in the figure above. If you want to change the colors, you can double-click on the tabs at the bottom of the Gradient Overlay palette.

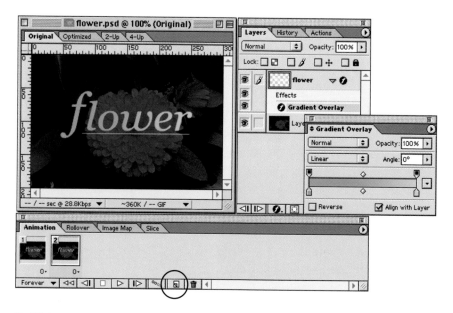

3. Click on the **New Frame** icon at the bottom of the **Animation** palette to add a new frame.

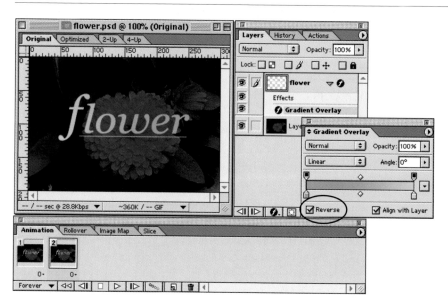

4. Change the gradient settings in the **Gradient Overlay** palette. We simply reversed the gradient by checking Reverse.

Tween

Layers: ◉ All Layers
○ Selected Layer

[OK]
[Cancel]

Parameters: ☑ Position
☑ Opacity
☑ Effects

Tween with: [Previous Frame ▼]

Frames to Add: [▲▼] 15

5. In the **Animation** palette, click on the **Tween** button. Choose **Tween with: Previous Frame**. Enter **Frames to Add: 15**. Make sure there's a checkmark next to **Effects**. Click **OK**.

6. Preview the results in a browser. You could also press the **Play** button on the **Animation** palette, but you would get less accurate feedback of the timing.

You should know how to make any adjustments that you want if you aren't pleased, but the main point is that you have now learned how to tween with effects. What you might not realize is that you can combine animating opacity, position, and effects in a single tween. Try your own experiments with this and you'll see.

7. Save and, finally, close the file.

NOTE | How Many Frames?

You might be wondering why we chose different numbers of frames to add in the **Tween** dialog box in different exercises. Some types of animations look better if they happen over a longer or shorter amount of time. Most animations will play more smoothly if they have more frames; but the more frames an animation has, the larger its file size and the longer its download time will be. How did we know how many frames to instruct that you add, or, more importantly, how will you know how many frames to add when you make your own animated GIFs? Experience has led us to have a good instinct about timing. We can imagine how something will look if it happens quickly versus if it happens slowly. You will be able to build this same skill if you make a lot of animated GIFs yourself. In the interim, don't be afraid to experiment! You can always delete the animation and try again, right?

[IR]

IO. _____Animated Slide Show

Let's say that you have a number of photographs from which you want to create a slide show. There are two types of slide shows that you can make. You can simply turn each image on and off and set a delay to last for a few seconds, which would be no different from what you did in Exercise 1. You can also create a slide show that fades up on one image and fades down on another (called a cross-fade in filmmaking). This is something that ImageReady does naturally without requiring that you set the opacity. You'll see how simple it is—just try it!

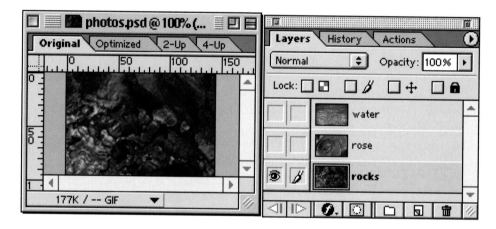

1. Open **photos.psd** from the **chap_13** folder.

This is a simple file that you could easily make. It contains three layers, each with a different image. The images could be photographic or graphic.

 MOVIE | slideshow.mov

To learn more about Exercise 10, "*Animated Slide Show*," check out **slideshow.mov** from the **movies** folder on the **H•O•T CD-ROM**.

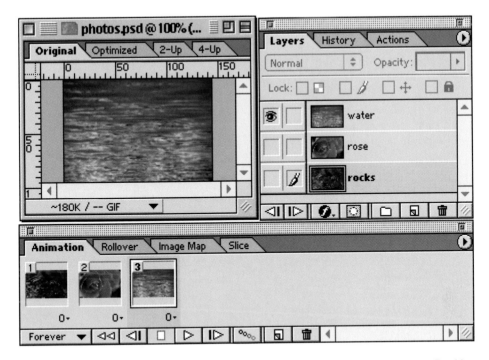

2. Make three frames and set three images so that only one appears on each frame. Do this by turning the layer for **rocks** on, and the layers for **rose** and **water** off. Click on the **New Frame** icon to add a second frame, which is a duplicate of the first frame. Turn off the layer for **rocks**, turn on the layer for **rose**, and turn off the layer for **water**. Click on the **New Frame** icon to add another frame. Turn off the layers for **rocks** and **rose**, and turn on the layer for **water**. The result should look similar to what you see here.

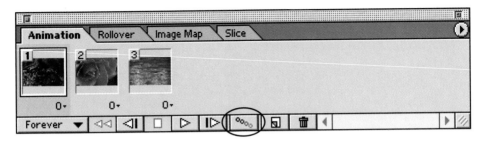

3. In the **Animation** palette, select the first frame, and click the **Tween** button.

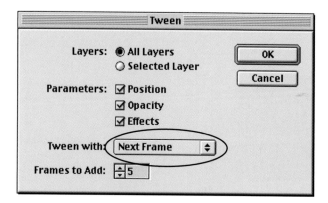

4. Notice that the **Tween** dialog box is already set to **Tween with: Next Frame**. Use the settings above (**Frames to Add: 5**), and click **OK**.

If you click on the first frame in the Animation palette, ImageReady defaults to Tween with: Next Frame but gives you the option of changing to Tween with: Last Frame .

5. Select the **last frame** in the **Animation** palette (**frame 8**) and click the **Tween** button.

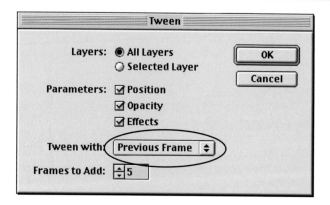

This time, ImageReady defaults to Tween with: Previous Frame because you selected the last frame in the sequence. Click OK.

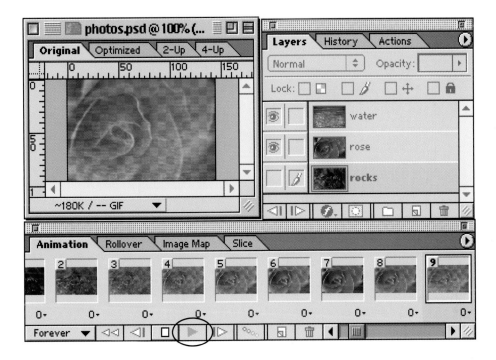

6. Click on the **Play** button or preview the animation in a browser.

It would be nice if it made a complete loop, wouldn't it?

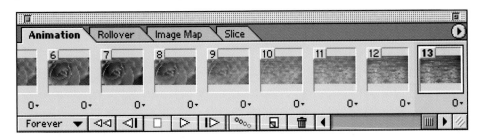

7. Select the **last frame** in the **Animation** palette (**frame 13**).

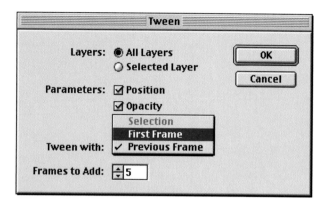

8. Click the **Tween** button. Notice that the **Tween with:** is set to **Previous Frame**. Press on **Previous Frame** and change this setting to **First Frame**. **Frames to Add** is still set to add **5** frames, which is perfect because all the other tweens were set to **5** frames, and this will be consistent. Click **OK**.

9. Click the **Rewind** button on the **Animation** palette. Then click the **Play** button. Notice that there is now a smooth fade between all the images.

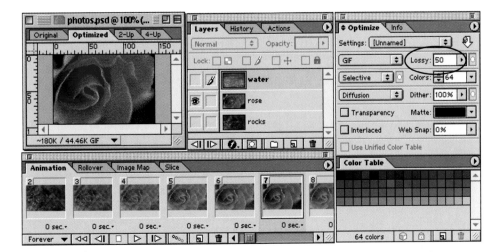

Now your animation is complete. The challenge will be to compress this to a small file size. Remember that your content is photographic, so lossy compression will really cut down on the file size. We got our version of this animation down to 44K. Without adding the lossy compression, it would have been double the size. If you'd like a refresher about optimizing animation, revisit Exercise 3 in this chapter.

10. To save the final animated GIF, choose **File > Save Optimized As**, and set the format field to **Images Only**. To save the Photoshop document, choose **File > Save**. Once you're finished saving your work, close the file.

[IR]

II. ——————————Animated GIF Rollovers

It might not be obvious to you, but it is also possible to combine animation and rollover techniques in a single ImageReady document. This is the only image editor we know of on the market that can easily do this. If you've never made animated rollovers in ImageReady before, it is likely that you might find the steps in this exercise a bit strange. The steps make sense once you've gone through them and have seen the results, but we find that many students in our lab have trouble understanding this exercise until they've tried it a few times.

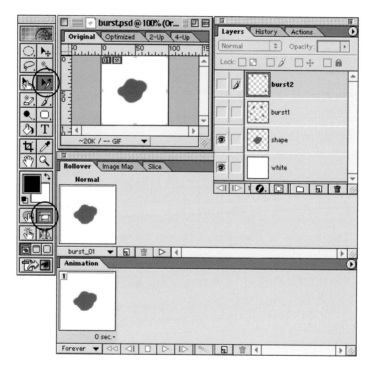

1. Open **burst.psd** from the **chap_13** folder. If you don't see a **Normal** state in the **Rollover** palette, it's because you haven't selected a slice. Click the **Slice Select** tool and click on the single slice, as shown above, and the **Toggle Slices Visibility** button in the Toolbox will automatically turn on.

MOVIE | animated_roll.mov

You might like to look at the movie **animated_ roll.mov** from the movies folder on the **H•O•T CD-ROM** before you embark on these steps.

When we create animation and rollovers in the same document, we like to dock the Animation and Rollover palettes together, as shown here. You learned to do this same kind of docking with the Optimize and Color Table palettes in Chapter 3, "Optimization."

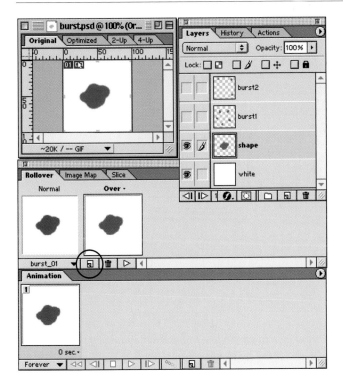

2. Click on the **New Rollover State** icon at the bottom of the **Rollover** palette. This will add a new frame (the Over state) to the Rollover palette, but won't affect the Animation palette.

Notice that the first frames in the Animation and the Rollover palettes are identical? This means that the Normal state will look just like what's on the screen. In other words, in the Normal state there will be no animation.

NOTE | Preload Issues

When designing animated rollovers, you need to set the animation to play at least two cycles (the **Forever** setting that generates an endless loop is our favorite). This is because ImageReady automatically writes a script that "preloads" the images. If the animation is set to play one time only, it will play in the preloading process and will not play when you finally see the image in the browser.

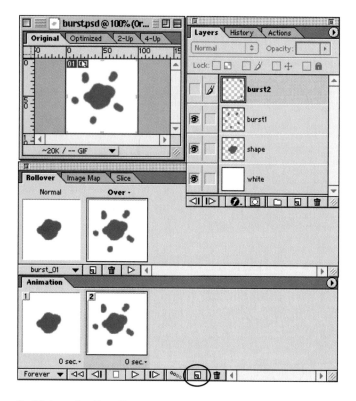

3. Click on the **New Frame** icon at the bottom of the **Animation** palette. In the **Layers** palette, turn the **Eye** icon on for the layer called **burst1** (leaving the Eye icons on for the white and shape layers).

This should result in two rollover states and two animation frames. If you click on the Normal *state in the Rollover palette, you'll see the animation* frame 2 *disappear, and if you click on the* Over *state, the animation frame will reappear. That's because the animation is going to be triggered by the* Over *state. Be sure that the* Over *state is selected before you go to the next step.*

WARNING | Netscape Animation Bug

Unfortunately, if you click on an animated rollover in Netscape, the animation will not resume if you move your mouse over the artwork again. This is not true in Internet Explorer. The problem is not with the code that ImageReady generates but in the way that Netscape renders animated GIF files. At this point, there is nothing we can suggest to get around this.

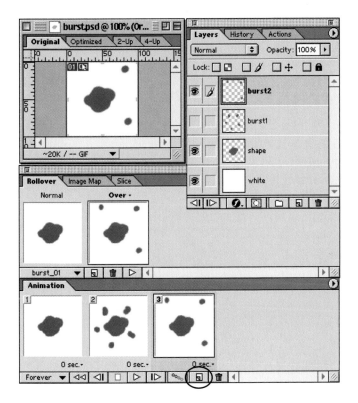

4. Click on the **New Frame** icon at the bottom of the **Animation** palette. This will create a third frame in the palette. In the **Layers** palette, turn on the layer **burst2** and turn off the layer **burst1**.

In the last step we suggested that you click on the Normal *and the* Over *states to watch the animation frames disappear. Now we're going to suggest that you click on* frame 2 *in the* Animation *palette. Notice that* frame 2, *like* frame 1, *appears in the* Over *state of the* Rollover *palette? That's because all of the frames of the animation will be triggered by the* Over *state of the rollover. This can be very confusing, but ImageReady is simply previewing whatever frame or state is selected. Be sure to select* frame 3 *in the Animation palette again before progressing to the next step.*

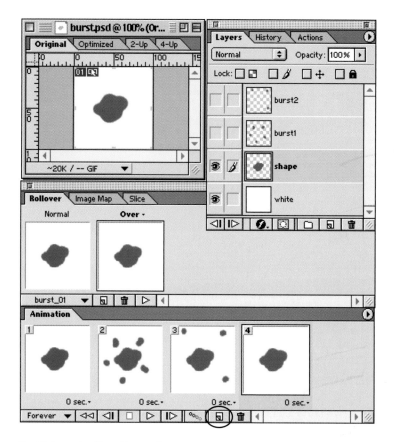

5. Click on the **New Frame** icon again at the bottom of the **Animation** palette, and turn off the **burst2** layer in the **Layers** palette.

You should see four frames of animation and two rollover states. This won't necessarily make sense until you preview the results of your work.

6. Click the **Preview in Default Browser** button and move your mouse over the artwork. Notice that the animation happens when the mouse is on the rollover artwork.

Assuming all went well, you just learned how to create an animated rollover. What's interesting about ImageReady is that any rollover can be made to have an animated state.

7. Return to ImageReady to save and close the file.

12. _____ Designing Entire Interfaces

In the past three chapters you've learned about slicing, rollovers, and animation. It might not seem obvious that all these techniques can be combined to design an entire Web interface. This next exercise should bring into practice a lot of skills that you've just learned and open your eyes to further possibilities. We'll be truthful with you, however–this is a very complex exercise. Don't be surprised if you have to try it a few times or watch the movies over and over. You won't be alone; when we teach this at our training center, most of our students suffer along until the big "aha!" moment comes and it finally makes sense. ImageReady is a powerful and complex tool, and this exercise really shows off its strengths and challenges.

1. Open **finished_layout.psd** from the **chap_13** folder.

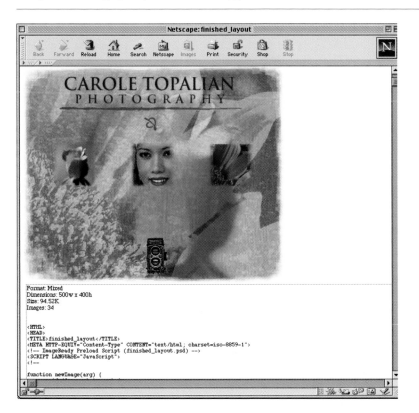

2. Preview it in a browser and notice that the camera at the bottom animates all the time. Move your mouse over the **rose**, the **portrait**, or the **sunflower** images. Notice that remote rollover words appear in the area below those images, and that when they do, the camera positions switch.

3. Return to ImageReady and make sure that the slices are visible (the shortcut is the letter **Q**). Use the **Slice Select** tool to click each of the three photographs in the middle of the image. You'll see that each has rollovers associated with it.

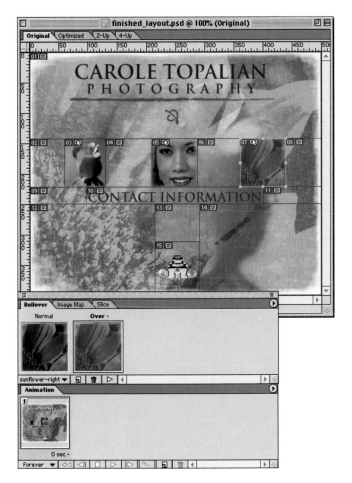

4. In the **Rollover** palette, click the **Over** state, and you'll see the screen change and that text appears in the area below the three photos. Notice that the Normal state of every single slice in this image contains the camera animation in the Animation palette. This means the animation will play before the end-user's mouse moves over any of the artwork. The Normal state is the default view of this document.

Deconstructing a finished piece can teach how to construct a complicated document like this.

 MOVIE | deconstructing.mov

To learn about deconstructing this piece, check out **deconstructing.mov** from the **movies** folder on the **H•O•T CD-ROM**.

5. Now that you have observed some of the techniques used in this exercise, **close** this file, and choose **File > Open > unfinishedlayout.psd** from the **chap_13** folder.

The first thing to set up is the camera animation. Why? Because you want this animation to take place on the Normal *state of every single slice in this document. Whenever you want animation to play at the onset of a page, you must set it up in the* Normal *state.*

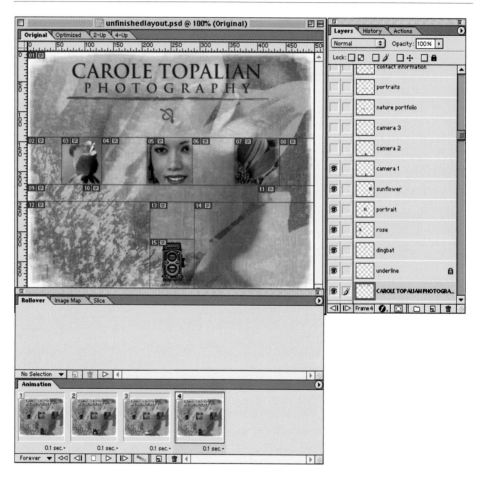

6. Do not select any slice just yet, because the goal here is to create an animation that is in the Normal state of the entire document. Add three more frames to the **Animation** palette by clicking three times on the **New Frame** icon. On **frame 1**, turn the layer **camera 1** on. On **frame 2**, turn the layer **camera 2** on and **camera 1** off. On **frame 3**, turn **camera 3** on and **camera 2** off. On **frame 4**, turn **camera 1** on and **camera 3** off.

7. Tween between each frame, and add three frames each. This can be tricky because you can lose track of the original frames as you start adding tweens. For this reason, we like to do this process backwards.

- Select **frame 4** and click the **Tween** button *(***Frames to Add: 4***, ***Tween with: Previous Frame***).*

- Select **frame 3** and click the **Tween** button *(***Frames to Add: 4***, ***Tween with: Previous Frame***).*

- Select **frame 2** and click the **Tween** button *(***Frames to Add: 4***, ***Tween with: Previous Frame***).*

This should result in a continuous loop of the animation. If you want to preview it right now, go ahead and look at it in the browser. No rollovers will work because you haven't specified any yet. Whenever we are building a document of this complexity we preview often and after each step. We usually preview in the browser because you can't preview the rollovers in ImageReady itself.

By the way, this is no different than what you learned in the last exercise, except that this is on a more complicated, sliced-up document. If you want to watch us set this up, check out **complex.mov** *from the* **movies** *folder.*

8. Using the **Slice Select** tool, select the **rose** slice (**slice #3**) inside the document window. Add an **Over** state in the **Rollover** palette by clicking on the **New State** icon.

9. The **Over** state should now be selected in the **Rollover** palette. From the **Layers** palette, select the **rose** layer and add a **Color Overlay** layer effect to it. We chose a red color and changed the **Opacity** to **30 percent**.

10. When you're finished, turn on the text layer **nature portfolio** in the **Layers** palette. In the **Animation palette**, click the upper-right arrow to choose **Delete Animation**. That's because you only want the animation to play on the Normal state, not on the Over state. Make sure that the layer **camera 1** is turned on and that the other camera layers are turned off.

You just specified that when your end-user's mouse rolls over the picture of the rose, it will change color, the words NATURE PORTFOLIO will appear, the animation will stop, and camera 1 will appear. Next you'll get to do the same for the rest of the pictures.

11. Using the **Slice Select** tool, select the **portrait** slice (**slice #5**). Add an **Over** state in the **Rollover** palette.

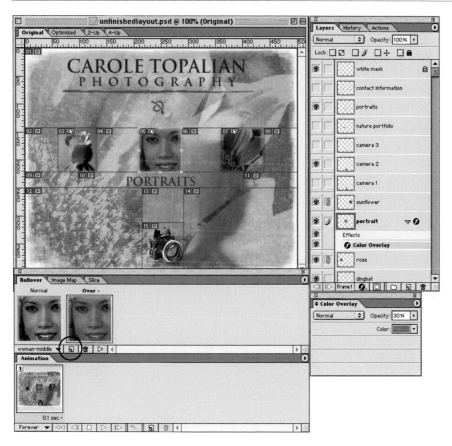

12. From the **Layers** palette, select the **portrait** layer and add a **Color Overlay** layer effect to it. We chose a red color and changed the **Opacity** to **30 percent**.

13. When you're finished, turn on the text layer **portraits**. In the **Animation** palette, click on the upper-right arrow to choose **Delete Animation**. Make sure that the layer **camera 2** is turned on and that the other camera layers are turned off.

You just specified that when your end-user's mouse rolls over the picture of the portrait, it will change color, the word PORTRAITS will appear, the animation will stop, and camera 2 will appear. Again, preview. If it doesn't work, retrace your steps to see if you can figure out what went astray. You might want to watch the movie complex.mov to see us do it.

14. Using the **Slice Select** tool, select the **sunflower** slice (**slice #7**). Add an **Over** state in the **Rollover** palette.

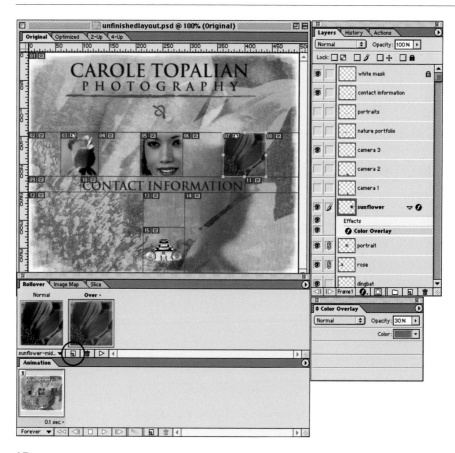

15. From the **Layers** palette, select the **sunflower** layer and add a **Color Overlay** layer effect to it. We chose a **red** color and changed the **Opacity** to **30 percent**.

16. When you're finished, turn on the layer **contact information**. In the **Animation** palette, click the upper-right arrow to choose **Delete Animation.** Make sure that the layer **camera 3** is turned on and that the other camera layers are turned off.

You just specified that when your end-user's mouse rolls over the picture of the sunflower, it will change color, the words CONTACT INFORMATION will appear, the animation will stop, and camera 3 will appear.

17. You're done. Preview in a browser to check to see if everything works. When you're finished, close and save the file. Remember that **Save Optimized As...** will save all the parts— the HTML, the JavaScript to make the rollovers function, and the images. **File > Save** will save the **.psd** file.

Whew! You survived this chapter. That truly is a feat. We know this is a rough one, but these skills afford wonderful bragging rights once you've mastered them!

14.

Automation

| Web Photo Gallery | Actions in Photoshop |
| Batch Processing with Actions |
| Actions in ImageReady | Droplets | Changing Droplets |

chap_14

Photoshop 6 / ImageReady 3
H•O•T CD-ROM

As we're sure you've realized by this chapter, there are tons of practical and creative things that you can do with Photoshop and ImageReady. This chapter addresses features you can use when you want to do something useful and creative, but to an entire folder of images at once. This can be a huge timesaver—who wants to repeat the same operation over and over when the computer can do it for you?

Photoshop and ImageReady both offer Actions, which allow you to store a series of operations as a recording that can be played back over a single image or multiple images that are in the same folder. Although it's possible to create actions in both Photoshop and ImageReady, they cannot be created in one program and played in the other.

ImageReady has another feature called Droplets, which store optimization settings that can be applied to a folder of images by drag-and-drop methods. Photoshop has a Droplets feature too, but Photoshop Droplets do not store optimization settings; they are just another way of storing and applying actions. Photoshop has other automation features, like the popular Web Photo Gallery. This chapter offers hands-on training in all these features: Actions, Droplets, and the Web Photo Gallery. This is the sort of stuff computers were made for. Enjoy!

What is the Web Photo Gallery?

The Web Photo Gallery is an exciting feature that automatically and quickly creates a Web site that displays a series of images in thumbnails and larger formats. This process automatically optimizes the images and writes HTML to produce a Web site suitable for publishing online. The Web Photo Gallery is a great tool for artists to display their work, for architects to show renderings to clients, for photographers to show proofs, for families to share personal photos on the Web, and for many other purposes too numerous to list here. In Photoshop 6 the Web Photo Gallery has been enhanced with more options and more opportunity for you to control the look of the Web sites Photoshop builds for you.

When you make a Web Photo Gallery, Photoshop starts with a folder of images you provide and does all of the following for you:

- The program copies, resizes, and optimizes the images, and then creates a thumbnail and a larger JPEG of each image in the folder.

- Photoshop also writes all the HTML code for a Web site that includes a page of thumbnails and a separate page for the larger version of each image.

- Photoshop even generates arrow keys for **next**, **previous**, and **home** buttons!

Photoshop gives you lots of options for customizing your Web Photo Gallery, but you can modify it even further by bringing it into an HTML editor like Adobe GoLive, a text editor, or a word processing application. To do so, you simply launch that other application and choose **File > Open** to open any of the **.htm** files that Photoshop generated. (At the end of each HTML file, Photoshop puts the file extension .htm, which works just the same as .html in any Web browser.)

It should be noted that in order to display a Web Photo Gallery live on the Web, you must first obtain an account for server space, plus know how to upload using a stand-alone FTP application like Fetch (Mac) or WS-FTP (Windows), or the uploading features in an HTML editor like Adobe GoLive. If you want to add a Web Photo Gallery to an existing Web site, you'll also need to know how to link to the Gallery from other pages in your site.

[PS]

I. _____Creating a Web Photo Gallery

This exercise walks you through the steps for creating a Web Photo Gallery in Photoshop. Once you learn how to do this to the folder of images supplied on the **H•O•T CD-ROM**, try it on a folder of your own images. We predict you'll be amazed at how simple it is to generate an entire Web site without needing any HTML coding knowledge whatsoever.

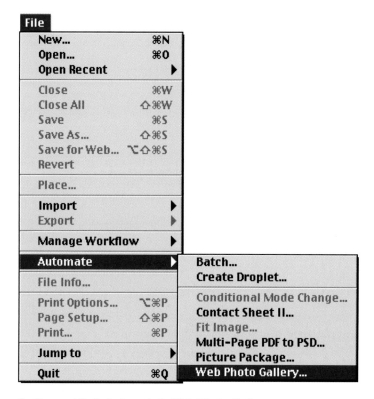

1. Choose **File > Automate > Web Photo Gallery**....

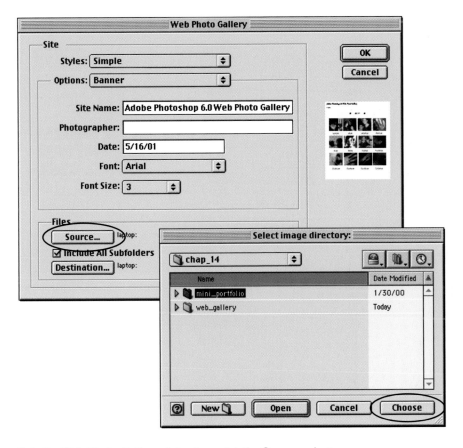

2. In the **Web Photo Gallery** dialog box, click the **Source...** button.

- **Mac:** In the **Select Image directory** window, navigate to the **Chap_14** folder you transferred to your hard drive from the **H•O•T CD ROM**. Select the **mini_portfolio** folder, and click **Choose**. This will return you to the Web Photo Gallery dialog box. The next steps will show you how to fill out the settings in the Web Photo Gallery dialog box, so don't click **OK** just yet.

- **Windows:** In the **Browse For Folder** dialog box, navigate to the **Chap_14** folder you transferred to your hard drive from the **H•O•T CD ROM**, select the **mini_portfolio** folder, and click **OK**. This will return you to the Web Photo Gallery dialog box. The next steps will show you how to fill out the settings in the Web Photo Gallery dialog box, so don't click **OK** there just yet.

The Web Photo Gallery accepts source images in many different formats, including .psd, .tiff, .pict, .bmp, .eps, and .ai.

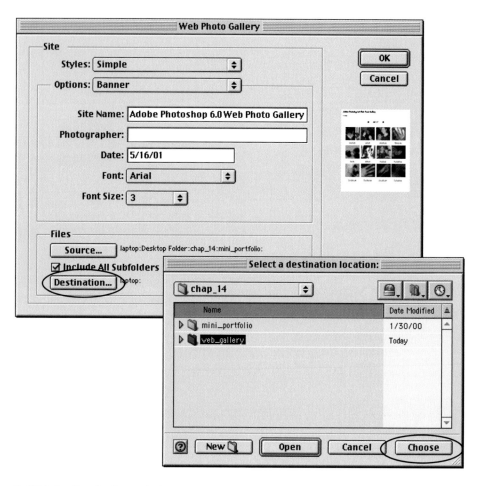

3. Click the **Destination...** button.

- **Mac:** In the **Select a destination location** window, navigate to the **web_gallery** folder in the **Chap_14** folder on your hard drive, and click **Choose**. This will return you to the Web Photo Gallery dialog box. Don't click **OK** yet.

- **Windows:** In the **Browse For Folder** dialog box, navigate to the **web_gallery** folder in the **Chap_14** folder on your hard drive, and click **OK** in the Browse For Folder dialog box. This will return you to the Web Photo Gallery dialog box. Don't click **OK** there yet.

Tip: When you make a Web Photo Gallery on your own, click the New Folder button to create a destination folder on your hard drive.

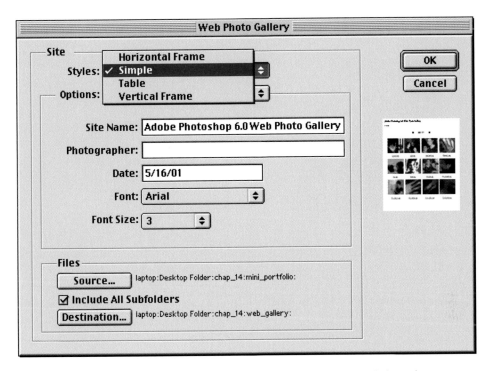

4. Press the **Styles** button, and choose **Simple** from the pop-up menu of site styles.

Styles may already be set to Simple if you've never used the Web Photo Gallery. Otherwise, you'll see the Styles setting you last used. Photoshop remembers all of the settings you chose the last time you made a Web Photo Gallery.

NOTE | Site Styles

Site styles are templates for the layout of a Web Photo Gallery site. Here's how the home page of this site would look with each of the four Style settings that ship with Photoshop 6.

Simple Style

Table Style

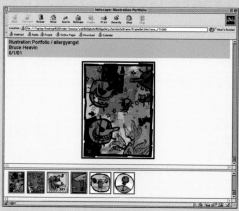
Horizontal Frame Style

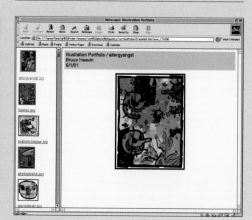
Vertical Frame Style

If you know HTML, you can build a custom style by altering the .htm files that ship with Photoshop. These files are located in the Presets > WebContact Sheet folder in the Photoshop 6 application folder on your hard drive. We don't suggest you try this unless you are an advanced user. It's easier to apply one of the four pre-made styles, and then bring the finished site into an HTML editor like Adobe GoLive to customize the site layout.

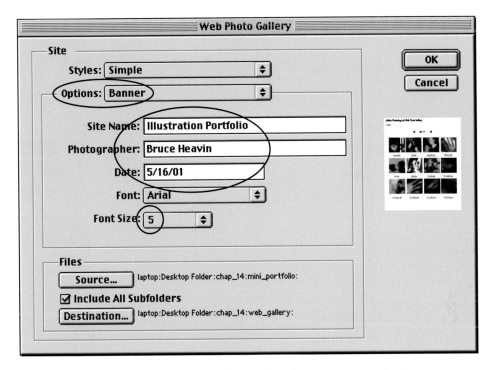

5. Press the **Options** button and choose **Banner** from the pop-up menu of options groups (if it's not showing already). Enter **Site Name: Illustration Portfolio,** and **Photographer: Bruce Heavin**. (Lynda's husband Bruce created these wonderful illustrations.) Photoshop automatically fills out the **Date** field, though you can manually enter a change if you'd prefer. Leave the **Font** setting at its default, **Arial**, and change the **Font Size** to **5**.

Choosing Options: Banner displays all the options for customizing the banner that will appear at the top of each page of the Gallery site. The information you enter into the Site Name, Photographer, and Date fields will be displayed as HTML text in the banner on the first page of the site.

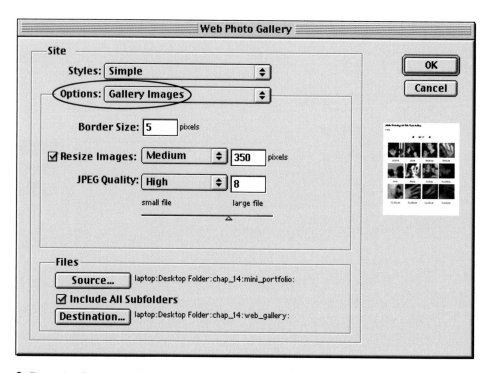

6. Press the **Options** button again, and choose **Gallery Images**. Leave all these settings at their defaults for now, so that they match the illustration above.

The Gallery Images settings affect the large version of each image that will appear on an individual page in the Gallery site. Notice that only JPEG (not GIF) optimization is available for images in a Web Photo Gallery. This is something we hope will change in future versions of Photoshop. For now, however, there isn't a way to change this setting.

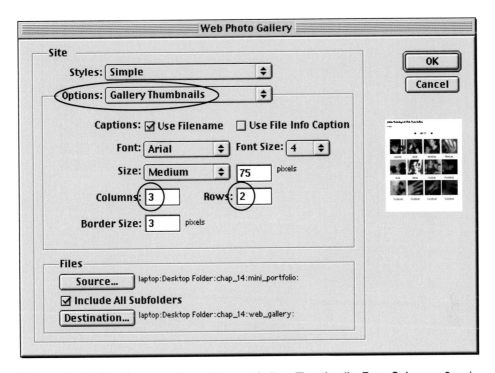

7. Press the **Options** button again, and choose **Gallery Thumbnails**. Enter **Columns: 3** and **Rows: 2**. Leave the other settings at their defaults for now.

This group of settings affects the way the thumbnails of all the images will appear on the first page of the site.

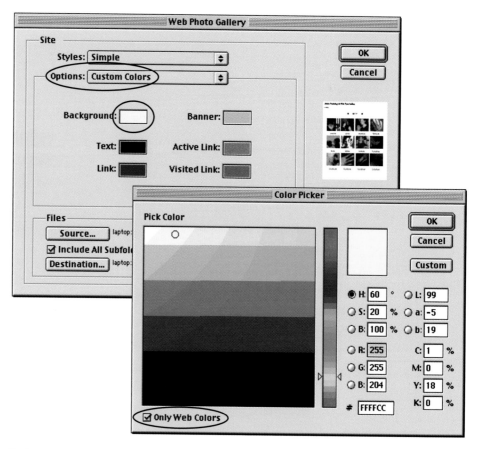

8. Click the **Options** button one more time, and choose **Custom Colors**. Click inside the **Background** color box in the **Web Photo Gallery** window. When the **Color Picker** opens, make sure **Only Web Colors** is checked. Choose a light yellow color, and click **OK**. Set colors in each of the other color boxes (**Banner**, **Text**, **Link**, **Active Link**, and **Visited Link**) the same way, choosing colors similar to those in the illustration above.

See the chart of Web Photo Gallery Options below for an explanation of what each color box controls.

 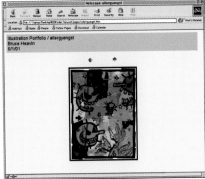

9. You can now click **OK** in the **Web Photo Gallery** dialog box. Photoshop will create the site, open a browser, and show you the Web site it just built in seconds. Click on a thumbnail image on the first page to jump to a page with a larger version of that image. Click on the navigation arrows that Photoshop generated to move between pages.

Warning: If you want to change the appearance of the site, you will need to return to Photoshop and change settings in the Web Photo Gallery dialog box, or edit the HTML file in an HTML or text editor.

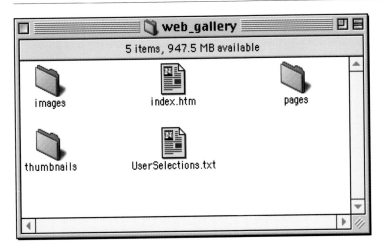

10. Go to your hard drive to look inside the **chap_14** folder; then open the **web_gallery** folder to see that Photoshop created folders for HTML pages, images, and thumbnails for you.

What Do All the Web Photo Gallery Settings Do?

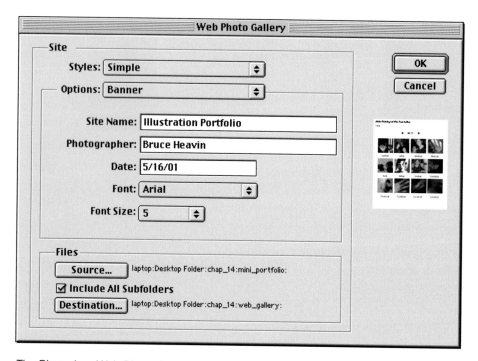

The Photoshop Web Photo Gallery contains many settings, most of which were left at their defaults in this exercise.

Web Photo Gallery Settings	
Setting	**Description**
Source	This button lets you select the folder of images from which Photoshop will build the Web Photo Gallery.
Destination	This button lets you select the destination folder to which Photoshop will write the images and HTML once it's finished creating the Web Photo Gallery.
Styles	Use this button to choose one of four site layouts. The Table style displays images in tables against a textured, gray background image. The Simple style also uses tables to position images, but these tables are invisible. There are two frame-based styles—Horizontal Frame and Vertical Frame.

continues on next page

Web Photo Gallery Settings *continued*

Banner Options

Site Name	The name you put in this field will appear in the banner on each page in the site and in the title bar of a Web browser displaying the first page of the site.
Photographer	Enter the name of the person who gets credit for creating the images here. Sadly, Photoshop uses the word *Photographer* for this field. The Web Photo Gallery is used for many types of artwork—and authors are not always photographers. The good news is that the word Photographer does not appear in the actual Gallery site.
Date	Photoshop automatically inserts the date on which the Web Photo Gallery is created. You can change this manually if you want.
Font	Choose Arial, Helvetica, Courier, or Times New Roman as the font of the HTML text in the banners.
Font Size	This setting determines the relative size of the HTML text in the banners on each page in the site. The higher the number, the larger the text will be. Unfortunately, you can't determine the actual size at which text will be displayed in a Web browser. Text size is relative to a default base text size, which a viewer can modify in his or her browser.

Gallery Thumbnails Options

Captions	Here you choose the captions that will appear beneath each thumbnail image on the first page of the site. Leave both boxes unchecked if you want no captions. Check *Use File Name* to create captions from the file names of each image in the source folder. Check *Use File Info Caption* to use custom captions you previously embedded in each image in the source folder. (To embed a caption in a source image, open that image in Photoshop, choose *File > File Info*, choose *Caption* from the drop-down *Section* menu, and type a name into the *Caption* field. Click *OK*, and choose *File > Save*).
Font and Font Size	This setting dictates the Font (*Arial, Helvetica, Courier,* or *Times New Roman*) and relative size of the text in the thumbnail captions.
Size	This setting determines the width in pixels of all of the thumbnail images on the first page of the site. If you start with images of unequal width, Photoshop will make all the thumbnails the same width, but different heights that are proportional to the originals.

continues on next page

Web Photo Gallery Settings *continued*	
Gallery Thumbnails Options *continued*	
Columns and Rows	This setting dictates the number of Columns and Rows in the arrangement of the thumbnail images on the first page of the site.
Border Size	This sets the size in pixels of the border around each of the thumbnail images on the first page of the site.
Gallery Image Options	
Border Size	This sets the size in pixels of the border around each of the larger images to which the thumbnails are linked (the Gallery images).
Resize Images	This setting dictates the width in pixels of all of the Gallery images Photoshop will generate. Check the *Resize Image* box, and choose from the presets, or type in a custom number of pixels. If you leave the Resize Image box unchecked, the Gallery images will be the same size as the original images in the source folder.
JPEG Quality	The Web Photo Gallery optimizes images only as JPEGs. You can choose a compression setting from 0 to 12 (0 applies the maximum amount of compression, and 12, the minimum). Use the slider or the presets, or type in a compression setting.
Custom Colors Options	
Background	The Background color you choose will fill the background of each page in the site.
Banner	The Banner color you choose will fill the horizontal banner at the top of each page.
Text	The Text color will affect the text in each banner.
Link, Active Link, Visited Link	Each thumbnail caption on the first page of the site will be the Link color initially, the Active Link color when clicked, and the Visited Link color after being clicked.

Actions that Ship with Photoshop and ImageReady

This chapter will show you how to create your own custom actions. Once you get acquainted with the Actions feature in both Photoshop and ImageReady, you'll notice that there are already actions inside the **Actions** palette. If you'd like to try some of these, you can simply click on the **Play** button at the bottom of the Actions palette to see what happens. On playback, certain actions contain prompts that explain how the action is supposed to work.

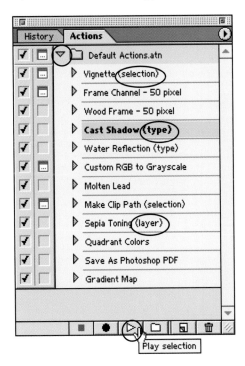

If you click on the arrow to the left of the **Default Actions.atn** folder in the **Actions** palette, you'll see the contents of that folder. Some of the actions have qualifying words in parentheses, such as **Vignette (selection)**, **Cast Shadow (type)**, and **Sepia Toning (layer)**. Those are hints that these actions only work under certain conditions, such as when there is a selection active, when there is editable or rendered type, or when there is an independent layer in a document. Note that the actions shown above are from Photoshop. ImageReady ships with different actions.

It's very easy to try out these default actions. Simply click on the action you want (exactly the same as you would select a layer in the **Layers** palette) and then click on the **Play** button at the bottom of the palette. If you don't have the proper condition set up for the action to play, it will either warn you or it will not work. That's the worst that can happen, so feel free to explore how these pre-built actions work.

[PS]

2. Creating an Action

Photoshop's Actions feature lets you streamline your workflow by recording a series of commands and automatically applying those commands to a single file or to many files at once. Actions are a great way to automate repetitive tasks, like creating Web-ready thumbnails of images, which you'll get to do in this exercise. Actions are good for zillions of other things, but we've chosen this example to teach you the basics of setting up your own actions recording. You'll create an action that resizes a copy of an image to thumbnail size and saves it as an optimized GIF. In the following exercise, you'll apply that action to a whole folder of image files in just a single step with Photoshop's **Batch** command. You can also create actions in ImageReady in an identical fashion, which you'll get to do later in this chapter.

1. Open **allergyangst.psd** from the **mini_portfolio** folder in the **chap_14** folder.

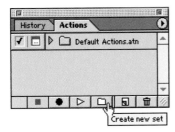

2. Choose **Window > Show Actions**, or click on the **Actions** tab to bring the **Actions** palette to the foreground. You'll notice that there is a folder called **Default Actions.atn**. These are actions you tried out in the last section that ship with Photoshop. Click on the **New Set** icon at the bottom of the **Actions** palette to create a folder to contain the actions you make yourself.

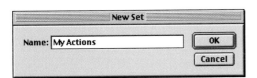

3. In the **New Set** window that opens, enter **Name: My Actions**, and click **OK**.

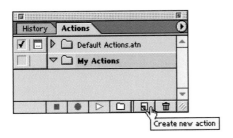

4. Click on the **New Action** icon at the bottom of the **Actions** palette.

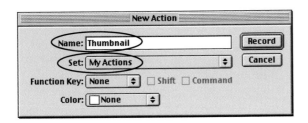

5. In the **New Action** window that will open, enter **Name: Thumbnail** to name the **Action** that you are creating. Make sure **My Actions** is selected in the **Set** field.

6. Click on the **Record** button in the **New Action** window to begin recording the **Thumbnail** Action. Everything you do in Photoshop from now until you stop recording will be part of the Action. The red dot at the bottom of the **Actions** palette indicates that you are now in recording mode.

7. Choose **File > Save for Web...**. This is the first step of the action.

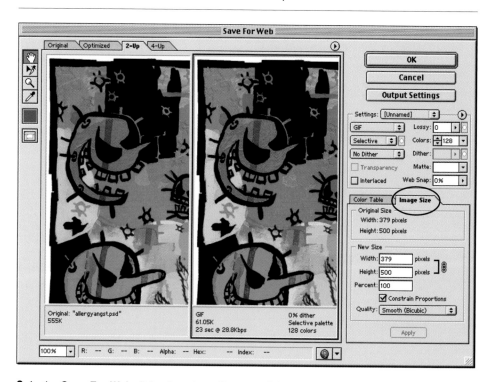

8. In the **Save For Web** dialog box that will open, click on the **Image Size** tab to bring the **Image Size** palette to the foreground.

We chose to work in the 2-Up tab so we could see more of the image while being able to compare it to the original.

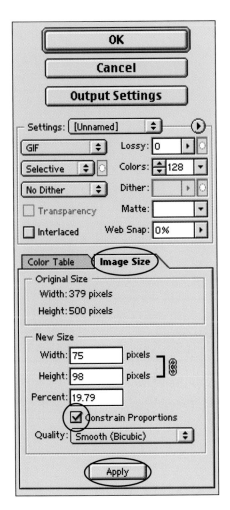

9. In the **Image Size** palette of the **Save For Web** dialog box, enter **Width: 75** to set the width of the thumbnail. This is measured in pixels. Make sure there is a check in the **Constrain Proportions** checkbox so that your image does not distort when resized. Click **Apply** to resize the image.

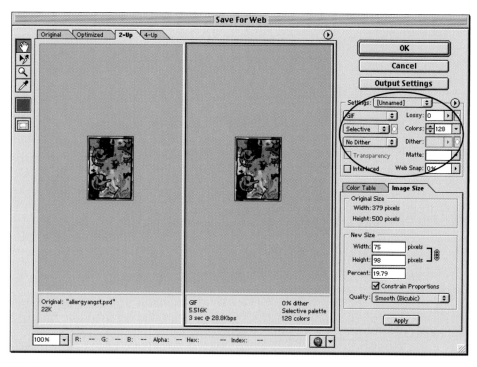

10. Choose image optimization settings. Try **GIF, Selective, Colors: 128, No Dither**, and **Lossy: 0**. Click **OK**. We suggest these settings because they seem to create the best-looking GIF.

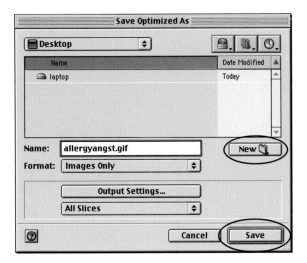

11. Next, you'll save the result inside a new folder that you'll create.

- **Mac:** In the **Save Optimized As** window that appears, navigate to the desktop, and click on the **New Folder** button. Name the new folder **thumbnails**, and click **Create**. Click **Save** to save a copy of the image as an optimized thumbnail named **allergyangst.gif**.

- **Windows:** In the **Save Optimized As** window that appears, navigate to the desktop, and click on the yellow **new folder** icon. Name the new folder **thumbnails**, and double-click on it so that it opens. Click **Save** to save a copy of the image as an optimized thumbnail named **allergyangst.gif** into the new folder called **thumbnails**.

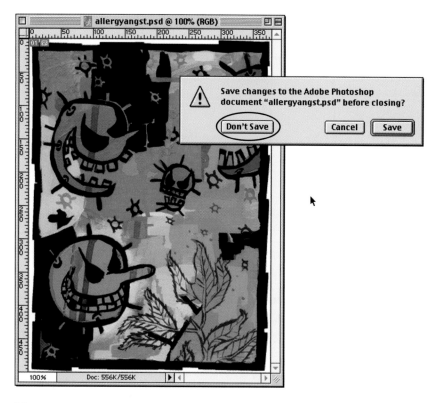

12. Back in Photoshop, close the original image without saving. This will preserve the **.psd** file without any changes.

This is the last step of the Action, and you'll program it as such in the next step.

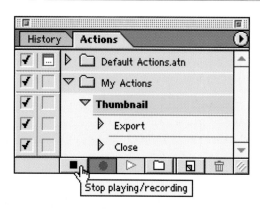

13. Click on the **Stop Recording** button in the **Actions** palette.

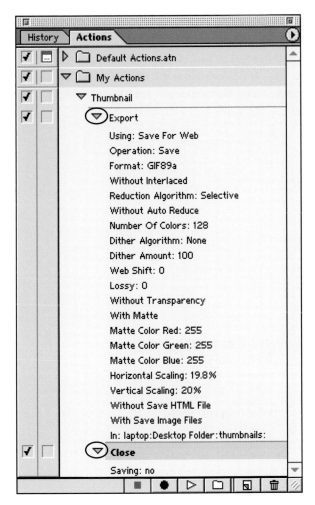

14. The arrow next to the **Thumbnail** action in the **Actions** palette will be pointing down, revealing all of the commands included in this action. Click on the arrows next to **Export** and **Close** (the action's two commands) to see the settings and steps included in each command.

You just successfully programmed an Action. Photoshop recorded everything you did, and now you can play back the recording on any images you like. The following exercise will show you how to take this Action and play it over a series of images contained in a folder.

[PS]

3.———————————**Batch Processing with an Action**

In this exercise, you'll use Photoshop's **Batch** feature to apply the Thumbnail action you created in the last exercise to a folder full of images. You can sit back and watch Photoshop automatically create thumbnails from each of the images in the folder. It's rather wondrous when you think how long it would take to do this process manually.

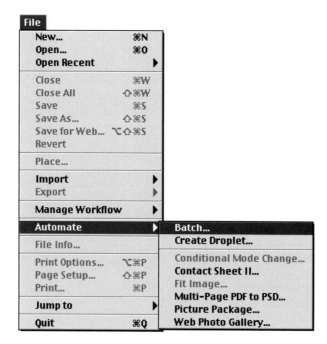

1. Choose **File > Automate > Batch....**

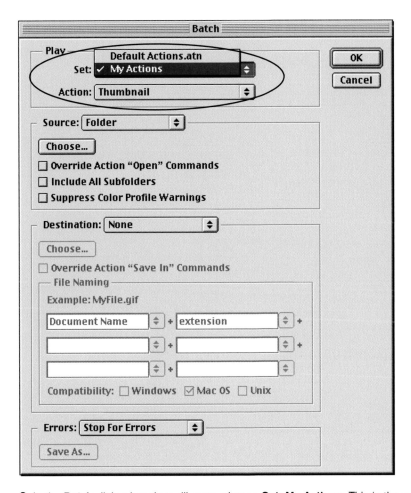

2. In the **Batch** dialog box that will open, choose **Set: My Actions**. This is the set of actions in which your Thumbnail action is located. Choose **Action: Thumbnail**, the action you created in the last exercise.

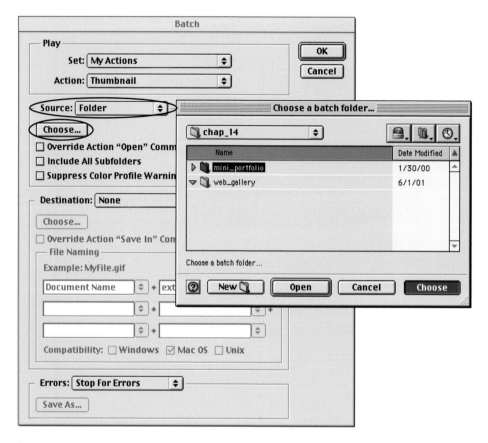

3. Choose **Source: Folder**. Then click on the **Choose…** button directly below it.

- **Mac:** In the **Choose a batch folder** window that will open, navigate to the **Chap_14** folder, click on the **mini_portfolio** folder, and click **Choose**.

- **Windows:** In the **Browse For Folder** dialog box that will open, navigate to the **Chap_14** folder, select the **mini_portfolio** folder and click **OK**.

If you want to try this Action on your own image files, first put your source files into a single folder.

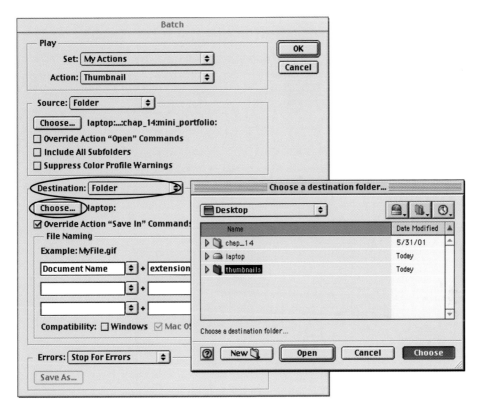

4. Back in the Batch dialog box, select **Destination: Folder**, then click on the **Choose...** button.

- **Mac:** In the **Choose a destination folder** window that will open, navigate to the desktop, select the **thumbnails** folder, and click **Choose**.

- **Windows:** In the **Browse for Folder** dialog box that will open, navigate to the desktop, select the **thumbnails** folder, and click **OK**.

You created a thumbnails folder on your desktop in Exercise 2 when you recorded this Thumbnail Action. If you can't find that folder, create a new thumbnails folder on the desktop using the New Folder button in the Choose a destination folder window (Mac), or the Browse for Folder dialog box (Windows).

> **WARNING | A Problem with Batch**
>
> The Batch dialog box is supposed to enable you to select a **Destination** folder by click-
> ing on the **Destination: Choose** button. Unfortunately, this doesn't work with Save For
> Web. If you record an action that involves Save For Web, as the Thumbnail action did,
> the Destination folder you select while recording will become the Destination folder
> regardless of whether or not you select a different folder in the Batch dialog box.
>
> The action you just recorded and batch processed will work correctly because you will
> have selected the same Destination folder in the action recording and the Batch dialog
> box. If you choose a different destination in the Batch dialog box, your thumbnails will
> still be saved in the destination you chose when you recorded the action.

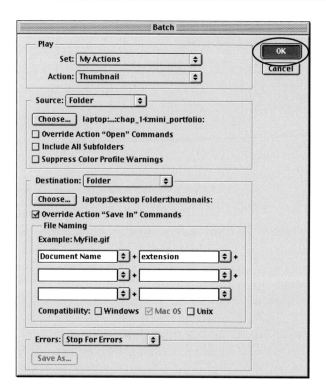

5. Click **OK** to begin playing the Thumbnail action on all the images in the **mini_portfolio**
folder.

*Kick back and watch Photoshop automatically resize, optimize, and save a thumbnail copy
of each image. This is the good life, isn't it?*

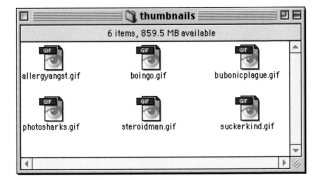

6. Open the **thumbnails** folder on your desktop to see all of the thumbnails that Photoshop just created for you.

TIP | Applying an Action to a Single File

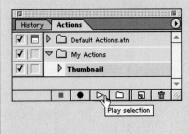

Batch processing is awesome, as you can already tell from Exercise 3. But what about those times when you want to work with only one file? As an alternative to batch processing, you can apply your Thumbnail action to just a single file.

Here's what to do: Simply open the file on which you want to apply the action and click on the Play button at the bottom of the Actions palette. The action will perform its task on the one file, and will still be a great timesaver.

NOTE | Actions in ImageReady

Now that you've learned to create an action in Photoshop, you might wonder if you can do the same thing in ImageReady. Yes, you can. ImageReady also contains an actions palette, and recording actions is done identically there. The difference is that there is no Automate menu item in ImageReady. If you want to apply an action you make in ImageReady to a folder of images, you will need to make a **Droplet** instead. You'll learn how to make Droplets later in this chapter.

Adding, Changing, Deleting, or Pausing an Action

Once you've created an action, you can always change it later. You can easily initiate a pause, and add or delete steps. Here's a chart to reference if you want to do any operations with actions beyond what the preceding exercises have taught.

Working with Actions	
Operations	**Methods**
To Add an Item	To add another item into an action, click on the upper-right arrow of the Actions palette, and choose *Start Recording* from the pop-up menu. Whatever you do at this point will be inserted at the end of the existing action. When you're finished, click the *Stop Recording* button at the bottom of the Actions palette. If you want to add another item somewhere in the middle of the recording, simply select whichever line item it should come after and then record your change.
To Delete an Item	To delete a portion of an action, simply select that portion in the Actions palette, and click on the *Trash can* icon at the bottom of the palette or click on the upper-right arrow at the top and choose *Delete*. Either way, you will be asked if you want to delete that section and you should click *OK*.
To Set a Pause	Setting a pause enables the action to stop in the middle of playback. Let's say you want to create a new document with an action. If you inserted a pause, you could enter the dimensions of the new document instead of having the new document always open at the same dimensions. To set a pause, wait until after you have completed recording the action. Click in the column to the left of the command in which you want to initiate a pause. The icon that will appear in that column indicates that a pause has been set at that point in the action.

[IR]

4. ————————Creating a Preview in Browser Action

In applications other than ImageReady, we're accustomed to using the **F12** key as a quick shortcut for previewing work in a browser. That's no problem, because you can set ImageReady up to honor the same shortcut if you program it as an action. This is a good example of when you'd want to program an action in ImageReady rather than Photoshop, because it's rare that you'll ever preview a Web graphic from Photoshop.

1. Switch to ImageReady. Open **bg.psd** from the **Chap_14** folder.

2. If the **Actions** palette isn't open, choose **Window > Show Actions**. Click on the **New Action** icon at the bottom of the palette.

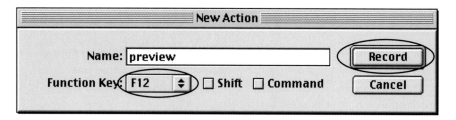

3. In the **New Action** window that will open, enter **Name: preview**. Click on the pop-up menu to the right of **Function Key:** to choose **F12**. Click **Record**.

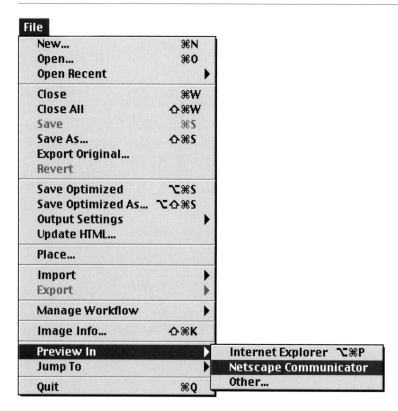

4. Choose **File > Preview In** and choose a browser.

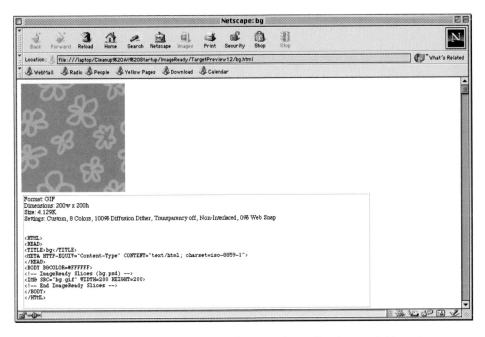

5. The image will appear inside the browser. Return to ImageReady to end this action.

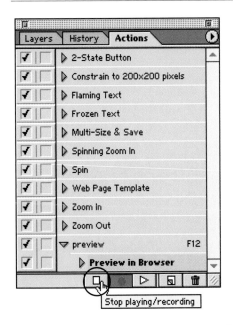

6. Click on the **Stop** button at the bottom of the **Actions** palette.

7. Choose **File > Open** to open a different image from the **Chap_14** folder, and press **F12** to run your new action on this image. You will grow to love how handy this shortcut will become to you.

Warning: If you're on a Mac and are having trouble using the F12 key, choose Apple > Control Panels > Keyboard, click the Function Keys button, and uncheck Use F1 through F12 as Hot Function Keys.

---

8. Leave **bg.psd** open for the next exercise.

From now on, any time you want to preview in the browser, simply press F12 and your wish will be ImageReady's command! This action *is stored and forever there until you alter or delete it. Another quick way to preview in a browser from ImageReady 3 is simply to click the Preview in Default Browser button on the Toolbox. However, you may prefer your custom F12 action if you're used to using that function key to preview in other programs.*

[IR]

5. —————————Previewing Backgrounds with an Action

That last action was great for previewing foreground images, but what about those cases when you want to preview an image as a background? This next exercise will show you how.

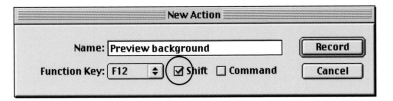

1. With **bg.psd** still open from the previous exercise, click on the **New Action** icon at the bottom of ImageReady's **Actions** palette. In the **New Action** window that will open, enter **Name: Preview background** and **Function Key: F12**, and put a check in the **Shift** checkbox. Click **Record**.

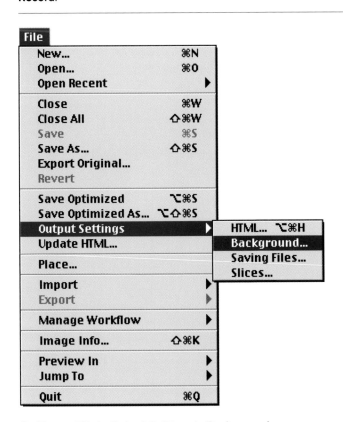

2. Choose **File > Output Settings > Background…**.

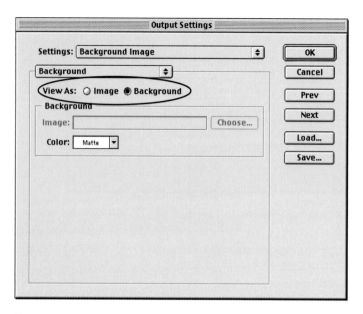

3. In the **Output Settings** window that will open, select **View As: Background** to set the optimized image as an HTML background image. Click **OK**.

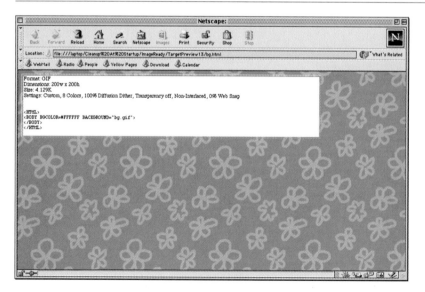

4. Choose **File > Preview in** and choose a browser. A preview of **bg.gif** will appear in the browser. This is the last step in this action.

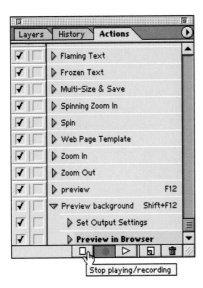

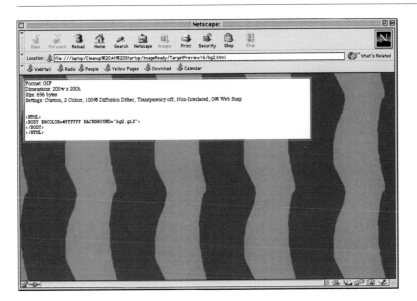

5. Return to ImageReady. Click on the **Stop** button in the actions palette. Now your action is recorded and good to try.

6. Close **bg.psd** and do not save. Open **bg2.psd** from the **Chap_14** folder. Press **Shift+F12** and watch it preview as a repeating background.

7. Close the file (you don't need to save), and you're ready for the next exercise.

[IR]

6. ———————————Automating Optimization with a Droplet

Optimizing images can be a time-consuming, repetitive process. ImageReady 3's **Droplet** feature makes optimization of multiple images efficient and easy. A droplet is a tiny application that runs an ImageReady action on images you identify by dragging and dropping. In this exercise, you will learn to create a droplet that stores the optimization settings of one image. You'll then automatically apply those settings to a folder full of images by simply dragging the folder onto the droplet.

1. Open **boingo.psd** from the **mini_portfolio** folder in the **Chap_14** folder.

2. Click on the **4-Up** tab on the screen to open four preview frames in which you can compare the look and size of the image at various optimization settings.

If the image previews look really terrible, it's because you haven't optimized them yet. You'll get to that in the next step.

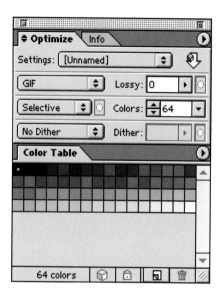

3. In the **Optimize** palette (Window > Show Optimize), choose compression settings that create the smallest image that is of acceptable quality. Try **GIF**, **Selective**, **Colors: 64**, **No Dither**, and **Lossy: 0**.

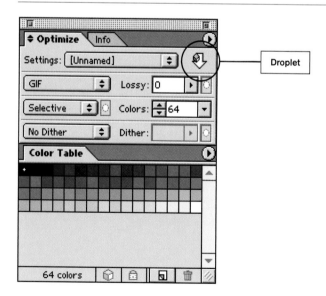

Droplet

4. Click on the **Droplet** icon on the **Optimize** palette. This will open the **Save optimized settings as droplet** dialog box.

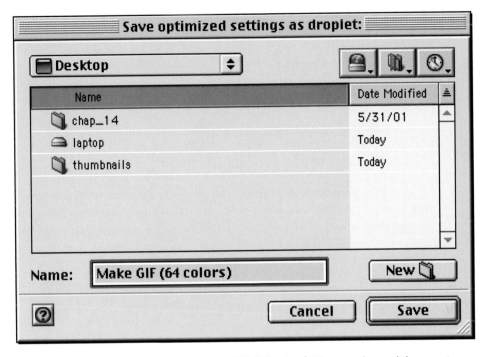

5. The default name of the droplet is **Make GIF (64 colors)**. You can change it here, or type over its title on the desktop. It's a good idea to give it a descriptive name, which the default name does well. Navigate to your desktop, and click **Save**. You can save a droplet to a folder or to your desktop. We're suggesting you save it to the desktop only because it's easy to find there.

6. Close the original version of **boingo.psd** without saving.

You needed the boingo *image open so you could judge the results of what kind of optimization to set. You can now use the droplet you just created to automatically optimize a folder full of images.*

Make GIF (64 colors)   mini_portfolio

7. Copy **mini_portfolio** from the **chap_14** folder on the **H•O•T CD-ROM** to your desktop. Click and drag the copy of the **mini-portfolio** folder directly on top of the **Make GIF (64 colors) Droplet** icon on the desktop in order to begin the automatic batch processing.

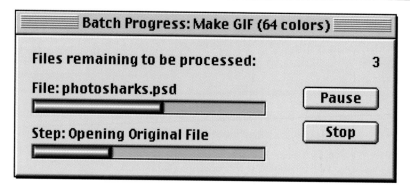

Progress bars in the Batch Progress window will keep track as the droplet optimizes each of the images your mini_portfolio folder.

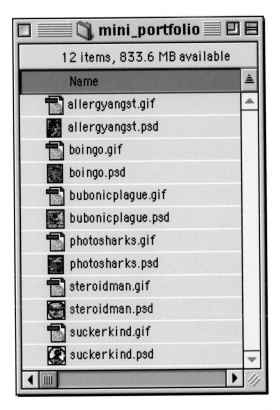

8. When the automatic optimizing is done, look in the **mini_portfolio** folder on your desktop and you will find the original .psd files and the optimized .gif files. The droplet processed all the original .psd files, optimized them, and saved the optimized versions back into the same folder.

 MOVIE | droplet.mov

To learn more about creating a droplet, check out **droplet.mov** from the **movies** folder on the **H·O·T CD-ROM**.

NOTE | Changing the Droplet

By default, droplets save the optimized images in the same folder as the original images. If you wanted to save the optimized images in a destination folder, you could use the **Batch Options** dialog box. This dialog box is only reachable by double-clicking on the droplet that you saved (in this case to your desktop).

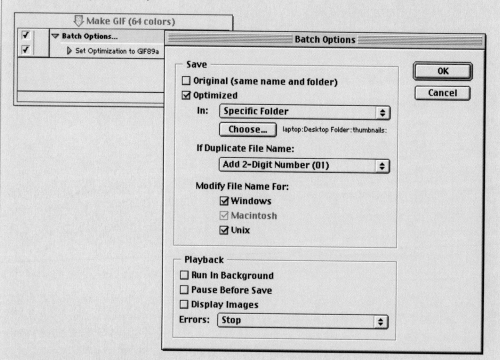

When it opens, you'll see a new window that resembles an action list labeled Make GIF (64 colors). Double-click on **Batch Options...** and the **Batch Options** dialog box will appear. Here, you can alter the way the droplet saves the results through a number of different settings and pop-up menus. For example, you could change the **Optimized In** field to **Specific Folder**, navigate to a particular destination folder, and click **Choose**.

More About Droplets

There are a few other neat things to share about actions.

- A droplet is similar to an action in that it records and plays back over a series of images. In the last exercise you saved the droplet to the desktop. That's where we like to store droplets because it's easy to drag and drop files onto them when we know where to find them! However, you can put them inside other folders on your hard drive and they will still function just fine.

- Photoshop 6 now offers a limited ability to make and apply droplets. In Photoshop you can create a droplet directly from an action, but you can't make or apply a droplet that stores Optimization settings.

- You can make droplets from the Actions palette in ImageReady and in Photoshop. In ImageReady, go to the Actions palette, select the action from which you want to make a droplet, and click on the upper-right arrow to choose Create Droplet... from the pop-up menu. In Photoshop, choose File > Automate > Create Droplet, click Choose to select a destination for the Droplet icon, select the Set and Action from which to create the droplet, and click OK.

- If ImageReady isn't open, you can drag a folder or image onto a droplet and it will launch that application for you to execute the optimization procedures. You can't really undo a droplet. If you want to change one, it's easiest if you just start over the process of creating it in the first place.

- Droplets are cross-platform, so you can share them between Mac and Windows users. However, for Windows machines to recognize that a droplet is an application, you need to add .exe to the end of the droplet name.

- ImageReady lets you drag and drop steps from the History palette into the Actions palette, which is a fast way to add steps to an action.

- For the true geeks, ImageReady actions are written in JavaScript, and can be edited or generated once you look at a sample action to see how the instructions and settings are structured.

Another chapter down, with just one more to go. If you have any files open in ImageReady, go ahead and close them without saving.

15.

Importing/Exporting

| Update HTML in ImageReady | ImageReady Rollovers Into GoLive 5 |
| ImageReady Rollovers Into Dreamweaver 3 or 4 |
| Illustrator 9 Into Photoshop 6 or ImageReady 3 |
| Exporting from Earlier Versions of Illustrator |
| ImageReady to QuickTime | QuickTime to Animated GIF |

chap_15

Photoshop 6 / ImageReady 3
H•O•T CD-ROM

This chapter addresses advanced issues of importing and exporting file formats (other than psd, gif, and jpg) to and from Photoshop and ImageReady. We don't know whether you have some of the programs described here, such as GoLive, Dreamweaver, or Illustrator, so we can't anticipate whether or not you'll know how to use those applications. It's obviously beyond the scope of this book for us to teach those applications as well as Photoshop and ImageReady. For that reason, keep in mind that parts of this chapter are for advanced users who know how to perform tasks in those applications (GoLive, Dreamweaver, or Illustrator) without much coaching.

This chapter will be helpful to those of you who are interested in importing and exporting HTML, Illustrator, JavaScript, and QuickTime files. Most books touch upon only a single application, but because Web development almost always involves more than one program, we had an idea that this chapter might be useful to many of you readers out there ;-).

[IR]

I. —————————Update HTML in ImageReady

Update HTML is an ImageReady command that writes over existing ImageReady-generated HTML files and updates only things that have changed. Suppose that you made a remote rollover in ImageReady and had saved the images and HTML in a folder on your hard drive. Your client looks at the work and likes everything but notices a spelling error. If you had saved the psd version of the file too, it would be easy to correct the spelling mistake, but it would require that you re-export all the optimized images and HTML. Or would it? The Update HTML command is useful when you make a change to an existing HTML file or its images. It saves you the headache of managing multiple versions of a document because it updates the HTML and images to reflect any changes you make to the psd file.

1. In ImageReady, open **remote_roll.psd** from the **chap_15** folder that you transferred to your hard drive from the **H•O•T CD-ROM**.

This is a sliced document with three remote rollovers that was made in ImageReady 3.

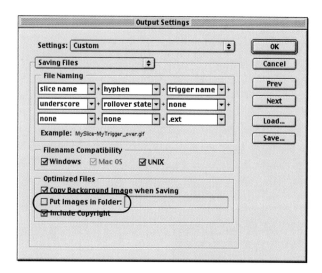

2. Choose **File > Output Settings > Saving Files....** Uncheck **Put Images in Folder**, and click **OK**.

Unchecking this box will cause ImageReady to write HTML and images to the same folder.

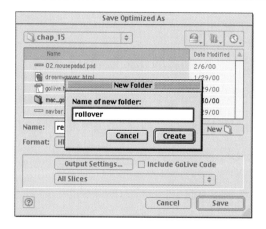

3. Choose **File > Save Optimized As...** and navigate to the **chap_15** folder.

- **Mac:** *Click on the* **New Folder** *button. Name the new folder* **rollover**, *and click on the* **Create** *button and then the* **Save** *button.*

- **Windows:** *Click on the yellow* **Folder** *icon to make a new folder. Name the folder* **rollover** *and double-click on it so that it opens. Click on the* **Save** *button, and all the files will populate the new folder you just created.*

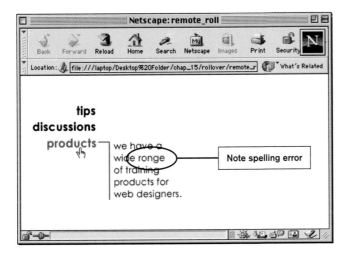

4. On your hard drive, open the **rollover** folder you just made, and double-click on **remote_roll.html**. This will open that HTML file in a browser. Move your mouse over the word **products**, and notice the spelling error in the word **ronge**. Return to ImageReady to fix this problem.

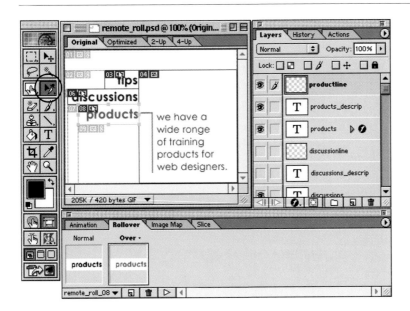

5. Back in ImageReady, select the **Slice Select** tool. (This will make the pre-built slices visible if they are not already.) Select the slice around the word **products** (slice **#08**). In the **Rollover** palette, click on the **Over** state. See the spelling error? Hey, spelling errors happen, right?

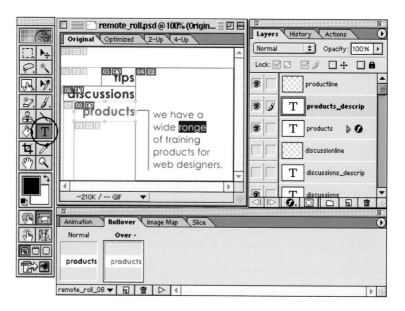

6. To fix the error, select the **Type** tool from the Toolbox and select the misspelled word **ronge**. Type **range** in its place.

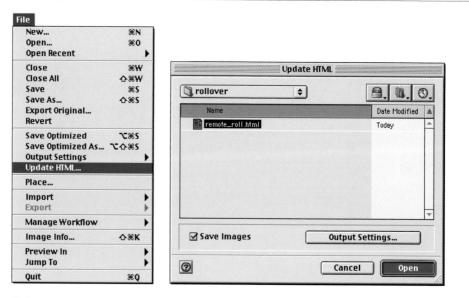

7. Once the spelling error is fixed, choose **File > Update HTML...**, and navigate to open the **rollover** folder you just created inside the **chap_15** folder. Select **remote_roll.html**, and click **Open**.

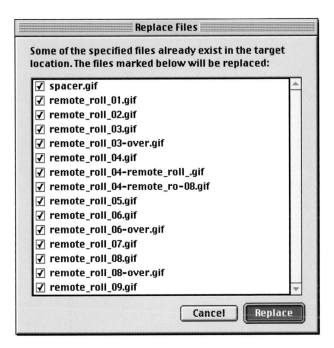

8. Click **Replace** when prompted. This will replace all the image files inside the **rollover** folder that are related to **remote_roll.html**, as well as the HTML file itself.

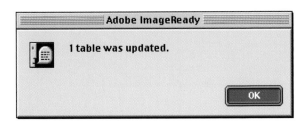

9. ImageReady will tell you that one table in the HTML file was updated. Click **OK**.

*ImageReady just rewrote all the files that you created in Step 3, and you avoided having to save a duplicate set just to make this one change to your file. Whenever we're making changes to an ImageReady-generated HTML file or images, we use **Update HTML** so we don't have multiple folders lying around with different versions of artwork and HTML.*

10. Close **remote_roll.psd**,and click **Save** when prompted.

How Does Update HTML Work?

In ImageReady, Update HTML uses comment tags to recognize where to replace code and images properly. Comment tags are an HTML convention that allows a programmer to write a comment inside the file without the browser showing that comment. When you use Update HTML, it's essential that ImageReady write its own comment tags.

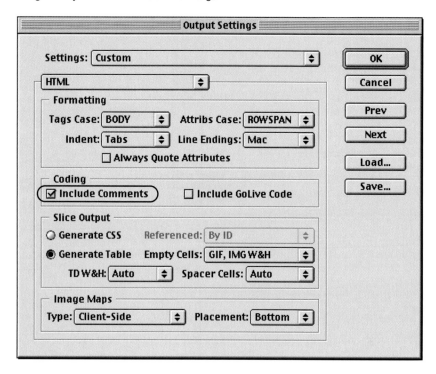

The setting to include comment tags is found under File > Output Settings > HTML…, and is on by default.

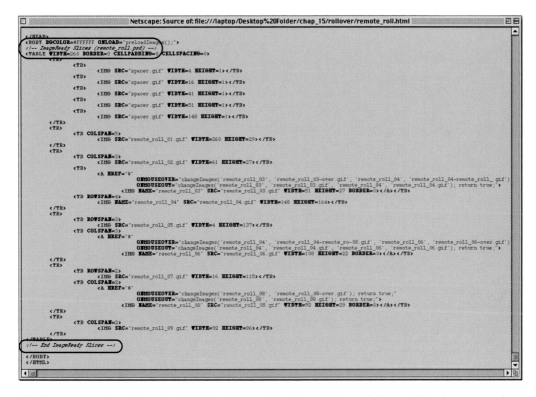

HTML comment tags always include brackets, exclamation points, and dashes. Here is an example:

`<! -- comment goes here --!>`.

If you copy and paste ImageReady code into a larger HTML document, Update HTML will still work if you leave the comment tags intact. For this reason, if you plan to use Update HTML and work with coders who might edit your code afterwards, be sure to tell them to leave the ImageReady comment tags alone.

[IR]

2. ———————————**Getting ImageReady Rollovers into GoLive**

Making rollovers in ImageReady was pretty fun back in Chapter 11, "*Rollovers*," but as you followed the exercises you were probably asking yourself, "How do I get this into an HTML editor?" You can open an ImageReady HTML file inside any HTML editor and it will work properly. The harder thing to do is to integrate something you made in ImageReady (like a rollover) into an existing HTML page that you made in the HTML editor. You might want to design the rollover in ImageReady and then use it on other pages inside an existing site. This exercise will show you how to accomplish this in **GoLive 5**. The instructions are different for GoLive than for other HTML editors, probably because it's an Adobe product and the engineers were able to make ImageReady files easier to use with GoLive. The main trick to getting ImageReady rollovers to work in GoLive is to be sure to set ImageReady to write GoLive code, which you'll learn how to do here.

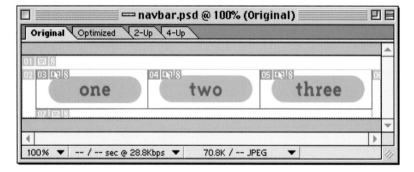

1. In ImageReady, open **navbar.psd** from the **chap_15** folder on your hard drive.

MOVIE | golive_rollovers.mov

To learn more about getting your ImageReady-created rollovers to work in GoLive, check out **golive_rollovers.mov** from the **movies** folder on the **H•O•T CD-ROM**.

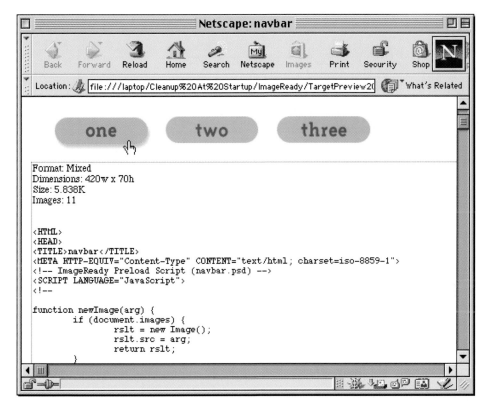

2. Click the **Preview in Default Browser** button in the ImageReady Toolbox to preview this file in a browser, and you'll see that it contains a series of three simple rollovers.

Next, you'll save this HTML file and images so they can eventually be copied into a GoLive site.

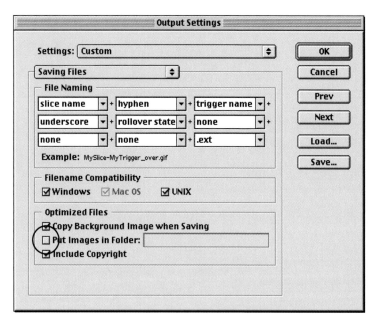

3. Return to ImageReady, and choose **File > Output Settings > Saving Files**. Uncheck **Put Images in Folder**, and click **OK**.

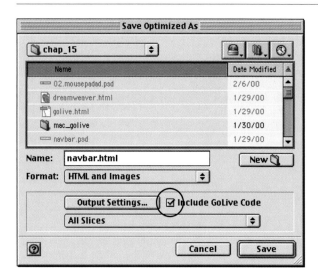

4. Choose **File > Save Optimized As…**, and put a checkmark in the box next to **Include GoLive Code**. Make sure that the **Format** field (Mac) or **Save as type** field (Windows) is set to **HTML and Images**.

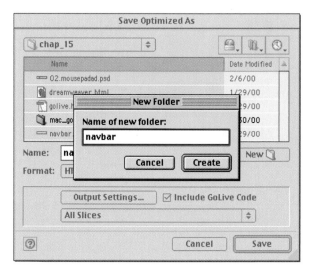

5. Navigate to the **chap_15** folder.

- **Mac:** *Click on the* **New Folder** *button. Name the new folder* **navbar**, *and click on the* **Create** *button and then the* **Save** *button.*

- **Windows:** *Click on the yellow* **Folder** *icon to make a new folder. Name the folder* **navbar**, *and double-click on it so that it opens. Click on the* **Save** *button, and all the files will populate the new folder you just created.*

This will create a navbar folder inside the chap_15 folder that contains the HTML and image files from navbar.psd.

---

6. In ImageReady, close **navbar.psd** without saving. You can leave ImageReady open, though you won't be using the program again for another couple of exercises.

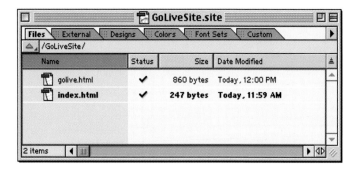

7. Open **GoLive 5.** Close the document named **untitled.html** that automatically opens. Choose **File > Open**, navigate to the **chap_15** folder > **GoLiveSite folder** > **GoLiveSite.site**, and click **Open**.

This will open a GoLive site that we made for you using GoLive 5. Note that you cannot open this site if you are using an earlier version of GoLive, because GoLive 5 files are not backwards compatible. Sorry.

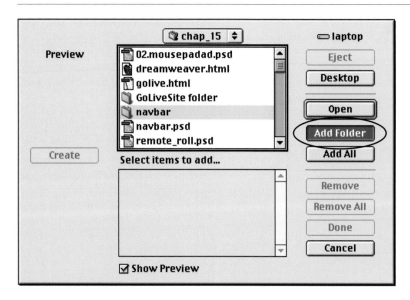

8. In GoLive, click inside the **Site** window (titled **GoLiveSite.site**) to activate the site. Choose **Site > Finder > Add Files** (Mac) or **Site > Explorer > Add Files** (Windows). In the window that opens, navigate to the **chap_15** folder. Select the **navbar** folder that you made earlier, and click on the **Add Folder** button.

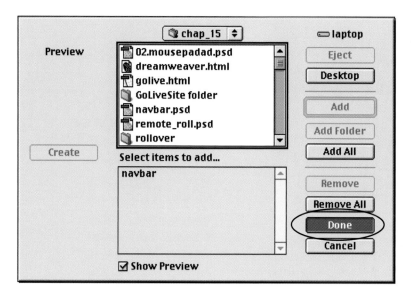

9. The folder **navbar** should now appear in the **Select items to add...** area. Click **Done**.

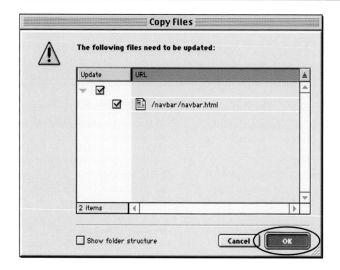

10. The **Copy Files** dialog box will appear. Click **OK**.

This is GoLive's way of updating the ImageReady HTML so that it is relative to the GoLive site. It's one of the strong points of GoLive's site management capabilities, because it ensures that all the links that were generated in ImageReady translate to GoLive properly.

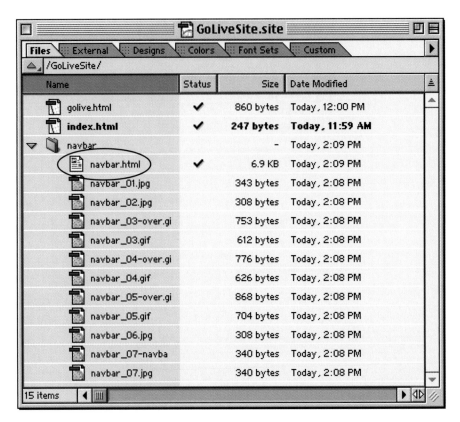

11. In the **Site** window, click on the **arrow** (Mac) or the **plus sign** (Windows) next to the **navbar** folder to reveal that folder's contents. Double-click on the **navbar.html** file to open it.

Warning: If you see an **images** folder in the **navbar** folder and **navbar.html** outside of that **images** folder, you neglected to follow Step 3, and will need to start this exercise over.

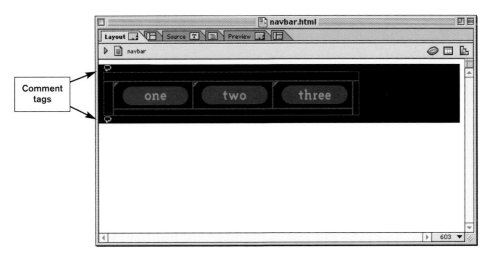

Comment tags

12. The file **navbar.html** will open in its own window in GoLive. Click and drag to select the contents of the file, including the **comment tags**. Choose **Edit > Copy**.

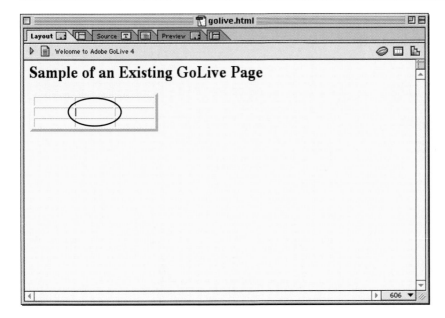

13. Return to the **Site** window by choosing **Window > GoLiveSite.site**, and open **golive.html** by double-clicking on it. This file will open in its own window in GoLive. Click on the table in the document to make it visible (it will look like a solid rectangle until you click on it), and click inside the middle table cell, as shown above.

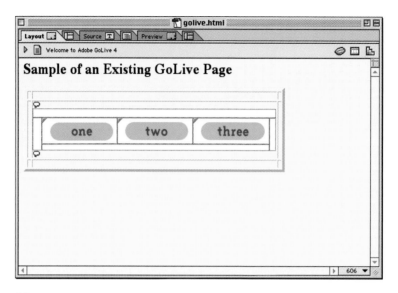

14. Choose **Edit > Paste**. This will paste the contents of the clipboard (the rollovers you copied from **navbar.html**) into the table on the **golive.html** page.

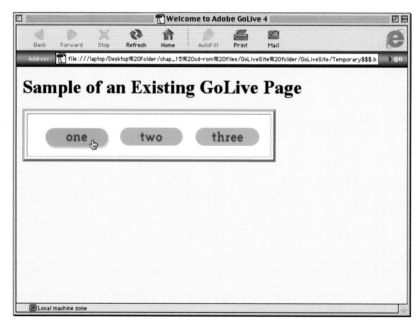

15. To preview this page in a browser, press **Command+T** (Mac) or **Control+T** (Windows). You'll see that it works in the browser just fine.

16. You're finished and can return to GoLive to choose **File > Quit**. If prompted to save your changes, click **Save**.

WARNING | Rollover Objects and GoLive

Notice the green corners on each of the rollovers? That indicates that GoLive is recognizing the ImageReady rollovers as GoLive **rollover objects**. If you are not familiar with rollover objects in GoLive, you can learn about them from the GoLive manual or the following book:

Real World Adobe GoLive 5
Jeff Carlson, Glenn Fleishman
Peachpit Press 0201704064
$44.99

Note: If you had not instructed ImageReady to **Include GoLive Code** in Step 4, the rollovers would not appear as a rollover objects in GoLive, and they would not work correctly in a browser. That's because the **Include GoLive Code** instruction in ImageReady tells ImageReady to format the JavaScript code it writes in a way that GoLive recognizes.

[IR]

3. ————————Getting ImageReady Rollovers into Dreamweaver

This next exercise shows how to put an ImageReady-generated rollover into **Dreamweaver 4**. These instructions also work for **Dreamweaver 3**. If all you want to do is use an ImageReady HTML file in its original form, you only need to open the file in Dreamweaver, and it will work just fine. This exercise shows you how to do something a little harder, which is to get the ImageReady rollover to work inside an existing HTML page that Dreamweaver generated. Unfortunately, this process is a little harder in Dreamweaver than it was in GoLive in the last exercise. It involves three different steps to copy and paste code between files, which will be outlined carefully in this hands-on exercise.

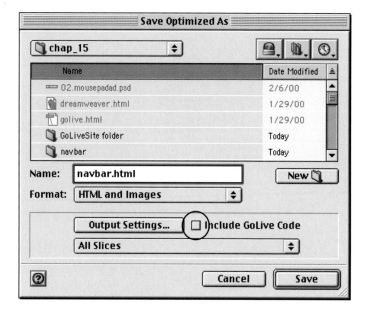

1. Go back to ImageReady and open **navbar.psd** from the **chap_15** folder again. The first thing to do is to save the HTML as **generic code** instead of GoLive code. This is the opposite instruction from the previous exercise. To do this, choose **File > Save Optimized As...**, and uncheck **Include GoLive Code**. Also, make sure the **Format** field (Mac) or **Save as type** field (Windows) is set to **HTML and Images**.

2. Navigate to the **chap_15** folder.

- **Mac:** *Click on the* **New Folder** *button. Name the new folder* **navbar_IR** *and click on the* **Create** *button and then the* **Save** *button.*

- **Windows:** *Click on the yellow* **Folder** *icon to make a new folder. Name the folder* **navbar_IR**, *and double-click on it so that it opens. Click on the* **Save** *button, and all the files will populate the new folder you just created.*

The files have been saved properly. Now it's time to move the files around in your **chap_15** *folder before progressing any further.*

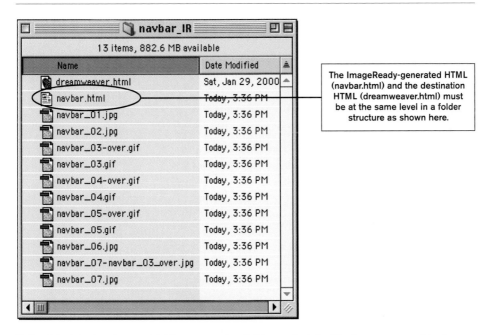

The ImageReady-generated HTML (navbar.html) and the destination HTML (dreamweaver.html) must be at the same level in a folder structure as shown here.

3. Look inside the **chap_15** folder on your hard drive to find the file **dreamweaver.html**, and move **dreamweaver.html** into the new folder you created there called **navbar_IR**.

When ImageReady wrote the file navbar.html, it contained references to all the images that appear in the rollover. If you move the HTML file away from those images, the links to them will break. That's why it's important that you bring the destination HTML file, dreamweaver.html, into the same folder as the target file, navbar.html, before opening Dreamweaver.

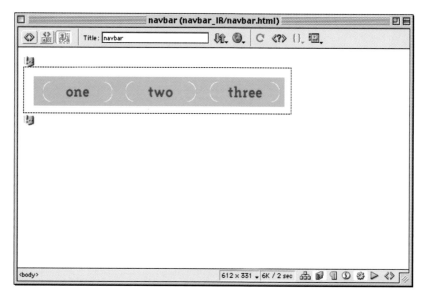

4. Open Dreamweaver 4, cancel any prompts, and close the untitled **Document** window that opens automatically. Choose **File > Open**. Navigate to **navbar.html** located inside the **navbar_IR** folder you just created, and click **Open**.

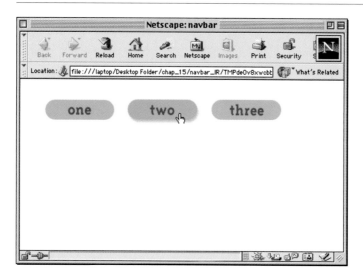

5. Press **F12** to preview in a browser. You'll see that the rollovers work just fine in a browser. The trick is putting this rollover into an existing Dreamweaver document, which is what you'll learn to do next.

6. Return to Dreamweaver 4, and press **F10** to open the **Code Inspector** (the **HTML Source** window in Dreamweaver 3). If line numbers are not visible, click the **View Options** icon at the top of the **Code Inspector** and choose **Line Numbers**.

```
                          navbar.html - Code Inspector
 Code Inspector                                                        ?

 1 <HTML>
 2 <HEAD>
 3 <TITLE>navbar</TITLE>
 4 <META HTTP-EQUIV="Content-Type" CONTENT="text/html; charset=iso-8859-1">
 5 <!-- ImageReady Preload Script (navbar.psd) -->
 6 <SCRIPT LANGUAGE="JavaScript">
 7 <!--
 8
 9 function newImage(arg) {
10     if (document.images) {
11         rslt = new Image();
12         rslt.src = arg;
13         return rslt;
14     }
15 }
16
17 function changeImages() {
18     if (document.images && (preloadFlag == true)) {
19         for (var i=0; i<changeImages.arguments.length; i+=2) {
20             document[changeImages.arguments[i]].src = changeImages.arguments[i+1];
21         }
22     }
23 }
24
25 var preloadFlag = false;
26 function preloadImages() {
27     if (document.images) {
28         navbar_03_over = newImage("navbar_03-over.gif");
29         navbar_04_over = newImage("navbar_04-over.gif");
30         navbar_05_over = newImage("navbar_05-over.gif");
31         navbar_07_navbar_03_over = newImage("navbar_07-navbar_03_over.jpg");
32         preloadFlag = true;
33     }
34 }
35
36 // -->
37 </SCRIPT>
38 <!-- End Preload Script -->
39 </HEAD>
40 <BODY BGCOLOR="#FFFFFF" ONLOAD="preloadImages();">
41 <!-- ImageReady Slices (navbar.psd) -->
42 <TABLE WIDTH=420 BORDER=0 CELLPADDING=0 CELLSPACING=0>
43     <TR>
44         <TD COLSPAN=5>
45             <IMG SRC="navbar_01.jpg" WIDTH=420 HEIGHT=15></TD>
```

7. The first step is to copy the section of ImageReady code that is located between the first set of comment tags. Notice that these comment tags begin right after the **META** element inside the **HEAD** of the document? Select the code exactly the way you see here, from the beginning of the **ImageReady Preload Script** comment to the **End Preload Script** comment (Lines **5** through **38**).

8. Copy the selected code using the command keys **Command+C** (Mac) or **Control+C** (Windows).

Note: This technique will not work unless you use the command keys to copy, instead of the menu. It's a strange Dreamweaver foible.

9. Choose **File > Open**. Navigate to **dreamweaver.html**, located inside the **navbar_IR** folder, and click **Open**.

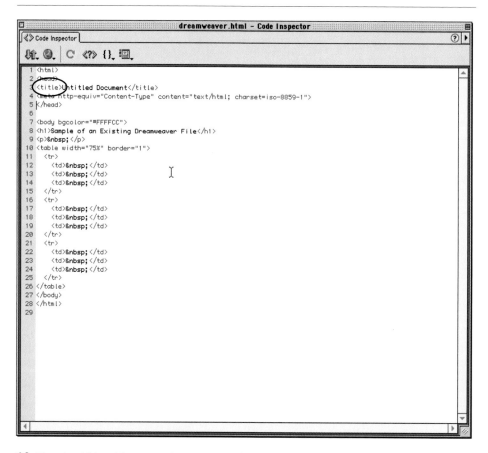

10. You should be able to see the source code of **dreamweaver.html** now. Locate the close of the **HEAD** tag (circled above in Line **5**) and click your cursor there.

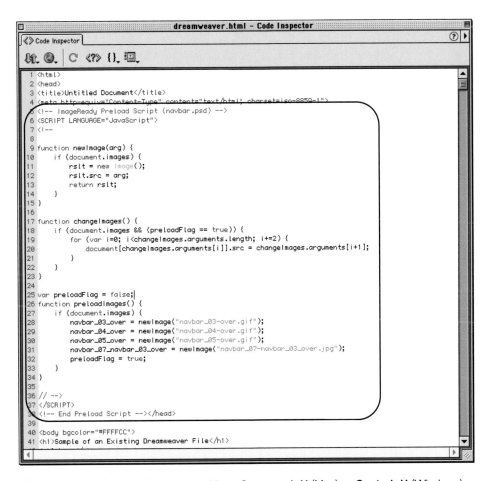

```
                    dreamweaver.html - Code Inspector
 Code Inspector

 1 <html>
 2 <head>
 3 <title>Untitled Document</title>
 4 <meta http-equiv="Content-Type" content="text/html; charset=iso-8859-1">
 5 <!-- ImageReady Preload Script (navbar.psd) -->
 6 <SCRIPT LANGUAGE="JavaScript">
 7 <!--
 8
 9 function newImage(arg) {
10     if (document.images) {
11         rslt = new Image();
12         rslt.src = arg;
13         return rslt;
14     }
15 }
16
17 function changeImages() {
18     if (document.images && (preloadFlag == true)) {
19         for (var i=0; i<changeImages.arguments.length; i+=2) {
20             document[changeImages.arguments[i]].src = changeImages.arguments[i+1];
21         }
22     }
23 }
24
25 var preloadFlag = false;
26 function preloadImages() {
27     if (document.images) {
28         navbar_03_over = newImage("navbar_03-over.gif");
29         navbar_04_over = newImage("navbar_04-over.gif");
30         navbar_05_over = newImage("navbar_05-over.gif");
31         navbar_07_navbar_03_over = newImage("navbar_07-navbar_03_over.jpg");
32         preloadFlag = true;
33     }
34 }
35
36 // -->
37 </SCRIPT>
38 <!-- End Preload Script --></head>
39
40 <body bgcolor="#FFFFCC">
41 <h1>Sample of an Existing Dreamweaver File</h1>
```

11. Paste the code using the command keys **Command+V** (Mac) or **Control+V** (Windows).
You should see the code you copied from **navbar.html** in Lines **5** through **38** of
dreamweaver.html, as shown above.

```
                           navbar.html – Code Inspector
 Code Inspector                                                                    ?  ▶

  ⇕.  ⬤.   C   ⟨?⟩  {}.  🖥.

25 var preloadFlag = false;
26 function preloadImages( ) {
27     if (document.images) {
28         navbar_03_over = newImage("navbar_03-over.gif");
29         navbar_04_over = newImage("navbar_04-over.gif");
30         navbar_05_over = newImage("navbar_05-over.gif");
31         navbar_07_navbar_03_over = newImage("navbar_07-navbar_03_over.jpg");
32         preloadFlag = true;
33     }
34 }
35
36 // -->
37 </SCRIPT>
38 <!-- End Preload Script -->
39 </HEAD>
40 <BODY BGCOLOR=#FFFFFF ONLOAD="preloadImages( );">
41 <!-- ImageReady Slices (navbar.psd) -->
42 <TABLE WIDTH=420 BORDER=0 CELLPADDING=0 CELLSPACING=0>
43     <TR>
44         <TD COLSPAN=5>
45             <IMG SRC="navbar_01.jpg" WIDTH=420 HEIGHT=15></TD>
46     </TR>
47     <TR>
48         <TD ROWSPAN=2>
49             <IMG SRC="navbar_02.jpg" WIDTH=16 HEIGHT=55></TD>
50         <TD>
51             <A HREF="#"
52             ONMOUSEOVER="changeImages('navbar_03', 'navbar_03-over.gif', 'navbar_07', 'navbar_07-
navbar_03_over.jpg'); return true;"
53             ONMOUSEOUT="changeImages('navbar_03', 'navbar_03.gif', 'navbar_07', 'navbar_07.jpg');
return true;">
54             <IMG NAME="navbar_03" SRC="navbar_03.gif" WIDTH=131 HEIGHT=44 BORDER=0></A></TD>
55         <TD>
```

12. Return to **navbar.html** by choosing **Window > navbar.html**. Select and copy the section of code you see highlighted above in Line **40**, using the command keys **Command+C** (Mac) or **Control+C** (Windows).

```
23 }
24
25 var preloadFlag = false;
26 function preloadImages() {
27     if (document.images) {
28         navbar_03_over = newImage("navbar_03-over.gif");
29         navbar_04_over = newImage("navbar_04-over.gif");
30         navbar_05_over = newImage("navbar_05-over.gif");
31         navbar_07_navbar_03_over = newImage("navbar_07-navbar_03_over.jpg");
32         preloadFlag = true;
33     }
34 }
35
36 // -->
37 </SCRIPT>
38 <!-- End Preload Script --></head>
39
40 <body bgcolor="#FFFFCC">
41 <h1>Sample of an Existing Dreamweaver File</h1>
42 <p> </p>
43 <table width="75%" border="1">
44   <tr>
45     <td> </td>
46     <td> </td>
47     <td> </td>
48   </tr>
49   <tr>
50     <td> </td>
51     <td> </td>
52     <td> </td>
53   </tr>
54   <tr>
55     <td> </td>
56     <td> </td>
57     <td> </td>
58   </tr>
59 </table>
60 </body>
61 </html>
62
```

13. Switch back to **dreamweaver.html** by choosing **Window > dreamweaver.html**. Locate the same spot in Line **40** inside the **BODY** tag, and click your cursor there.

```
                    dreamweaver.html - Code Inspector (modified)
  Code Inspector                                                              ?

  24
  25  var preloadFlag = false;
  26  function preloadImages( ) {
  27      if (document.images) {
  28          navbar_03_over = newImage("navbar_03-over.gif");
  29          navbar_04_over = newImage("navbar_04-over.gif");
  30          navbar_05_over = newImage("navbar_05-over.gif");
  31          navbar_07_navbar_03_over = newImage("navbar_07-navbar_03_over.jpg");
  32          preloadFlag = true;
  33      }
  34  }
  35
  36  // -->
  37  </SCRIPT>
  38  <!-- End Preload Script --></head>
  39
  40  <body bgcolor="#FFFFCC" ONLOAD="preloadImages();">
  41  <h1>Sample of an Existing Dreamweaver File</h1>
  42  <p>  </p>
  43  <table width="75%" border="1">
  44    <tr>
  45      <td> </td>
  46      <td> </td>
  47      <td> </td>
  48    </tr>
  49    <tr>
  50      <td> </td>
  51      <td> </td>
  52      <td> </td>
  53    </tr>
  54    <tr>
  55      <td> </td>
  56      <td> </td>
```

14. Paste the code using the command keys **Command+V** (Mac) or **Control+V** (Windows). The code should look identical to what is circled above.

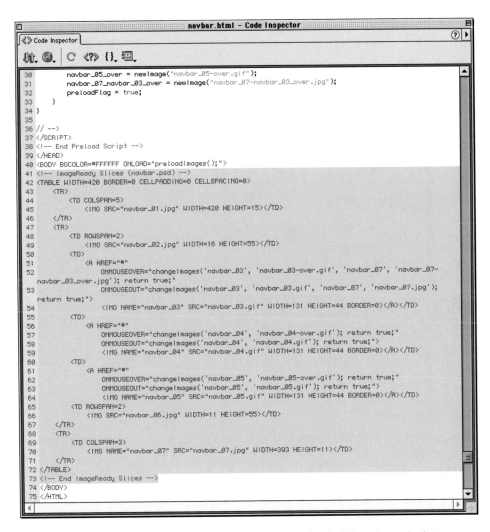

```
            navbar.html - Code Inspector

 Code Inspector                                             ?

  ↕  ⊕  │  C  <?>  {}  ▦

30          navbar_05_over = newImage("navbar_05-over.gif");
31          navbar_07_navbar_03_over = newImage("navbar_07-navbar_03_over.jpg");
32          preloadFlag = true;
33      }
34 }
35
36 // -->
37 </SCRIPT>
38 <!-- End Preload Script -->
39 </HEAD>
40 <BODY BGCOLOR=#FFFFFF ONLOAD="preloadImages();">
41 <!-- ImageReady Slices (navbar.psd) -->
42 <TABLE WIDTH=420 BORDER=0 CELLPADDING=0 CELLSPACING=0>
43      <TR>
44          <TD COLSPAN=5>
45              <IMG SRC="navbar_01.jpg" WIDTH=420 HEIGHT=15></TD>
46      </TR>
47      <TR>
48          <TD ROWSPAN=2>
49              <IMG SRC="navbar_02.jpg" WIDTH=16 HEIGHT=55></TD>
50          <TD>
51              <A HREF="#"
52                 ONMOUSEOVER="changeImages('navbar_03', 'navbar_03-over.gif', 'navbar_07', 'navbar_07-
   navbar_03_over.jpg'); return true;"
53                 ONMOUSEOUT="changeImages('navbar_03', 'navbar_03.gif', 'navbar_07', 'navbar_07.jpg');
   return true;">
54              <IMG NAME="navbar_03" SRC="navbar_03.gif" WIDTH=131 HEIGHT=44 BORDER=0></A></TD>
55          <TD>
56              <A HREF="#"
57                 ONMOUSEOVER="changeImages('navbar_04', 'navbar_04-over.gif'); return true;"
58                 ONMOUSEOUT="changeImages('navbar_04', 'navbar_04.gif'); return true;">
59              <IMG NAME="navbar_04" SRC="navbar_04.gif" WIDTH=131 HEIGHT=44 BORDER=0></A></TD>
60          <TD>
61              <A HREF="#"
62                 ONMOUSEOVER="changeImages('navbar_05', 'navbar_05-over.gif'); return true;"
63                 ONMOUSEOUT="changeImages('navbar_05', 'navbar_05.gif'); return true;">
64              <IMG NAME="navbar_05" SRC="navbar_05.gif" WIDTH=131 HEIGHT=44 BORDER=0></A></TD>
65          <TD ROWSPAN=2>
66              <IMG SRC="navbar_06.jpg" WIDTH=11 HEIGHT=55></TD>
67      </TR>
68      <TR>
69          <TD COLSPAN=3>
70              <IMG NAME="navbar_07" SRC="navbar_07.jpg" WIDTH=393 HEIGHT=11></TD>
71      </TR>
72 </TABLE>
73 <!-- End ImageReady Slices -->
74 </BODY>
75 </HTML>
```

15. Return to **navbar.html** by choosing **Window > navbar.html**. Select the code that you see selected above (Lines **41** through **73**), and copy it using the command keys **Command+C** (Mac) or **Control+C** (Windows).

```
                                   dreamweaver.html - Code Inspector
 Code Inspector                                                                      ?  ▶

 ↕ ⬤   C  <?>  {}  🖳

24
25 var preloadFlag = false;
26 function preloadImages() {
27     if (document.images) {
28         navbar_03_over = newImage("navbar_03-over.gif");
29         navbar_04_over = newImage("navbar_04-over.gif");
30         navbar_05_over = newImage("navbar_05-over.gif");
31         navbar_07_navbar_03_over = newImage("navbar_07-navbar_03_over.jpg");
32         preloadFlag = true;
33     }
34 }
35
36 // -->
37 </SCRIPT>
38 <!-- End Preload Script --></head>
39
40 <body bgcolor="#FFFFCC">
41 <h1>Sample of an Existing Dreamweaver File</h1>
42 <p> </p>
43 <table width="75%" border="1">
44   <tr>
45     <td> </td>
46     <td> </td>
47     <td> </td>
48   </tr>
49   <tr>
50     <td> </td>
51     <td> </td>
52     <td> </td>
53   </tr>
54   <tr>
55     <td> </td>
56     <td> </td>
57     <td> </td>
58   </tr>
59 </table>
60 </body>
61 </html>
62
```

16. Return to **dreamweaver.html** by choosing **Window > dreamweaver.html**. Click your mouse in Line **51** at the spot circled above.

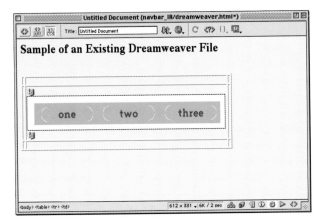

17. Use your command keys to paste. Press **F10** again and the **Code Inspector** will disappear. You should see the HTML file with the ImageReady rollover inside.

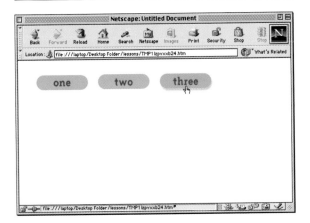

18. Press **F12** to preview this in a browser. The rollover works, and you're probably blown away by how hard this was. We agree with you that it's not an easy or fun task, but it does work.

19. Quit Dreamweaver (File > Quit), and **Save** when prompted.

 MOVIE | dreamweaver_rollovers.mov

To learn more about putting your ImageReady-created rollovers into Dreamweaver, check out **dreamweaver_rollovers.mov** from the **movies** folder on the **H•O•T CD-ROM**.

NOTE | Great News for Dreamweaver Users!

We've included a free "**Insert ImageReady HTML**" Extension for Dreamweaver on your **H•O•T CD-ROM.** You'll find it in your **chap_15** folder inside the **Mac_InsertIR** folder or **Windows_InsertIR** folder, along with detailed instructions on how to install and use this Extension and the Macromedia Extension Manager (which you can download from **www.macromedia.com/ exchange/dreamweaver**). This Extension will eliminate the tedious cutting and pasting that you learned to do in this exercise, by inserting your ImageReady code into any Dreamweaver document with a single instruction. This Extension was written by Massimo Foti (**http://www. massimocorner.com**) for Lynda.com. It was made originally for Dreamweaver 3, but works fine in Dreamweaver 4 too.

WARNING | Working with an Existing Dreamweaver Site

If you are an experienced Dreamweaver user and you already have a site with which you want to try the technique covered in this exercise, the instructions are a bit different than what you just did. Instead, you would want to move the **navbar_IR** folder into the root folder of that site. It would then appear inside the **Site** window (**F8**) (**F5** in Dreamweaver 3). You would also have to move the file **navbar.html** to the same level as the destination HTML file you want to paste it into. Be sure to move the files when you're in Dreamweaver's **Site** window, or you risk the possibility of all the links to the images breaking.

These are some resources we recommend for more information on learning about site management in Dreamweaver.

Learning Dreamweaver 4 (CD-ROM)
By Garo Green and Lynda Weinman
http://www.lynda.com/books/hot/dw4

Dreamweaver 4 Hands-On Training (H•O•T)
By Garo Green, developed with Lynda Weinman
lynda.com/books and Peachpit Press
ISBN: 0201741334
$39.99

Dreamweaver 4 Bible
Joseph W. Lowery
IDG Books
ISBN: 0764535692
$49.99

[PS/IR]

4. ——————————**Exporting Illustrator 9 Files**

The best way to prepare documents in Illustrator for ImageReady is to first work in layers in Illustrator. This example uses an Adobe Illustrator file (**tarpitdiscovery.ai**) that contains named layers. This exercise works in **Illustrator 9** or **Illustrator 8**.

1. Launch **Illustrator 9,** and choose **File > Open**. Navigate to the **chap_15** folder to select **tarpitdiscovery.ai**. Notice that this file contains three layers.

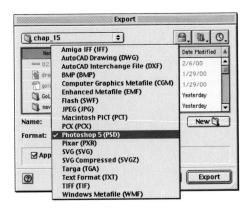

2. From Illustrator, choose **File > Export**. In the **Export** window, from the **Format** (Mac) or **Save as type** (Windows) pop-up menu, choose **Photoshop 5** (which works fine even if you're actually using Photoshop 6). Make sure there's a checkmark in the **Append File Extension** box. Navigate to the **chap_15** folder on your desktop, and click **Export** (Mac) or **Save** (Windows).

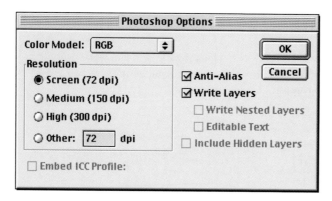

3. In the **Photoshop Options** dialog box that appears, match your settings to those shown above and click **OK**.

4. Launch ImageReady 3 (or Photoshop 6). Choose **File > Open** in that program, and navigate to the Photoshop document that you saved into the **chap_15** folder from Illustrator (**tarpitdiscovery.psd**). It will open with all the layers from the Illustrator file in Photoshop layers named exactly as they were in Illustrator.

The advantage to this technique is that the Illustrator file is brought into ImageReady with layers that were pre-named and separated correctly. Now you're ready to create rollovers or animated GIF files from this layered document.

5.————————**Exporting from Earlier Illustrator Versions**

If you own a version of Illustrator older than Illustrator 8, you will not be able to export in the Photoshop format. Don't worry. You can copy and paste between applications instead. This exercise works with Illustrator 8 and 9, as well as with older versions of Illustrator.

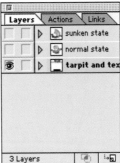

1. Open the **tarpitdiscovery.ai** file in Illustrator. Using the **Selection** tool (the black arrow), select the elements that you want to paste into Photoshop or ImageReady and choose **Edit > Copy**.

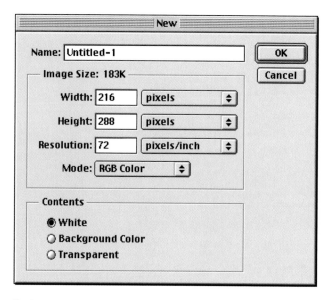

2. Open Photoshop or ImageReady, and choose **File > New**. Set up the document with the same settings as you see above (ImageReady won't give you a resolution option, but don't worry about that), and click **OK**.

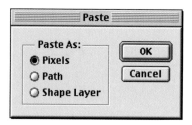

3. Choose **Edit > Paste**. In the **Paste** dialog box appears (Photoshop only), choose **Paste As Pixels** (and **Anti-Alias** if you're given that option). If you're prompted to **Place the File**, click **Place. Note:** Because ImageReady doesn't support paths, it knows to paste as pixels when you choose the **Paste** command. This will change the artwork from vector (Illustrator) to bitmap (Photoshop) format.

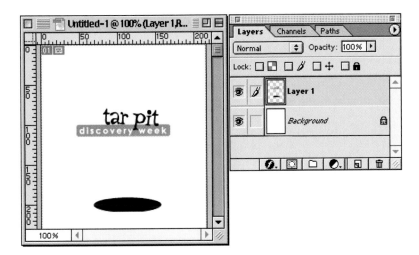

4. The artwork that you copied and pasted will appear on its own automatically-named layer. If your **Layers** palette isn't open for you to see this, choose **Window > Show Layers**. If you want to name the layer differently (which we suggest you do), **option+double-click** (Mac) or **Alt+double-click** (Windows) on that layer (or just double-click on it in ImageReady), and type in a better name.

You can go back and forth between Illustrator and Photoshop or ImageReady this way, copying and pasting whatever artwork you want onto new layers.

5. When you're finished with this exercise you can quit Illustrator and Photoshop, as neither is needed again.

[IR]

6. ——————————Exporting ImageReady to QuickTime

In addition to writing animated GIF files, ImageReady will also export animation files to QuickTime. You might want to do this if you are working on a multimedia project instead of an HTML project.

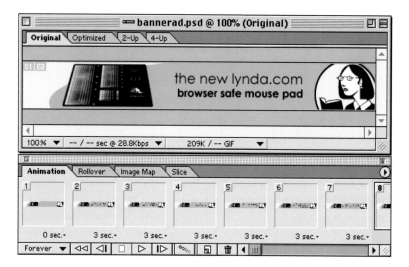

1. In ImageReady, open **bannerad.psd** from the **chap_15** folder on your desktop.

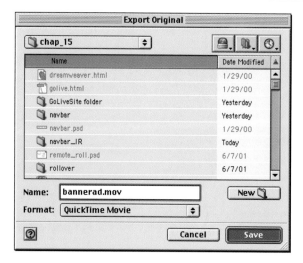

2. Choose **File > Export Original...** and choose **QuickTime Movie** in the **Format** field (Mac) or **Save as type** field (Windows). The .mov extension will automatically be added to the end of the file name. Navigate to the **chap_15** folder and click **Save**.

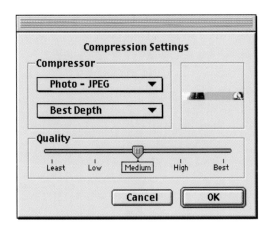
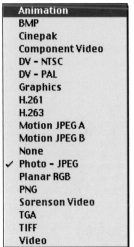

3. The **Compression Settings** dialog box will appear at its **Photo — JPEG** default. This is a good format if your animation includes continuous-tone imagery. The file you're working with is graphic in nature, so choose **Animation** from the top **Compressor** pop-up menu.

4. Click **OK** and the file will be saved. To see it, go to the **chap_15** folder where you saved it, double-click on the file **bannerad.mov**, and it should open up in the **QuickTime Player** that ships with QuickTime. **Note:** A version of the Quicktime Player is in the **software** folder on the **H•O•T CD-ROM** in case you don't have one.

5. Close **bannerad.mov** and **bannerad.psd**.

[IR]

7. ——————————**Converting from QuickTime to ImageReady**

You can also convert from QuickTime to an animated GIF in ImageReady. You might want to do this if someone gives you a QuickTime movie that was created for some other purpose (such as one that contained live action and was shot with a movie camera), but that you'd prefer to convert to an animated GIF.

1. In ImageReady, choose **File > Open**. Locate the **bannerad.mov** file that you just created and click **OK**. The **Open Movie** dialog box will appear.

You can choose to import the entire movie, a select range of frames, or skip frames to specified increments, such as every five frames or whichever setting is appropriate.

2. Click **OK** inside the **Open Movie** dialog box. These default settings will work perfectly for this example.

The file will be converted to layers and the frames will automatically appear inside the Animation palette. It will take whatever timing was set as the frame rate from the QuickTime movie.

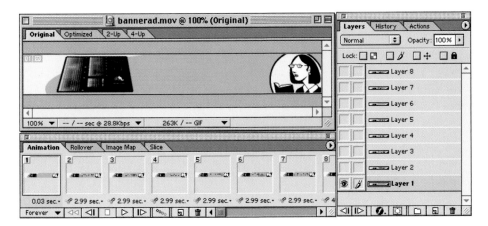

3. To save this as an animated GIF, make sure the optimization settings are in the **GIF** format and choose **File > Save Optimized As….** It's that easy, really!

This exercise showed how to convert a file from QuickTime to an animated GIF. This chapter covered a lot of loose ends that weren't easily defined by the other chapter categories. We hope some or all has been relevant to your work.

You're finished with the last chapter, and now it's time to go out into the world on your own and make great Web art and movies. Rock on!

16.

Troubleshooting FAQ

| H•O•T |

| Hands-On Training |

Photoshop 6 / ImageReady 3

For the Web

If you've run into any problems while following the exercises in this book, this Troubleshooting FAQ (Frequently Asked Questions) should help. This document will be maintained and expanded upon at this book's companion Web site: **http://www.lynda.com/ books/psirhot**

If you don't find what you're looking for here or in the companion Web site, please send an email to **psirfaq@lynda.com**.

If you have a question related to Photoshop 6 or ImageReady 3 that is not related to a specific exercise in this book, visit the Adobe site at: **http://www.adobe.com** or call their tech support hotline at: 206-675-6203 (Mac) or 206-675-6303 (Windows).

Q: I'm on Windows, and all the files on the **H•O•T CD-ROM** are locked, even though I transferred them to my hard drive. What should I do?

A: Unfortunately, Windows considers all files copied from a CD-ROM to be "read only" files. That means that you can't make changes to any of the files you've transferred to your Windows hard drive from the CD-ROM until you unlock them. Here's how:

1. Open the **Exercises** folder on the CD-ROM, and copy one of the subfolders (for example, the **chap_05** subfolder) to your desktop.

2. Open the **chap_05** folder you copied to your desktop, and choose **Edit > Select All**.

3. Right-click on one of the selected files, and choose **Properties** from the pop-up menu.

4. In the **General** tab of the **Properties** dialog box, uncheck **Read-only**. This will unlock all of the files in the **chap_05** folder on your desktop.

Q: I'm on a Mac, and I get weird refresh problems with my desktop flashing and everything running really slow. Do you have any ideas why this always happens to me?

A: You are probably running low on RAM. Close one or more applications and it should improve. You might have to quit ImageReady, Photoshop, or the browser during exercises so that you only keep one program open at a time. Consider getting more RAM if you plan to do this sort of work often.

Q: I'm noticing some odd behavior when I'm using Photoshop on my Mac. For example, I know a Color Picker is supposed to open when I click on the thumbnail on the left in a Shape layer, but my Color Picker doesn't open when I do that.

A: If Photoshop is acting strange, you may have a corrupt Preferences file. Go to **System Folder > Preferences > Adobe Photoshop 6 Settings**, find **Adobe Photoshop 6 Preferences** and drag that file to the Mac **Trash**. Launch Photoshop and go to **Edit > Preferences** to choose your preferences again. If you're experiencing similar behavior in ImageReady, trash the **Adobe ImageReady 3.0 Prefs** the same way.

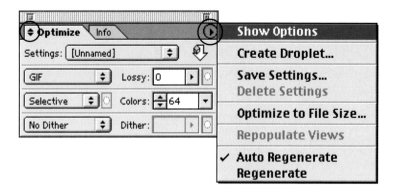

Q: My Optimize palette in ImageReady doesn't show all of the options that yours does. For example, I can't see the Transparency checkbox or the Matte setting. What's wrong?

A: There's nothing really wrong. All you need to do is press the arrow on the top right of the **Optimize** palette and choose **Show Options** from the drop-down menu. Or you can click on the small double-pointed arrow on the Optimize palette tab to cycle through a few expansions of that palette.

Q: What if I use color profiles in my print work? It's kind of disconcerting to turn them off, as you suggested in Chapter 1, *"Interface."*

A: You can always program an **action** that will turn them off and/or back on. You learned how to make actions in Chapter 14, *"Automation,"* but here's a brief refresher. Simply start recording an action before you turn profiles on or off, and the action will remember your steps. Once you've finished recording, press the **Stop** button. Bingo, you have an action for that task!

Q: What should I do about CMYK images that I created for print? Can I use them on the Web?

A: You won't be able to use CMYK images on the Web. You'll have to convert those images to RGB first. Do this in Photoshop by choosing **Image > Mode > RGB Color**. There might be some color shifting during this process because CMYK and RGB are two different color spaces that cannot achieve an exact translation.

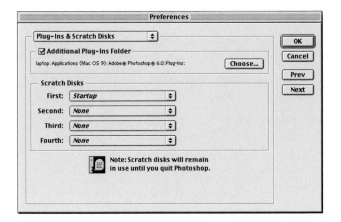

Q: In Chapter 3, *"Optimization,"* you suggest that I leave the Save For Web dialog box open for many exercises in a row. What happens if I have to quit and come back to the exercise another time?

A: You're in luck. The **Save For Web** dialog box will remember the last settings you used, even if you quit Photoshop. So you can quit, and you won't have to redo the exercises again from scratch.

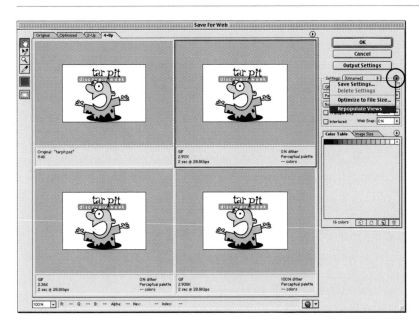

Q: What should I do when I'm in the Save For Web dialog box and see an orange warning triangle?

A: Click the menu arrow to the right of **Settings** in the **Save For Web** dialog box and choose **Repopulate Views**. This should cause all the views to refresh and the warning icon to disappear.

Q: My Layers palette doesn't look like yours! What's up with that?

A: To access any palette in its entirety, not just the Layers palette, just drag its bottom-right corner.

Q: Anytime I go to any file in ImageReady and click the Optimized tab, instead of seeing the image in the background, I get a checkerboard pattern.

A: If you're having trouble seeing an image in the **Optimized** tab, click on the menu arrow in the top-right corner of the **Optimize** palette and make sure that **Auto Regenerate** is checked in the pull-down menu. Remember, that checkerboard pattern indicates that this is a transparent GIF.

Q: Sometimes I don't see any color chips in the Color Table in ImageReady when I'm optimizing a GIF. Why not?

A: You may have to give the program a jump start by clicking the **yellow triangle** at the lower left of the **Color Table** palette. This will regenerate the Color Table.

Q: Please remind me what each of the optimization tabs in the ImageReady Document window means.

A: Glad to. The first is **Original** and that's self-explanatory. It's the original, non-optimized image. **Optimized** is self-explanatory, too. It shows you the optimized version of an image. We prefer to do all our work in Original, as Optimized constantly updates the image, which can really slow things down. The last two, **2-Up** and **4-Up**, offer two and four versions of the image, respectively. They're useful for comparing an image at different optimization settings.

Q: In Photoshop, when I'm working with type I can't see the effects of what I'm doing until I bail out of the dialog box. There's gotta be a better way.

A: You must be working in Photoshop 5.5. This was a problem in Photoshop 5.5, but in Photoshop 6.0 you type directly in the Document window, where you can see everything you're doing in real time. Thanks, Adobe!

Q: Every time I save a file I get this annoying box asking me where I want to update it.

A: We know what you mean when you say it's annoying. There's a simple way to fix this and it involves changing your Preferences. In both applications, choose **Edit > Preferences > General...**. In Photoshop, put a check next to **Auto-update open documents**; in ImageReady, put a check next to **Auto-Update Files**. Click **OK** and you'll never have to see that pesky box again.

Q: When I type, the type shows up behind the button, not over it. Why does this happen?

A: The stacking order of layers in the **Layers** palette is from bottom to top. If your type is under another layer it might be hidden. Drag the **type** layer above all the others and you will see it. Another problem is that you might be typing in the same color as your button. Hey, it happens even to the pros, we swear it does!

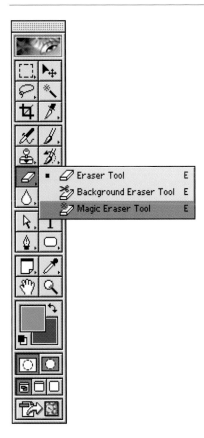

Q: I keep going to the Photoshop Toolbox to get to the Magic Eraser but it's nowhere to be found, though I do see the Eraser. How do I access it?

A: See the tiny **arrow** at the bottom right of the **Eraser** tool icon? Click there, leave your mouse depressed, and you'll see the other Eraser options, including the **Magic Eraser**. You can drag out to select any of the erasers in this fly-out menu. All the tools that have the same tiny arrow have more than one tool option, just like this one.

Q: Not to complain, but I get sick of zooming in and out of my files. Is there a quick way to get a big view?

A: If you double-click on the **Hand** tool inside the Toolbox the image will expand to fill your screen. If you double-click on the **Zoom** tool in the Toolbox it will change to **100%**. The trick is to double-click right in the Toolbox, not on your image.

Q: I am working away on an image in ImageReady, and it's taking forever for the program to accept my edits. I am slowly going crazy.

A: Our guess is you're working in the Optimized tab, which tells ImageReady to constantly optimize your graphic while you're editing it. Switch over to the Original tab. It will go faster, we promise.

Q: Is there a quick one-step way to hide all those palettes that are cluttering up my desktop?

A: Press the **Tab** key to toggle on and off all the palettes in either Photoshop or ImageReady. It's a beautiful thing!

Q: I keep trying to select a slice but for some reason I can't. Help!

A: Are you using the **Slice Select** tool? It's in a fly-out menu under the **Slice** tool in the ImageReady and Photoshop Toolboxes. Use the **Slice** tool to cut up an image into slices and then use the **Slice Select** tool to adjust those slices. The Slice Select tool lets you drag, reposition, delete, and select a single slice or more at one time. To select multiple slices, hold down the **Shift** key. The shortcut key for the Slice Select and Slice tools is the letter **K** on your keyboard.

Q: I want to create a rollover, but nothing is showing up in the Rollover palette. What am I doing wrong?

A: You must first select a slice (with the **Slice Select** tool) before the Rollover palette is operational. That's because you define rollovers according to a trigger slice. If you don't have a slice defined, ImageReady has no way of knowing which slice is going to trigger the rollover.

Index

H•O•T

Photoshop 6 / ImageReady 3
For the Web

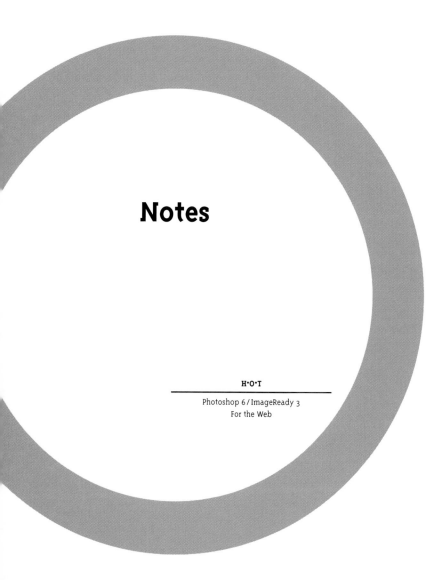

Notes

H•O•T

Photoshop 6 / ImageReady 3
For the Web